"Walter Kasper is a gentle giant within the Catho
ecumenical circles, and within the Catholic-Jewis
about this Festschrift is the ordering of the essays, the consistently high standard of contributions, and the constructive engagement with the work of Kasper over a period of fifty years. This collection reads like a mini-summa of what is best in Catholic theology. We are indebted to the careful work of the editors in putting together this handsome volume."

Dermot A. Lane
Mater Dei Institute of Education
Dublin City University, Ireland

"*The Theology of Cardinal Walter Kasper* is an exceptional volume from a remarkable range of leading scholars. As an introduction to a man who has served the church in so many capacities, this overview offers a unique vista on Catholicism over the span of Kasper's career through his writing in diverse areas of systematic theology. We see the mastery of Kasper through the lens of his scholarly admirers who together make a compelling case for the significance of the cardinal for his church and for its future."

Jeannine Hill Fletcher
Fordham University

"Cardinal Walter Kasper is undoubtedly a major figure in the church today, standing tall among contemporary theologians, epitomizing the theologian's task of mediating between the Christian tradition and contemporary culture. This book, which includes insightful surveys of Kasper's work by a stellar array of leading North American theologians as well as personal and pastoral statements by Cardinal Kasper, presents an excellent account of Kasper's theology—as consistently pastoral and insistently ecclesial—and his vision of the church in dialogue with the world. In all, it attests to Kasper's unswerving commitment to 'speak truth in love,' in service of God and of Christian faith, both within the Catholic communion and beyond it, through his remarkable contribution to the cause of Christian unity and in the promotion of Christian-Jewish relations. With its origins in a 2013 conference held at the University of Notre Dame, Indiana, this most welcome book will surely serve as a useful reference for evaluating Cardinal Kasper's extraordinary contribution as churchman, theologian, and pastor to the church, academy, and society."

Anne Hunt
Executive Dean, Faculty of Theology
and Philosophy
Australian Catholic University

"Warm thanks to Krieg and Colberg for editing these fifteen brilliant essays, describing the insights of the acclaimed cardinal-theologian Walter Kasper, shared at the University of Notre Dame colloquium (which I happily attended!) to celebrate his eightieth birthday. These North American professors provide a trusty GPS to navigate his doctrinal, ecumenical avenues while suggesting some still-unexplored lanes."

Michael A. Fahey, SJ
Scholar in Residence
Fairfield University, CT

"For much of the twentieth century Walter Kasper was overshadowed by theological greats such as Rahner, Schillebeeckx, von Balthasar, and Lonergan. Now is his time to emerge from the shadows to be revealed as a first-class theologian and exemplary churchman. This volume of contributions from leading Christian and Jewish theologians, and recent essays by Kasper himself, reveals the depth of his contribution both to theology and to the life of the church in the modern age."

Neil Ormerod
Professor of Theology
Australian Catholic University

"In this remarkable Festschrift, some of today's most distinguished theologians explore the achievements of Cardinal Walter Kasper as a systematician, a contributor to the ecumenical movement, and a leader in Jewish-Christian relations. Lucid and readily accessible, these essays will benefit both students and professional scholars. Personal anecdotes from Kasper's former students, colleagues, and dialogue partners complement the volume's general introduction to his life and career. The volume ends with three contributions from Kasper himself, so that its dialogue about Kasper becomes a dialogue with Kasper. This book deserves a place in every theological library."

Julia Fleming, Professor of Theology
Creighton University

"There is no comparable presentation and recent analysis of the theology of Walter Kasper in German."

Dr. Hermann Josef Pottmeyer
Professor Emeritus, Fundamental Theology
Ruhr University, Bochum, Germany

The Theology of Cardinal Walter Kasper

Speaking Truth in Love

Edited by
Kristin M. Colberg and Robert A. Krieg

Foreword by
Cardinal Walter Kasper

A Michael Glazier Book

LITURGICAL PRESS
Collegeville, Minnesota

www.litpress.org

A Michael Glazier Book published by Liturgical Press

Cover design by Jodi Hendrickson. Photo by Matthew Cashore.

1 2 3 4 5 6 7 8 9

Library of Congress Cataloging-in-Publication Data

The theology of Cardinal Walter Kasper : speaking truth in love / edited by Kristin M. Colberg and Robert A. Krieg.
pages cm
Includes index.
"A Michael Glazier book."
"A festschrift honoring Cardinal Walter Kasper, generated by his visit to Notre Dame in April of 2013."—E-Cip data view.
ISBN 978-0-8146-8315-6 — ISBN 978-0-8146-8340-8 (ebook)
1. Kasper, Walter, 1933– 2. Catholic Church—Doctrines. I. Kasper, Walter, 1933– honouree. II. Colberg, Kristin, editor of compilation.

BX4705.K21975T44 2014
230'.2092—dc23

2014010617

Contents

SECTION THREE

Reflections on Forgiveness, Vatican II, and Hope

Gratitude for an Unforgettable, Stimulating Symposium

Cardinal Walter Kasper
May 14, 2014

With the best of memories and deep gratitude, I recall the symposium, titled "The Theology of Cardinal Walter Kasper: Speaking Truth in Love," at the University of Notre Dame from April 25 to April 27, 2013.

This three-day assembly was an academic conference at which theologians presented and discussed scholarly essays of the highest quality. Revised versions of these essays are the chapters of this Festschrift.

Yet this assembly was much more a symposium that realized the original meaning of the term "symposium." It was an exchange of ideas in the context of an enjoyable, lively encounter of long-time friends and colleagues from both sides of the Atlantic Ocean. This gathering was akin to what St. Augustine described in his early writings as a dialogue among friends in the country home at Cassiacum. Our symposium too occurred at a lovely place: the beautiful campus of the University of Notre Dame, with its warm, generous hospitality, which included a grand banquet and the joyous celebration of the Eucharist in the Basilica of the Sacred Heart.

This event accentuated an important element in my symposium essay, titled "How to Do Theology Today," which is this Festschrift's chapter 16. To be sure, theology needs hard work at the desk, in libraries, and in classrooms. At the same time, it involves more than a discussion of scholarly papers, as useful and important are as they are. Theology matures by means of a vigorous, mutual giving and receiving of questions, insights, and lived convictions among friends and associates who often come from varied life experiences, different cultural backgrounds, and diverse academic orientations. Theology requires a sharing of a common faith, of a genuine willingness to participate in the one church whose unity embraces an enriching plurality, and of a commitment to speak to students and inquirers as they seek their way in faith, love, and hope within our global church and our complex world.

In sum, our symposium in April 2013 reminded me that theology flourishes only in an ongoing, never-ending dialogue that includes a challenging exchange of ideas, issues, and life. So I wish to express my heartfelt appreciation to the symposium's participants and, in particular, to the two people who initiated and organized this stimulating, fruitful event and who subsequently prepared this work for publication: Kristin M. Colberg and Robert A. Krieg.

Finally, my thanks also go to the people who generously sponsored the symposium and to the people who expertly published this Festschrift; the names of many of these men and women are acknowledged with gratitude in the introduction. In the symposium and this Festschrift, I have received a birthday gift that I will never forget. May the essays herein inspire their readers and convince them that it's worthwhile and invigorating to do theology today.

Tributes to Cardinal Kasper

From Gustavo A. Gutiérrez, OP
April 27, 2013

Dear Cardinal Kasper:

I greatly lament that health reasons prevent me from participating in the well-deserved honor the University of Notre Dame is offering to your theological work and to your personal testimony as a pastor and as a theologian.

We have much to thank you for your contribution to contemporary theology, though I only have time to mention your impact on the practice and thinking about ecumenical dialogue. I applaud you not only for the interest you have shown in personal encounters with representatives of different Christian confessions but also for the efforts to advance theologically the conditions for a truly fruitful dialogue. For example, your lucid and opportune works about collegiality in the church and the relation between the church universal and the local churches reflect the pastoral experience of a bishop.

At a more personal level I thank you for one of your earlier works about pluralism in theology, which inspired many of us in the beginnings of our theological efforts in Latin America. And also through your beautiful recent book, *Mercy: The Essence of the Gospel and the Key to Christian Life* (2012), which I am currently reading. You teach us the mercy of God that is manifest in the daily actions of Jesus and that is directed to all people and in the first instance to the poor and the socially insignificant.

I deeply regret that I am not able to be present in today's panel to which the conference organizers had the goodness to invite me, but I would like to reiterate my fraternal friendship and my solidarity with this tribute to your theological work.[1]

⁂

From Rabbi A. James Rudin, DD[2]

December 31, 2013

Cardinal Walter Kasper is a unique combination of a world-class theologian and an empathetic pastor. I was privileged to witness both attributes when he served as the Holy See's global leader in strengthening Catholic-Jewish relations between 2001 and 2010.

Cardinal Kasper's leadership came at a critical time. Three dozen years had passed since the conclusion of the Second Vatican Council when the world's Catholic bishops overwhelmingly adopted *Nostra aetate* with its declaration on Jews and Judaism. By 2001, some Catholics and Jews believed the task of building a new constructive relationship between the church and the Jewish people had been completed.

Because Cardinal Kasper knew this was not so, he devoted his academic head and his compassionate heart to make clear the council's historic achievement was not the "end" but rather the "beginning." He brought both intellectual and spiritual energy to that sacred task.

In a 2002 address at Boston College, he declared that "God's covenant with Israel by God's faithfulness is not broken (cf. Rom 11:29). . . . This is not a merely abstract theological affirmation, but an affirmation that has concrete and tangible consequences such as the fact that there is no organized Catholic missionary activity towards Jews."

A year later, the cardinal wrote: "Especially with regard to anti-Semitism and to the Shoah, we can justifiably speak of the need to embark on acts of repentance (*teshuvà*) . . . not limited merely to a few authoritative, meaningful gestures or even high-level documents. . . . In this spirit of rediscovered brotherhood a new springtime for the Church and for the world can bloom once more, with the heart turned from Rome to Jerusalem and to the land of the Fathers" (*L'Osservatore Romano English Weekly Edition*, n. 40 [January 10, 2003], p. 6).

Cardinal Kasper has helped free our two faith communities from the tight chains of the past, moved us to higher ground, and given all of us a mandate for further positive change.

Endnotes

1. This tribute was translated into English by Dr. Timothy Matovina.

2. Rabbi Rudin had prepared an invited presentation for the conference in honor of Cardinal Kasper, but he was unable to attend the conference because of a sudden health crisis from which he has fortunately recuperated. At our request he has crafted this statement.

Introduction

Kristin M. Colberg and *Robert A. Krieg*

A large crowd gathered in the University of Notre Dame's McKenna Hall for Continuing Education on the evening of Friday, April 26, 2013. The people broke into applause as Cardinal Walter Kasper entered the large atrium, accompanied by his sister Dr. Hildegard Kasper, who is emerita professor of philosophy, and walked to the table with the Bavarian chocolate cake in honor of the cardinal's eightieth birthday. Everyone joined in singing "Happy Birthday" to Cardinal Kasper and then cheered as he blew out the birthday candles, looked up with a large smile, and said, "Thank you!"

This birthday celebration was a high point of the conference in honor of Cardinal Kasper that was held at the university from April 25 to April 27, 2013. The cardinal's visit to campus generated all the chapters (except one) in this book. After recalling Cardinal Kasper's life and work, we give an overview of the nineteen chapters. In conclusion, we acknowledge the people and funding sources that made possible this *Festschrift* in honor of Cardinal Kasper.

Cardinal Walter Kasper's Life

Walter Kasper was consecrated the bishop of the Diocese of Rottenburg-Stuttgart on June 17, 1989. In accepting the church's call to ecclesial leadership, he chose as his episcopal motto, "Truth in Love," derived from Ephesians 4:15, "Speaking the truth in love, we must grow up in every way into him who is the head, into Christ." With these words, Kasper expressed the profound intention that has shaped his entire life.

Walter Kasper grew up in Swabia, Germany. He was born in Heidenheim an der Brenz on March 5, 1933, the day on which Adolf Hitler was "elected" Germany's national leader. Two years later his father, a schoolteacher, and his mother gave birth to Walter's sister Hildegard and after three more years to his sister Inge. During the war (1939–45), while Walter's father fulfilled mandatory military duty in national defense, the Kasper family resided in Wäschenbeuren, not far from Stuttgart. After the war when the father returned, the family moved to Wangen in the Allgäu Alps.

Beginning at an early age, Walter Kasper desired to become a priest and pastor. Thus, while studying at the University of Tübingen from 1952 to 1956, he resided at the Diocese of Rottenburg-Stuttgart's house of studies for seminarians, the Wilhelmstift. On April 16, 1957, after a year of diaconate studies in Rottenburg, Kasper was ordained a priest by the diocese's bishop, Karl Leiprecht. During 1957 and 1958, he engaged in parish ministry in Stuttgart, and in 1958 he commenced—at the bishop's request—his doctoral studies in theology at the University of Tübingen. In 1961, under the direction of Josef Rupert Geiselmann, he finished his doctoral dissertation, *Die Lehre der Tradition in der Römischen Schule*, "The Doctrine of Tradition in the Roman School." Soon after its completion, he embarked on the study, as suggested by the Dominican theologian Yves Congar, of the late philosophy of F. W. J. Schelling. In 1964, under the direction of Leo Scheffczyk, Kasper finished his Habilitation (the dissertation required in Germany for a university professorship), titled *Das Absolute in der Geschichte*, "The Absolute in History."

Walter Kasper was appointed professor of theology at the University of Münster in 1964 and remained there until 1970, when he accepted a professorship in theology at the University of Tübingen. Among his noteworthy publications while at Münster is his scholarly study "Verständnis der Theologie Damals und Heute" ("The Understanding of Theology Previously and Today," 1967) on the major shift occurring in Catholic theology during the mid-twentieth century. In 1967, Kasper became a member of the Study Commission of the Catholic Church and Lutheran World Federation.

At the University of Tübingen, Kasper wrote texts that brought him international recognition: *An Introduction to Christian Faith* (1972),

Jesus the Christ (1974), *The God of Jesus Christ* (1982), and "Die Kirche als universales Sakrament des Heils" ("The Church as Universal Sacrament of Salvation," 1984). At the request of the German bishops, Kasper was the primary writer and editor of a Catholic catechism for adults, titled the *Katholischer Erwachsenen-Katechismus*, which the German bishops' conference published in 1985. In that same year, Kasper served, at the request of Pope John Paul II, as the theological secretary of the Extraordinary Synod of Bishops in Rome. In this capacity, he proposed to the assembly of bishops that the Second Vatican Council's unifying theology of the church is *communio* ecclesiology. This proposal received an enthusiastic, positive response at the synod and subsequently among theologians around the world.

In light of these significant contributions to the church and theology, Pope John Paul II singled out Kasper for ecclesial leadership. During the spring of 1989, at the pope's request, Walter Kasper relinquished his professorship at the University of Tübingen, and on June 17, 1989, he was consecrated the bishop of the Diocese of Rottenburg-Stuttgart. At the helm of Germany's fourth-largest Catholic diocese, Kasper devoted himself to pastoral leadership and ministry, visiting on every weekend a different parish, where he presided and preached at the Sunday Masses. At the same time, he continued to participate in the Catholic-Lutheran dialogue, which produced the "Joint Declaration on the Doctrine of Justification" on October 31, 1999.

After ten years leading the Diocese of Rottenburg-Stuttgart, Bishop Kasper was asked by John Paul II to move to Rome. On March 3, 1999, the pope appointed Kasper to serve as the secretary of the Pontifical Council for Christian Unity and of its Commission for Religious Relations with the Jews. On February 21, 2001, the pope named Kasper a cardinal and two weeks later appointed him president of the Pontifical Council and its Commission. In this position, Kasper assumed international leadership in ecumenism and also in Christian-Jewish dialogue. His publications during this time include his books *Sacrament of Unity: The Eucharist and the Church* (2005) and *Handbook of Spiritual Ecumenism* (2006).

On July 1, 2010, Cardinal Kasper retired from his ecclesial office. Since then, he has continued to contribute to the church, ecumenism, and Christian-Jewish dialogue. In particular, he has published *The Catholic Church: Nature, Reality and Mission* (2011) and *Mercy: The Essence of the Gospel and the Key to Christian Life* (2012). Translated into

Spanish, *Mercy* was read during the papal conclave by Argentina's Cardinal Jorge Mario Bergoglio, who became Pope Francis on March 13, 2013. Much to Cardinal Kasper's surprise, the new pontiff publicly praised and quoted *Mercy* on March 17—twelve days after the cardinal's eightieth birthday! Moreover, Pope Francis has continued to accentuate in his words and deeds that God is mercy.

This Book's Content

This book's essays are arranged in three sections. Section 1's seven chapters discuss important aspects of Cardinal Kasper's major theological writings from 1964 to 1989 when Kasper was professor of theology. Section 2's nine chapters present Kasper's vision of the church and his contributions to ecumenism and Christian-Jewish relations from 1989 to the present. Section 3 contains three texts by Kasper himself.

Section 1: God, Freedom, and History

In chapter 1, "The Task of Theology," Kristin M. Colberg explains that Kasper has persistently sought to translate or interpret the church's Gospel into a language accessible to contemporary people, and in chapter 2, "A Distinctive Theological Approach," Francis Schüssler Fiorenza highlights how Kasper understands divine revelation, freedom, and history and unites these key notions in a theology distinct from the theologies of Karl Rahner and Joseph Ratzinger.

Anthony J. Godzieba elucidates in chapter 3, "The Promise and the Burden of Natural Theology," that Kasper acknowledges human beings' potential in the Holy Spirit of discerning God's presence and action in limited experience, and he has crafted a personalist language concerning God that is readily accessible to men and women in today's secular, consumer society. In chapter 4, "The Mystery of Being Human," Mary Catherine Hilkert develops Kasper's theological understanding of becoming a human person in relation to the mystery of Jesus Christ as "the key" to hope, freedom, and identity.

Chapters 5, 6, and 7 treat Kasper's Christology, pneumatology, and trinitarian theology, respectively. In "*Jesus the Christ* in Retrospect and Prospect," William P. Loewe illumines the creativity and continuing validity of Kasper's critical inquiry into Jesus' life, death, and

Acts 20:7-12

On the first day of the week when we gathered to break bread, Paul spoke to them because he was going to leave on the next day, and he kept on speaking until midnight. There were many lamps in the upstairs room where we were gathered, and a young man named Eutychus who was sitting on the window sill was sinking into a deep sleep as Paul talked on and on. Once overcome by sleep, he fell down from the third story, and when he was picked up, he was dead. Paul went down, threw himself upon him, and said as he embraced him, "Don't be alarmed; there is life in him." Then he returned upstairs, broke the bread, and ate; after a long conversation that lasted until daybreak, he departed. And they took the boy away alive and were immeasurably comforted.

resurrection. In "Pneumatology and Beyond: 'Wherever,'" Elizabeth A. Johnson highlights Kasper's emphasis on the Holy Spirit in relation to the church's understanding of the triune God, the historicity and humanity of Jesus Christ, and the Nicene Creed, and she asks that Cardinal Kasper develop his pneumatology in relation to an ecological theology of creation. In "*The God of Jesus Christ* in Continuity and Discontinuity," Cyril J. O'Regan clarifies, on the one hand, Kasper's adoption of the theological paradigm at work in Karl Rahner's *The Trinity*, and, on the other hand, Kasper's development and correction of important elements of Rahner's work.

Section 2: The Church, Ecumenism, and Christian-Jewish Relations

In chapter 8, "A Theology of Church and Ministry," Thomas F. O'Meara sketches the emergence of Kasper's ecclesiology, culminating in *The Catholic Church: Nature, Reality and Mission*, with its attentiveness to history, ecclesial forms, and the Holy Spirit.

The next five chapters study Kasper's efforts toward Christian unity. In chapter 9, "Dialogue, Communion, and Unity," Brian E. Daley locates the cardinal's ecumenical achievements in relation to the ecumenical movement beginning in the early 1900s. Catherine E. Clifford uncovers the theological roots of Kasper's vision of Christian unity in chapter 10, "The Catholic Tübingen School and Ecumenism," in which she reviews the ecclesiology of Johann Adam Möhler and its influence on Kasper's *The Catholic Church*. In chapter 11, "Catholicism in a New Key," John R. Sachs sheds further light on Kasper's vision of Christian unity as he discusses how Johann Sebastian Drey's theology of the church shaped Kasper's emphasis on the Spirit in the church. Susan K. Wood demonstrates in chapter 12, "Unity at the Table," how Kasper has advanced ecumenism as he has worked for new theological agreements concerning the Eucharist in his dialogues with the Lutheran, Reformed, Anglican, and Methodist churches.

Chapters 13 and 14 examine Kasper's leadership of the Vatican's Commission for Religious Relations with the Jews. In "New Paths of Shalom in Christian-Jewish Relations," Elizabeth T. Groppe highlights five major contributions to understanding, respect, and collaboration between Catholics and Jews. Moreover, she includes tributes to Cardinal Kasper by Susannah Heschel, Adam Gregermann, Shire Lander, Ruth Langer, and David Rosen. In "Celebrating Judaism as a 'Sacrament of Every Otherness,'" Philip A. Cunningham describes how Kasper turned ecclesiastical "problems" into fresh opportunities for improved communications, insight, and respect between Catholics and Jews.

In chapter 15, "Faith Seeking Understanding," John C. Cavadini lauds Kasper's achievement—on which Kristin M. Colberg focuses in chapter 1—of "translating" the Gospel in ways that express discovery and intelligibility. In chapter 16, Cardinal Kasper concludes the book's first and second sections by reflecting on "How to Do Theology Today."

Section 3: Reflections on Forgiveness, Vatican II, and Hope

Chapter 17, "Forgiveness and the Purification of Memory," was a public lecture by Cardinal Kasper at the Tantur Ecumenical Institute, Jerusalem, on May 25, 2004, when he participated in a conference sponsored by the University of Notre Dame's Office of the President, Theology Department, and Institute for Church Life. In this lecture, Kasper gives a theological reflection on Pope John Paul II's public request in March 2000 for forgiveness for the sins committed by the church's members throughout history, especially in the Shoah.

Chapter 18, "Renewal from the Source: The Interpretation and Reception of the Second Vatican Council," is Kasper's Keeley Vatican Lecture, sponsored by the Nanovic Institute for European Studies, at the University of Notre Dame on April 24, 2013. It highlights three phases in the church's reception of Vatican II and its teachings, and it envisions the path ahead during the pontificate of Pope Francis.

Chapter 19, "Be Joyful in Hope: A Homily," is Cardinal Kasper's homily at the University of Notre Dame's Basilica of the Sacred Heart on Saturday evening, April 27, 2013.

Acknowledgments

The Theology of Cardinal Walter Kasper has come to fruition thanks to the efforts of many people, not all of whom can be thanked here.

As already noted, the essays here, except one, are the fruit of Cardinal Kasper's visit to the University of Notre Dame in April 2013. This sojourn, including the Keeley Vatican Lecture, the conference in honor of Cardinal Kasper, and the homily in the Basilica of the Sacred Heart, was made possible through grants at the University of Notre

Dame from the Reverend John J. Jenkins, CSC, the Office of the President; the Institute for Church Life; the Institute for Scholarship in the Liberal Arts' Henkels Lectures; the Nanovic Institute for European Studies; and the Theology Department's Berner Lecture Series and Crown-Minnow Lecture Fund for Christian-Jewish Relations.

Over three years of collaboration, the editors drew on the wise counsel of J. Matthew Ashley, George Augustin, John C. Cavadini, Shawn M. Colberg, Michael A. Fahey, Mary Catherine Hilkert, A. James McAdams, and Thomas F. O'Meara. They received invaluable assistance from Harriet Baldwin and Lauri Roberts in the University of Notre Dame's Office of Academic Conferences; Monica Caro, Sharon Konopka, and Melanie Webb in the Nanovic Institute for European Studies; and Emily Hammock Mosby in the Theology Department. Moreover, the editors benefitted during the conference from the generous collaboration of Reverend William M. Lies, CSC, university vice president for mission engagement and church affairs, and Peter D. Rocca, CSC, director of the Basilica of the Sacred Heart. Finally, in April 2013, they relied on Mr. and Mrs. Harald and Patricia Bellm who helped in hosting Cardinal Walter Kasper and Dr. Hildegard Kasper during their stay at the University of Notre Dame.

The book's essays were initially prepared for publication with the assistance of the theology graduate students Michael Anthony Abril and Brandon R. Peterson. The essays rapidly changed into a publishable manuscript through the enthusiasm, expertise, and diligence of Hans Christoffersen, publisher; Lauren L. Murphy, managing editor; and the production team at Liturgical Press.

The book's editors remain grateful to the people and funds named above and also to the many other people who generously gave assistance so that this book could reach publication. Finally, the editors owe a debt of gratitude to Cardinal Kasper himself. Beginning in March 2011, he assisted the editors as they planned the conference and this volume. Most important, he graciously participated in five intense days at the University of Notre Dame that reached highpoints in the eightieth birthday celebration on April 26 and in the Eucharist on April 27, 2013. As an expression of gratitude for his extraordinary contributions to the church, the academy, and society, we dedicate this *Festschrift* to Cardinal Walter Kasper.

SECTION ONE

God, Freedom, and History

CHAPTER 1

The Task of Theology

Kristin M. Colberg

Few Catholic theologians or church leaders have done more than Walter Kasper to translate effectively the Christian message into the language and practice of our times. The scope of his efforts stretches from his work as a university professor at Münster and Tübingen to his service as bishop of Rottenburg-Stuttgart and ultimately to his leadership of the Pontifical Council for Christian Unity. Throughout that span, he has worked tirelessly to find expressions of the Gospel that best present its truth, hope, and joy. When he was asked in anticipation of his eightieth birthday (March 5, 2013) about how he would want scholars to celebrate his achievements, he responded that he prefers not to think of himself strictly as a church diplomat, an ecumenist, or an academic. Instead of being identified with any of these roles, he has always seen himself primarily as a pastor. Commenting on his career of more than five decades, he observed that he has pursued a single aim: "My question is, and was always, how to translate the Christian tradition in the present context and the present context in the Christian tradition."[1]

Kasper's view of himself as a pastor and his goal of communicating successfully the "good news" to our contemporaries go hand in hand. Agreeing with the Tübingen theologian Johann Sebastian Drey, Kasper holds that "it is the fundamental task of pastoral work to keep the Church alive into the future" and to perpetuate the "transmission of the faith to a continuous present."[2] This task faces serious challenges, however, in the contemporary context in which Christian hope often appears unintelligible or unimportant to people with modern and postmodern sensibilities. Therefore, Kasper's commitment "to translate the Christian tradition in the present context and the present context in the Christian tradition" requires ongoing attempts to interpret Christian belief in ways that respond to today's urgent, existential questions.

This commitment to mediate between the Christian tradition and the world determines Kasper's way of doing theology and illumines the divine mystery on which this theology reflects. For Kasper, the interpretation of the Gospel for people today is not solely a strategy for advancing the "good news." The act of transmission is much more than a technique applied exteriorly to a neutral content. Rather, it corresponds interiorly to the message itself.[3] The inherent translatability of Christian belief discloses the character of Christ's revelation and its significance. Being attentive to this reality, Kasper consistently identifies questions of proper interpretation with questions about the Gospel's content.

This essay elucidates Kasper's understanding of the task of theology and traces its influence on his constructive dialogue between the church and the world. It proceeds in three steps. First, it sheds light on Kasper's thought concerning theology's task in relation to the Christian message itself. Second, it recalls his analysis of modernity's unique challenges, which can convey a sense of Christian incoherence. Third and finally, it reviews Kasper's recent proposals for improving the transmission of the Gospel to today's world.

1. Theology's Task and Challenges

According to Walter Kasper, theology's task is to render "an account of the Christian hope to every human being."[4] This endeavor is inspired by 1 Peter 3:15-16: "Always be ready to make your defense to anyone who demands from you an accounting for the hope that is in you; yet do it with gentleness and reverence." This seemingly straightforward aspiration is not, however, easily realized. It faces a number of challenges. In every age, theology—that is, critical, systematic reflection on the Christian faith—should unfold, Kasper observes, in relation to its "subject," its audience or recipients, and its two foci: God's Word and a specific society. The nature of theology's task introduces at least three distinct challenges.

First, Christian discourse seeks to give expression to a reality that is fundamentally ineffable or transcendent. It strives to proclaim the ultimate mystery that, as such, exceeds our full comprehension and eludes complete articulation in human words and forms. Employing the distinction between a problem and a mystery highlighted by Gabriel Marcel, Kasper asserts that theology is concerned not with resolving a problem but with attempting to "grasp mystery as mystery."[5] Efforts to express the subject matter or content of the Christian faith in concepts risk misrepresenting this limitless, complex reality. Hence, theologians must adopt theological methods that are appropriate to the "subject" or "subject matter" of their critical, systematic reflection.[6] Despite good intentions, a theologian may speak of God in ways that reduce the divine mystery to the linguistic and conceptual economy of this world. Kasper writes: "A theology that has managed to conceive God has in fact misconceived him. . . . [F]or the theological mind, God is not a problem comparable to the many other problems which a person can, at least in principle, solve one after the other. God is an abiding problem; he is the problem par excellence which we describe as mystery."[7]

Second, if it is to be effective, theology must employ a discourse that is meaningful for the communities and individuals to which it is addressed. Christian belief was not intended for monolithic transplantation from one culture to another.[8] An intelligible presentation of Christian hope to a specific society rests on difficult decisions concerning the form of presentation. It must articulate the mystery of Jesus Christ so as to relate to people's experiences and to engage their questions about life's meaning and purpose. For this reason, there is no one account of Christian hope that suffices for all people in all times and places. Thus, in Kasper's judgment, theologians must think about the method of their critical, systematic reflection on the Christian faith; they must ask themselves, "Is it still possible for theology to speak about God? How can it do so?"[9]

Third, theology must hold together two foci: God's revelation and a specific people's questions and ideals. If it is to unite these two realities, it must engage in interpretation. Kasper writes: "Understood in this way dogmatic theology is a hermeneutic activity, a process of translation. It stands midway between two poles: The Word of revelation in Scripture and the present-day realities of Christian proclamation."[10] On the one hand, theology must retrieve the Gospel as expressed in the Bible and the Christian tradition. Yet, on the other hand, it must communicate this "good news" in a way that is intelligible to the people of a specific time and place. A theologian's method, Kasper holds, must "show that this Word can be understood, made operative, and brought to fulfillment today. To state it in methodological terms: Dogma has exegesis as its starting point and missionary proclamation as its goal."[11] In this vein, Kasper's theological method embraces what Aidan Nichols has called a "twin stress" on the Christian tradition and philosophical intelligibility in a given historical moment.[12]

Referring to theology's two foci, Kasper stresses that theologians face the challenge of keeping a proper balance between the Gospel's "identity" and its "relevance."[13] That is, they uphold the identity of the Christian tradition as they maintain an authentic witness to Jesus Christ, and they advance the relevance of the "good news" when they highlight its intelligibility, importance, and relation to the needs, questions, and values of a particular audience. On the one hand, the identity or continuity of Christian belief is rooted in efforts "to represent the person, work and word of Jesus Christ" so that, even if Christians produce a variety of articulations, "they have one starting point and one center."[14] It is comprised by fidelity over two thousand years to the Word expressed in scripture and the Christian tradition. It is this common faith in the unity of God's revelation in Jesus Christ that unites Christians amid vast geographic and cultural differences as well as throughout expansive periods in history. On the other hand, the relevance or significance of the Christian message derives from the fact that the Gospel should ultimately reveal to us both God and ourselves in God's presence. The Gospel's inherent relevance ensures that while Christians are bound together in a common identity, they respect and value a diversity of legitimate expressions of belief in Jesus Christ.[15]

As Kasper points out, the church sometimes errs by one-sidedly emphasizing either the identity or the relevance of the Gospel. Why does this imbalance occur? It results from the church's unwillingness or inability to abide the tensions inherent to witnessing to the divine mystery, to the transcendent reality that—as we noted above—is beyond our full understanding. Attempts to eliminate this tension only intensify the church's struggle with incoherence by forfeiting God as the ultimate mystery and also the church itself as mystery. Highlighting the difficulty of keeping the balance between continuity and significance, Kasper states that "when the Church tries to be relevant, it runs the risk of surrendering its unambiguousness for the sake of openness. Yet, whenever it tries to speak straightforwardly and clearly it risks losing sight of men and their actual problems. If the church worries about identity, it risks a loss of relevance; if on the other hand it struggles for relevance, it may forfeit its identity."[16]

Theology in particular faces the challenge of holding together the Gospel's identity and relevance. Giving voice to this issue, Kasper asks:

> How can theology escape from the identity-relevance dilemma in which it finds itself? How can it escape the deadly logic of preserving its relevance at the cost of identity, or keeping its identity at the cost of relevance—and at the price of retreat into the ghetto? Without a clear, unequivocal individual identity there is no relevance; but of course without relevance there is no identity.[17]

If theology is to give an intelligible account of Christian hope, it must show that Christian belief's continuity and significance are inseparable from one another. As Kasper points out, the Gospel's identity is inherently relational; it always emerges in relation to a people's particular questions and aspirations. Conversely, the Gospel's relevance is vacuous without a substantive and definitive contribution to offer. Thus, when theology witnesses appropriately to God's revelation in Jesus Christ, it communicates the identity of Christian belief as it discloses that which is absolutely relevant: the truth of human existence. It reflects on the Word that is always new and yet always at the heart of human life. "If this newness is abandoned," Kasper states, "the relevance of Christianity is destroyed." But this "newness" remains anchored in continuity, in identity. "Once identity is lost, relevance is lost as well. Only the one who has identity can have relevance."[18] In sum, if theology is to give an authentic translation or interpretation of God's revelation in scripture and tradition, it must maintain the balance between the identity and the relevance of the Gospel.

2. Contemporary Challenges to Theology

Since its inception, the church has continually sought to balance the Christian tradition's identity and its relevance. While this endeavor is inherently difficult, it is especially formidable, Kasper observes, in our contemporary context. Today, the Christian community's ability to present the Gospel effectively has been strained by the apparent abyss between the experience of Christian faith and the experience of the modern/postmodern world. In light of this separation, the church's teachings may seem irrelevant and incoherent to many people. Reflecting on this dilemma, Kasper writes:

> The real question is: How does this central concept of the Christian faith (the relationship between nature, grace and culture) relate to our modern and frightfully secular culture? How does it relate to our everyday experiences and those social, economic and political issues which confront us on a daily basis? How can we keep the message of salvation alive in a world that is characterized by the experience of destructive forces? How can we speak of reconciliation in a world that is not reconciled but is deeply alienated? What is the meaning of the message of grace for the Church and our culture on our way into the third millennium?[19]

In response to these questions, Kasper has explained (1) what he perceives to be the central issue, (2) the post-Enlightenment notion of autonomy, and (3) the Christian notion of freedom.

(1) *The Central Issue: The Notion of Freedom*

In Kasper's judgment, the apparent separation between the church and the modern world is inauthentic and artificially compartmentalizes that which should be understood as one reality.[20] Fresh answers to the question of the relationship between the church and the world require that we shed light on the seeming dissonance. As Kasper notes, "No answer is intelligible unless people can first grasp the question to which it is the answer."[21] As the issue comes into sharper focus, then it must be shown that the church has something meaningful to say to the world, something that human beings cannot say by themselves and to which they are unconditionally related. Yet, to achieve this aim the church must acknowledge its actual discomfort with the secular world and deliberately become more engaged in it. As the church does so, it will find that contemporary thought could provide the church with resources for successfully conveying its message of hope. Keeping the balance between identity and relevance, church leaders and theologians could translate the Christian tradition into the modern/postmodern idiom.

Analysis reveals, Kasper argues, that while the estrangement between the church and today's world appears to be the result of the collision of two mutually exclusive worldviews, it actually occurs because of the intersection of the church's internal weaknesses and also of modernity's internal weaknesses. Given their respective weaknesses and crises, the Christian community and the secular society perceive the other as a threat.[22] In other words, the underlying issue is that the two meet at a moment when each is too weak to interact constructively with the other. As a consequence, they fail to recognize their authentic relationship and common goals.[23] Unable to consider appropriately the challenges presented by the other, both respond to the encounter with a resounding no. In this way, the rupture between the church and the modern/postmodern world stems from a lack of authentic engagement between the two rather than their fundamental incompatibility. What they encounter is a distorted version of the other, and thus what they reject are not the principles of modernity or Christianity but unrealized caricatures of them.[24]

According to Kasper, the locus for the apparent collision between Christian and modern/postmodern sensibilities is the issue of human freedom. At the center of people's self-understanding is a strong sense of personal authority that stands side by side with an inchoate yearning for a transcendent source of life and values. The challenge of construing the relationship between personal autonomy, that is, self-determination, and theonomy, that is, faithfulness of God, frustrates both the cohesion of the church and contemporary society and also the ability of each to communicate with the other.[25] The Christian community and the secular society must attain a coherent, intelligible view of the relationship between personal autonomy and theonomy if each is to engage contemporary men and women who are demanding an account of how to reconcile human freedom and God's grace. As things stand, neither the church nor the contemporary world has so far succeeded in speaking meaningfully about the relationship between human freedom and divine freedom. The inability of each to offer an inclusive account of freedom or liberation leads both the church and society to a lack of intellectual cohesion and hence to a defensive stance in relation to the other.

Nevertheless, the point of apparent difference and defensiveness has the potential, Kasper proposes, to be the point of rapprochement between the church and society. The issue of freedom can become the source of the interdependence between the Christian community and today's world. For this shift to happen, each must consider anew its understanding of the relationship between personal autonomy and divine presence and action.[26]

(2) *Clarifying the Secular Notion of Personal Autonomy*

The underlying crisis in the contemporary world, Kasper avers, is secular society's inability to answer the very question it has proposed concerning human freedom. Having highlighted the human potential for personal autonomy, it has not made available the primary resource that would enable people to realize their liberation. Society has ignored this resource because it has denied the roots of its notion of personal autonomy and, given this denial, it cannot respond effectively to questions of how we as individuals and communities can realize our full selves. The notion of human freedom, which is the starting point and centerpiece of the modern/postmodern worldview, has its origins in the Judeo-Christian tradition. But secular society rejects that foundation and thereby separates itself from the wellspring that nourishes authentic self-realization.

Kasper argues that the concept of human freedom is born "on the very first page" of the Judeo-Christian scriptures with their witness to the fundamental distinction between God and the world.[27] The notion of a transcendent Source outside the cosmos who freely creates a world that otherwise could not have existed inaugurates "an epoch-making revolution" by establishing both the ontological difference between God and creation and also creation's absolute reliance on God, who respects creation as "the other."[28] The understanding of the world as a relative reality ruptures the univocal view of the relation between God and creation that dominated the ancient and medieval worldviews, and it serves as the basis for the idea of the relative independence of men and women in relation to God. Kasper writes:

> It is precisely when God's divinity was taken seriously that the world could be demythologized and dehumanized. And the logical result was that the worldliness of the world could be

> taken seriously too. It is precisely the world's radical dependence on God which makes the general independence before God possible: this is the special character of the Bible's definition of the relation between God and the world. As what is radically dependent, the world is what is not divine. It therefore stands over against God in relative independence.[29]

The Bible's acknowledgment of the ontological distinction between God and the world democratizes the *imago Dei* and establishes the equality of all men and women in their relationship with God. Because every person equally bears the divine image, he or she has an innate sacred dignity and should be free from domination or manipulation by other human beings.[30] Further, since all men and women are unconditionally oriented to God, they do not experience fulfillment in the things of this world and should be free in relation to them. According to Kasper, it is the idea of a relative world, rooted in the notion of an ontological distinction, that serves as the ultimate ground for asserting the fundamental equality and dignity of every human being.

The crisis of our modern/postmodern era has resulted from the idea of a "worldly world," a world that is detached from its transcendent source and *telos*. With its turn to the knowing subject, contemporary thought often eliminates God as the ontological reference point that defines and determines reality, including personal autonomy. It consequently offers an account of freedom that regards self-determination as an independent starting point in human life. As such, the ideal for men and women is no longer deification but rather humanization. Accordingly, human freedom is understood no longer in relation to its goal or *telos* but as a goal in itself, as wholly autonomous and self-legislating. As a result, there emerges the view of human persons as self-contained and "liberated" from an ultimate source of truth and meaning; in short, there is only a "self-sufficient humanism."[31] But with the assertions of the world as the totality of reality and of each human subject as the determinant of its own reality, men and women lose the "all-embracing unity of reality" and become wanderers, "homeless" in the world.[32] Without a clear sense of its relation to theonomy, the sense of personal autonomy loses its ability to engage the crucial questions of human existence, and the world becomes fragmented by competing claims of authority. Thus, the desire for human freedom awakened in modern/postmodern thought cannot be realized in post-Enlightenment categories, and the secular system of thought dissolves into incoherence. In effect, the modern/postmodern era loses the capacity to function as the organizing principle of reality.

(3) *Clarifying the Christian Notion of Freedom*

In Kasper's judgment, the church currently suffers in its encounter with secular society because of its inability to articulate effectively the relationship between nature and grace that is the basis of the relationship between personal autonomy and theonomy. Christian theology has struggled in every era to give an intelligible account of the unity-in-difference between creation and God. It has time and again sought to clarify the bond between God's immanence and God's transcendence; the former is expressed in Genesis 2:4b-25 and the latter in Genesis 1:1–2:4b. Although the book of Genesis attests to the union and yet ontological distinction between the natural and the supernatural realms, theologians have had difficulty, especially since the Enlightenment, in speaking in readily understandable terms about the ultimate mystery. They tend to give an insufficient exposition concerning divine immanence, divine transcendence, and their paradoxical unity. As a result, today's church is unable to communicate well its claims about the transcendent God's presence and action in human affairs. It lacks coherent statements concerning the God who is both wholly other and yet intimately related with humankind and creation. Given this inability, the Christian community has not realized its synthetic or unifying role in contemporary society; it appears to be one social sector or mode of reality amid others instead of being the primary interpreter of reality.

A devastating consequence of the nature-grace issue is, Kasper holds, that the church remains unable to articulate a noncompetitive relationship between personal autonomy and theonomy. This inability gives rise to society's perception that post-Enlightenment notions of freedom are incompatible with Christian conceptions of freedom. Moreover, the church's claim to present the truth of human existence seemingly stands in fundamental tension with contemporary society's view of personal autonomy, leaving little or no common ground for meaningful dialogue. Gaining the attention, interest, and respect of an audience today depends on the church's ability to show that its notions of an omnipotent God and an institutional church are not incompatible with a dynamic concept of personal freedom. According to Kasper, the church must give evidence that "freedom and institution are not antithetical terms"; it must demonstrate and explain institutionalized freedom.[33] Further, ecclesial officials, pastoral leaders, and theologians must show that "being bound to the church does not mean being bound to an abstract system of doctrine. It means being woven into a living process of tradition and communication in which the gospel of Jesus Christ is interpreted and actualized."[34] In sum, meaningful translations of the Gospel for our world rely on the church clarifying how the modern/postmodern notion of freedom and the Christian life are not contradictory. Without a clear articulation of the relationship between personal autonomy and theonomy the church's interpretations of its scripture and tradition will suffer from a lack of intelligibility and import.

Given its current dilemma, the church must turn not only outward, *ad extra*, to comprehend our modern/postmodern society world but also inward, *ad intra*, to understand some central elements of its identity. While it asks about its relevance, that is, about *how* it might effectively address today's society, it must develop a deeper grasp of *what* it has to say. Regarding this ecclesial self-examination, Kasper writes:

> The present crisis facing Christianity in the West does not touch merely on peripheral concerns; rather, it specifically addresses this very question. We are dealing here primarily with a crisis of relevance. We hear daily dogmatic teachings and, even more, moral rules of the Church no longer reach a large segment of believers. They appear to offer answers to questions that are no longer asked. Nonetheless, the crisis of relevance represents the merely superficial side of the problem. It has long since led to a much deeper crisis within Christian churches. The question is no longer *how* the Church will be able to reach out to the modern, secularized world; rather the question is *what* constitutes Christianity as such. What can, *must* Christianity say to the modern world? Does it have something of its own to say, something unmistakeable?[35]

In Kasper's judgment, the church is currently struggling to articulate more accurately and intelligibly two key aspects of its identity:

the complementarity between nature and grace and also the compatibility between personal autonomy and theonomy. It must advance its insight into and expression of these two crucial relationships if it is to engage in a more fruitful dialogue with our modern/postmodern society. In short, it must undertake a scrutiny *ad intra* in order to communicate more effectively *ad extra*. Until it knows its own identity more fully, the Christian community will not succeed in its relevance, that is, in translating the Gospel into the contemporary world.[36]

3. Communicating the Christian Hope Today

The primary task of theologians, Walter Kasper insists, is to communicate the Christian view of God's presence and action in human life. As mentioned at the outset, it is to give "an accounting of the hope that is in you" (1 Pet 3:15-16). Achieving this goal today, however, is, as Kasper readily acknowledges, no easy endeavor.

From the mid-1800s into the mid-1900s, most Catholic theologians aimed at imparting what was perceived to be the church's unchanging or timeless theology, its *theologia perennis*. But over that century, they increasingly realized that their message was not making sense to more and more people, even to Catholics. In light of the unintelligibility of their neoscholastic teaching, they realized and the Second Vatican Council affirmed that the church and its theologians must continually interpret the Gospel anew for its specific time and place. Commenting on this new approach to theology, Kasper writes: "Theology cannot choose its time. It has to convey the Christian message to men and women of its own era, and has to give an account of the Christian hope. A *theologia perennis*—a theology that is in principle timeless—is of no use to anyone. This commits theology today to a critical and creative reception of modern thought."[37]

What is involved in undertaking "a critical and creative reception of modern thought"? According to Kasper, theologians today must clarify the Christian notion of freedom. In particular, they must show how it reconciles the best elements of the contemporary concept of personal autonomy and the church's concept of theonomy. They must explain the Christian insight that true freedom is liberation *for* God and not freedom *from* limitations. This idea gives direction and meaning to the otherwise vacuous secular notion of personal autonomy. In Kasper's words, Christianity "gives human freedom, which by itself is empty, the content which is alone adequate for it: that which completes freedom cannot be something else than freedom; that which fulfills freedom can only be freedom itself."[38] The post-Enlightenment notion of personal autonomy that has collapsed amid competing claims of various authorities attains content when it is associated with the Christian notion of the ultimate mystery or "the Absolute," God, who transcends the world and yet moves within it seeking both to emancipate all men and women from the innate tendency to absolutize or deify temporal realities and also to empower them for their full personal existence. In sum, theologians must explain that "Christian freedom presupposes human freedom, [and] gives it its final determination and provides it with its final fulfillment."[39]

As Kasper reiterates in numerous places, the "final determination" of personal autonomy is not an abstract principle but Jesus Christ, alive in the Holy Spirit. Thus, the strength to attain our "final fulfillment" comes not solely from within human beings or from an idea but from the living Christ and the Spirit whom Christ has released within creation. In other words, Jesus Christ and the Holy Spirit now liberate our constricted human freedom so that human persons might realize their authentic selves in union with God. Kasper explains: "In the life of Jesus we are given the definition that could come to us through no other means—a lived, acted out model which defines and fulfills the nature of human freedom. Christ reveals that the self-emptying love which appears as 'foolishness' in the 'light of reason' is, in fact, the pattern which makes sense of our lives."[40]

To be sure, these reflections could move at this point into rich themes in Kasper's theology, themes that this book's other chapters pursue. It suffices here to conclude with Kasper's three proposals for improving the church's translation or interpretation of the Gospel in our modern/postmodern world. These proposals appear in Walter Kasper's recently published *The Catholic Church: Nature, Reality and Mission* (2011).

First, the church must prove itself to be a symbol and a safeguard of the dignity and freedom of every human person. As it does so, it must admit that in today's society "the religious-transcendent orientation is no longer seen as normal. . . . Where once transcendence pointed towards a different, mysterious, mysteriously divine world, this place has been taken by a big yawning void and where the gods once were, there now reigns the fear of constantly new ghosts."[41] Given the secular mentality, the church must deliberately witness to God as the transcendent ground or Source of all reality. As Kasper notes, what is needed today is "new joy in God and new enthusiasm for him. In a largely secularized world we need a theocentric turn." Theologians must speak again of God as the source and goal of all reality, indeed as the fulfillment of our human longing. "In our situation the Church becomes a prophetic-critical sign against the innerworldly secularism that thinks it can cope with life out of personal insights and achievements and that believes it can plan and forge the fortune of life on its own."[42]

Second, the church's theocentric turn must lead to a Christological concentration.[43] Jesus Christ—the one person who is fully divine and fully human—is the key for interpreting the relationship between personal autonomy and theonomy as well as between nature and grace. The Word made flesh (John 1:14) reveals that divine agency does not compete with human agency. Rather, Jesus Christ manifests that the unity and the difference between nature and grace, between personal autonomy and theonomy increase *not in inverse proportion but in direct relation*. This perfect union of God and humanity, where nothing is truncated or excluded, is represented in the Council of Chalcedon's formula concerning Jesus Christ in whom the human nature and the divine nature remain "unmixed and undivided" in one person. This ancient doctrine is the lens through which men and women can make sense of their lives as part of a larger transcendent experience of God.[44] In this reality, men and women can see that opening oneself to the divine is not self-destructive; on the contrary, it is the condition for the possibility of gaining one's authentic personal identity.

Third and finally, the church must continue to undergo a spiritual renewal in relation to Jesus Christ and the Holy Spirit. Kasper writes: "Jesus Christ did not simply live two thousand years ago and then depart from us. He lives and continues to work through the Holy Spirit in the Church and in the world. So the Church is more than an institution; it is, as an institution, time and again a new event in the Holy Spirit." Although it may seem contradictory, the church must adopt forms of life that manifest its ability to institutionalize freedom as it lives in faithfulness to Jesus Christ in the Spirit. "In this way, the theocentric turn and the Christological concentration should become fruitful in a spiritual deepening."

More than fifty years ago, Walter Kasper set out "to translate the Christian tradition into the present context and the present context into the Christian tradition." As he has pursued this goal, he has realized that theologians need to find ways to overcome the gap between the church and secular society. For his part, he saw that while their respective notions of freedom had brought about their estrangement from each other, these differing notions shared a common wellspring and could mutually enrich each other. In his judgment, the question of freedom that served as the point of impact in the collision between the church and contemporary society could become the point at which they could speak meaningfully to each. He writes: "The proclamation of the Gospel of Christian freedom is the primary service the Church can offer the world."[45] For this reason, running as a dominant thread through many of Kasper's writings is the theme of Christian freedom, the freedom or liberation that Jesus Christ has accomplished and now offers to all people in the Holy Spirit through the church. As Walter Kasper has developed key aspects of Christian freedom, he has pursued the primary task of theology today; namely, he has rendered "an account of the Christian hope to every human being."[46]

Kasper's ability to bring together the issues of the church and the world in a truly synthetic way illumines a fundamentally hopeful path for theology in the twenty-first century. If the church seeks a renewed understanding of its own identity as meaningful and relevant to contemporary men and women, then it must engage the secular world in earnest. A reception of modernity and a quest for greater self-understanding that is mutually critical, creative, and ongoing means that there are no once-for-all translations of the Gospel. The work of translating is never complete, for even the most successful interpretations of the good news are always incomplete relative to the reality they seek to express. This theological commitment has led Kasper to insist on dialogue throughout his career, and, as a result, his work of translation has made invaluable contributions to our efforts to render an "account of the hope that is within us."

Endnotes

1. Walter Kasper, e-mail message to author, March 18, 2011.

2. Walter Kasper, *The Catholic Church: Nature, Reality and Mission*, trans. Thomas Hoebel (London: Bloomsbury Academic, 2014), 9.

3. On Walter Kasper's theological method and the mystery it seeks to express, see his *Die Methoden der Dogmatik—Einheit und Vielheit* (Munich: Kösel-Verlag, 1967).

4. Walter Kasper, *Theology and Church*, trans. Margaret Kohl (New York: Crossroad, 1989), 32.

5. Walter Kasper, *Jesus the Christ*, trans. V. Green (Mahwah, NJ: Paulist Press, 1985), 14. On Marcel's distinction and its significance, see Thomas G. Weinandy, *Does God Suffer?* (Notre Dame, IN: Notre Dame Press, 2000), 27–39.

6. Kasper, *Die Methoden der Dogmatik*, 6.

7. Walter Kasper, *The God of Jesus Christ*, trans. Matthew J. O'Connell (New York: Crossroad, 1996), 13. According to Kasper, "to preserve the transcendence of God is also to preserve the transcendence of the human person and therefore the freedom and inalienable rights of humanity" (p. 15).

8. See Walter Kasper, *Faith and the Future*, trans. Robert Nowell (New York: Crossroad, 1982). On Christianity's inherent translatability, see Lamin Sanneh, *Translating the Message: The Missionary Impact on Culture* (New York: Orbis Books, 1989).

9. Kasper, *Die Methoden der Dogmatik*, 1.

10. Ibid., 25.

11. Ibid.

12. Aidan Nichols, "Walter Kasper and His Theological Programme" (1986), in *Scribe of the Kingdom: Essays on Theology and Culture*, vol. 2 (London: Sheed and Ward, 1994), 44–53, 50.

13. On the contemporary "dilemma" of relevance and identity, see Kasper, *Jesus the Christ*, 15–25; idem, *Theology and Church*, 1–16, 73–79; idem, "Nature, Grace and Culture: On the Meaning of Secularization," in *Catholicism and Secularization in America*, ed. David L. Schindler (Notre Dame, IN: Communio Books, 1994), 31–51. When I spoke with Kasper regarding his use of the concepts of relevance and identity, he commented that "this is the center of it all and not enough has been done to explore it." In *Jesus the Christ*, Kasper cites Jürgen Moltmann, *The Crucified God*, trans. R. A. Wilson and John Bowden (New York: Harper and Row, 1974).

14. Kasper, *Jesus the Christ*, 15.

15. Kasper's understanding of translation is a form of critical correlation whereby he attempts to reconceive of truths of Christian faith in terms assessable to contemporary readers. On the development of critical correlation as a theological method, see Francis Schüssler Fiorenza, "Systematic Theology: Task and Methods," in *Systematic Theology: Roman Catholic Perspectives*, ed. Francis Schüssler Fiorenza and John P. Galvin (Minneapolis: Fortress Press, 2011), 3–77, esp. 41–47;

David Tracy, "The Uneasy Alliance Reconceived: Catholic Theological Method, Modernity and Postmodernity," *Theological Studies* 56 (1989): 548–70.

16. Kasper, *Jesus the Christ*, 15.

17. Kasper, *Theology and Church*, 4.

18. Kasper, "Nature, Grace and Culture," 44.

19. Ibid., 31.

20. See Walter Kasper, *The Christian Understanding of Freedom and the History of Freedom in the Modern Era: The Meeting and Confrontation between Christianity and the Modern Era in a Postmodern Situation*, trans. Joseph A. Murphy (Milwaukee: Marquette University Press, 1988); idem, "Nature, Grace and Culture," esp. 36–44.

21. Kasper, *The God of Jesus Christ*, 12.

22. Ibid., 41–45.

23. See Walter Kasper, "Autonomy and Theonomy: The Place of Christianity in the Modern World," in *Theology and Church*, 32–53.

24. See Kasper, *The Christian Understanding of Freedom*, 18–29.

25. Kasper, *Theology and Church*, 32–45.

26. Here Kasper is drawing on the later work of F. W. J. Schelling, in particular, his ideas that human freedom needs to be freed by God's freedom and that Jesus Christ fulfills the need for a "new beginning in history." See Walter Kasper, *Das Absolute in Geschichte* (Mainz: Matthias Grünewald, 1965). Concerning Schelling's influence on Kasper's Christology, see Robert A. Krieg, *Story Shaped Christology: The Role of Narratives in Identifying Jesus Christ* (New York: Paulist Press, 1988), 34–64, esp. 38–40.

27. Kasper, *The Christian Understanding of Freedom*, 6.

28. Ibid.

29. Kasper, *Theology and Church*, 35.

30. Concerning Genesis 1:26-27, Kasper writes: "The idea of the image of God is now transferred to every human being; the result of this democratization is that everyone, irrespective of his ethnic, racial, or religious affiliation, is God's direct partner, and as such enjoys an unconditional dignity that no one can dispose" (see Kasper, *Theology and Church*, 36).

31. Kasper, *The Catholic Church*, 33.

32. Kasper, "Nature, Grace and Culture," 38.

33. Kasper, *Theology and Church*, 70.

34. Ibid., 6.

35. Kasper, "Nature, Grace and Culture," 32; Kasper's emphasis.

36. It is important to be clear that Kasper's call for greater *ad intra* clarity for the sake of more effective *ad extra* dialogue does not exclude or diminish the value of pursuing dialogue and self-understanding from the other direction, that is, moving from *ad extra* to *ad intra*. Kasper often affirms that engagement with the world is an essential element of developing awareness of the church's own identity and mission. For him, these two impulses always work together and inform one another.

37. Kasper, *Theology and Church*, 80.

38. Kasper, *The Christian Understanding of Freedom*, 41.

39. Ibid, 37.

40. Kasper, *Theology and Church*, 67.

41. Kasper, *The Catholic Church*, 333.

42. Ibid., 334.

43. Ibid., 336.

44. On Kasper's use of Chalcedon's teaching, see his *Theology and Church*, 94–108; idem, "Neuansätze gegenwärtiger Christologie," in *Wer ist Jesus Christus?*, ed. J. Sauer (Freiburg: Herder, 1977).

45. Kasper, *The Christian Understanding of Freedom*, 40.

46. Kasper, *Theology and Church*, 32.

CHAPTER 2

A Distinctive Theological Approach

Francis Schüssler Fiorenza

I am delighted to have the opportunity to be back at the University of Notre Dame among friends in order to honor Cardinal Kasper. As my teacher in Münster, Walter Kasper had a formative influence on me. My wife Elisabeth and I have always greatly appreciated his friendship and encouragement, especially during our years in Münster.

In 1964, convinced of the importance of theology for the church's ministry, I obtained a fellowship to study at the University of Munich with Karl Rahner, who then held the university's Romano Guardini Chair in the philosophy department. When I learned that Rahner's students in Munich could not earn their doctorates in theology, I decided at the last minute to transfer to the University of Münster. This change made sense because I was interested in studying both with Johann Baptist Metz, Rahner's former student, who had just been appointed to Münster's chair for fundamental theology (my specific area of interest), and also with Joseph Ratzinger, who had recently joined Münster's faculty to teach systematic theology. Moreover, the biblical scholar Rudolf Schnackenburg had received an invitation to join Münster's faculty, and there were rumors that Rahner himself might eventually move to the University of Münster.

When I arrived in Münster, I found that my fellow students in the Marianum, a residence hall for Catholics, were excited that the young professor Walter Kasper had recently joined the faculty in systematic theology. They knew nothing about him except that he was, at that time, the youngest professor in West Germany. He was offering "Christology" four times a week at eight o'clock in the morning. Despite the early hour, I eagerly went to Kasper's classes because of their content and clarity. Elisabeth, then a student in biblical studies, also attended these lectures, and so we indirectly owe our marriage to Walter Kasper. After we met each other through mutual friends on the feast of the Epiphany, we often ate breakfast together right after Kasper's class in the university's cafeteria, and we discussed that day's lecture.[1]

My years in Münster from 1964 to 1970 corresponded to the years that Walter Kasper taught there. Thus, I had the opportunity to take many courses with him. At the same time, I took courses with Joseph Ratzinger and Karl Rahner, who accepted an appointment to Münster's faculty in 1967. As things turned out, Rahner even lived down the hall from me in the Marianum. As a student, I wrestled to sort through the differences among these three German theologians—differences that have become more evident today. Walter Kasper's approach to theology came to influence my own understanding of systematic theology.

In this chapter, I compare the writings of that time by Kasper, Ratzinger, and Rahner on two related sets of topics: (1) revelation, scripture, and tradition and (2) history, freedom, and modernity. Their differences provide the context for me to profile the distinctiveness, importance, and legacy of Cardinal Kasper's theology. Although Johann Baptist Metz was also teaching in Münster during those years, I do not discuss his theology here because I do not want to overextend this comparison and because he has dealt primarily with the second set of issues but not with the first set.

1. Revelation, Scripture, and Tradition

In May 1964, Karl Rahner gave a lecture on divine revelation at the University of Münster when the university awarded him an honorary doctorate. A few months later, when I arrived there, an unpublished copy of his lecture was circulating among the students in the Marianum.[2] A year later, Rahner published that lecture along with an essay by Joseph Ratzinger on the relation between scripture and tradition.[3] In late 1965, Walter Kasper discussed the same topic in his *Dogma unter dem Wort Gottes* ("Dogma under the Word of God").[4]

Karl Rahner contends in his lecture that, in reaction to modern thought, Catholic neoscholastic theology had developed a too extrinsic understanding of God's presence and action in human life. In contrast with that prevailing view, he argues that revelation despite its divine origin belongs to the innermost realm of human history in general. The relation between divine causality and human causality should be understood in such a way that God as the transcendent ground of his creation is not one categorical cause beside others in the world. Instead, God's creative activity takes place in and through the self-transcendence of human persons. Rahner concludes: "If that is correct, then the transcendental and the categorical revelation and the history of revelation are co-extensive with the spiritual history of human beings in general."[5] Pursuing this theme, Rahner underscores more consistently than before in Catholic theology the transcendental character of revelation in relation to the categorical symbolization of revelation. In doing this, he highlights that the transcendental dimension of human life is universal.

Joseph Ratzinger discusses two theses upheld at that time by Josef Rupert Geiselmann of the Catholic Tübingen School. The first is that the Council of Trent (1545–63) did not explicitly define the truth of revelation as divided into two separate sources, one being scripture and the other being tradition, and the second is that Roman Catholic theology, in agreement with Martin Luther, can accept the material sufficiency of scripture.[6] Regarding the second thesis, Ratzinger responds that "the sufficiency of scripture is a secondary problem."[7] The primary issue, he holds, lies in the concepts of abuse and authority and especially in the "relationship between the authority of the church and the authority of Holy Scripture. Everything else depends on this relation."[8] To resolve the issue of the relation between the church and scripture, Ratzinger argues that divine revelation is greater than scripture. God is present in the Christ event, and Christ's Spirit is present in the church, Christ's body. Moreover, the Christian tradition originates in the Father's sending of his Son, and the organ of this tradition lies in the church's full power and teaching office.[9] According to one of Ratzinger's formulations, while God's Word and the church's tradition are the causes of Christian unity, the church's teaching office is the condition of this unity. The authority of the church's teaching office is central to Ratzinger's interpretation of Catholic theology since the Council of Trent.[10]

Walter Kasper, a student of Geiselmann, places the Christian tradition at the center of his theology. In his doctoral dissertation (completed in 1961), he studies the notion of tradition in the theology of the Roman School, whose members included Carlo Passaglia, Giovanni Perrone, and Clemens Schrader. The dissertation's seminal idea was initially contained in a seminar paper that Kasper wrote for Geiselmann in 1955.[11] In his dissertation's treatment of Perrone's theology and in its conclusion, Kasper discusses the notion of the "living tradition" developed by Johann Adam Möhler of the Catholic Tübingen School.[12] Moreover, he also points to the understanding of the "active tradition" in the work of Johann Baptist Franzelin.

Building on his doctoral work, Kasper clearly outlines in *Dogma unter dem Wort Gottes* a constructive position on divine revelation that is distinct from Rahner's and Ratzinger's views. He starts with an analysis of the Gospel's truth. Appropriating the later notion of language of Martin Heidegger, he maintains that theologians should begin their intellectual inquiries, not as René Descartes and Immanuel Kant do, with human thinking or with our transcendental subjectivity, but "rather with language because language first makes possible thinking."[13] Those of us who have worked with the ideas of Hans-Georg Gadamer and Paul Ricoeur recognize the importance of Kasper's starting point.[14] Kasper rightly emphasizes the unity of event and word, of our experience and our talk about it. The ultimate point of unity has occurred, according to Christian faith, when the Word became flesh in Jesus Christ (John 1:14). By beginning with the importance of language, Kasper differentiates his theological method not only from the extrinsic approach in neoscholastic theology but also from the exclusively transcendental approach in Rahner's fundamental theology. Indeed, he explicitly disagrees with Rahner's presupposition that one should "bypass the word of revelation and ask for the conditions of the possibility of revelation and thereby demonstrate that humans are 'hearers of the word.'"[15]

In *Dogma unter dem Wort Gottes* Kasper proposes a theology of the Gospel, the *Evangelium*, a theology that in his judgment the church has not yet fully developed. He clarifies that scripture is not the Gospel itself but "a manifold testimony of the Gospel."[16] In this regard, he refers to understanding of scripture's "spiritual sense," promoted by Origen, with reference to Jesus Christ, salvation, the church, and eschatological hope. Kasper also points out that Thomas Aquinas's exposition of Gospel takes place within his teaching on grace. In other words, the Gospel exists in the grace of the Holy Spirit, and it is present in our faith in Jesus Christ.[17] Thus, the Gospel is primarily the grace of the Holy Spirit, and it is secondarily the written scripture.

Turning to the Council of Trent, Kasper discusses Cardinal Cervini's three principles—principles to which Ratzinger also refers in his essay—concerning the foundation of our faith: scripture, the Gospel (implanted in the hearts of the faithful), and the Holy Spirit in the hearts of the believers and in the church. The conclusion that Kasper draws from Trent's teaching is this: "The living Gospel in the church is a manifold source of all truth of salvation and all disciplines of praxis."[18] Further, Kasper affirms the material sufficiency of scripture in a way that is close to Geiselmann's position. In sum, in *Dogma unter dem Wort Gottes*, Kasper works out the dynamic and reciprocally illuminating interaction that scripture, tradition, and dogma have with one another as the church seeks to understand and communicate the Gospel.

The relation between scripture and tradition receives further discussion in Kasper's writings. In an essay of 1966, the theologian discusses the Second Vatican Council's progress on this topic. As he observes, in its Dogmatic Constitution on Divine Revelation, *Dei verbum* (DV), the council teaches the unity of scripture and tradition, it rejects the view of tradition as being only oral tradition, and it describes tradition as grounded in the Holy Spirit's life-giving function in church. Kasper underscores that the council views the Christian tradition as the living understanding and actualization of the Gospel. Further, he proposes that a hermeneutic of mission for tradition could work out of the council's pastoral intent.[19]

In a later essay, Kasper distinguishes among three models concerning the relation of scripture and tradition: (1) the ancient church's model of tradition and traditions, (2) the Council of Trent's and the post-Tridentine model of scripture and the church, and (3) the post–Vatican II model of dogma and history.[20] The post-Tridentine model stresses the teaching office's primary role in the interpretation of scripture and in the transmission of tradition. According to this view, the church's hierarchy realizes in its teachings with full power and authority the charism of truth, which (according to Irenaeus of Lyons and other patristic writers) the Holy Spirit has given to the church. In other words, the magisterium becomes the proximate "rule of faith" (*regulae fidei*), whereas scripture and tradition become the remote rule of faith.[21]

In Kasper's judgment, the modern model is positive to the extent that it does not relegate scripture and tradition to a purely antiquarian, historical, and documentary role as occurs in Gallicanism or Jansenism. Instead, it regards tradition as an active process of transmission. This dynamic view of tradition as the living appropriation of the truth is present in the writings of Johann Adam Möhler, Cardinal John Henry Newman, and Matthias Scheeben. It relates scripture to God's Word, and it understands the church's tradition and teaching office as giving witness to this Word. According to Kasper, *Dei verbum* makes another decisive contribution insofar as it affirms the ancient model's conviction that "this magisterium is not superior to the word of God, but is rather its servant" (DV 10). Kasper presents a vision in which scripture and tradition interrelate so that the church's various charisms, offices, and ministries work together to give witness to God's Word. In this perspective, one church office should not therefore monopolistically rule over the other offices, charisms, and ministries.

To sum up, while Karl Rahner accentuates the transcendental aspect of revelation and while Joseph Ratzinger emphasizes the role of the church's magisterium in the interpretation of scripture and tradition, Walter Kasper outlines the complex and dynamic interaction of scripture, the living tradition, and the Spirit's action as the church attempts to proclaim the Gospel.

2. History, Freedom, and Modernity

Turning to the topic of history, freedom, and modernity, I shall now focus on what Joseph Ratzinger, Karl Rahner, and Walter Kasper said on these topics in their publications in the mid-1960s.

(1) *Joseph Ratzinger on History, Freedom, and Modernity*

In 1965, Joseph Ratzinger made two relevant points concerning history, freedom, and modernity in his introductory lectures at the University of Münster, lectures that appeared as *Introduction to Christianity* (1968). First, he commented on a paradigmatic anecdote in Harvey Cox's *The Secular City* (1965), which in translation gained as much attention in Germany as it had in the United States. Cox relates the story that when a fire breaks out in a circus, one of the circus's clowns runs to the village to get help. The villagers immediately notice that the man is wearing the antiquated dress of a clown, and they laugh at him. Unfortunately, distracted by his attire, they disregard the man's words and gestures, and they do not go to help put out the fire. As a result, the circus burns to the ground.

In Ratzinger's judgment, despite its merits, Cox's interpretation "is still a simplification."[22] Our contemporary "situation is by no means so different from that of others."[23] Faith ultimately concerns that which cannot be "supported on the visible and tangible" because the decision of faith entails "that which cannot be seen" and yet is a "necessity for our existence."[24] The problem of faith in God lies not in specific historical conditions but in the truth that the foundation of our existence is that which is eternal and invisible. At the same time, Christian faith concerns not simply what is eternal but also what has been revealed in Jesus. And, this "most radical revelation" in Jesus possesses "the most extreme obscurity and concealment."[25] The decision of faith does not depend on the visible. There is a freedom in faith, and faith is a free decision.

Second, Ratzinger gives a specific description of the modern understanding of reality in relation to history and faith. He sees modernity beginning with Giambattisa Vico, who turned away from the scholastic and traditional conviction that *verum est ens*, "being is truth," to the axiom *verum quia factum*, "we know what we have ourselves made."[26] Further, Ratzinger draws a line from Vico's thought not only to the contemporary Promethean emphasis on action over thought, for example, in the writings of Karl Marx, but also to today's technocratic rationality, that is, to limiting our knowledge to how things operate or come about. According to Ratzinger, this mind-set operates even in contemporary historiography, and thus modern historical studies do not reach to the heart of the Christian faith.

Ratzinger concludes his study with the observation: "The primacy of the invisible over the visible and that of receiving over making run directly counter to this basic situation . . . and [explain] why it is so difficult for us today to make the leap of entrusting ourselves to what cannot be seen."[27] Interestingly, although Ratzinger contests Cox's emphasis on historical change, he himself acknowledges a significant historical shift when he interprets modernity as the dominance of a technocratic rationality and as the restriction of knowledge to what humans can make and control. That said, Ratzinger's conclusion is, in another sense, a further radicalization of his critique of Harvey Cox's emphasis on the importance of one's historical dress.

(2) *Karl Rahner on History, Freedom, and Modernity*

One year after Ratzinger's introductory lectures, Karl Rahner taught his course on the introduction to Christianity, which he eventually published as *Foundations of Christian Faith* (1976).[28] This large work is well-known and too complex to summarize here. The subtitle of the German edition refers to the "idea of Christianity" that has overtones from German idealism, overtones that American scholars have not sufficiently discussed.[29] For the purpose of our comparisons among Ratzinger, Rahner, and Kasper, a few points are significant.

First, Rahner starts out with a description of what makes our historical situation different: our contemporary world experiences pluralism and the insecurity of believers' faith.[30] The pluralism that characterizes contemporary expressions of faith means that theology cannot rely on a particular philosophy as the mediating link to faith. Instead, it is important to justify faith in relation to a first level of reflection. This initial kind of inquiry concerning what Newman called the "illative sense" involves the whole person and embraces the basic content of faith. As a first level of reflection, it mirrors the unity between a formal fundamental theology and systematic theology.

Second, Rahner himself engages in this first level of reflection by means of a transcendental analysis. That is, he discusses our transcendental experience, which Rahner defines as "the subjective, unthematic, necessary and unfailing consciousness of the knowing subject that is co-present in every spiritual act of knowledge, and the subject's openness to every spiritual act of knowledge."[31] This transcendental experience involves not only knowledge but also will and freedom. Rahner explains that this "experience . . . can never be objectively represented in its own self, but only by an abstract concept of it. . . . [It] is not constituted by the fact one speaks of it."[32] A transcendental experience involves one's whole person and, in a sense, precedes its expression in human language.

Note here Rahner's view of the relation between experience and language. His transcendental analysis of the question of God does not start out with the importance and significance of language, which—as I have emphasized—is significant for Kasper's analysis of the *Evangelium*. Instead, Rahner goes beyond or beneath language, even though he acknowledges there is a mediated character to the immediacy of experience. The role of the Christian experience of what it means to be a Christian is important to his proposal of an indirect method in the approach to Christianity. It is much more an experiential demonstration than a historical argument as occurs in traditional fundamental theology.[33]

Third, Rahner's interpretation of modernity differs from Ratzinger's critique of technocratic rationality with its Promethean subjectivity. In February 1966, speaking to the Catholic students at the University of Münster, Rahner gave a lecture titled "The Experiment with Man: Theological Observations on Man's Self-Manipulation."[34] In this essay, Rahner argues that human persons should keep themselves open to the infinite mystery and to the concrete possibilities of human freedom. Self-manipulation is a manifestation of the essential freedom of the human being. This modern historical breakthrough "not only corresponds to Christianity's fundamental understanding of man, but also how the historical breakthrough from theory to practice, from self-awareness to self-actualization was essentially a *product* of Christianity."[35] Nevertheless, the centrality of Christology to his anthropology and his interpretation of the death of Jesus display his Christian modification of contemporary subjectivity and freedom.[36]

Rahner's understanding of the human subject in terms of freedom and self-manipulation is a very "modern" subject. Indeed, in his *Foundations of Christian Faith* he devotes a significant essay to the meaning of Christ in an evolutionary and progressive world.[37] In this inquiry as elsewhere, Rahner seeks to come to terms with the evolutionary notion of the world that Pierre Teilhard de Chardin had integrated with a Christian vision of creation and history. In this respect, Rahner's vision is modern and progressive. It stands in contrast to Ratzinger's view of modernity and is prior to the current postmodern criticisms that Kasper is aware of and seeks to incorporate into his later analyses.[38]

(3) *Kasper on History, Freedom, and Modernity*

Unlike Ratzinger and Rahner, Kasper did not write a general introduction to Christian faith during his time in Münster, though he did this afterward.[39] Rather, in the fall of 1964 he taught a seminar on the theology of history and in the spring of 1965 he lectured on the thought of F. W. J. Schelling. This second course dealt with the philosophical and theological importance of Schelling's later philosophy, which is the topic of Kasper's Habilitation *Das Absolute in der Geschichte* (1964).[40] This book is surely important for understanding Kasper's approach to modernity, history, and freedom.

While taking Kasper's seminars on history and Schelling, it became clear to me how these topics are interrelated.[41] Kasper's interpretation of the later Schelling underscores Kasper's philosophy of history and his understanding of God's revelation in relation to our knowledge of God and God's freedom. Kasper critically appropriates Schelling's thought. He is sympathetic with Schelling's effort to overcome German idealism, and yet he is *critical* of Schelling's accomplishment. According to Kasper, Schelling does not fully take into account God's radical freedom and the free expression of this divine freedom in history. This critique foreshadows the contours of Kasper's own theology. It expresses Kasper's understanding of freedom and history, and it underlies his interpretation of modernity.

In his later writings, Schelling takes up Kant's transcendental question on the possibility of synthetic a priori judgments and turns it into a metaphysical question about the ground of being and the origin of the finite in "the Absolute," that is, in God.[42] He responds that in German idealism there is no transition from the infinite to finite. As a result, one cannot think of the Absolute by ascending to it from below.[43] For Schelling, Hegel's dialectical philosophy is insufficient to mediate the Absolute in history because, in this view, the Absolute remains outside the dialectical process, which is itself only a moment in the unfolding or maturation of the finite consciousness.

Schelling proposes the solution that the infinite realizes itself in time and space and thus is able to create a transition from the finite to the infinite.[44] Because the Absolute, God, has entered into creation and history, God may be knowable in events and in the human drama. Moreover, history becomes the presupposition for reason itself.[45] History does not run according to laws because it is subject to human freedom. Therefore, the correct understanding of the relationship between history and human freedom is central to any philosophical understanding of history. In his late philosophy, Schelling acknowledges the weakness of his earlier attempts to think of history as shaped by necessity rather than "as that which [involves] God in freedom, and so the free history is understood in the light of the eternal mystery of God."[46]

Kasper maintains, however, that even the late Schelling did not escape idealism and that his philosophy falls into a theosophy. In particular, he raises two reservations about Schelling's later philosophy that are important to Kasper's own distinctive theological approach. First, according to Kasper, scripture points to God's Wisdom as freely given to humans as a *gift* and an *event*. In this perspective, the Wisdom of Christ in the Gospel is the summit of God's free self-revelation. Christian belief cannot be a priori deduced but has to be understood as God's free gift. For this reason, scripture is not simply a set of documents that theology appropriates; it is the written witness to God's self-revelation in human affairs.[47] Second, since the Wisdom of God is historical, its historical forms of expression cannot be reduced to a philosophical system. Rather, they express the Absolute, the divine mystery that is too complex and free for full articulation in human thought.[48]

Kasper himself draws out the implications of his two criticisms of Schelling's thought. He highlights that God's free self-revelation is rooted in God's self and in history. Freedom is not simply that which humans have and can exercise as they wish. Rather, humans must receive their freedom. To put it another way, we must accept our liberation by God so that we can live in freedom. In particular, we are set free in and through Jesus Christ. Kasper's conception of freedom underlies his critical reflection on God, who is not called the ground or arche of Being but—as expressed in the title of Kasper's book—*The God of Jesus Christ*.[49] This book's Trinitarian conception of God shows Kasper's difference to Schelling. Given Kasper's emphasis on God's freedom, Kasper undertakes a dialogical or communicative approach to understanding God in history rather than Schelling's dialectical approach. Further, with this dialogical approach, Kasper is able to move beyond Schelling's negative philosophy as he appropriates the Christian tradition's negative or apophatic theology and as he approaches the Christian tradition as the living and active communication of God's Wisdom.

(4) *The Distinctive Gestalt of Kasper's Theology*

What is the distinctive gestalt or character of Kasper's theology? In order to get to the heart of this theology one has to combine Kasper's understanding of freedom, drawn in his critique of Schelling's philosophy in his Habilitation of 1964, with Kasper's reflections in his doctoral dissertation of 1961 concerning the Christian tradition and the relation between the Christian tradition and the Gospel, the *Evangelium*. The implications of this unity of thought are significant for his theology. Indeed, I propose that one can grasp the distinctiveness of Kasper's theological trajectory by linking his Habilitation's emphasis on freedom and history and his doctoral dissertation's view of the Christian tradition as an epistemological principle.[50]

Kasper ends his Habilitation with a reflection on the various conceptions of theology that were current in 1964. He asks, what or who is the final subject of theology? Is it God as God, which is the view of Thomas Aquinas? Is it Jesus Christ, as held by Émile Mersch? Is it an anthropological interpretation of revelation in which Christology is the radical realization of anthropology, which is the view of Karl Rahner? Refusing to regard these concepts as mutually exclusive, Kasper unites elements of them in the trajectory of his thought. In his judgment, God is known only historically and primarily in Christ. At the same time, God may be known only in the horizon of the human person, just as human persons are understood only in the horizon of God. Moreover, he holds that the "historical-dialogical situation is the final presupposition behind which we can no longer go."[51]

What Kasper calls the "historical-dialogical situation" in his Habilitation expresses well what he has developed into his distinctive theological approach. According to Kasper, "the question of the meaning of totality is for us today a question about the meaning of history. The question about the possibility of experiencing God becomes the question of how we can experience God as the meaning of history or, biblically expressed, the Lord of history."[52] He is intent on showing that the God of Christian revelation has the power to illumine reality and history.

Since the question about God entails a question about the meaning of reality and history, the relation between history and freedom is central for Kasper's description of the historical experience of God. He differentiates his position from metaphysical thinking with its hierarchical order of being that understands God to be the culmination and the encompassing ground of this order.[53] In advocating the God of history, Kasper is clear that God is not that which is far and beyond us as the eternally unattainable horizon. Instead, God encounters us in a historical and unconditioned claim. In this orientation, Kasper goes beyond a cosmological approach and beyond a transcendental or anthropological approach. To be sure, one can point to the significance of the metaphysical and the transcendental dimensions for his theology, as Kasper himself does.[54] Yet, it is crucial that the metaphysical and the transcendental approaches include within themselves the recognition of freedom in and through history. The question of the experience of God cannot be abstracted from how one experiences God as the meaning of history and human life as a free response to God's gift of freedom.

Here the distinctiveness of Walter Kasper's views on the knowledge of God in difference to Karl Rahner's views becomes clear. Rahner speaks of our transcendental experience of God, and he primarily refers to the intellectual dynamism of self-transcendence in knowing and willing (though he also includes freedom). In so doing, he is following the orientation of Joseph Maréchal.[55] Kasper maintains, however, that human experience is always a historical experience, and he places more much emphasis on freedom and on freedom as a gift made possible through Christ. It is this understanding of freedom that makes Kasper critical of antiquity's cosmic natural theologies and of the Enlightenment's natural theologies. Instead, in Kasper's judgment, freedom points more to the limitations of the self and simultaneously to the self's openness for the gift of freedom from "the Other," God.[56]

Kasper's approach shows that he not only takes the freedom of divine revelation more seriously than Rahner but also conceives of the freedom of God more radically than Schelling. This emphasis has important consequences for his theology. He writes: "Thinking of God as absolute freedom means understanding God as a liberating God and the world as a place of freedom."[57] Moreover, when Kasper understands this freedom in relation to the totality of history, he includes the emphasis on freedom in the contemporary world. He offers an interpretation of modernity that does not simply view modernity as the appearance of technocratic rationality and Promethean subjectivity, which is Joseph Ratzinger's view, or as a rationalistic rejection of religion, or as a progressive development of spiritualization as in Teilhard de Chardin's evolutionary model.[58]

To be sure, Kasper is aware of currents in modernity that entail a rejection of religion, which is the view that Henri de Lubac argues in *The Drama of Atheistic Humanism*.[59] At the same time, Kasper is also conscious of modern attempts to appropriate religion or at least some of the values of religious belief. In this regard, he traces the roots of human freedom back to the Christian tradition and in highlighting these origins he attempts to enrich our contemporary concept of freedom. This dual approach to modernity and the Christian tradition approach is also evident in his treatment of the theological foundation of human rights.[60] Further, it is present in his interpretation of religious freedom in modernity, which he discusses in his article on Vatican II's discussion of freedom, "The Church and Modern Process of Freedom."[61]

Kasper's twofold approach is manifest, too, when he interprets autonomy, i.e., our desire for individuation, and theonomy, i.e., our orientation to God, in relation to the place of Christianity in the modern world.[62] In an essay written for Alfons Auer, who was an advocate of an autonomous ethic and a teacher of Kasper's former Tübingen colleague, Dietmar Mieth, Kasper highlights the Christian roots of autonomy in the biblical belief in creation. In this discussion, he concurs with Rahner's dialectic between autonomy and dependence, that is, between freedom and love.[63]

In this perspective, Kasper differentiates among three models of freedom in modernity. A *restorative* model, such as operative in the thought of Joseph Ratzinger, interprets modern freedom only in categories of decay, according to which the rise in freedom has resulted in a falling away from theonomy. A *progressive* model perceives today's emphasis on freedom as conducive to mature faith in God. In this regard, he refers to Rahner and Metz, pointing to their nuanced interpretations. He also locates Trutz Rendtorff, a teacher in the Protestant theology faculty of Münster and then Munich, as an unambiguous advocate of the progressive model. Kasper himself proposes a third model that mediates between the restorative and progressive models. This model is *dialogical* and *historical*. It combines correlation and analogy in order to show that one can understand modern autonomy positively, but one must enrich it by a correct, Christian theological interpretation of autonomy.

These differences among Ratzinger, Rahner, and Kasper with regard to modernity are evident in their publications of the 1960s. Joseph Ratzinger is critical of modernity's emphasis on a technological rationality and a Promethean subjectivity. He adopts a restorative model, already in his early writings. Karl Rahner clearly relies on a progressive model, though not uncritically. Walter Kasper promotes a dialogical and historical model of freedom. Anchored in his engagement with Schelling's later philosophy, he develops a mediated position, which continues in his later writings. Kasper enters into a dialogue with modernity in which he reflects on the enduring significance of Christian tradition and yet simultaneously calls attention to the transformation of freedom in the ongoing practices of modernity.

If space permitted, we could consider other important points of comparison. For example, while Rahner took a positive interpretation of pluralism in modernity, Ratzinger has held a more reserved interpretation. Also, Rahner's view of Vatican II manifesting how the contemporary church is on its way to becoming a world church finds its confirmation in Kasper's interpretation that during the fifty years since the Second Vatican Council there has occurred the radical shift from a European-centered Christianity to a Christianity centered in the Americas, Asia, and Africa. Further, Kasper has taken over Rahner's quasi-Hegelian notion of the dialectic between autonomy and dependence. But Kasper's ideas here differ in emphasis from Rahner's. While Rahner accentuates the transcendental nature of freedom and the importance of freedom as an "existential," an essential aspect of human life, in relation to the "supernatural existential," Kasper emphasizes the dialogical nature of freedom in relation to history.

3. A Dialogical Conception of Theology

In this essay, I have shed light on the distinctive gestalt of Walter Kasper's theology by focusing both on his notions of revelation, scripture, and tradition and also on his thought concerning history, freedom, and modernity. His distinctive views were already evident in 1964 and 1965, as has become clear through my comparison of his lectures and writings with those of Karl Rahner and Joseph Ratzinger at that time. To be sure, there are theological elements that Ratzinger, Rahner, and Kasper share. I have neglected these similarities, however, because I have focused on the theological differences that were already evident in the 1960s.

Kasper's later writings show the further lines of his trajectory and its concrete applicability. Moreover, Kasper's dialogical and communicative historical approach to understanding God entails a distinctive conception of theology.[64] This conception, as I have suggested, can be formulated as such: Kasper appropriates the notion of an active living tradition as a theological and epistemological principle, and he combines it with the dialogical and historical approach that emerges from his thought on divine and human freedom and on the totality of history. This understanding arose from his confrontation with Schelling's late philosophy.

Kasper's emphasis on God's freedom in his critique of Schelling has a significant implication for his theology. That is, he focuses not only on God's free self-revelation in history but also on the living and active tradition of interpreting that revelation in history and yet in a responsive active dialogue with the development of history and the future of history. An idealistic system such as Schelling's affirms the identity of freedom and necessity, of reality and truth, and of thinking and being. Such an identity philosophy seeks a philosophical conception of history. When freedom in history is taken seriously, however, then history cannot be reduced to a system. For theologians, this conclusion means that theology too should not be reduced to a system. It is at this crucial point that Kasper underscores the freedom of God's revelation and the active tradition of this free dialogical engagement with God's revelation and the process of history.

We can shed further light on Kasper's notion of a living tradition by relating it to Hans-Georg Gadamer's understanding of hermeneutics and to the role that tradition has in it. According to Gadamer, tradition is not so much what we have but what we are. It informs our self-understanding and our horizon. We appropriate our tradition within a horizon that is always informed by that tradition itself. According to this hermeneutic theory, as we make the tradition our own, we continue the tradition. This continuation involves a fusion of our contemporary horizon with the tradition's horizon. Our effort to understand something in human life involves the application and the continuation of a tradition; it goes hand in hand with bringing into praxis tradition's claim upon us and with living in the horizon of our contemporary lives and contexts.

Going beyond Gadamer's discussion, Kasper also explains that the Christian tradition possesses a distinctive focus and freedom because it is rooted in the Gospel, the *Evangelium*.[65] In his view, the church's tradition is its ongoing living interpretation and appropriation of the Gospel as the church engages with modernity. This theological view is evident in Kasper's notion of freedom. As Kasper reflects on freedom in modernity or on modern freedom, he does not adopt either a restorative model or a progressive model. Instead, he promotes a dialogical model in which he seeks to deepen the modern idea of freedom by drawing on the Christian tradition, while he is also open to the transformations of freedom in modernity's emphasis on human rights and religious freedom.

I am aware that my interpretation of my former teacher's ideas might be inadequate. Nevertheless, I remember that my first paper delivered in German was in Kasper's seminar. In it, I examined Max Seckler's understanding of history and salvation as presented by Thomas Aquinas.[66] After the seminar, Kasper walked over to where I was standing with friends and praised my paper, saying that it hit the central point and raised a crucial question. His encouragement at that time and generous view of my work were important to me.

This kind act by Walter Kasper shows something about him that goes contrary to the American stereotype of a German professor: Professor Kasper was always pastoral in his approach to his students. I can vividly remember my first time in his office in 1964 when I told him about my theological interests and my last time in his office in 1970 when we both knew we were leaving Münster. He would move back to the University of Tübingen, and I would begin teaching at the University of Notre Dame. In these interactions, he exemplified toward me the generosity and charity that his new book on mercy expounds.[67] Therefore, I conclude by publicly expressing thanks to Cardinal Kasper for all that he has done not only for Elisabeth, me, and many other people but also—through his teaching, writing, and service—for the church and Christian unity.

Endnotes

1. The lectures appeared in Walter Kasper, *Jesus the Christ*, trans. V. Green (New York: Paulist, 1976; German original, 1974).

2. Karl Rahner, "Bemerkungen zum Begriff der Offenbarung," in idem and Joseph Ratzinger, *Offenbarung und Überlieferung* (Freiburg: Herder, 1965), 11–24. ET: *Revelation and Tradition*, trans. W. J. O'Hara (New York: Herder and Herder, 1966).

3. Joseph Ratzinger, "Ein Versuch zur Frage des Traditionsbegriffs," in Rahner and Ratzinger, *Offenbarung und Überlieferung*, 25–69.

4. Walter Kasper, *Dogma unter dem Wort Gottes* (Mainz: Matthias-Grünewald, 1965).

5. Rahner, "Bemerkungen zum Begriff der Offenbarung," 16–17. See Rahner and Ratzinger, *Revelation and Tradition*, 16; translation by F. S. Fiorenza.

6. Ratzinger refers to Josef R. Geiselmann, *Die Heilige Schrift und die Tradition* (Freiburg: Herder, 1962).

7. Ratzinger, "Ein Versuch," 33.

8. Ibid.

9. Ibid., 45–46.

10. See Joseph Ratzinger, "Das geistliche Amt und die Einheit der Kirche," in *Das Neue Volk Gottes* (Düsseldorf: Patmos, 1969), 119.

11. For the 1954–55 Winter Semester.

12. Walter Kasper, *Die Lehre von der Tradition in der römischen Schule: Giovanni Perrone, Carlo Passaglia, Clemens Schrader* (Freiburg: Herder, 1962).

13. Kasper, *Dogma*, 61.

14. See, for example, my use of Gadamer, Jauss, and Ricoeur, in Francis Fiorenza, *Foundational Theology: Jesus and the Church* (New York: Crossroad, 1983).

15. Kasper, *Dogma*, 64. This difference in regard to language does not rule out a similarity between Rahner and Kasper on the issues of the sufficiency of scripture and its normative function; see Karl Rahner's essays "Scripture and Theology" and "Scripture and Tradition," in *Theological Investigations*, vol. 6, trans. Karl H. Kruger and Boniface Kruger (Baltimore, MD: Helicon, 1969): 89–97, 98–112.

16. Kasper, *Dogma*, 87.

17. Ibid., 88.

18. Ibid., 90.

19. See the essays in Walter Kasper, *Glaube und Geschichte* (Mainz: Matthias-Grünewald, 1970), 159–257, especially "Schrift-Tradition-Verkündigung," 159–86.

20. Walter Kasper, "Das Verhältnis von Schrift und Tradition: Eine pneumatologische Perspektive," in *Theologie und Kirche*, vol. 2 (Mainz: Matthias-Grünewald, 1999), 51–83; originally published in *Theologische Quartalschrift* 170 (1990): 170–93.

21. Kasper, "Das Verhältnis," 66

22. Joseph Ratzinger, *Introduction to Christianity*, trans. J. R. Foster (New York: Seabury, 1969), 16.

23. Ibid., 17.

24. Ibid., 24

25. Ibid., 28.

26. Ibid., 31.

27. Ibid., 43–44.

28. Karl Rahner, *Foundations of Christian Faith: An Introduction to the Idea of Christianity*, trans. William V. Dych (New York: Crossroad, 1982).

29. A leitmotiv of German Idealism is reconciliation or mediation in history through the development of concepts.

30. Rahner, *Foundations*, 1–14.

31. Ibid., 20.

32. Ibid., 21.

33. Ibid., 346–69. See Fiorenza, *Foundational Theology*.

34. In Karl Rahner, *Theological Investigations*, vol. 9, trans. Graham Harrison (New York: Herder and Herder, 2004), 205–24. In the same volume, see "Christian Humanism" (pp. 187–204) and "The Problem of Genetic Manipulation" (pp. 225–52).

35. Ibid., 214. Freedom was a central topic for Karl Rahner. See his early essays, "Freedom in the Church" and "The Dignity and Freedom of Man," in *Theological Investigations*, vol. 2, trans. Karl H. Kruger (Baltimore, MD: Helicon, 1963): 89–107, 235–65; and "Theology of Freedom," *Theological Investigations*, vol. 6, 178–96. The theme of freedom is the explicit topic of several of Rahner's later essays. For a comparison, see Ratzinger's essay of 1981: "Freedom and Constraint in the Church," in *Church, Ecumenism, and Politics*, trans. Michael J. Miller et al. (New York: Crossroad, 1988), 183–203.

36. On this point, see Francis Schüssler Fiorenza, "Method in Theology," in *The Cambridge Companion to Karl Rahner*, ed. Mary E. Hines and Declan Marmion (New York: Cambridge University Press, 2005), 65–82.

37. Rahner, *Foundations*, 178–203, titled "Christology within an Evolutionary View of the World."

38. Walter Kasper, "Die Kirche angesichts der Herausforderung der Postmoderne," in *Theologie und Kirche*, vol. 2.

39. See Walter Kasper, *Einführung in den Glauben* (Mainz: Matthias-Grünewald, 1972). ET: *An Introduction of the Christian Faith*, trans. V. Green (New York: Paulist Press, 1980).

40. Walter Kasper, *Das Absolute in der Geschichte. Philosophie und Theologie der Geschichte in der Spätphilosophie Schellings* (Mainz: Matthias-Grünewald, 1965). Kasper's research on Schelling has sparked several theological dissertations concerning Schelling's influence on theology.

41. Kasper's book on Schelling was his wedding gift to Elisabeth and me; we suggested this gift in response to his indirect inquiry. The book's title is an appropriate label for a Christian marriage!

42. Kasper, *Das Absolute*, 43–54.

43. Ibid., 43–124.

44. Ibid., 124.

45. Walter Kasper, "Die Freiheit als philosophisches und theologisches Problem in der Philosophie Schellings," in *Glaube und Geschichte*, 33–47.

46. Kasper, *Das Absolute*, 433. There has, of course, continued to be an interest in Schelling's early conception of freedom; see, especially, Martin Heidegger, *Schelling's Treatise on the Essence of Human Freedom*, trans. Joan Stambaugh (Athens, Ohio: Oxford University Press, 1985); Christian Brouwer, *Schellings Freiheit Schrift. Studien zu ihrer Interpretation und ihrer Bedeutung für die theologische Diskussion* (Tübingen: Mohr Siebeck, 2011).

47. Kasper, *Das Absolute*, 436.

48. Ibid., 434–37.

49. Walter Kasper, *The God of Jesus Christ*, new ed., trans. Matthew J. O'Connell (London: Continuum, 2012).

50. See also his later essay, "Tradition als theologische Erkenntnisprinzip," and "Kirchengeschichte als historische Theologie," *Theologie und Kirche*, vol. 1 (Mainz: Matthias-Grünewald, 1987), 72–100 and 101–16.

51. Kasper, *Das Absolute*, 434.

52. Walter Kasper "Möglichkeit der Gotteserfahrung heute," in *Glaube und Geschichte*, 120–43, 135.

53. Ibid., 139.

54. Walter Kasper, "Zustimmung zum Denken. Von der Unerlässlichkiet der Metaphysik für die Sache der Theologie," *Theologische Quartalschrift* 169 (1989): 257–71.

55. On the relation between transcendence and experience with reference to Rahner and Schleiermacher as well as in relation to a linguistic and historical approach, see Francis Schüssler Fiorenza, "The Experience of Transcendence or the Transcendence of Experience: Negotiating the Difference," in *Religious Experience and Contemporary Theological Epistemology*, ed. Yves de Maeseneer and S. van den Bossche (Louvain: University Press, 2005), 183–218; idem, "Being, Subjectivity, and Otherness: The Idols of Gods," in *Questioning God*, ed. John D. Caputo, Mark Dooley, and Michael Scanlon (Indianapolis: University of Indiana Press, 2001), 320–50.

56. See Kasper, "Möglichkeit," 120–43; idem, *The God of Jesus Christ*, 65–130. On the question of the natural knowledge of God; see Hermann J. Pottmeyer, "Kontinuität und Innovation in der Gotteslehre. Die Vermittlung der Gotteslehren des 1. und 2. Vatikanums—ein Anliegen der Gotteslehre von Walter Kasper," in *Gott Denken und Bezeugen*, ed. George Augustin and Klaus Krämer (Freiburg: Herder, 2008), 171–87.

57. Walter Kasper, "The Timeliness of Speaking of God: Freedom and Communion as Basic Concepts of Theology," *Worship* 83 (2009): 293–311, 304.

58. Whereas Kasper points to what is negative and positive in modernity, Ratzinger tends to emphasize the negative. See Joseph Ratzinger, "Truth—Tolerance—Freedom," in *Truth and Tolerance* (San Francisco: Ignatius, 2004), 210–58; he concludes: "we must also bid farewell to the dream of the absolute autonomy of reason and of its self-sufficiency" (p. 258). This statement encapsulates Ratzinger's interpretation of the Enlightenment's ideal of emancipation.

59. Henri de Lubac, *The Drama of Atheist Humanism*, trans. Edith M. Riley, Anne Englund Hash, Mark Sebanc (Cleveland, OH: World Publishing, 1950).

60. Walter Kasper, "The Theological Foundations of Human Rights," *The Jurist* 148 (1990): 253–69.

61. Walter Kasper, "Kirche und neuzeitliche Freiheitsprozesse," in *Theologie und Kirche*, vol. 2, 213–28.

62. Walter Kasper, "Autonomie and Theonomie. Zur Ortsbestimmung des Christentums in der modernen Welt," in *Theologie und Kirche*, vol. 1, 149–75.

63. Rahner, *Foundations of Christian Faith*.

64. See Walter Kasper, *Die Methoden der Dogmatik. Einheit und Vielheit* (Munich: Kösel-Verlag, 1967); idem, "The Timeliness of Speaking of God."

65. See Walter Kasper, "Neue Evangelisierung als theologische, pastorale, und geistliche Herausforderung," in *Das Evangelium Jesu Christi*, vol. 5, *Gesammelte Schriften*, ed. George Augustin and Klaus Krämer (Freiburg: Herder, 2007).

66. Max Seckler, *Das Heil in der Geschichte. Geschichtstheologisches Denken bei Thomas von Aquin* (Munich: Kösel, 1964).

67. See Walter Kasper, *Mercy: The Essence of the Gospel and the Key to Christian Life*, trans. William Madges (New York: Paulist Press, 2014).

CHAPTER 3

The Promise and the Burden of Natural Theology

Anthony J. Godzieba

Three decades after Cardinal Walter Kasper's *The God of Jesus Christ* was first published, it remains a stunning achievement.[1] The book has been hailed as an utterly trustworthy exposition of the Christian doctrine of the triune God, a reliable guide to the doctrine's historical development, and a brilliant theological explication of the role that the Trinity plays in Christian life today. It is truly a "classic" in Hans-Georg Gadamer's sense of the term: timeless because it is always timely.

And our discussion of this book could not be more timely. We are in the midst of intense debates over the existence of God, the nature of transcendence, the quality of human life in a fragile and dangerous world, and the role of religious belief in contemporary culture. In this context, Kasper's thesis—that the Trinity is the answer to the mystery of the world and human beings—makes an especially substantive and hopeful contribution. It also reveals the pastoral orientation of his theology, his view that the answer to the contemporary challenges to Christian faith cannot be a "watered-down theism" but rather "a new reflection on the message that God is the living and liberating God of history, the God of hope (Romans 15:13) who is Love itself."[2]

Alongside this Trinitarian focus, three other aspects should be noted. First, the book presents a persuasive history of how God became a problem in Western culture and how critical was modernity's role in the shift toward the "abstract theism of a unipersonal God,"[3] a still-influential stance that Kasper does not hesitate to label "heretical."[4] Second, as an alternative to this thin and outmoded theism, he offers a reformulation of the Catholic tradition of natural theology that points to what he calls a "theological theology," where faith and reason mutually explore the reality of God as Trinity. Finally, there is Kasper's insistence that the doctrine of the Trinity is "the summary of the entire Christian mystery of salvation" and the fundamental "grammar" of Christian belief.[5]

Commentators have tended to focus on Kasper's Trinitarian theology—his "theological theology." But I want to focus on what precedes this and has often been bypassed, namely, his development of a natural theology. He argues that it is an urgent contemporary task in light of both a resurgent atheism and the resurgent yet ambivalent embrace of religion and spirituality.[6] I would add that this urgency is heightened by a contemporary aspect that Kasper, at the time, could hardly address but now looms ever larger: the feeling of social, political, and economic entrapment fed by a narrative of pure immanence and commoditized happiness defined by late capitalist consumer culture.[7] Using Charles Taylor's terms, we can say that the limits experienced by the modern and postmodern "buffered self" have become tighter and meaner, not simply by the constriction of the "social imaginary," but also because Max Weber's "iron cage" has finally reached into each home, but now in the form of rigidly policed choices based on quick-changing images and their short-term satisfactions. Today, when the commoditized image often equals reality for many, the lack of imaginative human possibilities leads to a dehumanization so subtle that it literally goes without saying and becomes the new "normal."

Is there an alternative interpretation of human life and its possibilities—a more likely story—that describes an encounter with transcendence in the midst of finitude? That "more likely story" is the basic *promise* of Christian natural theology: that the finitude of the human condition is a means, not an end; that humanity can experience a trace or glimpse of transcendence within its limited experience, not in spite of it. On the other hand, natural theology also carries a *burden*. It must think and talk about God without colonizing the divine or reducing the supernatural to the limits of human understanding. Both the promise and the burden are summed up in Maurice

Blondel's famous characterization of the role of reason in apologetics: its correct employment with regard to God, the "method of immanence," will consider the supernatural "as indispensable and at the same time as inaccessible for man."[8] That paradox is both the promise and the burden of natural theology, and *The God of Jesus Christ* attempts to respect it and make a convincing appeal that belief in God is the authentic way of being human in the contemporary context.

1. Kasper's Natural Theology

Kasper defines natural theology as thinking that seeks "the natural 'access-point' of faith."[9] It seeks to demonstrate "the internal reasonableness of a faith which has its substantiation in and from itself."[10] In other words, its task is to show how human experience is inherently open to transcendence and participates in a dynamic movement toward God. That movement can be more fully articulated through a faith commitment to God's further self-revelation, a fuller relationship to God than can be achieved by rational reflection alone and yet one not opposed to reason, since it fulfills reason's intentional drive.

Kasper acknowledges our post-metaphysical context and notes how modern and contemporary philosophy, especially after Friedrich Nietzsche and Martin Heidegger, has forced theology to raise the most fundamental issue, namely, "whether we must ask the question of God within the horizon of the question of being, or the question of being within the horizon of the question of God."[11] But rather than agree completely with the critique of metaphysics, Kasper offers instead a general defense. Our talk about God, "the reality that includes and determines everything," demands a metaphysics "which enquires not about individual beings or realms of being but about being as such and as a whole."[12] "Without a transcendent ground and point of reference," he says, "statements of faith are finally only subjective projections or social and ecclesial ideologies."[13] Discourse about God becomes impossible, and theology itself is thereby plunged into crisis.

Kasper is careful, however, to delineate the type of metaphysics he believes is necessary. It must be open to the overarching horizon of mystery that grounds the transcending character of human experience[14] and must rigorously avoid absolutizing the finite.[15] Thus he distances himself from any "substance" metaphysics.[16] He takes seriously Heidegger's criticism of metaphysics' objectifying and calculative tendencies, and this sensitivity provides a basis for Kasper's negative evaluation of modernity's various attempts to prove God's existence: the traditional onto-theological arguments simply lead to modern atheism. "In the final analysis," he says, "it is impossible to prove God's existence from some authority external to him; he must show himself."[17]

This conviction is why Anselm of Canterbury can be considered one of the book's major influences, because he points out precisely *where* God can be disclosed to human experience. In the ontological argument—for Kasper, the one "to which all the other arguments boil down"[18]—Anselm demonstrates the dynamic openness of finite human subjectivity to the infinite without attempting to constrain the infinite to fit a certain determination. Anselm's fundamental achievement is that he has shown how "in the end thinking necessarily transcends itself, inasmuch as it thinks something which it is essentially incapable of thinking out any further, because the infinite cannot be captured in any finite concept. God, therefore, can be known only through God; he can be known only when he himself allows himself to be known."[19]

Kasper rehabilitates natural theology by demonstrating how "thinking necessarily transcends itself" and supports the reasonable character of a "prophetic" faith that gives us access to "the ultimate ground and the ultimate meaning and goal of all reality."[20] He does this in two major steps. In the first he analyzes the structure of human experience to show its fundamental relation to transcendence and faith. Indeed, faith and experience are joined in a hermeneutic circle: faith is necessarily mediated by our contextually situated experience, while experience itself exhibits a transcendental faith in meaning and can be expanded by its encounter with the transcendental object of faith, the word of God.[21]

The analysis of the structure of experience reveals five crucial aspects that, when taken together, testify to its intentional drive beyond any finite closure.[22] First, experience involves both *objective and subjective elements in a dialectical relationship*; that is, the person is affected by reality and interprets this interaction in a meaningful way through words, images, and symbols. Next, experience is *historical, emerging over time*; it involves past memories and future hopes, both converging in the present. It is open to what is new and is never closed or completed. Third, experience is *historical* in another way: it never occurs in general but is always situated and inflected by historically particular horizons of understanding. Fourth, experience is always *hermeneutical*, always *interpreted experience*. "We never experience reality in itself; we always experience it as something that has a specific meaning for us; objective experience and interpretation of experience can never be completely separated."[23] Finally, experience always involves us with *what is other than us*, the crucial "non-I" element that is not a projection but that *offers resistance* to us and *contrasts* with our expectations.[24]

In sum, the convergence of these five aspects reveals experience to be both thoroughly contextual and thoroughly open beyond itself because of its inherent incompleteness. A practical example is the "depth dimension" of language: the very act of communication expresses a longing for an interpersonally shared understanding not yet empirically present and "an anticipation of a life unmarked by alienation."[25] But, in the end, no finite experience can ever give us the fully settled certainty we crave; there is always more that expands our fund of experience or shatters our expectations. Our finitude brings us suffering as we chafe against our inherent limits, and yet suffering is a positive sign, for it underscores our openness to a future: "experience becomes a way . . . into a mystery that is even greater and never to be completely plumbed."[26]

The very structure of experience, then, opens us to infinite mystery that is nothing less than the transcendental horizon of all human experience. And here, for Kasper, we discover the religious dimension of human experience: "Religious experience is an indirect, not a direct type of experience; it is an experience which we have 'in, with and under' our other experiences. It is therefore not just one experience alongside other experiences, but rather the basic experience present in our other experiences; it is an experience that presides over and gives a pervasive tone to all other experience."[27] The *indirection* of religious experiences has the character of everyday "disclosure situations" that points beyond themselves to the overarching mystery, the unifying horizon that forms the "background" of the thematic "foreground" of our everyday experience.[28] This mystery can never be apprehended directly as such but known only in traces and hints.[29] Since perfect clarity escapes us, religious experiences can be profoundly ambiguous: as "an inaccessible horizon of all our experience, it encounters us as the Wholly Other, a frightening abyss, a wilderness of nothingness. Insofar as it is close to us in everything, it appears to us as a protecting Ground, as grace and fulfillment."[30]

This first step, then, is a transcendental anthropological argument demonstrating the fundamental openness of historically situated human experience to all-encompassing mystery. Kasper's second step is to articulate this mystery's character insofar as it is possible, highlighting the natural access point of faith while respecting reason's limits. The crucial clue can be found in modern philosophy's insistence that *freedom*, not substance, is the true overarching condition of reality. "Not observable fact but free activity is the reality that alone brings the self-disclosure of the world. Being, therefore, is act, accomplishment, happening, event. Not self-contained being but existence, or freedom that goes out of itself and fulfills itself in action, is now the starting point and horizon of thought."[31] The "melancholy of fulfillment" that permeates our experience alerts us to the unconditioned fulfillment we fully intend but that is unavailable within the realm of human action.[32] "Only in encounter with absolute freedom can the person reach inner peace and inner fulfillment."[33] Absolute freedom is the transcendental condition of the possibility of all individual free acts. But we have no objective grasp of this, only a pre-apprehension and "fragmentary anticipations" of its character.[34]

How, then, can we ever be fulfilled? Only in a *personal* way, through relationships where the non-I catalyst of experience has a *personal* character. The key to Kasper's entire argument is his understanding of "person": at the same time both a unique, irreplaceable individual and "ordered to reality in its entirety," as one "who exists only in self-actualization in response to another person and as ordered to other persons."[35] Our fulfillment occurs "only by emptying ourselves out in love, so as to realize our own intentional infinity."[36] But this too seems blocked: every relationship, no matter how intense, shares in the limits imposed by our human condition. Is experience merely intentionality without fulfillment?

The possibility of fulfillment does indeed exist. Kasper writes:

> The human person can reach definitive fulfillment only if it encounters a person who is infinite not only in its intentional claims on reality but in its real being; that is, only if it encounters an absolute person. Thus a more appropriate concept of person as

> the always unique "there" of being leads necessarily to the concept of an absolute, a divine person. If we understand the person as an always unique realization of being, then the category of person as applied to God does not mean an objectification of God. On the contrary, the concept of person is able to express in a new way the fact that in God being subsists in a unique way, that is, that God is *ipsum esse subsistens* ["subsistent being itself," echoing Thomas Aquinas].[37]

Natural theology, then, recognizes infinite mystery as the all-pervasive ground that is present "in, with and under" everyday experience. And Kasper, working in an Anselmian mode where "thinking transcends itself," goes further: he believes rational reflection can detect something of the fundamental character of infinite mystery and of its inherent relationship with us. Reality manifests a logic of *giving* that traditional metaphysics misses. The only proper language for the all-encompassing mystery is that of the *personal*, which necessarily implies relationality, one's openness to an other. If we use the word "God" to refer to the total meaning of reality that forms the horizon of our life and actions, then our desire for an inherently *personal* fulfillment can give us a pre-apprehension of the character of that horizon: the hope for a gracious *giver* who takes the initiative to encounter us in a *personal* fashion, the absolute mystery that graciously grants us the free space that makes our life and our actions possible. "Seen in the horizon of the person, the meaning of being is love. . . . To call God a person is to say that God is the subsistent being which is freedom in love."[38] But as to a fuller description of the authentic character of that person and the extent and specific performance of that love, natural theology can say no more.

Kasper thus succeeds in depicting how experience, faith, and revelation, while obviously nonidentical, are related in a hermeneutical circle: human experience, desiring fulfillment, points toward revelation, which fills out and provides the true explanation of human experience, which in turn responds to revelation in faith. Faith is not defined in opposition to reason but describes a mode of life where one is personally open to absolute mystery that embraces all aspects of human activity, including rationality. And so the *promise* of natural theology is kept: it is possible for humanity to experience a glimpse of divinity and its character within its limited experience, not in spite of it. And the *burden* is respected as well: thinking, while transcending itself, reaches a limit: it describes a clearing where human intentionality can meet supernatural revelation, without overstepping its boundaries, imposing definitions, and colonizing the supernatural.

But even within these limits something is gained: "being" is redefined. "The meaning of being is therefore to be found not in substance that exists in itself, but in self-communicating love."[39] This redefinition marks a farewell to any of the usual understandings of metaphysics even if Kasper, as we saw earlier, desires to retain the term.[40] The description of experience at the natural access point of faith also reveals that supernatural revelation (of the character of God, of God's inner life, and of God's relationship to the world) is not extrinsic to that experience. Rather, revelation is the superabundant fulfillment of the intentional openness of finite experience and of the natural knowledge of God that flows from that experience.

2. A Changed Situation: An Entrapment Culture

Is Kasper's transcendental and personalist argument, with its origins in a modern analysis of subjectivity, still convincing? Does it still resonate after the peak years of postmodernism and in a context where selves are considered socially, politically, and economically determined, or where the self is simply seen as the residue of various power vectors?

Let me return to the entrapment thesis that I mentioned at the outset. Of the many diagnoses of the contemporary situation, I will mention two that, in my view, interlock.

The first diagnosis is Charles Taylor's from *A Secular Age*. His analysis of secularization describes a retreat that typifies Western culture after 1600: an "exclusive humanism" rooted in Nominalism, developed throughout early modernity, and eventually characterizing and dominating the modern secular order. Unlike the premodern "porous self" open to transcendent influences and forces, the modern "buffered self" disavows any possible transcendence and rather "giv[es] its own autonomous order to its life."[41] This moral order infiltrates what Taylor terms the "social imaginary," that is, "the generally shared background understandings of society, which make it possible for it to function as it does."[42] The social imaginary is accompanied by a "cosmic imaginary" that envisions a vast, unfathomable, disenchanted universe without a sense of God or purpose,[43] and a shift in the conception of time, from either an eschatological or a teleological understanding to one that makes us anxious by imagining an infinite stretch of time both before us into the future and behind us into the past, hiding "the process of our genesis."[44]

The other diagnosis comes from the American cultural critic Chris Hedges. We now live not only commoditized consumer lives, he argues, but consumer lives measured by a celebrity culture that denigrates ordinary life and defines "authenticity" in terms of vast material excess.[45] Celebrity consumer culture creates an overarching narrative where image equals reality, attractive images generated by the entertainment industry become the dominant objects of aspiration, and personal identity and dignity are measured by standards set by those who are famous because they are celebrities and who are celebrities because they are famous. The narrative paints a fantasy world of short-term material pleasures undergirded by narcissism, where we are urged "to generate, almost unconsciously, interior personal screenplays in the mold of Hollywood, television, and even commercials."[46] Cultural participants are divided into "haves" and "have-nots." "Have-nots" are encouraged to think of themselves as possible celebrities, but they are offered impossible-to-fulfill aspirations. They are thus left permanently defeated and yet hungry for more; they become willing participants in their own degradation, "shut out of television's gated community," "mocked, even as they are tantalized, by the lives of excess they watch on the screen in their living rooms," and left with "feelings of inferiority and worthlessness."[47] The result, Hedges argues, is a "cultural retreat into illusion" that is "a form of magical thinking."

Both Taylor and Hedges underscore the *limits* confronting human experience and chronicle the truncated possibilities available in the contemporary West in the wake of modernity. Taylor emphasizes epistemic limits that over time have developed into social and cultural limits of pure immanence, what he calls "the immanent frame." Yet he finds hope in a widespread yearning for long-term fulfillment that a flattened-out secularization fails to satisfy and sees the real possibility of a spiritual ascent "beyond the boundaries."[48] Hedges's relentlessly downbeat portrayal of societal decay takes pure immanence a step further and makes a reasonable case that the buffer around the buffered self has become narrower, tighter, offering less and meaner possibilities for human existence.[49] The limits on human possibilities are more economic than epistemic: consumer capitalism's ability to co-opt and colonize everything, only now more insidiously as commoditized celebrity culture, denigrates ordinary life and defines authenticity in terms of the twin dreams of media influence and grandiose success at material consumption.[50] In this context, so-called fulfillment is only ever short term, if it occurs at all; it depends completely on therapeutic metaphors and consumerism's definition of "freedom" as merely the freedom to choose among attractive images. Hedges's intensification of the "immanent frame" thereby provides a necessary corrective to any naive theological approach that may tend to forget capitalism's "hybridizing, transgressive, promiscuous" nature.[51]

3. Natural Theology in a Post-Postmodern Age

Let's ask our question again: is Kasper's natural theology still convincing? In fact, it may be even more convincing in the present context than when it was first proposed three decades ago.

There is no need to rehearse the critiques of transcendental arguments that have been made ever since the mid-1960s.[52] But there is no need to apologize for those arguments either. With continental philosophy's "theological turn" since the 1980s—the current philosophies of the "event," the "call," and the "gift"—and with speculative realism's pursuit of a purely immanent absolute existing prior to all cultural constructions, transcendental thinking is again back on the table (if it ever really left) and has become central to recent discussions of subjectivity, culture, and religion. And with various social, political, and economic discourses, of all shades of adequacy, attempting to describe what counts as human flourishing and then deliver the means to achieve it, it is clear that in the midst of difference and contextual particularity there remains the intense need for a fundamental phenomenology of the human condition, a way to articulate some essential and universal aspects of humanity in order to guard against dehumanization and protect human rights.[53]

Kasper is keenly aware that natural theology's task has both anthropological and metaphysical elements. The anthropological is the more immediately evident. It serves as the portal, so to speak, with its argument about experience, its fundamental historicity, its limits, and its transcending orientation. Already at this point one can sketch a narrative of human life and its possibilities that differs from the entrapment narrative. Kasper's analysis is phenomenological more than merely transcendental because it attempts to expose the essential intentional structure of experience while at the same time insisting on its historical particularity and interpreted character. His argument closely parallels those of Hans-Georg Gadamer, Edward Schillebeeckx, Max Müller, and others in speaking of experience as fundamentally dialectical, historically situated, contrasting with our expectations, and grounded in freedom.[54] Discussions of experience in this more phenomenological vein have continued to play a crucial role in explicating the mediating relation between faith and everyday life.

Kasper's major contribution comes, however, by showing how the anthropological task is rooted in the metaphysical. That connection itself is not new, but his insight into it is daring: the claim that being itself can be adequately disclosed only in active and personalist terms—freedom, love, gift—and that any static or "substance" language is a distortion. This means that three decades ago, Kasper was among the first to use the concept of "gift" in the context of philosophical theology: before Jacques Derrida and his commentators, and contemporaneous with Jean-Luc Marion, whose *Dieu sans l'être* was published in 1982, the year *The God of Jesus Christ* first appeared.[55]

Kasper defines the fundamental structure of reality as relational and as freedom-in-gift, the gratuitous granting of open space in order for the possibilities constituting the incommunicable individuality we call "the person" to be discovered and actualized in relationship to other persons. The transcending openness that marks human selfhood thus mirrors the character of the transcendent freedom that is its ground and in which it participates. And that intentional and paradoxical selfhood, incommunicably particular and yet constituted in relation to all others, can be fulfilled as person only when it experiences love and relationship without constraint, when it experiences, as Kasper puts it, "an absolute, a divine person."

The crux of Kasper's natural theology is thus metaphysics in an anthropological key. In making metaphysics the issue he is situated squarely in the long tradition of Western thought. In speaking about reality and about God, the issue has always been the ability to think and speak about what exceeds the limits of the material-empirical. Reflection on religious claims—no matter how one defines the term "religious"—needs a discourse that takes seriously both the particular and the universal, and starts in particularity and moves to what transcends it. In the wake of the critique of metaphysics, stretching back to Immanuel Kant, some other thinking has always rushed in to fill the vacuum; the powerful critique and the resulting displacement elicits an equally powerful counterreaction. These reactions include Nietzsche's emphasis on the will to power, Heidegger's call to overcome metaphysics with a meditative "god-less thinking" still open to the divine, Derrida's evocation of *différance* that functions as a transcendental, blatant calls for a return to metaphysics in the midst of radical materialism (Alain Badiou's mathematical ontology, Quentin Meillassoux's "the real"). These all compensate for the end of metaphysics by thematizing the overarching horizon that exceeds and conditions the contingent.[56] There is clearly an obsession with metaphysics, even when metaphysics has been officially declared off the table and "buffers" have been raised to screen out the transcendent. That itch needs to be scratched, even when one denies any scratching is going on.

Kasper's natural theology thus makes a unique contribution by keeping its eye on the hermeneutic circle of experience and faith: faith mediated by our particular experience, while experience exhibits a transcending faith in meaning. In other words, *some* form of faith is *a priori*, always already present in experience. And that experience already shades over into "religious experience" by virtue of its intentional orientation to absolute fulfillment, *trusting that such fulfillment is possible, even if beyond our means.* It is precisely this faith—held in the midst of finitude—that provides a more likely story of the human condition than the entrapment narrative. This is Kasper's contemporary translation of Blondel's insight that the supernatural is indispensable yet inaccessible by rational means. But Kasper's "method of immanence" dares to go a step further, joining Anselm in exploring how "thinking necessarily transcends itself," and arrives at the furthest limits of experience, where we touch on the character of reality as free gift, the fundamental structure of reality as relational, and the pivot of reality as love.

The "burden" of natural theology is thus double edged: respecting reason's limits while providing a bridge to the "theological theology" of Trinitarian reflection. For when the overarching mystery is seen from the angle of freedom and love, as Kasper insists, theological theology can show more readily how the revelation of the Trinity is not extrinsic to human life but responds directly to experience's desire for "that than which nothing greater can be thought."[57] The rereading of ontology from a relational perspective creates a clearing wherein one more readily encounters the revelation of the Trinity as a communion of persons in love and as the ground of all reality. The "secret" of this Trinitarian ontology, as Klaus Hemmerle once wrote, "is called love, self-giving. From this structure all being, all thinking, all activity opens out," impelling the believer to see everyday phenomena anew and "reread" them for signs of revelation.[58] Before this step, though, natural theology from a transcendental-personalist perspective can act as a pre-apprehension of the fundamental sacramental structure of all reality, even if the fuller definition of what counts as "sacramental" relies on the revelation of the Incarnation and indeed the Trinity.

This pre-apprehension of the sacramental view explodes the limits of the entrapment imagination and releases the Christian believer's imagination from the tyranny of buffered thinking. Natural theology shows that the tighter and meaner buffers described by Taylor and by Hedges are not the only description of the human condition, even if they are so pervasive that they appear to be the norm. In fact, the truncation of experience by epistemic, economic, or class buffers appears, in the light of natural theology, as sheer dehumanization. The remaining questions, of course, are how to link the liberation that natural theology represents with the Trinitarian "theological theology" that Kasper argues is the true answer to the mystery of human life and how to translate this ensemble of theologies into a contemporary Christian narrative and practices that can blunt the effects of centuries of buffering and the ascendance of late capitalist consumer culture. The question of *practices* that incarnate the Christian belief that "God is love" (1 John 4:16)—in biblical terms, discipleship—and the *rhetoric* needed to recommend these practices as essential to human flourishing is perhaps most important of all. The task of natural theology, though, is more limited: by describing the "natural access-point of faith" as that place where the human experience touches on the absolute mystery of reality, a mystery of love and personal relationship, Kasper makes the case that in the very structure of human experience a clue may be found that renders the revelation of God as love and as grace the most plausible story of the human condition. To counteract the dominant narrative of meaner and tighter limits one must start somewhere in human experience. This is the place.

Endnotes

1. Walter Kasper, *Der Gott Jesu Christi* (Mainz: Matthias-Grünewald-Verlag, 1982). ET: *The God of Jesus Christ*, trans. Matthew J. O'Connell, new ed. (London: Continuum, 2012); hereafter, referred to as *God*. Idem, *Der Gott Jesu Christi*, ed. George Augustin and Klaus Krämer, rev. ed., *Gesammelte Schriften*, vol. 4 (Freiburg: Herder, 2008); hereafter, referred to as *Gott*.

2. Walter Kasper, "Vorwort," in *Der Gott Jesu Christi*, 3rd ed. (Mainz: Matthias-Grünewald-Verlag, 1995), 1.

3. *God*, 294; *Gott*, 451.

4. *God*, 285; *Gott*, 437.

5. *God*, 311; *Gott*, 473.

6. *God*, xv–xvii; *Gott*, 19–22.

7. On the "entrapment culture" that has developed in the West since the nineteenth century, see Eyal Chowers, *The Modern Self in the Labyrinth: Politics and the Entrapment Imagination* (Cambridge, MA: Harvard University Press, 2004).

8. Maurice Blondel, "The Letter on Apologetics," in *The Letter on Apologetics and History and Dogma*, trans. Alexander Dru and Illtyd Trethowan (1964; reprint, Grand Rapids, MI: Eerdmans, 1994), 160–61; idem, *Lettre sur les exigences de la pensée contemporaine en matière d'apologetique* (1896), in *Œuvres complètes*, vol. 2: *1883–1913: La philosophie de l'action et la crise moderniste*, ed. Claude Troisfontaines (Paris: Presses Universitaires de France, 1997), 131: "Bref la théologie ne peut admettre ne que la philosophie atteigne la réalité de l'ordre surnature . . . il n'y a qu'une relation qu'elle requière; et c'est celle que détermine la méthode d'immanence en considérent le surnaturel . . . comme indispensable en même temps qu'inacessible à l'homme."

9. Walter Kasper, *An Introduction to Christian Faith*, trans. V. Green (New York: Paulist Press, 1980), 20.

10. *God*, 71; *Gott*, 145. Regarding the relationship between natural theology and faith, "natural theology does not substantiate the faith; rather the faith grounds natural theology, although only as a relatively independent entity" (*God*, 78; *Gott*, 153).

11. *God*, 64; *Gott*, 136.

12. *God*, 15; *Gott*, 61–62.

13. Walter Kasper, "Postmodern Dogmatics: Toward a Renewed Discussion of Foundations in North America," trans. D. T. Asselin and Michael Waldstein, *International Catholic Review: Communio* 17 (1990): 181–91, 189.

14. *God*, 84–85; *Gott*, 159–60.

15. *God*, 114; *Gott*, 204.

16. *God*, 100; *Gott*, 184–85.

17. *God*, 109; *Gott*, 197.

18. *God*, 109; *Gott*, 197.

19. *God*, 113; *Gott*, 202.

20. *God*, 78; *Gott*, 154.

21. *God*, 80; *Gott*, 157.

22. This paragraph summarizes the analysis of experience in *God*, 82–87; *Gott*, 158–65.

23. *God*, 81; *Gott*, 158.

24. Kasper writes: "The experiences that are fruitful are not our everyday experiences but rather those contrasting experiences that challenge us to a decision. In other words: experiences are dis-illusioning, in the positive sense of the term; they dissolve previous illusions and delucive coherences and thus reveal the truth about our previous experience" (*God*, 84; *Gott*, 161).

25. *God*, 92; *Gott*, 172. Kasper relies here on the communicative action theories of Karl Otto Apel and Jürgen Habermas. See *God*, 347 nn. 55 and 56; *Gott*, 171 nn. 55 and 56.

26. *God*, 84; *Gott*, 162.

27. *God*, 84–85; *Gott*, 162.

28. Kasper borrows the term "disclosure situation" from Ian T. Ramsey, *Religious Language: An Empirical Placing of Religious Phrases* (London: SCM Press, 1969); see *God*, 85, 90, 346 n. 37, 347 n. 51; *Gott*, 163 n. 37, 169 n. 51.

29. Again, language can serve as an example. According to Kasper, its essential character as "a pre-apprehension of the total meaning of reality" is "a remembering of an unfulfilled hope of the human race and an anticipation of this hope." Thus "even before language becomes explicitly religious language, it always already implies a religious dimension" (*God*, 94; *Gott*, 175).

30. *God*, 86; *Gott*, 164.

31. *God*, 153; *Gott*, 255.

32. See Kasper, *An Introduction to Christian Faith*, 28–35, especially the claim (framed in terms of critical theory's analysis of modernity) that the history of suffering generates "the strongest objections to belief in God" (29–30).

33. *God*, 105; *Gott*, 191.

34. *God*, 105; *Gott*, 191.

35. *God*, 154–55; *Gott*, 257–58. Kasper here combines Boethius's classical definition of person as "an individual substance of a rational nature" ("naturae rationalis individua substantia" [*De persona et duabus naturis* 3]), Thomas's understanding of human nature "in so far as it is immaterial," as "in some way all things" ("Secundum vero esse immateriale . . . est etiam quodammodo omnia" [*In libros de anima* 2, 5, 5]), and Richard of St. Victor's definition of person as "an intellectual nature existing incommunicably" ("naturae intellectualis incommunicabilis existentia" [*De trinitatae* 2, 22, 24]), and he retrieves them in more contemporary terms (*God*, 153–54; *Gott*, 256–57).

36. *God*, 155; *Gott*, 258.

37. *God*, 154; *Gott*, 257–58.

38. *God*, 155; *Gott*, 258.

39. *God*, 156; *Gott*, 260.

40. See also Walter Kasper, *Theology and Church*, trans. Margaret Kohl (New York: Crossroad, 1989), 29–30, where Kasper states: "By defining God, the all-determining reality, in personal terms, *being as a whole* is personally defined. This

means a revolution in the understanding of being. . . . To put it in more concrete terms: *love is the all-determining reality* and the meaning of being. . . . So wherever there is love, we already find, here and now, the ultimate meaning of all reality" (Kasper's emphases).

41. Charles Taylor, *A Secular Age* (Cambridge, MA: Belknap Press, 2007), 38–41.

42. Ibid., 323. On this same page, there appears another definition: "the ways in which [people] imagine their social existence, how they fit together with others, how things go in between them and their fellows, the expectations which are normally met, and the deeper normative notions and images which underlie these expectations."

43. Ibid., 363. It is "impersonal in the most forbidding sense, blind and indifferent to our fate."

44. Ibid., 326–27.

45. Chris Hedges, *The Empire of Illusion: The End of Literacy and the Triumph of Spectacle* (New York: Nation Books, 2009).

46. Ibid., 16, citing the argument of Neal Gabler's *Life: The Movie; How Entertainment Conquered Reality* (New York: Vintage, 1998).

47. Hedges, *Empire of Illusion*, 26.

48. Taylor, *A Secular Age*, 770–72.

49. Hedges's only sustained expression of hope comes in the book's concluding pages and ends this way: "Love will endure, even if it appears darkness has swallowed us all, to triumph over the wreckage that remains (*Empire of Illusion*, 193).

50. See Vincent J. Miller's precise formulation of this phenomenon: "We face a cultural infrastructure that is capable of absorbing all other cultures as 'content' to be commodified, distributed, and consumed," in idem, *Consuming Religion: Christian Faith and Practice in a Consumer Culture* (New York: Continuum, 2004), 179.

51. Terry Eagleton, *The Illusions of Postmodernism* (Oxford: Blackwell, 1996), 39.

52. For a range of criticisms, see Michel Foucault, *The Order of Things* (New York: Pantheon, 1971; French orig. 1966), 424; Johann Baptist Metz, *Faith in History and Society*, trans. J. Matthew Ashley (New York: Crossroad, 2007), 144–55. For a summary from a theological point of view, see Francis Schüssler Fiorenza, "Systematic Theology: Task and Methods," in *Systematic Theology: Roman Catholic Perspectives*, ed. idem and John P. Galvin, 2nd ed. (Minneapolis: Fortress, 2011), 31–32.

53. For a human rights argument predicated on a universal human "ontological frailty," see Bryan S. Turner, *Vulnerability and Human Rights: Essays on Human Rights* (University Park: The Pennsylvania State University Press, 2006).

54. See Hans-Georg Gadamer, *Truth and Method*, trans. Joel Weinsheimer and Donald G. Marshall, 2nd rev. ed. (New York: Continuum, 1989), esp. 346–79; Edward Schillebeeckx, *Christ: The Experience of Jesus as Lord*, trans. John Bowden (New York: Crossroad, 1981), esp. 27–79; idem, *Interim Report on the Books* Jesus *and* Christ, trans. John Bowden (New York: Crossroad, 1981), esp. 3–19. See also

Max Müller, *Erfahrung und Geschichte: Grundzüge einer Philosophie der Freiheit als transzendentale Erfahrung* (Freiburg: Herder, 1971) and the additional literature cited in *God*, 345 n. 30; *Gott*, 154 n. 30.

55. Jean-Luc Marion, *Dieu sans l'être: Hors-texte* (Paris: Librairie Arthème Fayard, 1982); ET: *God without Being: Hors-Texte*, trans. Thomas A. Carlson (Chicago: University of Chicago Press, 1991).

56. Friedrich Nietzsche, *Thus Spoke Zarathustra*, ed. Adrian Del Caro and Robert Pippin, trans. Adrian Del Caro (Cambridge: Cambridge University Press, 2006); Martin Heidegger, "The Onto-Theo-Logical Constitution of Metaphysics," the second essay of Heidegger's *Identity and Difference*, trans. Joan Stambaugh (New York: Harper and Row, 1969), 42–74; Jacques Derrida, "Différance," in *Margins of Philosophy*, trans. Alan Bass (Chicago: University of Chicago Press, 1982), 1–27; for summaries of Alain Badiou's difficult argument, see Frederiek Depoortere, *The Death of God: An Investigation into the History of the Western Concept of God* (New York: T. & T. Clark, 2007); Quentin Meillassoux, *After Finitude: An Essay on the Necessity of Contingency*, trans. Ray Brassier (New York: Continuum, 2008).

57. Anselm of Canterbury, *Proslogion*, chap. 2, in *The Prayers and Meditations of Saint Anselm*, trans. Benedicta Ward (1973; reprint, Harmondsworth, PA: Penguin, 1986), 244–45.

58. Klaus Hemmerle, *Thesen zu einer trinitarischen Ontologie. Kriterien* 40 (Einsiedeln: Johannes Verlag, 1976), 54 (my translation).

CHAPTER 4

The Mystery of Being Human

Mary Catherine Hilkert, OP

The first and, to date, only systematic treatment of theological anthropology to issue from an ecumenical council is the Second Vatican Council's Pastoral Constitution on the Church in the Modern World, *Gaudium et spes*. Cardinal Walter Kasper, whose life and work this volume celebrates, once remarked that the core insights from that document can be summed up in the short formula in its article 22: "In reality it is only in the mystery of the Word made flesh that the mystery of humanity truly becomes clear."[1] The same might be said of Kasper's own writings on the mystery of being human. Although anthropology is not one of the theological topics for which Kasper is most well-known, important insights from that discipline are integral to all of Kasper's writings, and several of his essays set out an agenda for the field that still remains to be fulfilled.

Three decades after the church's promulgation of *Gaudium et spes* (GS), Kasper observed that in theological anthropology, as in so many other areas of theology and church life, the reception of Vatican II still lies before us. Specifically, he called for "the systematic development of a christologically grounded and defined anthropology and the fully articulated formulation of corresponding individual and social ethics" as "an urgent *desideratum*."[2] The challenge to articulate that anthropology and to develop a corresponding ethics in a global village marked by radical suffering, plural worldviews, increasing economic disparities, fear of the stranger, violence, terrorism, and ecological devastation has grown all the more urgent in the past two decades.

Three of Kasper's contributions to the field of theological anthropology deserve particular attention. Each of them derives from his conviction that Christology—and, more recently, a fully Trinitarian theology—provide the key to a Christian understanding of what it means to be human. Kasper is not unique in making that claim, but his writings differ, both in method and in substance, from many other Christian theologians, both Protestant and Catholic, who write in that vein.[3] The first contribution to be considered in this chapter is the question of the appropriate starting point for a truly *theological* anthropology. As he has done on many other questions, Kasper has carved out a judicious both/and position in this debate, which began at the time of the council and which has continued since then in ongoing disputes about the interpretation and reception of the conciliar documents. A second creative contribution follows from the first. For Kasper, the anthropological symbol of *imago Dei*, "image of God," provides the systematic hinge between Christology, soteriology, and anthropology rather than a faulty starting point for a truly *theological* or *Christological* anthropology. Kasper's third and major contribution to the field is to be found in a careful rereading of his well-known volumes *Jesus the Christ* and *The God of Jesus Christ* with an eye toward how the life, death, and resurrection of Jesus disclose "the key, center, and purpose of human life." Although Kasper does not address in detail how a Christological and Trinitarian anthropology provides a theological basis for individual and social ethics, including ethical dialogue with those who don't share those faith convictions, he does at least point in that direction. This chapter concludes with the ethical hints, which he himself offers, and suggests some related questions that he, and those who study his thought, might pursue further.

1. Christological Anthropology: The Question of Starting Point

Kasper himself has reviewed the disputed issues surrounding the appropriate starting point for *Gaudium et spes* at the time of the council. Once the decision had been reached to add a document to the conciliar agenda that would address the question of what the church could contribute to the most pressing problems facing human persons and the world in the mid-1960s, it became clear that the audience for this document needed to be all human beings, not only Christians. A more disputed point was the question of whether the church's message should be framed as a dialogue *with* the world or a proclamation *to* the world.[4]

Closely related was the question of whether to begin the document from an anthropological starting point or from a more explicitly Christological and ecclesiological point of view. In the background were concerns about the relationship of nature and grace, which had been at the forefront of the theological renewal that led to the council but which had also been identified as a cause of major doctrinal concern since the time of the Modernist crisis at the beginning of the twentieth century. The major specific concern voiced in the papal encyclical *Humani Generis* (1950) was that various forms of the so-called *nouvelle théologie* threatened to compromise the gratuity of grace and to collapse the supernatural order into the natural.

Various drafts of *Gaudium et spes* shifted back and forth between alternative starting points, some of which were explicitly Christological, but the final decision was to begin with the contemporary anthropological crisis. Before turning to reflection on the mystery of Christ, the pastoral constitution identifies human persons as created in the image of God and destined for communion with God, a supernatural vocation to be realized precisely in and through active engagement of one's life in the world and activity on behalf of the kingdom of God in the world. The final draft of *Gaudium et spes* affirms that the followers of Christ are called to solidarity not only with other Christians or religious believers but also with the whole human family.[5] In the now well-known opening words of the pastoral constitution: "The joys and hopes, the grief and anguish of the people of our time, especially of those who are poor or afflicted, are the joys and hopes, the grief and anguish of the followers of Christ as well. Nothing that is genuinely human fails to find an echo in their hearts" (GS 1).

The pastoral constitution's rationale for the call to the church to stand in solidarity with the world is equally significant: "For theirs is a community of people united in Christ and guided by the holy Spirit in their pilgrimage towards the Father's kingdom, bearers of a message of salvation for all of humanity. That is why they cherish a feeling of deep solidarity with the human race and its history" (GS 1).

As *Gaudium et spes* confirms, Christians share the challenge of all other human beings in the modern—and now postmodern—world to "read the signs of the times." And, if faithful to their Christian vocation, they do so from a specific faith perspective: "the light of the Gospel" (GS 4). Thus, in his reading of the pastoral constitution, Kasper emphasizes that although anthropology is the starting point for the document, "Christology is nevertheless the criterion of all its statements about anthropology and remains the horizon in which they are to be understood."[6] In contrast to a number of other commentators on the document, Kasper distinguishes the text's starting point from its interpretive lens and insists that *Gaudium et spes* truly does present a Christological anthropology precisely because "it proclaims Jesus Christ as the origin and end of true humanity," as the one mystery who unlocks the mystery of human life.[7]

2. *Imago Dei* as the "Systematic Clasp"

Rather than seeing the symbol of human beings in the "image of God" as providing an alternative to a Christological starting point for Christian anthropology, Kasper describes the concept of *imago Dei* as the "systematic clasp" that holds together anthropology and Christology. Some theologians view the goodness of creation in the image of God, as described in the first creation account in Genesis 1:26, as that which has been destroyed by human sin and cast soteriology solely, or at least primarily, in terms of redemption from sin. Other scholars view the gift of creation in the image of God as enduring in spite of "the Fall" (Gen 3), but relegate that goodness to the realm of "nature" as distinct from the redeeming grace of Jesus Christ, which belongs to the order of the "supernatural." Kasper, however, maintains that there is a continuity as well as a distinction between the order of creation and the order of redemption, arguing that, for Christians, Genesis 1:26 needs to be interpreted in light of Colossians 1:15. He notes that that was the precise strategy the authors of *Gaudium et spes* employed by concluding the discussion of the dignity of the human person in the pastoral constitution's chapter 1 with the climactic article on "Christ the New Man" (GS 22).

In a later essay, which goes beyond an interpretation of *Gaudium et spes* and its reception, Kasper expands the council's intertextual reading of biblical texts related to Christian anthropology with his interpretation of Romans 5:12-21. Agreeing with Karl Barth, he argues that Adam is to be understood in light of Christ, not Christ in light of Adam. At the same time, he disagrees with Barth's negative reply to the question of whether human beings remain "hearers of the word," affirming, in contrast to Barth, that human persons are fundamentally open to receive the good news of the Gospel in spite of sin.[8] Kasper agrees that Christology surpasses and perfects anthropology. But unlike many who highlight that point, he also argues that, in the modern context, Christology also presupposes anthropology, that is, human persons who are truly open to receive and respond to the saving grace of Jesus Christ. Otherwise, the Gospel would remain a heteronomous command that has no resonance with the joys and the hopes, the grief and the anguish of human beings, rather than being the "good news" freely received and embraced as the deepest truth of humanity and human longings.

The human subject that Christology presupposes remains radically free before God's self-offer. This conviction flows from Kasper's Trinitarian convictions that God is love and that God desires to persuade and draw the human response of friendship, but never to coerce that response. That same respect for human dignity and the inviolability of conscience, Kasper argues, should characterize the church, especially in light of its own teaching that "only truth can persuade conscience" (*Dignitatis humanae* 1). Further, precisely because of its conviction that the human person has a vocation that transcends this world, the church should be an advocate for genuine human freedom and respect for conscience in the public arena.

The symbol of *imago Dei* serves as a systematic clasp not only between Christology and anthropology but also between anthropology and soteriology. For Kasper, the latter term refers not only to Christ's death on the cross for the sake of the redemption of humanity from sin but also to Christ as the final fulfillment of human hope. Salvation in Jesus Christ promises a relationship that goes beyond the restoration of broken relations distorted by sin. Final salvation includes an unimaginable form of humanization, the participation in divine life that goes beyond reconciliation to include divinization. This is the promised destiny of human persons, the concrete fulfillment of human hopes, which exceeds the human imagination, let alone human deduction. In view of the "shock of revelation" in Jesus Christ, the true destiny of all human persons is revealed to be communion with God, and human freedom is redefined as freedom *for* God and for one's neighbor, freedom-in-love.[9]

If, as Christian faith professes, only Jesus Christ can be fully identified as the very "image of God," all other theoretical or practical claims to define human life, meaning, and purpose are called into question or measured by the norm of Jesus Christ. In Kasper's terms, Christology "*outbids* anthropology by defining the meaning and purpose of human beings as the humanization of men and women through their divinization, which cannot be brought about by human beings themselves."[10]

3. Paschal Christology and the Human Dilemma

The fear of many church leaders and theologians at the time of Vatican II and beyond was that a theological document that emphasizes the goodness and vocation of all of creation and the continuity between anthropology and Christology, even if the latter "trumps" the former, would not be able to deal adequately with the reality of human sin and the radical need for human redemption and reconciliation. These sobering realities receive greater emphasis when the mystery of the cross, rather than the mystery of creation or even that of incarnation, forms the starting point for a theological anthropology. Kasper agrees that at least one earlier draft of the pastoral constitution (the Ariccia text) did not do justice to realities of human sinfulness and divine judgment, something that both of his German colleagues Karl Rahner and Joseph Ratzinger stressed during the council.

In Kasper's assessment, however, the incarnational Christology in the final text (which both Rahner and Ratzinger helped to revise) "was broadened by a theology of the cross and a paschal Christology."[11] If Jesus the Christ, who is the very icon of God, discloses the meaning and destiny of human life, then there is no question, Kasper holds, that a theology of the cross is essential to a proper understanding of human life, especially to the grief and the anguish of human life. The real questions are: *which* theology of the cross, and *how* is the cross related to human life? Kasper is quite clear that human beings as sinners can never arrive at an adequate self-understanding on their own and that the cross is integral to human existence. But he is equally clear that sin is not a part of human nature; the cross is a form of liberation rather than a destruction of human life. The cross carries a message of judgment and calls for a radical change of life, a *metanoia.*

This conversion is not, however, a diminishment or rejection of human life but a crucial element in a larger journey toward the fullness of life. Kasper states that "the cross which breaks sinful nature is not the crucifixion of the human being. What exodus and *metanoia* do is to break down the sin through which human beings have become curved in upon themselves (sin as *incurvatio hominis*). They lay bare man's [*sic*] original *ekstasis* once more and bring it to fulfillment. To enter into the *pascha domini* is therefore the way to human perfection."[12]

A fuller understanding of the meaning of the cross for human life and of the significance of a paschal Christology for Kasper's approach to theological anthropology requires a turn to his classic books *Jesus the Christ* and *The God of Jesus Christ*. Both volumes make clear that, for Kasper, as for any theologian who insists on a historical starting point for understanding the mystery of Jesus as the Christ, the cross cannot be interpreted apart from the life and ministry of Jesus that led to his execution on a cross. Kasper also stresses, more strongly than some others who share a historical approach, that the cross cannot be understood apart from the resurrection of Jesus. Jesus' resurrection is, Kasper insists, not only revelatory of God but also salvific. It is not only a confirmation of the validity of Jesus' life and ministry and of his implicit claim to a unique relationship with God but also the definitive defeat of evil and death and the final realization of Christian hope.

Although Kasper's *Jesus the Christ* and *The God of Jesus Christ* focus on biblical revelation and the development in Christological and Trinitarian doctrines, both texts begin with Kasper's own reading of "the signs of the times" and the specific anthropological challenges that Christian theologians, pastors, and preachers need to address if faith in the God of Jesus Christ is not to be dismissed. Kasper's lifelong apologetic and pastoral concern that theology remain talk about God, which for Christians is always talk about the God of Jesus Christ, was evident in an address that he delivered on his reception of an academic award in 2009 from Saint John's University in Collegeville, Minnesota. He argues there, as he has elsewhere, that the most central and fundamental question of theology as well as the most challenging problem for theology is "the God question."[13]

But that address and all of Kasper's writings make clear that "the God-question" is at the same time "the human-question," the question of the ultimate meaning and purpose of human life. What

Gaudium et spes identifies as the task that is essential to the future of humanity—"providing generations to come with reasons for living and for hope" (GS 31)—ultimately depends on whether reality itself can be considered trustworthy. In Trinitarian terms, the challenge of faith is whether one can believe that love and communion are the source and goal of all that is, in spite of all of the historical evidence to the contrary. Kasper's fruitful attempts to reinterpret—and therefore to retrieve—the most basic Christological and Trinitarian doctrines are directed not only toward human *understanding* but more deeply toward undergirding and empowering human dignity, freedom, and hope. In this regard, he writes, "If [theology with the church] speaks in a new and fresh way of the living, liberating God who is love, then it will render a service to life, freedom, justice, solidarity and love, then it can serve the dignity of humanity and the truth of reality, and open up perspectives of hope in all the *aporia* [doubts] of the present."[14]

These rich thoughts flow into three specific themes in Kasper's theology: Jesus' suffering as the revelation of God's love and communion with us, Jesus' saving death as the source of liberation and hope, and Jesus' resurrection as the key to hope.

(1) *Jesus the Christ: God as Love and Communion in the Flesh*

What, then, is the light that Christian faith can shed on the mystery of being human, especially in the face of innocent suffering? In spite of his insistence that theology requires an adequate metaphysics and is a search for rational understanding, Kasper stands with the vast majority of theologians who recognize that no doctrine, not even that concerning the triune God, offers an intellectual answer to why innocent suffering exists and how God—if there is a God—can permit tragedies, ranging from natural disasters to the *Shoah*. Yet he remains convinced that Christian faith can shed some light in the darkness precisely because the unfathomable mystery of God has shed light on the depths of the human situation by becoming one with humankind in the person of Jesus of Nazareth. The concrete history of Jesus, and especially his death interpreted in light of resurrection faith, reveals the love and communion that the Christian tradition identifies as the very mystery of God freely shared with God's beloved creation. Emphasizing that Christology is the key to theology as well as to anthropology and theology of creation, Kasper declares that Jesus' "life is the answer to the question 'Who is God?' "[15]

At the same time, in speaking about a properly theological anthropology, Kasper is equally clear that Jesus's life is the answer to the question of what it means to be human. This view is most fully developed in *Jesus the Christ*, where Kasper presents Jesus as a prophetic preacher who responded to the human hopes and the longing for salvation in his first-century Jewish context by announcing the reign of God as a rule of justice, peace, and unconditional love. That reign is not only an eschatological promise but also present and active here and now. This good news is, at the same time, a judgment on all interpretations of human life and freedom that fall short of that promise. In his preaching and teaching, Jesus breaks open human hopes for peace, freedom, justice, and life, promising their fulfillment in the kingdom of God while also revealing human alienation from true freedom and justice and the impossibility of fulfilling those hopes with human resources alone. In his discussion of Jesus' parables, Kasper further emphasizes that God's free offer of salvation requires a free response. The unconditional love of the God of the parables beckons those who have received that love to accept each other unconditionally as well.[16]

In Kasper's account, Jesus' revelation of God and authentic human life is equally evident in his actions. In particular, his table fellowship with outcasts and sinners and his miracles are concrete signs that God's salvation includes the well-being of the whole person, body and soul. The gospels also depict Jesus' confrontation with demonic powers, forces of evil that are hostile to creation and to the coming of the new creation—the creation that, according to Kasper, is marked by life, freedom, peace, reconciliation, and love. Through his preaching in word and deed of God's reign, Jesus discloses that the meaning of human life is to be found in a love that includes, but goes beyond, the demands of justice, a love that is grounded in absolute dependence on God and absolute surrender to God.[17]

In Kasper's reading, Jesus not only announces the reign of God in word and deed; he *is* the reign of God in person; he is God's unconditional love made visible, but at the same time he is concealed in lowliness and poverty.[18] Expressing this revelation of the mystery of what it means to be human in a way that speaks to contemporary concerns for emancipation and liberation, Kasper describes Jesus as the "free [person]" *par excellence*, both because of his utter dependence on the Father (Christian freedom is always given by God) and because his life, death, and resurrection bring about the possibility of true freedom for the rest of humankind.

(2) *Jesus' Saving Death as Source of Liberation and Hope*

It is only in the context of his life, mission, and implicit claim to a unique relationship with God that Jesus' death can be interpreted as the liberation and source of hope for human beings in a world of suffering and violence. In his discussion of Jesus' death in *Jesus the Christ*, Kasper begins with the political dimension of Jesus' execution: Jesus was sentenced to death as a political rebel by Roman authorities with the deceitful collaboration of some Jewish authorities. In Kasper's reading, Jesus' death, historically speaking, was brought about by the worst that humanity is capable of: "Jesus was caught between millstones of power. Misunderstanding, cowardice, hatred, lies, intrigues, and emotions brought him to destruction."[19]

How, then, can that same death be a saving act of God and Jesus' free self-sacrifice? In engaging the question of later theological interpretations of Jesus' death, Kasper grants that the biblical sources don't give direct access to Jesus' own interpretation of his death. Turning to the final actions of Jesus, Kasper calls attention to the cleansing of the temple as a provocative prophetic action symbolizing the end of one era and the beginning of a new one (Mark 11:15-19). He likewise reads Jesus' final meal with his disciples as providing evidence that Jesus saw his approaching death as somehow connected with the coming of the kingdom of God (Mark 14:17-25).[20] Finally, Kasper highlights the anguished prayer of lament in the Marcan and Matthean accounts of the death of Jesus in which he cried out, "My God, my God, why have you forsaken me?" (Mark 15:34; Matt 27:46). Whether Jesus uttered those lines from Psalm 22 or they were the addition of the gospel writers based on post-resurrection faith, Kasper remarks that the faith and the anguish expressed in Psalm 22 are consistent with Jesus' faith in Abba throughout his life. At this point, Kasper offers his theological interpretation of the death of Jesus as salvific: "[Jesus] experienced God as the one who withdraws in his very closeness, who is totally other. Jesus experienced the unfathomable mystery of God and his will, but he endured this darkness in faith. This extremity of emptiness enabled him to become the vessel of God's fullness. His death became the source of life. It became the other side of the coming of the Kingdom of God—its coming in love."[21]

Jesus' death on the cross was the ultimate consequence of his life and ministry. But it was, Kasper observes, at the same time "the resumé and sum of his message," which was one of saving service. The Christological basis for Kasper's later reflection on both divine and human personhood as radically relational is evident in Kasper's brief remark about the one who freely accepted death, even death on the cross: "He showed himself to be a "man for others"; he personified God's unconditional love for all.[22] Taking a stand in the exegetical and theological disputes about whether Jesus saw his death as saving, Kasper judged that, based on the whole of Jesus' life, it was reasonable to conclude that "he saw his death as a representative and saving service to many."[23] Nevertheless, he confirms that the salvific dimension of Jesus' death remained hidden in his death as it was throughout his life. Highlighting this connection, Kasper writes, "The helplessness, poverty and insignificance with which the Kingdom of God appeared in his person and in his activity came to a final, even scandalous culmination in his death. Jesus' life ended in a final uncertainty. The story of Jesus and its end remain a question which only God can answer."[24]

This stark admission returns theodicy to center stage in discussions of anthropology, Christology, and Trinitarian theology: Where is God to be found in innocent suffering? What empowers radical hope in the face of failure, death, and destruction? In the face of death, whether one's own death or that of others—and especially when confronted with the death of innocent victims—it is impossible to offer a human explanation of the ultimate meaning and purpose of life. If there is some final significance to life, it is not evident to the human mind; it escapes any human control and exceeds even the human imagination. As *Gaudium et spes* points out, it is not only the tragic deaths of the innocent that haunt humanity and raise questions about God but all human death: "It is when faced with death that the enigma of the human condition is most evident. People are tormented not only by pain and by the gradual diminution of their bodily powers but also, and even more, by the dread of forever ceasing to be. . . . The imagination is at a loss before the mystery of death" (GS 18).

Although Kasper is more explicit about the saving significance of Jesus' death than are many others who engage that question, he writes in the mode of paradox when he speaks of the cross as "failure and disgrace" as well as the vanquishing of death and the foundation of new life. He likewise emphasizes that the cross provides "the passage to Resurrection and transfiguration."[25] Although he joins the ranks of those who speak about the cross as revealing "a God who suffers with us," he explicitly distances himself from any kind of valorization of suffering. Maintaining the paradox of life emerging from the crucible of death, he writes: "God does not glorify or deify suffering, nor does he simply eliminate it; he redeems and transforms it. The cross is the passage to resurrection and transfiguration. So the theology of the cross and kenosis . . . becomes an Easter theology of transfiguration; it becomes a hope against hope in the living God who gives life (Rom 4:19). '*Spe salvi*' (Rom 8:20, 24; 1 Pet 1:3), we are, so Scripture says, redeemed in hope."[26]

(3) *Resurrection Faith: Christ the Key to Human Hope, Freedom, and Identity*

In the end, Christian hope in the face of death and the tragic dimensions of human life is sustained only by the conviction of faith that the Spirit of God raised Jesus to new life and has defeated the power of sin and death. Here, Christology, anthropology, and pneumatology intersect in the mystery of resurrection faith. The faith of all later believers is dependent on the testimony of the first human witnesses, yet their faith in turn was empowered by the Spirit of God who made possible the encounter with the risen Christ as both fully human and radically transformed. The basic faith claim of the first witnesses to the resurrection—that God raised Jesus from death (1 Cor 15:3-5)—is not historically verifiable beyond the testimony of those witnesses whose lives were radically transformed and who were willing to give their lives rather than to deny that belief.

The relationality and interdependence that are constitutive of human life also become evident in the transmission of Easter faith. The encounter with the risen Christ that the first disciples claimed to have experienced is mediated to others only through the testimony and the trustworthiness of their witness. The classical claim that the faith of later generations stands on the foundation of the apostolic testimony is transposed into anthropological terms when the focus is put on the possibility of later generations having a similar experience of resurrection faith as only possible within a tradition mediated by the narratives of the "believing-seeing" of the first witnesses. Nevertheless, both the originating experience of the first witnesses to the resurrection—the birth of their faith and the restoration of their hope—and that of later believers remain the work of the Holy Spirit who makes possible any encounter with the resurrected Christ.

Kasper argues that the depths of hope of which human beings are capable and the experience of salvation that is available during human life are most fully disclosed in the resurrection accounts. Each of these biblical narratives points both to an experience of the risen Jesus whom his followers recognize through some kind of revelatory encounter and also to the radical novelty of what has happened to Jesus and to his witnesses. In this event, which Paul describes with the language of "new creation" (1 Cor 15:42ff.), God confirms Jesus' identity as unique Son of the Father and the validity of his preaching of the in-breaking of the eschatological reign of God. Further, Kasper emphasizes that the resurrection not only *reveals* that final era of salvation but also *inaugurates* the end time. The definitive love and loyalty of God are not only manifest but also *effective* in the resurrection of Jesus.[27] God is shown to be faithful to God's promises even when all human potentiality has been exhausted or quenched in personal, interpersonal, and social situations of impasse.

The anthropological risk of a human life lived in faith is one that Jesus himself faced—and embraced freely—during his life, especially when anticipating his death. Kasper describes the challenge of choosing to live by Easter faith and contrasts a Christian understanding of freedom with modern notions of autonomy:

> In making such a decision [for Easter faith], what has to be considered is whether one feels one can live from one's own potentialities or whether one dares to live from what absolutely cannot be controlled, from God. Easter faith has confidence in God's possession of a potential far beyond existing reality, far beyond death, and dares to bet on that God "with whom all things are possible" in life and in death. Hence the faith of Easter is an attack on that enclosed view of the world which sets itself absolute limits and leaves no space for the non-deducible new creative potentialities of God.[28]

Kasper explicitly distinguishes Christian hope from modern abstract utopias as well as from progressive evolutionary or revolutionary ideologies of history. Reemphasizing the necessary unity of cross and resurrection, he insists that Easter hope returns the Christian to the way of the cross, which involves concrete bodily engagement in everyday life lived in obedience to one's Christian vocation. Resurrection faith and the claim of the early baptismal creeds—"I believe in resurrection of the body"—carries specific significance for human hope since human persons are inconceivable without a body. Without pretending to be able to fully define what Paul means by the "pneumatic body," Kasper's review of what is meant by "body" (*soma*) in scripture leads him to conclude that the resurrection of the body refers to "the totality of the person (not just the soul) that is finally in the dimension of God, that has entered entirely into the Kingdom of God."[29] In one of his rare cosmological and ecological references in *Jesus the Christ*, Kasper further notes that this bodily engagement extends to a loyalty to the earth itself. He writes: "As hope in eternal life, it not only respects life but turns lovingly towards all that is living and alive."[30]

The new creation in Jesus Christ that is the fruit of God's Spirit poured forth in the radically new event of resurrection is characterized in many ways in scripture, including talk about life, justice, redemption, peace, and forgiveness. But in Kasper's judgment, the new existence of the Christian life in the Spirit is best characterized in modern and late modern eras as freedom. The notion of Christian freedom and its difference from the contemporary notion of autonomy are the heart of Kasper's writings. He has embraced the horizon of the post-Enlightenment philosophy of freedom as the most relatively adequate metaphysical framework for theological reflection on reality as a whole, yet he also clearly affirms that no philosophical system will be adequate to the mystery and that biblical revelation surpasses the categories of philosophical thought. To speak of God as Absolute Freedom, Kasper asserts, is to stress that the living God of biblical revelation is also a liberating God, "a living, speaking, and self-bestowing God who can be called upon and addressed."[31]

That claim, in turn, has implications for the addressees of the invitation to share in the communion of divine love. Thus, Kasper stresses that God's creation is a place of freedom and also that human persons, because they are created in the *imago Dei*, discover their fullest freedom in complete surrender to God. For this reason, the human person remains a mystery that exceeds and relativizes any attempts to understand what it means to be human in naturalistic, deterministic, political, or economic terms. The human person is made for love and called to communion, which—from a Trinitarian perspective—is the only context in which freedom can flourish. Trinitarian love, as concretized in Jesus' life and death and confirmed in his resurrection, is a freely bestowed noncoercive invitation to communion that respects the otherness of the other and extends solidarity and unconditional love to all people, including to enemies or those who reject that love.

Because Kasper is convinced that Jesus' life, death, and resurrection as well as the triune God of love, whom Jesus revealed, provide the key for understanding all reality, Kasper joins a host of theologians, many of them from the Orthodox tradition as well as Catherine Mowry LaCugna and others, in calling for a metaphysical revolution from a metaphysics of being or substance to a relational and personal ontology. That shift of linguistic and philosophical framework has implications for speech about God but also for speech about those created in the divine image. Kasper describes this framework more simply: "Love is the all-encompassing horizon of reality and the meaning of existence."[32] The identity of human persons, created in the image of the triune God, remains a mystery grounded in that mystery of love which can never be fully defined or captured in concepts or human constructs.

4. Ethical Concerns and Further Questions

Although human identity remains a mystery that can never be fully defined, Kasper is clear about what is ruled out and what really matters for those who share the "open identity combined with solidarity" that *Gaudium et spes* proposes. The brief ethical mandate included in his address at Saint John's University might be seen as providing the broad strokes of the Christologically grounded individual and social ethics for which Kasper called two decades ago. Basing his ethical summons on the Trinitarian conviction that God is love and the Christological conviction that Jesus' life and death are the fullest articulation of what that love means in human terms, Kasper affirms, "Neither personal nor national distinction, neither ethnic affiliation nor even academic greatness, nor force, money, power and influence, nor the self-assertion 'of the fittest' will be what counts in the end, but instead tolerance, respect, solidarity, forgiveness, goodness and practical love will be what remains as the definitive reality."[33]

Kasper grounds his ethical claims in a biblical and historical Christology in continuity with early Christian Wisdom and Logos Christologies.[34] His explicit reference to the writings of Justin Martyr, who developed his second-century Logos Christology in response to the religious and philosophical currents of his time and culture, suggests that others who do not share Christian faith might embrace many of the same ethical convictions that Kasper expresses, but on grounds drawn from their own religious, philosophical, or humanist convictions.

Although theological anthropology and ethics have not been at the center of Cardinal Kasper's recent theological writings or ecclesial concerns, research in both areas would benefit from Kasper's further theological reflection, along with that of students of his thought. Three questions, in particular, come to mind.

First, if the Christian "call to solidarity" extends not only to the entire human family but to all creatures, as recent ecclesial documents have confirmed, what are the implications of a broader ecological theology for a Christian anthropology that focuses on the human person and human freedom? How might Kasper's call for a Wisdom Christology contribute to that dialogue?

Second, Kasper agrees that contemporary theology needs to take the concrete experience of suffering humanity as its starting point, yet at the same time he has expressed clear reservations in the past about forms of political and liberation theology.[35] Although Kasper has called for attention to the concrete history of Jesus of Nazareth in his Christological writings, Kasper's analysis of "the signs of times" and his proposals for "Christian humanism" remain abstract, for the most part. If all human subjects have to realize their freedom, subjectivity, and personal existence in concrete historical and social contexts, which include and are often dominated by sinful social structures and systems of power that limit and compromise the exercise of that freedom—as Johann Baptist Metz, Gustavo M. Gutiérrez, M. Shawn Copeland, and other political and liberationist theologians have argued—what are the implications of Kasper's ideas for theological anthropology, solidarity, and practical love/ethics?

Third, Kasper has argued that the question of God in the presence of evil and suffering can be answered only in terms of Christology and a theology of the cross. How does his concern about the centrality of concrete human suffering for all aspects of theology impact the way he and other theologians develop a soteriology that acknowledges that Jesus' death is salvific and that the cross provides the essential transition to resurrection and yet avoids the legitimation of human suffering?[36]

These and the many other questions emerging in the fields of theological anthropology and ethics call to mind the insight of the Trappist monk Thomas Merton in "Untitled Poem":

> Each one who is born comes into the world with a question
> For which old answers are not sufficient.
> So all theology is a birthday. A way home to where we are.[37]

On the occasion of Cardinal Kasper's eightieth birthday and this *Festschrift* in his honor, I join my colleagues in giving thanks for his theology in which the "old answers are not sufficient" and for his steadfast focus on the mystery of God, our only "home."

Endnotes

1. On this conciliar statement, see Walter Kasper, "The Theological Anthropology of *Gaudium et Spes*," *Communio* 23 (Spring 1996): 129–40, 137.

2. Ibid., 140.

3. For the dispute on this point at the time of the council, see Kasper, "The Theological Anthropology of *Gaudium et Spes*," and Joseph Ratzinger, "The Dignity of the Human Person" [commentary on *Gaudium et spes*, introductory article, and chapter 1], in *Commentary on the Documents of Vatican II*, vol. 5, ed. Herbert Vorgrimler (New York: Herder and Herder, 1969), 115–63, esp. 119–23 and 159–63. For a later call for a more explicitly Christological reading of *Gaudium et spes*, see David L. Schindler, "Christology and the *Imago Dei*: Interpreting *Gaudium et Spes*," *Communio* 23 (1996): 156–84. For a doctrinal rather than a historical approach to a Christological anthropology, an approach that places a greater impact on the power of sin to distort human creation in the image of God, see Kathryn Tanner, *Christ the Key* (Cambridge, UK: Cambridge University Press, 2010); idem, *Jesus, Humanity and the Trinity: A Brief Systematic Theology* (Minneapolis: Fortress, 2001).

4. Shortly after the council, Karl Barth raised that precise concern about *Gaudium et spes*: "Is it so certain that dialogue with the world is to be placed ahead of proclamation *to* the world?" See Karl Barth, *Ad limina apostolorum* (ET: Edinburgh, 1969), 9, as cited by Aidan Nichols, "Twenty-Five Years On: A Catholic Commemoration of Karl Barth," *New Blackfriars* 74 (1993): 538–49, at 548.

5. One of the major developments in the fifty years since the council is the recognition that solidarity extends not only to the human family but also to all creatures and to the earth. See this volume's chapter 6 by Elizabeth A. Johnson.

6. Kasper, "Theological Anthropology of *Gaudium et Spes*," 137.

7. Ibid.

8. Karl Barth, *Christ and Adam: Man and Humanity in Romans 5*, trans. T. A. Smail (Edinburgh and London, 1956), 43, as cited by Walter Kasper, "Christology and Anthropology," in *Theology and the Church*, trans. Margaret Kohl (New York: Crossroad, 1989), 73–93, 82 and 210 n. 37. Kasper's critique of Barth is similar to the critique by Hans Urs von Balthasar in his *The Theology of Karl Barth*, trans. John Drury (Garden City, NY: Anchor Books, 1972), 191–262.

9. Walter Kasper, *The Christian Understanding of Freedom and the History of Freedom in the Modern Era*, trans. Joseph A. Murphy (Milwaukee, WI: Marquette University Press, 1988), 41.

10. Kasper, "Christology and Anthropology," 92; emphasis in original.

11. Kasper, "Theological Anthropology of *Gaudium et Spes*," 139. Concerning Rahner's and Ratzinger's dissatisfaction with earlier drafts of Schema XIII, which became *Gaudium et spes*, see Brandon R. Peterson, "Critical Voices: The Reactions of Rahner and Ratzinger to 'Schema XIII' (*Gaudium et Spes*)," *Modern Theology* (October 2014). Peterson cites a speech by Cardinal Hermann Volk that summarizes the widely voiced criticism of the Ariccia text of Schema XIII: "The whole world . . . has been so afflicted by sin that this situation can only be overcome in Christ. In the Schema, however, the world appears as a creation only slightly injured by sin. . . . I propose that the clear preliminary statement in the first part of the schema, especially the description of the present condition of the world and humanity . . . be shortened while an earlier theological view of the world be expressly declared: namely, the world is created by God and therefore has a definite and inexterminable disposition toward God; the world is in sin; it is redeemed by Christ; it is destined toward a supernatural end, which can be obtained neither by evolution nor natural history, but only by means of the advent of Christ" (trans. Brandon R. Peterson). Volk's full speech is available in *Acta Synodalia* 4.2, 406–8.

12. Kasper, "Christology and Anthropology," 84.

13. Walter Cardinal Kasper, "The Timeliness of Speaking of God: Freedom and Communion as Basic Concepts of Theology," *Worship* 83, no. 4 (2009): 293–311, at 293.

14. Ibid., 311.

15. Walter Kasper, *Jesus the Christ*, trans. V. Green (New York: Paulist Press, 1976), 70.

16. Ibid., 86.
17. Ibid., 86–110.
18. Ibid., 101.
19. Ibid., 114.
20. Here Kasper puts significant weight on the apparent historicity of Jesus' declaration, "Truly I say to you, I shall not drink again of the fruit of the vine until the day when I drink it new in the kingdom of God" (Mark 14:25; cf. Luke 22:16, 18).
21. Kasper, *Jesus the Christ*, 118–19. See Kasper's "The Timeliness of Speaking of God," in which, writing later from the perspective of Trinitarian faith, Kasper expands on the self-sacrificing love of God to be found in the death of Jesus: "This kenotic, self-relinquishing mode of existence enables God on the cross to identify himself with that which is most alien to him, the sinner who has deserved death, and to enter into his opposite, into the night of death. God can take this death upon himself without being conquered by it, but instead thereby vanquish it and establish the foundation of a new life. Thus the cross is the utmost that is possible to God in his self-relinquishing love, it is the *id quo maius cogitari nequit*" (pp. 307–8).
22. Kasper, *Jesus the Christ*, 120.
23. Ibid.
24. Ibid., 121.
25. Ibid., 150. Adopting a Johannine perspective in *Jesus the Christ*, Kasper observes, concerning the resurrection, "It is . . . not a separate event after the life and suffering of Jesus, but what is happening at the most profound level in the death of Christ: the act and suffering of a human being's bodily surrender to God and the merciful loving acceptance of this devotion by God. . . . Cross and Resurrection together form the one *Pascha Domini*" (p. 150).
26. Kasper, "The Timeliness of Speaking of God," 308–9.
27. Kasper, *Jesus the Christ*, 156.
28. Ibid., 145. For that reason Kasper stresses that Easter faith is not one dimension of Christian faith but rather "the entirety and essence of that belief" (p. 145).
29. Ibid., 151.
30. Ibid., 155.
31. Kasper, "The Timeliness of Speaking of God," 302.
32. Ibid., 309.
33. Ibid., 310.
34. On the affirmation that a Wisdom Christology is coherent with and demanded by a biblical Christology in a new cultural context, see Kasper, "The Timeliness of Speaking of God," 301; idem, "Gottes Gegenwart in Jesus Christus," in *Weisheit Gottes–Weisheit der Welt*, ed. W. Baier (St. Ottilien: EOS Verlag, 1987), 311–28.
35. See Walter Kasper, *The God of Jesus Christ*, trans. Matthew J. O'Connell (New York: Crossroad, 1984), 160–63. For Kasper's critique of political and liberation theologies, see idem, "Christology and Anthropology," 211–12 n. 72, where he expresses concern about theologies that begin from the relationship of theory

and praxis. Kasper's specific concern is that faith will be viewed as a configuration or *Gestalt* of a "socially critical freedom" rather than as "transcending the sphere of political praxis." See also Kasper, *The Christian Understanding of Freedom*, 17.

36. See Walter Kasper, "Das Kreuz als Offenbarung der Liebe Gottes," *Catholica* 61 (2007): 1–14.

37. Thomas Merton, "Untitled Poem," in *Eighteen Poems* (New York: New Directions, 1968).

CHAPTER 5

Jesus the Christ in Retrospect and Prospect

William P. Loewe

This man is "[a] tireless worker in the vineyard of the Lord, an esteemed theologian, scholar and teacher of theology . . . deeply rooted in the faith [and] in touch with the church." These words, penned in praise of Cardinal Karl Lehmann, apply equally to their author, Cardinal Walter Kasper.[1]

With great esteem for Cardinal Kasper, I focus in this chapter on the cardinal's Christology as articulated in his *Jesus the Christ*. This benchmark book of 1974 (in German) was recently republished in German, with a new introduction by Kasper, as volume 3 of his collected works.[2] Since its first appearance, this book has enjoyed enormous success. It is with good reason, therefore, that the cardinal has expressed the hope that, even though Christology has changed in the last four decades, *Jesus the Christ* can continue to be of service.[3]

The year 1974 also saw the appearance (in their original languages) of *On Being a Christian* by Hans Küng[4] and also *Jesus: An Experiment in Christology* by Edward Schillebeeckx.[5] Although these two books as well as Kasper's *Jesus the Christ* differ in their specific agendas, thus prompting controversy among their authors, their combined impact brought about a theological breakthrough.[6] Indeed, they accomplished a paradigm shift in Catholic Christology. For Kasper, as for Küng and Schillebeeckx, this shift was fully conscious and deliberate. Since this new paradigm remains appropriate and valid today, its specific form in *Jesus the Christ* is worthy of our analysis and evaluation.

1. Toward a Paradigm Shift in Christology

Neoscholasticism, which emerged in the nineteenth century, provided the dominant paradigm for Catholic Christology until the Second Vatican Council. Its theologians followed the theology of Thomas Aquinas in that they looked to the Christological dogma of the Council of Chalcedon for the framework, terms, and issues that, in their judgment, define Christology. Yet, they ignored the exploration of "the mysteries" of the life and destiny of Jesus Christ that Thomas had integrated into that paradigm. The medieval Dominican theologian pondered at length Christ's virginal conception and birth, baptism, way of life, preaching, and miracles; he also accorded equal space to Jesus' resurrection as to Jesus' passion.[7] All of these elements vanished, however, from the Christology of neoscholasticism. Truncating Thomas's Christological framework, the neoscholastic scholars contented themselves with an ahistorical, metaphysical mediation of Chalcedon's teaching that Jesus Christ is "truly God" and "truly man" in "one person." Even when, especially after 1951, these theologians set about the task of recovering Christ's full humanity, they did so within their appropriation of Chalcedon's framework.[8]

(1) *The Transition from Neoscholasticism*

In the 1960s, as Walter Kasper began his theological career, he found himself in what he regarded as a transitional period.[9] In his view, neoscholasticism had produced a "clerical" theology, that is, a theology for seminarians and priests. As a result, the preaching and catechesis informed by this theology often proved unintelligible and hence irrelevant to the laity.[10] By contrast, Vatican II called for a scripturally based and pastorally dynamic theology, a theology capable of rendering the Bible's witness to the living Christ effective in the lives of contemporary men and women. In this perspective, the council recognized that if the church was to fulfill its mission in the modern world, it needed a new kind of theology. In response, the young Kasper laid the foundations for the church's theological renewal in his doctoral dissertation, Habilitation, and a series of essays running through the 1960s, essays that remain quite fresh today.

During his theological studies, Walter Kasper discerned that historical consciousness—that is, an awareness of the historical character of all finite reality—provides the key to contemporary culture and the defining horizon within which Catholic theology must proceed.[11] While neoscholastic theologians had conducted a rearguard action against the incursion of historical consciousness into Catholic thought, Catholic scholars intent on communicating with their modern contemporaries now had to adopt a historical form of thought. This orientation was not a mere adjustment to the spirit of the times but, Kasper argued, an exigency arising from the character of divine revelation.[12]

Moreover, Kasper saw that his forebears in the Catholic Tübingen School had started this new orientation during the nineteenth century.[13] The University of Tübingen's Catholic theologians such as Johann Sebastian Drey and Johann Adam Möhler had focused on the Christian tradition as a central theological category designating the dynamic process through which the Spirit renders the risen, living Christ present to and through the church in every time and place. Theology, anchored in the tradition, should operate as a moment within and in service to that process, tradition's leading edge, as it were. In other words, according to the Catholic Tübingen School, theology is the ecclesial, intellectual discipline that seeks to mediate between the Christian tradition and the cultural matrix in which the church finds itself. This mediatory function, in turn, demands theologians' dialogical engagement with their culture and society. In particular, given this view, Tübingen's Catholic theologians undertook a lively and enlivening critical interaction with German romanticism (e.g., Friedrich Schlegel) and German idealism (e.g., G. W. F. Hegel and F. W. J. Schelling).

Walter Kasper has made his own the Catholic Tübingen School's understanding of the theologian's task of entering into a conversation between the Christian tradition and the contemporary world. In this vein, he recently wrote, "My question is, and was always, how to translate the Christian tradition in the present context and [how to translate] the present context in the Christian tradition."[14]

(2) *Kasper's Post-idealist Foundations*

In particular, one specific form of Kasper's dialogue with modernity was his engagement with German idealism, specifically, with the late philosophy of Schelling. In Schelling, Kasper discovered a figure who, on his reading, overcame German idealism from within and, in doing this, provided some of the ideas from which Kasper fashioned the categories for his own historically based dogmatic or systematic theology.[15]

In his late period, Schelling recognized that German idealism's project of mediating the Absolute through human consciousness misfired insofar as in its view (a) the Absolute, God, is subjected to creation's limitations and (b) history and human beings are controlled by necessity. Animated by the human will to know, the idealist quest for the Absolute proved powerless and self-defeating. Further, Schelling perceived that human freedom is neither self-grounding nor self-fulfilling. Requiring a foundation or source outside of itself, human freedom must be empowered by the freedom of a self-existing or subsistent being, namely, God, the Absolute. To put it another way, human reason has to forgo its autonomy for a stance of receptivity; it must await a free act of self-communication into history from God. If that act were to occur, it would ignite the freedom of human beings who were open to this act. In sum, according to Schelling, German idealism's view of a dialectic process in history has to give way to the understanding that history depends on a dialogue between God and the human community.

Schelling's discernment that the issue of human freedom—which lies at the heart of modernity—can be resolved only in relation to God, the Absolute, means that Christian faith remains a meaningful possibility in the modern era. This recognition, in Kasper's judgment, constitutes the final significance of Schelling's post-idealism.[16] Philosophical inquiry of the sort pursued by Schelling can highlight the human need for divine revelation. It cannot, however, deduce the occurrence or the form of this act of divine self-communication. Philosophy has its limits. Thus, Kasper holds that when Schelling went on to expound his positive philosophy of divine revelation, he produced a hybrid; he overstepped the limits of philosophy and simultaneously yielded an illegitimate sort of theology. In light of Schelling's mistake, Kasper has seen that no comprehensive synthesis of reason and faith is possible, for any such synthesis will weave a web of necessity inimical to the freedom of both God and human beings. Kasper has clarified that "Christian faith rests on history, in which God acts freely and indeducibly, in which he proves his freedom and promises freedom to humanity."[17]

(3) *Kasper's Theological Categories*

Walter Kasper's encounter with Schelling's late philosophy proved decisive for Kasper's effort to forge the theological categories for his description of the horizon or framework within which he would construct his theology.[18] With Schelling, Kasper adopted the fundamental categories of *history* and *historicity*, and his reflection on these brought others into view.[19] History cannot be reduced to a series of brute facts. It is the all-embracing reality in which human beings participate and seek their lives' significance and direction. History is invested with meaning, but this meaning becomes evident only through and in human *language*. Language has a constitutive role in our understanding of our lives, creation, and God. Further, because language embodies the experience and insight of the generations of people who precede us, language relies on *tradition*. In turn, tradition requires a vehicle to carry it; it would end if it were not passed on in some formal way. Thus, there arises the role of an *institution* such as the church. Finally, if history is not driven by necessity, then it is the fruit of *freedom*. It comes about through God's freedom, and yet, to some extent, history is itself the product of human freedom.

History and historicity, meaning, language, tradition, institution, and freedom are Kasper's general theological categories. He has relied on these concepts as he has pursued the vision of the Catholic Tübingen School for the renewal of the church and theology. In particular, he has employed them to unlock the intelligibility of specific theological categories such as revelation, grace, redemption, Spirit, and church.

Beyond drawing on Schelling's thought for his general theological categories, Kasper has also taken his compass bearings from Schelling's discussion of divine revelation. At the center of Kasper's theological work is his effort to shed light on the singular event in which God's freedom entered history in order to liberate human freedom and bring it to fulfillment. As known in Christian faith, that unique, cosmic turning point is the life, death, and resurrection of Jesus Christ. For this reason, Kasper has looked to Jesus Christ as the key to the identity and relevance of the Christian faith as well as to the meaning of human life.[20] Given his recognition of history as the horizon of contemporary thought, Kasper constructed his *Jesus the Christ* as a Christology in a historical mode. In this, he separated his work from the neoscholastic paradigm of Christology and grounded this book in the heritage of the Catholic Tübingen School, especially in the Christological writings of Karl Adam and Josef Rupert Geiselmann.[21]

2. A Three-Source Christology

According to Robert Krieg, Kasper's Christology draws on and achieves a balance among "three sources: the church today, history, and scripture and tradition."[22] At this point, I would like to explore why these are the sources that Kasper employs and just how he deploys them.

(1) *Making Use of the "New Quest"*

Kasper's basic intent—as we have seen—is to mediate between the Christian tradition and contemporary culture. Such a project generates two questions. Retrospectively, what has the Christian tradition been? Prospectively, what should it be? With regard to Christology, these two questions direct scholars to give a genetic and dialectical account of the origin and development of the tradition (what has it been?) toward the goal of mediating the tradition's critical, healing, and transformative potential into the concrete, specific present (what should it be?).

The Christian tradition begins, of course, with Jesus of Nazareth, and it includes elements that received little or no attention until they were noticed by modernity. Because of the rise of historical-critical studies, tradition now makes available a resource that was not yet accessible to Tübingen's Catholic theologians during the nineteenth century. This resource bore the promise of recapturing historically who it is that Christians confess as the Christ. As exegetes pursued their historical-critical approach to the Bible, scholars generated criteria for determining the infelicitously termed "authentic" sayings and deeds of Jesus among the New Testament traditions.

By 1974, when Kasper published *Jesus the Christ*, the "new quest" for the historical Jesus had been underway for two decades. Unlike the "original quest," which sought to write a biography of Jesus of Nazareth, this "second" or "new quest" attempts to highlight the lines of continuity between Jesus' ministry and the early church's proclamation. After twenty years of this kind of research, something of a consensus regarding its results had emerged among theologians.[23] For Kasper, the study of the historical Jesus can make a constructive contribution to Christian faith and Christians' critical reflection on the "person" and "work" of Jesus Christ.

(2) *The Historical Jesus: A Once-for-All Yardstick?*

For Kasper the genesis of the Christological tradition lay in a reciprocity between the earthly Jesus and the risen Christ: Jesus' full identity as the Christ is disclosed to faith by his resurrection, but what it means to be Christ is defined in part by his earthly career. Hence, in a renewal of the ancient two-stage Christology (e.g., Rom 1:3-4), Kasper anchors *Jesus the Christ* in an account of Jesus' ministry, death, and resurrection, titled "The History and Destiny of Jesus Christ." On this basis he could proceed in the rest of his book to read the Council of Chalcedon's dogma as an interpretation of precisely this biblical pattern. Beginning with the history of the earthly Jesus, Kasper presents a synthetic survey of the historical reconstruction of Jesus' eschatological message, miracles, claim, and death proposed by exegetes of the day.

In this account, "the earthly Jesus" and "the historical Jesus" are not equivalent categories. The former is Jesus "as he really was, as he moved and lived," but the latter is "that Jesus whom we take from the kerygma by a complicated method of subtraction, and with the aid of modern historical methodology." Given this distinction, Kasper holds that "the earthly Jesus *and* the risen, exalted Christ" are "the content and primary criterion of Christology."[24] And access to the earthly Jesus is available through a reconstruction of the historical Jesus, for which theologians draw on the work of the biblical exegetes.

Kasper's account of the historical Jesus has drawn criticism insofar as it seems at points to over-read the historical data. As Krieg puts it, "the results of historical and exegetical study appear at times to be forced to align with tradition."[25] For example, Jesus' crucifixion is an unimpeachable historical fact, but to affirm that Jesus suffered more than any other human being is quite another matter.

More important, in his introduction to the new edition Kasper recognizes that exegesis has not stood still since 1974. As a result, he says, "many questions and particular answers have changed."[26] Perhaps, however, more is at issue. In 1974 Kasper could affirm that we possess "in the earthly Jesus, as he is made available to us through historical research, a relatively autonomous criterion, a once-for-all yardstick" for Christian belief.[27] At present, however, the exegetical consensus that yielded that "once-for-all yardstick" has collapsed. One speaks of a "third quest" for the historical Jesus, namely, of critical research (since the late 1970s) aimed at locating Jesus of Nazareth in his historical, cultural, and religious world. The participants in this quest differ heatedly on which sources are relevant and which methods appropriate, ensuring that the results at which they arrive vary widely.[28] In this state of affairs, one has to ask, whose historical Jesus among the welter of candidates now proposed can serve as a "relatively autonomous criterion" for the faith of Christians?

Given this development, the historical Jesus who, in *Jesus the Christ*, serves to partially constitute the starting point for the Christological tradition turns out to be a period piece. The cardinal himself indicates why this is so when in his new introduction he writes that "it has become impossible to see Jesus only in contrast to the Judaism of his time."[29] This view, of course, is precisely how Günther Bornkamm in the 1950s and 1960s, following a long tradition of German biblical scholarship, arrived at his portrait of Jesus. Bornkamm presented the historical Jesus as a figure like a prophet and like a rabbi and yet different, distinguished by an unparalleled implicit claim to exercise the authority of God himself. In this perspective, Jesus' outrageous claim drew down upon Jesus the fate of a blasphemer but found vindication, so Christians believe, in the resurrection.[30] Bornkamm's portrait thoroughly informs Kasper's depictions of the historical Jesus in *Jesus the Christ*.[31]

Subsequent scholarship, however, has demonstrated how the portraits of Bornkamm and Kasper rest on an untenable construal of the Judaism of Jesus' day.[32] Further, this construal is one in which a Lutheran Law/Gospel dialectic has been projected onto the data.[33]

What, then, remains? In the logic of Kasper's two-stage Christology, Jesus' implicit claim to be the Son of God provides the hinge, the link, between the earthly Jesus and the risen Christ, between what Jesus explicitly proclaimed and what the early church proclaimed about Jesus. In retrospect, in his new introduction, the cardinal affirms that "we can indisputably prove an implicit Christological claim" made by the earthly Jesus. As evidence he offers, first, "the wholly unique way in which Jesus addresses God as *abba*," which reveals "in the earthly Jesus a unique consciousness of being God's Son." Second, "by forgiving sins Jesus implicitly claimed to act with full divine authority and to stand in God's place." Third, this manner of acting "was regarded as scandalous and blasphemous by his opponents, and without that accusation of blasphemy, we cannot explain why Jesus was condemned to be crucified."[34]

Unfortunately, the probative status of this evidence is no longer indisputable. Today, some scholars question the distinctiveness of Jesus' use of *abba*. For example, Mary Rose D'Angelo rightly observes that "E. Schillebeeckx's *Jesus* seems to have nearly canonized this reconstruction of Jesus' consciousness among Roman Catholic theologians."[35] Building on earlier work by James Barr,[36] for whom *abba* neither connoted familial intimacy nor reflected Jesus' usage, and also work by Joseph A. Fitzmyer,[37] for whom the title *abba* was used by Jesus but in close continuity with prior Jewish usage, D'Angelo goes on to painstakingly deconstruct this popular theological trope of Jesus' unique filial consciousness as historically grounded. Similar lines of critique might be adduced regarding Jesus' alleged practice of declaring sins forgiven[38] and regarding the charge of blasphemy as the explanation for Jesus' execution.[39]

Perhaps, however, Jesus' implicit claim as Christological hinge may be rescued if, as John P. Meier has it, Jesus' message presented a "peculiar mix of present-yet-future eschatology that implicitly put Jesus himself at the center of the eschatological drama that he proclaimed."[40] We may recall that for Karl Rahner it was historically credible that Jesus "understood himself rather as the *eschatological* prophet," that is, in Rahner's language, as "the absolute and definitive savior."[41] Rahner further proposed that "the absolute event of salvation and the absolute mediation of salvation by a man mean exactly the same thing as [what] church doctrine expresses as Incarnation and hypostatic union."[42] This line of thought is pursued by Meier. In his unfolding construal of Jesus, Meier portrays Jesus of Nazareth as, among other things, an Elijah-like eschatological prophet. This depiction within Meier's form of the third quest may yet provide a usable historical Jesus for Kasper's revitalization of a two-stage Christology. At present, however, Meier's is but one voice among many discordant voices. Unlike the situation in 1974, one cannot confidently appeal to a consensus of exegetes to supply the lineaments of one's historical Jesus and hence of one's earthly Jesus.

(3) *Christology's Starting Point*

Recent research concerning the historical Jesus renders problematic the account in *Jesus the Christ* of one element in the genesis of the Christological tradition, namely, the earthly Jesus. Yet this ambiguity does not of itself invalidate Kasper's project of a Christology in an historical mode. For Kasper, the starting point of the Christian tradition and the starting point of contemporary Christology are not identical.

The new quest for the historical Jesus began with a theological agenda, namely, to discern an underlying continuity between the Jesus of history, as reconstructed by historical-critical methods, and the Christ of faith. This quest's apparent success generated an enthusiasm that made it seem possible to assume the identity of the Jesus of history with the earthly Jesus to whom Christian faith is a possible and plausible, though not necessary, response. Within this framework, the historical Jesus might easily stand forth as *the* ground and norm of that faith.

Nevertheless, Kasper opposes the reduction of Christology to "Jesus-ology." While he adopts historical inquiry as one source of Christology, he refuses to regard the new quest as Christology's point of departure. Rather, Kasper holds on both historical and theological grounds that "the starting point of Christology is the phenomenology of faith in Christ; faith as it is actually believed, lived, proclaimed and practiced in the Christian churches."[43]

This appeal to a phenomenology itself harbors an ambiguity. As Kasper is fully aware, the classical heresies live on in the imaginations of many modern Christians. In this vein, Kasper notes that "we can scarcely say that the doctrine of the true humanity of Christ and its meaning for salvation have been clearly marked in the consciousness of the average Christian. What is often found there often amounts to a mythological and Docetist view of Jesus Christ."[44] It follows that the starting point for Christology that Kasper is commending cannot be gleaned from an opinion poll of contemporary Christians.[45]

In the early nineteenth century, Friedrich Schleiermacher had to deal with the same ambiguity, and it is significant that Schleiermacher's programmatic *Brief Outline of the Study of Theology* (1811) found an appreciative reception by Johann Sebastian Drey, the founder of the Catholic Tübingen School.[46] Agreeing with Drey, the

Catholic Tübingen theologian Johannes Evangelist von Kuhn ranked Schleiermacher's *The Christian Faith* (1821) in a class with Thomas Aquinas's *Summa Theologiae.*[47] Schleiermacher conceived dogmatic/systematic theology as the culminating moment of historical theology, under which he also subsumed exegesis and church history. In this perspective, he held that the task of dogmatic/systematic theology is to give a critical and systematic account of the church's teaching to its contemporary age. In other words, it should begin with the present-day church's belief. At the same time, in order to engage in its critical task, it should employ a norm. That norm, Schleiermacher judged, lay in what he held to be the essence of Christianity, namely, the Christian "consciousness" of being redeemed by Christ in which is disclosed the character of God as love.[48]

This is hardly the occasion on which to probe the ambiguities of Schleiermacher's notion of the Christian's "immediate self-consciousness."[49] The point remains that for Schleiermacher dogmatic/systematic theology should begin from the present faith of the church, so that the foundation of the practice of theology as a historical discipline ultimately lies in the religious transformation of consciousness that is Christian conversion. With this acknowledgment Schleiermacher's theological program proved revolutionary by joining radical historicity with normativity.[50]

Kasper follows in Schleiermacher's path when he locates the starting point of Christology in the church today, in "faith [that is, *authentic* faith] as it is actually believed, lived, proclaimed and practiced in the Christian churches."[51] Contemporary faith, he goes on to show, is constituted by the Christian tradition. It encounters its "object," Jesus Christ, by accepting the church's witness to the risen one who was crucified as "the Christ." Further, this witness is carried by the Christian tradition into the present-day church from the church's origin. As Kasper emphasizes, this constitutive function of the Christian tradition is, theologically speaking, the work of the Holy Spirit.

3. Turning to the Subject, the Believing Christian

Perhaps Schleiermacher can help us further articulate what is implicit and unsaid in Kasper's position concerning Christology's starting point. Patricia Plovanich points toward this further dimension when she remarks that she does not find in Kasper's work a full treatment of the recipient of revelation.[52] To complement Kasper's position on the starting point of Christology, I should like to follow Schleiermacher in turning to Christology's subject, the believing Christian.

The faith that constitutes the starting point of Christology is a matter of a transformed consciousness. Its root is grace, the gift, according to Saint Paul, of "God's love [having] been poured into our hearts through the Holy Spirit that has been given to us" (Rom 5:5). The influx of divine love transforms a person's horizon. It generates light, the *lumen cordium*, as the hymn for Pentecost has it, by which one discerns the value of accepting as true the meanings constitutive of the Christian community's identity. The inner word of God's gift finds its mediation by the meaning in the outer word of Christian beliefs. The articulation of those constitutive meanings takes its rise from the church's original witness to Jesus as the Christ, to the risen though crucified one whose saving presence is mediated precisely through the ongoing life of the community. On this account, the Holy Spirit—to bow in the direction of Cardinal Kasper's work in pneumatology and to Elizabeth Johnson's essay on this topic (see chapter 6)—that is, God's love poured out, is active in generating the Christian tradition, in providing the illumination that guides the process of discernment by which the tradition develops, and in equipping today's theologians with the criteria with which to read the signs of the times. The gift of God's love transvalues all other values and sets them in their proper order.

By insisting on the faith of the Christian community today as the starting point of Christology, Kasper implicitly recognizes the foundational role of religious conversion in the practice of theology, and that basic reality enabled young Professor Kasper to respond with equanimity to one of the signs of the times, namely, to the rise of historical consciousness and, with it, to the emergence of the intellectual discipline of critical history. Often wielded antagonistically by the church's critics as a weapon,[53] the historical-critical method continues even now to be disparaged in some church circles as diabolical. But from Geiselmann, however, Kasper learned there was nothing to fear from this quarter.[54]

Kasper rightly identifies the kerygma or confession concerning Jesus as the Christ (Mark 8:29) as the heart of Christian belief. As a faith confession it satisfies different criteria for objectivity—criteria inhering in the transformative gift of grace—that govern the efforts of the contemporary historians. Critical history may require a shift, a development, in the self-understanding of faith, but that faith remains ever itself. Since, further, the confession concerning Jesus Christ employs a time-bound symbol, Kasper is also correct in pointing to the necessity of a hermeneutical tradition to carry that symbol and its transformative power through history, a tradition that includes both doctrinal decisions and also contemporary theology. No historical reconstruction of Jesus, not even one so congenial to Christian theology as that of the new quest, provides the foundation or ultimate criterion of Christology. That foundation lies in the gift of God's love in the light of which one recognizes the truth of the biblical witness to Jesus as the personal entrance of that divine love into history.

In sum, I am proposing that such notions as conversion, symbol, and the imagination might profitably enlarge Kasper's set of general theological categories as he seeks, in his Christology, to give an account of the hope that is in us (1 Pet 3:15). On this score we might invoke the example of Hans Urs von Balthasar's project of a theological aesthetics.[55] The term *aesthesis* refers, of course, to feeling, and it may be on the level of intentional feeling that the gift of God's love first registers in our consciousness. Be that as it may, at the heart of both his Christology and his Trinitarian theology, Kasper, like Balthasar, celebrates the overwhelming mystery of God's love enacted historically in the life, death, and resurrection of Jesus Christ.

4. Redemptive Mediation

In its prospective moment, theology's task is to serve the ecclesial community in mediating the Christian tradition into the contemporary context. In this regard, Kasper's appropriation of Schelling's later philosophy fulfilled both apologetic and critical purposes. As apologetics, it found in the thought of Schelling a key to securing the meaningfulness of Christian faith in a modern Western context defined by concerns with historicity and human freedom. At the same time, it functioned as a critique of the modern project of autonomous self-liberation.

There is, however, a further dimension to the prospective task of theology. The final challenge of historical consciousness is for human beings to assume responsibility for the history they make. Now Kasper found it to their credit that "Schelling and all the idealists attempted to grasp freedom [i.e., the human person] concretely: in its concrete social and historical determinations."[56] Contemporary theology, he observed, must do the same. Christian truth, for Kasper, is a truth to be performed; it involves doing.

In *Jesus the Christ* Kasper identifies the saving truth of Christianity as the Gospel of Jesus the Christ in whom God and humanity are personally made one. Jesus Christ is himself salvation, the kingdom of God in person, and through union in faith with him human beings come to share in God's own life as they await in hope the consummation of history. This truth, for Kasper, is the *novum* toward which Schelling pointed, the historical intervention of divine freedom that cannot be deduced by the human mind. It is God's act, not humankind's. But this divine intervention does not leave human beings passive. We are to respond in faith and repentance.[57] Doing so, we come to participate in God's kenotic or self-emptying love (Phil 2:5-11) and so open ourselves to other people in freedom and solidarity.

Kasper is concerned to emphasize the religious and theological character of the salvation enacted in and through Jesus Christ. Echoing Johannes Weiss's devastating critique of his nineteenth-century liberal counterparts,[58] Kasper affirms that for Jesus, "the Kingdom is totally and exclusively God's doing. It cannot be earned by religious or moral effort, imposed by political struggle, or projected in calculation."[59] The cardinal insists that "Jesus is not interested in a better world, but in the new world."[60] Like Weiss, Kasper draws conclusions concerning the current theological scene. Political theology errs in affirming that "Jesus' message of the Kingdom of God is a political and social utopia, to be created by kindness and brotherly love."[61] With regard to poverty, Kasper writes, "The New Testament is here completely realistic: 'You always have the poor with you' (Mark 14:7)." He continues: "Jesus' glorification of the poor is not related to any social stratum and implies no social programme."[62] Without naming names, in his introduction to the new edition of his Christology he refers to "radical forms of liberation theology [which] betray . . . a sociological reduction of Jesus' character and message."[63] He abjures as banal any "hermeneutics strongly influenced by a fashionable neo-Marxism."[64] He also warns against "neo-integralist movements which . . . seek on left-wing lines to make the church itself form the advance guard of political liberation movements."[65]

One might ask whether Kasper has painted with too broad a brush the projects of liberation theology and also of political theology. From another angle, the question arises whether his insistence on the priority and exclusive efficacy of God's initiative is in danger of veering toward an un-Catholic notion of *sola gratia.* More on Kasper's own terms, one may inquire what becomes of the theological imperative "to grasp freedom [i.e., the human person] concretely: in its concrete social and historical determinations." How does the freedom won in Christ engage the principalities and powers of this age in their concreteness?[66]

Kasper makes a start toward answering this latter question when he links the animating principle of Christian praxis with self-sacrificing love, the redemptive participation in the kenotic love of God enacted in and by Jesus Christ. He recognizes that "the only possible redemption is one that is concrete and historical."[67] In what he takes as Jesus' historical practice with regard to fasting, purity laws, dining with sinners, and associating with the ritually unclean, he discerns, if only indirectly, a "connection with criticism of society and social change."[68] Finally, in his introduction to the new edition, he notes that a Christology within a Trinitarian perspective will find precisely in the doctrine of Chalcedon—as a doctrine of unity-in-permanent-difference—"far-reaching anthropological, social-political, and also ecclesiological significance."[69]

The theologian José Vidal Taléns has taken Kasper at his word. Given that Kasper envisioned *The God of Jesus Christ* as the first volume of a complete dogmatic theology, Taléns has speculated on the Christological book that Kasper would have written if his vocation had not taken him on a different path in ecclesial leadership. Remaining Trinitarian and kenotic, this book would have likely continued to emphasize the mediating roles of the church and the Holy Spirit in Christology. In addition, Taléns allows himself to wish that this book would have been devoted with no less vigor to the other mediations—for example, the anthropological, sociological, and political mediations—that he regards as no less necessary if the Christian message of salvation is to become concretely effective in contemporary society.[70]

With all that said, we can continue to learn how to do Christology from Kasper's *Jesus the Christ*. For in this classic book Christology is at once a thoroughly *historical discipline*, which is one moment in the ongoing tradition it seeks to serve and confidently open to the historical scholarship of the present age, and a thoroughly *theological discipline*, grounded in the grace that the Christian tradition mediates and the light that grace sheds on the tradition's origins, its development, and its reading of the signs of the current times. For this crucial instruction in Christology, we are grateful to Cardinal Kasper as we celebrate this milestone birthday.

Endnotes

1. Cardinal Walter Kasper, ed., *Logik der Liebe und Herrlichkeit Gottes: Hans Urs von Balthasar im Gespräch. Festgabe für Karl Kardinal Lehmann zum 70. Geburtstag* (Ostfildern: Matthias-Grünewald-Verlag, 2006), 9.

2. Walter Kasper, *Jesus der Christus* (Freiburg: Herder, 2007). ET: *Jesus the Christ*, trans. V. Green, 2nd ed. (New York: Continuum Books, 2011). Unless otherwise noted, references and citations are this edition.

3. Kasper, *Jesus the Christ*, viii.

4. Hans Küng, *On Being a Christian*, trans. Edward Quinn (Garden City, NY: Doubleday, 1976).

5. Edward Schillebeekx, *Jesus: An Experiment in Christology*, trans. Hubert Hoskins (New York: Seabury Press, 1979).

6. Kasper has taken issue with the Christological approaches of Küng and Schillebeeckx. See Kasper's exchange with Küng in *Grundfragen der Christologie Heute*, ed. Leo Scheffczyk, *Quaestiones Disputatae* 72 (Freiburg: Herder, 1975), 141–83. On Schillebeeckx's *Jesus*, see Walter Kasper, "Neuansätze Gegenwärtiger Theologie," in *Wer ist Jesus Christus*, ed. Joseph Sauer (Freiburg: Herder, 1977), 121–50, 134–36; idem, "Christologie—Zum Jesus-Buch von Edward Schillebeeckx," *Evangelischer Kommentar* 9 (1976): 357–60. See Zdenko Joha, *Christologie und Anthropologie. Ein Verhältnisbestimmung unter besonderer Berücksichtigung des theologischen Denkens Walter Kaspers, Freiburger Theologische Studien* 148 (Freiburg: Herder, 1987), 100–157.

7. Thomas Aquinas, *Summa Theologiae*, III, 27–59.

8. On the significance of this point, see John P. Galvin, "From the Humanity of Christ to the Jesus of History: A Paradigm Shift in Catholic Christology," *Theological Studies* 55 (1994): 252–73.

9. Walter Kasper, *Glaube und Geschichte* (Mainz: Matthias-Grünewald-Verlag, 1970), 5.

10. Walter Kasper, "Möglichkeit der Gotteserfahrung Heute," in ibid., 120.

11. Kasper, *Glaube und Geschichte*, 5.

12. Walter Kasper, "Kirche und Theologie Unter dem Gesetz der Geschichte," in ibid., 52–53.

13. See Walter Kasper, "Theologie Damals und Heute," in ibid., 9–32.

14. Kasper, e-mail message to Kristin M. Colberg, March 18, 2011; see Kristin M. Colberg's chapter 1 in this volume; Kristin M. Colberg, "Walter Kasper on Translating the Message of Christian Hope Today," in *Translating Religion*, ed. Mary Doak and Anita Houck, College Theology Society Annual, vol. 58 (Maryknoll, NY: Orbis Books, 2013), 58. Aidan Nichols holds that "Kasper is, in fact, a pure product of the Catholic Tübingen School, and . . . his theological programme is a re-statement of the historic aims of that school" (see "Walter Kasper and His Theological Programme," *New Blackfriars* 67, no. 1 [1986]: 16–24, at 16).

15. See Walter Kasper, *Das Absolute in der Geschichte: Philosophie und Theologie der Geschichte in der Spätphilosophie Schellings* (Mainz: Matthias-Grünewald-Verlag, 1965); idem, "Die Freiheit als philosophisches und theologisches Problem in der Philosophie Schellings," in *Glaube und Geschichte*, 33–66. See also Thomas F. O'Meara, "Christ in Schelling's *Philosophy of Revelation*," *Heythrop Journal* 27 (1986): 275–89.

16. For an interpretation of Kasper's Christology from the viewpoint of the idealist problematic of mediating the Absolute, see José Vidal Taléns, *El Mediador y La Mediación. La Cristología de Walter Kasper en su Genesis y Estructura* (Valencia: Artes Gráficas Soler, 1988).

17. Kasper, "Die Freiheit als philosophisches und theologisches Problem," 46.

18. On general and special theological categories, see Bernard Lonergan, *Method in Theology* (New York: Herder and Herder, 1972), 281–94.

19. Kasper, "Kirche und Theologie unter dem Gesetz der Geschichte," 60.

20. Kasper, *Jesus the Christ*, 3.

21. Kasper, *Jesus the Christ*, xxiii. See Josef R. Geiselmann, *Jesus der Christus*, 2nd ed. (München: Kösel Verlag, 1965).

22. Robert A. Krieg, *Story-Shaped Christology: The Role of Narratives in Identifying Jesus Christ* (New York: Paulist Press, 1988), 53. Chapter 2 is devoted to Kasper's Christology.

23. For a summary, see Gustaf Aulén, *Jesus in Contemporary Historical Research*, trans. Ingalill H. Hjelm (Philadelphia: Fortress Press, 1976).

24. Kasper, *Jesus the Christ*, 34–35.

25. Krieg, *Story-Shaped Christology*, 55.

26. Kasper, *Jesus the Christ*, ix.

27. Ibid., 23.

28. On the third quest, see Ben Witherington, III, *The Jesus Quest: The Third Quest for the Search for the Jew of Nazareth* (Downers Grove, IL: InterVarsity Press, 1995); Mark Allen Powell, *Jesus as a Figure in History: How Modern Historians View the Man from Galilee* (Louisville, KY: Westminster John Knox Press, 1998).

29. Kasper, *Jesus the Christ*, x.

30. Günther Bornkamm, *Jesus of Nazareth*, trans. Irene and Fraser McLuskey, with James M. Robinson (New York: Harper & Row, 1975). The original appeared in 1956.

31. This also seems true of Kasper's Trinitarian theology. See Walter Kasper, *The God of Jesus Christ*, trans. Matthew J. O'Connell (New York: Crossroad, 1984), 166–72.

32. See Charlotte Klein, "'Late Judaism' and 'Jewish Religious Community,'" in *Anti-Judaism in Christian Theology*, trans. Edward Quinn (Philadelphia: Fortress Press, 1984), 15–38.

33. See E. P. Sanders, *Jesus and Judaism* (Philadelphia: Fortress Press, 1985), 23–58.

34. Kasper, *Jesus the Christ*, xii.

35. Mary Rose D'Angelo, "*Abba* and 'Father': Imperial Theology and the Jesus Traditions," *Journal of Biblical Literature* 111, no. 4 (1992): 611–30, at 612.

36. James Barr, "Abba Isn't Daddy," *Journal of Theological Studies* 39 (1988): 28–47.

37. Joseph A. Fitzmyer, "Abba and Jesus' Relation to God," in *À Cause de l'Évangile: études sur les Synoptiques et Actes offertes au P. Jacques Dupont, O.S.B. à l'occasion de son 70e anniversaire* (Paris: Cerf, 1985), 14–38.

38. Questions of the historicity of individual pericopes aside, Geza Vermes insists on the distinction between forgiving sins oneself and declaring them forgiven by God; see G. Vermes, *Jesus the Jew: A Historian's Reading of the Gospels* (Philadelphia: Fortress Press, 1981), 68.

39. See, for example, Ellis Rivkin, "What Crucified Jesus?," in *Jesus' Jewishness: Exploring the Place of Jesus in Early Judaism*, ed. James H. Charlesworth (New York: Crossroad, 1991), 226–57.

40. John P. Meier, *A Marginal Jew: Rethinking the Historical Jesus*, vol. 3, *Companions and Competitors* (New Haven, CT: Yale University Press, 2001), 338.

41. Karl Rahner, *Foundations of Christian Faith. An Introduction to the Idea of Christianity*, trans. William V. Dych (New York: Seabury Press, 1978), 246.

42. Ibid., 299.

43. Kasper, *Jesus the Christ*, 16.

44. Ibid., 187.

45. For an idea of what such a poll might reveal, see Ann Christie, *Ordinary Christology: Who Do You Say I Am? Answers from the Pews* (London: Ashgate, 2012).

46. See Kurt Nowak, *Schleiermacher: Leben, Werk, und Wirkung* (Göttingen: Vandenhoeck & Ruprecht, 2002), 233.

47. See Brian A. Gerrish, *Continuing the Reformation* (Chicago: University of Chicago Press, 1993), 148.

48. Perhaps this is why Karl Barth, in his "Concluding Unscientific Postscript on Schleiermacher," mused that he "would like to reckon with the possibility of a theology of the Holy Spirit, a theology of which Schleiermacher was scarcely conscious, but which might actually have been the legitimate concern dominating even his theological activity"; see idem, *The Theology of Schleiermacher: Lectures at Göttingen, Winter Semester of 1923/24*, trans. Geoffrey W. Bromiley (Grand Rapids, MI: Eerdmans, 1982), 278.

49. See Louis Roy, "Consciousness in Schleiermacher," *Journal of Religion* 77 (1997): 217–32. This idea generated the "experiential-expressive" notion of doctrine; see George A. Lindbeck, *The Nature of Doctrine: Religion and Theology in a Postliberal Age* (Philadelphia: Westminster Press, 1984).

50. See Nowak, *Schleiermacher*, 251.

51. Kasper, *Jesus the Christ*, 16.

52. Patricia Ann Plovanich, *The Theological Method of Walter Kasper* (PhD diss., Fordham University, 1990), 102.

53. See Kasper, *Jesus the Christ*, 27, concerning Rudolf Augstein's *Jesus Son of Man*, trans. Hugh Young (New York: Urizen Books, 1977), preface by Gore Vidal.

54. Kasper, *Jesus the Christ*, xi.

55. For a brief statement of this project, see Hans Urs von Balthasar, "The Third Way of Love," in *Love Alone Is Credible*, trans. David C. Schindler (San Francisco: Ignatius Press, 2004). On the use of symbol as a theological category, see Avery Dulles, *Models of Revelation* (Garden City, NY: Doubleday, 1983), 131–73.

56. Kasper, "Die Freiheit als philosophisches und theologisches Problem in der Philosophie Schellings," in *Glaube und Geschichte*, 44 (translation mine).

57. Kasper, *Jesus the Christ*, 69.

58. Johannes Weiss, *Jesus' Proclamation of the Kingdom of God*, trans. Richard Hyde Hiers and David Larrimore Holland (Philadelphia: Fortress Press, 1971).

59. Kasper, *Jesus the Christ*, 69.

60. Ibid., 84.

61. Ibid., 60.

62. Ibid., 72–73.

63. Ibid., xi.

64. Ibid., 7.

65. Ibid., 253.

66. See Kasper, "Grundlinien einer Theologie der Geschichte," in *Glaube und Geschichte*, 67–100, at 71.

67. Kasper, *Jesus the Christ*, 192.

68. Ibid., 89.

69. Ibid., xviii.

70. Taléns, *El mediador*, 463.

CHAPTER 6

Pneumatology and Beyond: "Wherever"

Elizabeth A. Johnson, CSJ

I am genuinely pleased to be participating in this celebration of the life and work of Walter Kasper, who has made such an outstanding contribution to theology and the life of the church. He is "a clever theologian, a good theologian," whose book on mercy "has done me a lot of good," in Pope Francis's own words.[1] Happy eightieth birthday, Cardinal Kasper, and in the salute traditional among theologians, *ad multos annos!*

Theological consideration of the Holy Spirit runs like a golden thread through all of Cardinal Kasper's work. In his position as president of Pontifical Council for Promoting Christian Unity, he wrote numerous articles and gave public speeches addressing the Spirit in relation to matters concerning the church. These include such issues as the renewal of Catholic life, the Petrine ministry, the Eucharist, the call to unity, the work of ecumenical dialogue and its spirituality, *rapprochement* with Eastern Orthodox churches, relations with the Jews, and the challenges and opportunities for self-criticism raised by Pentecostalism. Prior to those years, during the time Kasper humorously calls his "pre-existence" as a professor and scholar, his reflections on the Holy Spirit focused on matters related to the doctrine of God. As seen especially in his books *Jesus the Christ*[2] and *The God of Jesus Christ*,[3] he thought through pneumatology in relation to Christology and Trinitarian theology in groundbreaking ways that continue to influence the field. This chapter considers these early works, starting with an observation about style.

In his writings about the Holy Spirit, Walter Kasper is a scholar in the Germanic tradition, which means he carefully mounts arguments that can be tested by reason, traces in detail the historical background of different points of doctrine, backs everything up with voluminous footnotes, and in general gifts his readers with rigorous discussions of pneumatology that can only be called *wissenschaftlich*, "scholarly." The theologians who use his books, myself included, benefit greatly from this learned approach.

As a careful reader, I have also been struck with his periodic departure from this approach. Every now and then, taken with the beauty of what he is studying, this author departs from lines of logic and soars into poetry. The signal that this is about to happen comes when a sentence begins with the word "Wherever." Three examples from *The God of Jesus Christ*:

- "Everywhere that life breaks forth and comes into being, everywhere that new life as it were seethes and bubbles, and even, in the form of hope, everywhere that life is violently devastated, throttled, gagged and slain. Wherever true life exists, there the Spirit of God is at work."[4]
- "Wherever there is love, the Spirit of God is at work, and the reign of Christ becomes a reality even without institutional forms and formulas."[5]
- "Wherever something new arises, whenever life is awakened and reality reaches ecstatically beyond itself, in all seeking and striving, in every ferment and birth, and even more in the beauty of creation, something of the activity and being of God's Spirit is manifested."[6]

When these kinds of sentences appear, Walter Kasper's heart is being borne up by the power of that which he is writing about, by the Holy Spirit, Giver of life, who is also the gift, the one who is "the gravitational pull of love,"[7] who works to bring all things to their eschatological completion in God. Kasper's "Wherevers" indicate that there is more here than can be articulated in our systematic theology.

In this brief festival presentation, I highlight three areas where Kasper makes particularly telling use of pneumatology: the problem of God and modern atheism, the historical Jesus of the gospels, and the church-dividing, Trinitarian question of how the Spirit proceeds. In conclusion, I make bold to suggest a new subject for his attention, a new "Wherever."

1. Atheism and the Trinitarian God

The denial of God in modern atheism poses a massive challenge to belief in our day. Kasper takes seriously the masters of suspicion Ludwig Feuerbach, Karl Marx, Friedrich Nietzsche, and Sigmund Freud, analyzing their arguments that God is a projection, one that needs to be rejected in the name of the autonomy of nature and the autonomy of the free human being. But who is this God that atheism rejects? It is not the God of Christian revelation. Kasper traces how the pressure of dealing with Enlightenment philosophy led Christian theology to speak about God as a person in the singular. This idea of a unipersonal God is the root of the problem. It forms what Kasper calls "the heresy of Christian theism."[8] Contemporary critics had an easy time of it when they set out to show that this idea *is* a projection of human consciousness, an ideological construct of the bourgeois subject. Kasper writes: "The situation of atheism . . . has been brought about by Christian theism."[9]

Such an analysis points to the urgent task of retrieving the understanding of the Trinitarian God as disclosed in Christian revelation. This is Kasper's thesis: the Trinitarian confession can serve as an answer to modern atheism. Far from being an individual acting subject whose overwhelming power is a threat to the autonomy of human beings and the natural world, the ineffable God is the Trinitarian communion of love whose outflow creates and empowers the world.

Even if this thesis be granted, major problems persist. For one, Kasper notes, the modern shift that understands a person to be a self-conscious, free center of action and an individual personality makes Trinitarian language of three such persons in one nature logically impossible for people to understand. Beyond that, the Holy Spirit in particular presents a suite of additional difficulties. While the Son has shown himself to us in human form, and we can form at least an image of the Father, Kasper muses, the Spirit has no face. Like the wind, it blows where it will, uncontrollable and free (cf. John 3:8). In addition, the Western tradition has forgotten the Spirit, often replacing the triad Father-Son-Spirit with the triad God-Christ-church. Even when the Spirit is remembered, the struggle against enthusiasts in the Middle Ages resulted in the Spirit being tied very tightly to church office and relegated to reflections on the inner life of the Trinity, with little fruit in the actual life of the church. Indeed, the Spirit is "the unknown God."[10]

Kasper's strategy in the face of these and a host of other problems is to turn from the meaning of spirit in the speculative modern philosophy of consciousness and, instead, to begin with the Spirit of God in the history of salvation. He uses biblical images of wind, fire, and water; shows the close identification of the Spirit with Wisdom, holy Sophia; interprets these biblical texts via patristic and medieval concepts of "gift" and "love poured out"; and synthesizes these into a theology that honors the mystery of God's graciousness. In so doing, he soars on the wings of pneumatology to develop a robust Trinitarian theology capable of responding to contemporary atheism.

As Kasper himself has noted, this elevation of discourse is the case because as soon as one introduces the Spirit into the discussion of God, one departs from the stereotype of God rejected by atheism:

> The Holy Spirit reveals, and is, the giftness of God as gift, love as love. The Spirit thus expresses the innermost nature of God—God as self-communicating love—in such a way that this innermost reality proves at the same time to be the outermost. . . . The Spirit is as it were the ecstasy of God; [the Spirit] is God as pure abundance, God as the overflow of love and grace. On the one hand, then, the immanent love of God reaches its goal in the Spirit. But at the same time, because in the Holy Spirit the Father and the Son as it were understand and realize themselves as love, the love of God in the Spirit also moves beyond [God's own self].[11]

This loving streaming-out-beyond is God's gracious self-communication that creates and makes holy the world. "In the Holy Spirit God is eternally givable."[12] With this in mind, Kasper observes, early Christian writers compared the Spirit to the wafted fragrance of a perfumed ointment or to beauty radiating from God, traces of which can be seen in natural beauty, in the abundance that marks creation.

Wherever the Spirit of God abides, there exists the God of love of Christian revelation. The God whom theism abstractly describes and atheism rejects, it turns out, is not the true God at all.

2. The Historical Jesus of the Gospels

In *Jesus the Christ* Kasper construes the entire life and ministry, death and resurrection, history and mystery of Jesus of Nazareth as the fruit of the Spirit working to bring about the redeeming, eschatological fulfillment of the whole world. Given this book's publication in German in 1974, this date makes Kasper one of the very first to develop a Spirit Christology in Catholic theology. To do so he first corrals a multitude of gospel texts that connect Jesus with the Spirit, and then uses them to construe Jesus' life and destiny as a phenomenon wrought by the Spirit. Jesus was conceived by the Holy Spirit and sent into mission by the Spirit at his baptism. In an early scene in Luke's gospel, he interpreted his ministry in the words of Isaiah: "The Spirit of the Lord is upon me" (4:18)—and this Spirit anointed him to proclaim good news to the poor, release to captives, and recovery of sight to the blind (Luke 4:16-22; Isa 61:1-2). Jesus preached and healed the sick by the power of the Spirit. After his tortured death on the cross, he was raised from the dead by the power of the Spirit. Early Christians gave him the title of the Messiah, the Christ, the Anointed, believing that he is the one whom the Spirit anointed to bring about the reign of God.

Fully aware of how Spirit Christology along these lines led in the early church to the problem of Adoptionism, Kasper skillfully employs Trinitarian and ontological perspectives to root Jesus' Spirit-filled person in the being of God. Especially in light of the resurrection, which divinely vindicates Jesus as the one who now sends the Spirit to others, a theology of the soteriological *mission* of Jesus in the power of the Spirit (*Sendungstheologie*) necessarily cannot be separated from a theology of the *being* of Jesus in relation to God (*Seinstheologie*): "A pneumatologically defined Christology can in fact best convey the uniqueness of Jesus Christ and his universal significance. . . . Jesus Christ, who in the Spirit is in person the mediator between God and [humans], becomes in the Spirit the universal mediator of salvation."[13]

It is interesting to note that in his later book *The God of Jesus Christ*, Kasper presents a more traditional Logos Christology, focused on Jesus as Son of God. Some years back I directed a doctoral dissertation at Fordham University on these two books and the seeming disjunction between their two Christologies. In a letter to my former student Ph.D., Thomas Petriano, Kasper wrote that he had no particular reason for shifting from a Spirit Christology to a Logos Christology and saw no opposition between the two approaches. Be that as it may, they do read very differently, and in 1985 we had a faculty seminar at The Catholic University of America to discuss this very point.

I underscore the fact that Spirit Christology in Kasper's hands has had a lasting impact. It has supported the move to make concern for the historical Jesus and for the humanity of Jesus theologically significant while remaining coherent with the church's confession of faith. Kasper's work rebuts the criticism that such a human, historical emphasis betrays an orientation that is not interested in Jesus' relation to God. To the contrary, Jesus' Spirit-filled existence as "the Mediator" of the Spirit actually accounts for his unrivaled uniqueness and the universal significance that Christian faith professes.[14]

3. The *Filioque* Dilemma

In 1054 the Eastern Orthodox Church and the Western Roman Catholic Church split from each other. Against an emotional political background, the doctrinal issue was the *filioque* phrase, inserted into the Nicene-Constantinopolitan Creed by the Western church earlier in the eleventh century. Disagreement over whether the Father alone is the source of the Spirit, as the creed originally confessed and the Eastern church maintains, or the Spirit proceeds from the Father "and the Son," *filioque*, as the West came to think, has divided these two ecclesial bodies for nigh unto one thousand years. Kasper's way of exploring this division is an exemplary piece of ecumenical theologizing. Beginning with a search for common ground, he discusses how both traditions share the same faith as attested in scripture and tradition. The point to note, however, is that over long centuries they came to think about the Spirit using different images and concepts. The Latin West interprets the Spirit as the mutual love between Father and Son, as their ineffable communion. Proceeding from the Father and the Son, the Spirit links them in mutual and reciprocal unity, the way the bond of human love unites lover and beloved, to use one of Augustine's eloquent analogies.[15] Kasper observes that this results in a symmetrical model according to which the Trinitarian life is rounded off in the Holy Spirit in a kind of circular movement *ad intra*. Starting instead with the monarchy of the Father, the Greek East envisions the Spirit proceeding from the Father alone, not by way of generation like the Son, but as the breath of his mouth which accompanies his word and reveals its efficacy. Within the Trinity, the three "persons" are joined in a *perichoresis* ("going around," Greek) or circling movement of life, like a divine round dance. Moving "outside," the Son and Spirit are like the two hands of the Father in the loving work of creating and redeeming the world. Kasper judges that the Eastern pattern brings out more clearly the relation of God's Spirit to divine activity in the world.

These different representational models of how the three Trinitarian "persons" relate are accompanied by different theological concepts and by vocabulary with different evocative resonances. Carefully tracing the history of Trinitarian theology in East and West, which employed these two representational models with their different concepts in two different languages, and assessing the strengths and weaknesses of each, Kasper makes several important judgments. Each formulation is internally consistent. Each developed the way it did to deal with different problems. Neither is reducible to the other. Hence, the formulas are complementary. To say that the Spirit proceeds from the Father alone, or from the Father and the Son together, may sound on the surface like contrary positions, but both bear witness to one and the same faith, only in different conceptual forms.

Interestingly, Kasper notes a little-known historical fact. In the eighteenth century, Pope Benedict XIV decreed that the Eastern Catholic churches in union with Rome could use the original form of the Nicene-Constantinopolitan Creed, which says only that the Spirit proceeds from the Father, a usage which continues to this day. So there are Catholics in communion with Rome who do not confess the *filioque*. This exception would seem to support the position that the two articulations are complementary. Perhaps someday, Kasper suggests, genuine dialogue can move both churches toward a third, common formula. But even if not, each can acknowledge the unity in truth we share despite different representational images, theological concepts, and vocabularies. Unity in multiplicity rather than a monolithic confession is the appropriate ecumenical goal. Kasper's conclusion is rigorously logical but daring: the *filioque* "do[es] not amount to a difference that should divide the churches."[16] The question of how the Spirit proceeds within the Trinity should not be church dividing. Extraordinary!

There are other areas where Cardinal Kasper's pneumatology has developed the thinking of the theological community, but these must suffice for now to show how rich his contribution has been.

4. Going Forward

We are gathered to celebrate the life and work of Walter Kasper on the occasion of his eighty years of life. For an agile, curious mind such as his, the gift of a new question may be the best possible birthday present of all. And so I would like to end this presentation by proposing in an open-ended way a new pneumatological issue that desperately needs this good scholar's attention, namely, the Spirit in creation.

In our day we have become familiar with the image of our home planet, Earth, seen from space, a blue marble swirled around with white clouds against an endless vista of black. We stand in awe at the wonder that this is the only planet we know of that hosts life. Earth is home for our human species as well as for teeming millions of species that evolved here and nowhere else, starting with single-celled creatures that came alive in the ancient seas and diversifying over billions of years into "endless forms most beautiful," as Charles Darwin wrote.[17] But even as we marvel, we know that in our day human beings are inflicting deadly damage on our planet, ravaging its identity as a dwelling place for life. The way we consume, exploit resources, and pollute with sewage and chemicals is dealing a sucker punch to life-supporting systems on land, sea, and air. This ruining of habitats has as its flip side the extinction of the plant and animal species that live therein. We have now crossed a threshold. By a conservative estimate, in the last quarter of the twentieth century 10 percent of all living species went extinct. One-quarter to one-third of current species may well be extinct by the end of this twenty-first century. Their perishing sends an early warning signal about the death of our planet as a habitat for life itself. In the blunt language of the World Council of Churches, "The stark sign of our times is a planet in peril at our hands."[18]

Pope John Paul II rightly called the ecological crisis a moral issue and articulated a radical principle for Christian behavior: "Respect for life and for the dignity of the human person extends also to the rest of creation, which is called to join humanity in praising God."[19]

Pope Francis preached at his inaugural Mass that we must step up with a mantle of care: "Protect creation . . . protect all creation, the beauty of the created world . . . respect each of God's creatures and respect the environment in which we live . . . care for creation and for our brothers and sisters . . . protect the whole of creation, protect each person, especially the poorest. . . . Let us protect with love all that God has given us!"[20] To do its part, theology needs to bring back into view a full understanding of creation based on the ongoing *cosmic* presence and activity of the Spirit, the Lord and Giver of life.

While creation often gets pinned to the beginning of things in the past, and rightly so, it is a doctrine with unsuspected depths. Classical theology speaks of creation in three senses: *creatio originalis, creatio continua, creatio nova,* that is, original creation in the beginning, continuous creation in the present here and now, and new creation at the redeemed end time. While creation in the beginning and creation at the end appear in the Nicene-Constantinopolitan Creed recited weekly, the doctrine of continuous creation has suffered an eclipse. The reality is, however, that in addition to their origin and end in God, all creatures, including plants and animals, continue to be held in life and empowered to act in every moment by the Giver of the gift. Without this sustaining power, they—and we!—would sink back into nothingness. The living God did not retire after the six days of creation. Divine creativity is active here, now, in the next minute, or there would be no world at all. A stunning metaphor from the British philosopher Herbert McCabe expresses this insight: the doctrine of continuous creation means that the Creator "makes all things and keeps them in existence from moment to moment—not like a sculptor, who makes a statue and leaves it alone, but like a singer who keeps her song in existence at all times."[21]

Theology traditionally speaks about this music in language of the Spirit, the Holy Spirit, the Creator Spirit, the Spirit of God, the personal presence of the transcendent God in the world, whom the Nicene-Constantinopolitan Creed calls the "Lord and Giver of life," or in Latin, *vivificantem*, the Vivifier. Empowering the flow of energy in sea, air, and land and the life of animals and plants, the Spirit poured out on all flesh, as prophesied by Joel (2:28-29) and occurring at Pentecost (Acts 2:1-21), is not limited to humans only but fills the earth. The natural world is the dwelling place of God. In truth, I think neglect of the Spirit is a key factor that has contributed to the natural world being relegated to secondary importance in the life of people of faith.

In *The God of Jesus Christ*, a book of over three hundred pages, Kasper devotes two pages to "The Spirit of God in creation"[22] and one short passage to Paul's text in Romans (8:18-25) about all creation groaning, waiting for redemption. If Cardinal Kasper decides to remain active in retirement, the idea of the Spirit in creation could be the seed of a good monograph on ecological pneumatology, a theology of continuous creation in the power of the Spirit, with implications for the church's preaching and praxis of ecological ethics.

An anecdote reveals why I think this might appeal. In 1981 Walter Kasper spent a semester as visiting professor at Catholic University in Washington at the invitation of Carl Peter, dean of the School of Religious Studies, who was himself born and brought up in Omaha, Nebraska. During the term, our visitor was invited to give a lecture at the University of Notre Dame, which is situated geographically on the same broad expanse of level prairie land as Omaha. When he returned, I overheard him say to Carl Peter, "How did you ever discover your vocation to be a priest, living out there where it is so flat?" You need to have the "Alps experience," Walter Kasper went on, describing how being in the mountains lifted his mind and heart to God. A bit nonplused, Carl Peter responded that being in the mountains gave him claustrophobia. To be on the plains, where you can see to the horizon in every direction with the big sky overhead, that is where you can sense God. My own experience as a New Yorker who grew up close to the beach led me to intervene with the wisdom that the best place to encounter God was neither the mountains nor the plains but at the edge of the vast Atlantic Ocean. We had a little discussion, then, about the geography of spirituality, each of us so different, but God finding us through nature.

Listen again to one of Kasper's "Wherever's" in the light of the current ecological crisis: "everywhere that life breaks forth and comes into being, everywhere that new life as it were seethes and bubbles, and even, in the form of hope, everywhere that life is violently devastated, throttled, gagged and slain. Wherever true life exists, there the Spirit of God is at work."[23] To this I add: wherever in the Alps the glaciers are melting and the tundra flowers are going extinct; wherever the plains are burning in drought, wiping out nourishment for migratory birds and monarch butterflies; wherever the ocean beach has disappeared due to rising sea levels, and the deeps themselves are depleted of plankton and fish; wherever this great earth is groaning, there the Spirit of God groans with it (cf. Rom 8:22-23). Wherever someone acts on behalf of life, there the Spirit of God is at work, empowering nature's resilience, to the glory of God.

The church and the world would benefit from Walter Kasper turning the power of his craft on this aspect of pneumatology. In good *wissenschaftliche* fashion, he could trace how the theme of the Spirit in creation is present in the Bible but got lost in Western theology, filling in historical details about alternative Christian traditions that kept this intuition alive, finding sources, mounting arguments, filling out footnotes, bringing a discussion of the Holy Spirit in creation back into prominence, and sailing off into a new "Wherever" when overcome by the beauty and distress of the real natural world. It is a suggestion.

The British poet T. S. Eliot in *Four Quartets* wrote a memorable line that is pertinent as we celebrate Cardinal Kasper's eightieth birthday: "Old men ought to be explorers."[24]

At the age of eighty, Cardinal Kasper has earned the right to be called a wise elder among us. And we hope that he will want to keep on exploring. But whatever he decides to do next, we remain grateful to him for what he has done, and we wish him Godspeed on his days to come.

Endnotes

1. Pope Francis, sermon, March 17, 2013.

2. Walter Kasper, *Jesus the Christ*, trans. V. Green (New York: Paulist Press, 1976).

3. Walter Kasper, *The God of Jesus Christ*, trans. Matthew J. O'Connell (New York: Crossroad, 1984). All citations in point 1 are from this book.

4. Ibid., 202.

5. Ibid., 229.

6. Ibid., 227.

7. Ibid., 202.

8. Ibid., 285.

9. Ibid., 286.

10. Ibid., 198.

11. Ibid., 226.

12. Ibid.

13. Kasper, *Jesus the Christ*, 252.

14. Ibid., 252–68.

15. Augustine, *The Trinity*, trans. Edmund Hill (Brooklyn, NY: New City Press, 1991), 6.7; 15.10, 27–31.

16. Kasper, *The God of Jesus Christ*, 222.

17. Charles Darwin, *On the Origin of Species*, annotated by James Costa (Cambridge, MA: Harvard University Press, 2009), 490.

18. World Council of Churches, Canberra Assembly, "Giver of Life Sustain Your Creation!," in *Signs of the Spirit*, ed. Michael Kinnamon (Grand Rapids, MI: Eerdmans, 1991), 55.

19. John Paul II, *Peace with God the Creator, Peace with All of Creation* (January 1, 1990), 16; also published as "The Ecological Crisis: A Common Responsibility."

20. Pope Francis, Inaugural Mass, March 19, 2013.

21. Herbert McCabe, *God, Christ and Us*, ed. Brian Davies (New York: Continuum, 2003), 103.

22. Kasper, *The God of Jesus Christ*, 200–202.

23. Ibid., 202.

24. T. S. Eliot, "East Coker," in *Four Quartets* (New York: Harcourt, Brace, 1971), 32.

> Old men ought to be explorers
> Here and there does not matter
> We must be still and still moving
> Into another intensity
> For a further union, a deeper communion
> Through the dark cold and the empty desolation,
> The wave cry, the wind cry, the vast waters
> Of the petrel and the porpoise. In my end is my beginning.

CHAPTER 7

The God of Jesus Christ in Continuity and Discontinuity

Cyril J. O'Regan

This essay focuses on the Trinitarian theologies of Karl Rahner and Cardinal Walter Kasper as it examines the relation between Rahner's *The Trinity* (1967) and Kasper's *The God of Jesus Christ* (1982).[1] It provides merely an X-ray of the relation between Rahner's precursor text and Kasper's magisterial reflection, without reducing the latter to the former. Like an X-ray, this essay is limited: it picks out skeletal structures but misses the muscle and flesh of these significant theological contributions. Also, it overlooks entirely the principles that make both texts so alive. The aim here is twofold: on the one hand, to bring to light the conversation between these two major contributions to Catholic Trinitarian thought and, on the other, to inquire into their similarities and differences concerning theological starting point, view of scripture, and the Trinitarian tradition as well as their critical understanding of modernity.

At first brush, *The Trinity* and *The God of Jesus Christ* appear to differ in terms of style, method, and theological agenda. In terms of style, the earlier work is a set of fragments and a program, and the latter is a treatise with a sustained, complex argument. In terms of method, the earlier book shows a commitment to transcendental method and a method of correlation, and the latter (which relies to some degree on correlation) is committed to the biblical God of history who loves in freedom and who enters into dialogue with free human beings. In terms of agenda, *The Trinity* is intended to retrieve the Trinitarian tradition and recover the salvation-history experience that begot Trinitarian symbols in the first case, while *The God of Jesus Christ* is meant to call on the symbol of the Trinity, as suitably replanted in biblical soil, as an answer to the various forms of naturalism and atheism that have seemingly put the biblical God in the docks.

Although these differences are far from trivial, they do not define the relationship between these two highly influential Catholic texts on the Trinity, nor do they suggest a real theological chasm between the theological projects of Rahner and Kasper. I propose that the relations between the two texts show broad patterns of continuity and complementarity and that one sees the discontinuities best in light of the broader agreements. In pursuit of this proposal, this essay is divided into two parts. The first part attends to the "grammatical" continuities between the Trinitarian theologies of Rahner and Kasper, and the second part sketches some of the ways in which *The God of Jesus Christ* develops and corrects *The Trinity* while still operating within its parameters.

1. Continuities

In order to illumine the continuities between *The Trinity* and *The God of Jesus Christ* let us view these two achievements from two perspectives. First, we shall see them in relation to the new paradigm concerning the Trinity that Rahner introduced and that Kasper has presupposed in his theology of the triune God. Second, we will consider how this new paradigm yields a twofold genealogy concerning discourse on the Trinity in theological scholarship and also in the Christian tradition.

(1) *A New Paradigm in Trinitarian Theology*

The Trinity is a powerfully generative text in theology, despite its slightness and despite the fact that its three parts do not hold together well and also have minor inconsistencies, if not in substance, then in defining the book's agenda. Rahner's text makes an eloquent appeal for a reordering of priority between the "immanent Trinity" and the "economic Trinity" in Catholic theology, that is, between God as God and God in relation to us. Before Rahner's text, theologians had prioritized the immanent Trinity in the order of theological reflection largely on the grounds that God as God is the ontological basis of the missions of the Son and the Spirit. *The Trinity* challenges this starting point as exhibiting an overcommitment to explaining God's nature. Rahner's text represents a paradigm shift. It directs attention away from explanation to description, that is, away from an intellectual or metaphysical analysis of God as God to a critical, systematic reflection on the saving or salvific actions of the Son and Spirit in history. History is the matrix in which we come to experience the triune God. It is also the matrix in which the triune God has real pertinence, for we in fact respond to God's outreach to us with our whole selves, not just with our minds.

A crucial feature of Rahner's paradigm shift is its epistemic proviso against our claiming too great an intellectual competence concerning God as God. This implicit claim is one that the classical tradition was not fully successful at preventing—at least in the Western tradition—despite manifold appeals to apophasis, that is, to a negative theology.[2] Rahner's epistemic proviso is not, however, Kantian in nature. That is, it does not implicitly demand a split between the economic Trinity and the immanent Trinity, with the latter totally unavailable to thought as if it were a "thing in itself," a reality outside of human apprehension.[3] The theory of truth operative in Rahner's text more nearly follows the personal disclosure model of truth, held by Martin Heidegger, which corrects the view of Immanuel Kant concerning the external rather than expressive relation of reality to appearance.[4]

In studies of Rahner's theology, a common error is not to distinguish sufficiently between Kant's epistemology and Rahner's. One consequence of this mistake is to misinterpret Rahner's famous axiom, "The immanent Trinity is the economic Trinity and vice versa."[5] While it is true that Rahner is recommending, in a restricted sense, a reduction of the immanent to the economic Trinity, he means "reduction" here neither in the sense that the immanent Trinity has been totally sidelined nor in the sense that it has become purely notional. Rather, in Rahner the term "reduction" connotes something like a return to the experiential basis of the doctrine of the Trinity. This orientation is totally in line with the general commitment to the Heideggerian pattern of destruction and recovery that Rahner first tendered in his

Geist in Welt (1936). Further, it involves a reduction similar to Bonaventure's aim of *reducere*, "to reduce," that is, to trace how one discourse "leads back" to another discourse that can account for it.[6]

One can supplement these observations regarding *The Trinity* by appealing to the important distinction between two kinds of mystery articulated in Rahner's famous essays on the topic.[7] There exists, Rahner argues, a significant difference between mystery as the exhaustion of knowledge and mystery as ontological surplus that provokes interrogation in the very same measure that it denies satisfaction. The former, a privative mystery, is a reality that we can in principle fully know, such as whether there is extraterrestrial life. The latter, a positive or true mystery, is a reality that we can increasingly know but never fully comprehend, for example, a human person and God.

The misguided kind of interpretation of Rahner's axiom that would reduce, in the strict sense, the immanent to the economic Trinity operates in terms of a deficient view of mystery common both to the Enlightenment and neoscholastic thought. It fails to regard Rahner's axiom in relation to a positive or true mystery in which divine revelation is a personal manifestation. Such a view is supported not only by Heidegger but also by the broad Catholic theological tradition. For Rahner, the divine mystery is not a secret but God's self-communication, which is ontologically excessive. Intentional or not, Rahner's definition of mystery finds its basic pattern in the dominant trope of Christian neoplatonism, that is, *Bonum diffusivum sui*, "The good is copious." Certainly, when reading Rahner's account of the saving operations of the Son and the Spirit in history, it is difficult not to think of Bonaventure's view of the Trinity as self-communicating persons.[8]

In *The God of Jesus Christ* Kasper quite intentionally places his work within this new paradigm, starting with the economic Trinity and also giving salvation history concreteness and determinacy by speaking of the biblical witness concerning the activities of the Son and the Spirit (part 2). As he does so, Kasper is careful not to slide from defocusing on the ontological and personal ground of the soteriological activities of the Son and Spirit to subtly questioning the ontological status of this ground. In other words, while he anchors his critical, systematic reflection in the economic Trinity, he also acknowledges the immanent Trinity. Nowhere does he give a one-sided interpretation of Rahner's axiom that would effectively reduce all valid Trinitarian discourse to a discourse of salvation history.[9] Kasper grasps that even with a momentous shift in perspective, there is not a complete throwing aside of a Catholic grammar of Trinitarian discourse that forbids the reduction of the triune God to history.[10]

The reasons provided by Kasper are not in the slightest nostalgic; rather, the distinction is necessary in order to guarantee the freedom of the God of history and to underscore the gratuity of creation, redemption, and sanctification. As Kasper notes, to read Rahner's axiom as a tautology would violate the "non-deducible, free, gracious, historical presence of the immanent Trinity in the economic Trinity."[11] It would be a mistake to deny Rahner's commitment to the historical realm as well as historicity, and it would also be a mistake to fail to acknowledge Rahner's emphasis on God's freedom when it comes to revelation.[12]

Kasper has no interest in gainsaying any of this. Rather, he wishes to underscore this commitment to history and divine freedom, which supersedes its conditions of reception. He is intent on emphasizing God's freedom. For this purpose, he relies in *The God of Jesus Christ* not on Heidegger's thought but rather on Schelling's later philosophy. In choosing this philosophical foundation, he builds on the work of the Catholic Tübingen School in general and on Johann Sebastian Drey in particular.[13] Thus, in *The God of Jesus Christ* Kasper fully accepts Rahner's distinction between privative mystery and positive mystery, for only the latter is consistent with divine self-manifestation or self-communication. As Kasper insists, the triune God remains utterly mysterious in self-communication.[14]

(2) *A Genealogy Concerning Discourse on the Trinity*

As we have seen, the paradigm for Trinitarian discourse, introduced by Rahner and continued by Kasper, favors first what is given in the order of knowledge rather than what is prior in the order of being.[15] What we also should note is that starting with the economic Trinity rather than the immanent Trinity generates a genealogical account of Trinitarian discourse throughout history and especially in the modern period. Indeed, it yields—as conveyed in Rahner's *The Trinity* —a genealogy or account that sheds light both on pre–Vatican II Catholic theology concerning the triune God and also on the Christian tradition, including the church's pastoral disaster in which there is a disconnect or dissonance between the church's doctrine of the Trinity and most Catholics' inadequate monotheist view of God.

a. Manualist / "Textbook" Theology. In the case of theology, Rahner conveys that the problem definitely has an intramural dimension (that is, within the Christian tradition) without necessarily ruling out an extramural dimension (that is, in relation to secular thought). Although he does not fully identify the intramural-dimension issue in *The Trinity*, he refers to it when he speaks about the church's "textbook theology."[16] He is speaking of the Manualist theology, written in Latin, of the late nineteenth and early twentieth centuries that repeated and simplified neoscholastic propositions concerning the truths of Christian belief. This theology was the subject matter that all Catholic seminarians studied in preparation for ordination to the priesthood and upon which priests relied in their preaching, catechesis, and religious instruction. When Rahner speaks of Catholics' functional monotheism with its disregard for the Trinity, he implicitly blames the church's Manualist or textbook theology for this state of affairs.

According to Rahner, the textbook theology was unable to counter an inadequate monotheistic view of God because it lacked a soteriological orientation. Further, the prioritizing of the immanent Trinity over the economic Trinity, along with the scholastic and the neoscholastic differentiation between theology "concerning the one God," *de Deo Uno*, and theology "concerning the triune God," *de Deo Trino*, had a lasting impact on how Catholics think about the God who gives himself to us in the Son and the Spirit.[17] Although he does not clearly argue the case, Rahner implies in *The Trinity* that there is a causal link between textbook theology's approach to the mystery of God and today's impoverished understanding of God. Of course, given Rahner's reflections on atheism, he would also recognize that there are extramural or non-Christian reasons for contemporary Christians' faulty understanding of God.[18]

b. The Trinity in the Christian Tradition and Contemporary Thought. Rahner's genealogy of discourse on the Trinity also sheds light on the Christian tradition over the centuries, especially concerning the Trinitarian theologies of Augustine and Thomas Aquinas. This discussion has influenced Kasper's *The God of Jesus Christ*.

In light of Rahner's shift in paradigms, what are the systemic defects in Augustine's and Thomas's theologies of the triune God? Three are noteworthy. First, these theologies privilege the immanent Trinity over the economic Trinity. Second, they theologically establish God's unity before proceeding to discuss God as three "persons." Third, they only conventionally assign acts in salvation history to specific divine persons.[19] Rahner himself does not pursue these three aspects of Augustine's and Thomas's theologies. Confining his observations and concerns to his notes in *The Trinity*, he encourages such work.[20]

In *The God of Jesus Christ* Kasper agrees with Rahner's linking of the reordering of priority between the economic and immanent Trinity (in Kasper's part 2) with a genealogy of how the classical view ceased to have intellectual and existential purchase (in Kasper's part 1). Unlike Rahner, Kasper does not discuss neoscholasticism and Manualist theology.[21] Instead Kasper provides an expanded account of extramural or secular systems of thought such as naturalism, atheism, and apologetically "thin" theism. In his view, these bodies of thought have hindered the reception of any "thick" or full doctrine of God. Significantly, as Kasper discusses these specific challenges to Christian belief, he approaches them as an opportunity rather than as a suffering. He is convinced that a robust articulation of the Trinity can effectively respond to all challenges from contemporary life and thought.

Kasper is critical of the Christian tradition's emphases in the West on the unitary essence of the Trinity and also on the classical doctrine of the divine appropriations, which cuts against the grain of the biblical data. He does not, however, explicitly speak of a causal link between these two problematic emphases and the modern problems regarding the Trinity. To be sure, if he had done so, he would have followed the critical drift of *The God of Jesus Christ*. Other Catholic theologians, such as Catherine Mowry LaCugna, however, have done so, arguing that the contemporary "defeat" of the doctrine of the Trinity is coded in the tradition itself.[22] Kasper does not follow this possible and plausible Rahnerian trajectory. If there is a causal link between classical Western Trinitarian thought and the palpable absence of the imaginative and argumentative force of the Trinity in the contemporary periods, it is not part of Kasper's agenda to underscore it.[23]

c. Further Lines of Continuity. At this point, I shall highlight other lines of continuity from Rahner's theology of the Trinity to Kasper's. Conspicuous features of continuity/complementarity between *The Trinity* and *The God of Jesus Christ* include the preference for the East's emphasis on the communion of the divine persons over the West's emphasis on the unity of divine essence and the recognition that the church may revise its doctrine of the Trinity.[24] Concerning the first emphasis, Rahner's favoring of the East's orientation reflects both his judgment of theological adequacy and his cultural diagnosis—to which he gives greater weight—that Christians in the West hold a functionally monotheist view of God. While Kasper acknowledges both the theological adequacy of the East's orientation and the cultural influence in the West, he lends more weight to the question of theological adequacy, since theology is obliged to rhyme with the givens of divine revelation. In light of biblical testimony, Kasper is inclined toward the Greek Trinitarian theology with its emphasis on the communion of the divine persons, the innascibility (i.e., unbegottenness) of the Father as well as the determinate activity of the Son and Spirit in salvation history.[25]

Rahner holds that contemporary theologians must attempt to interpret the Trinitarian creed and assess its authority. While he upholds in principle that the church can revise its doctrine of the Trinity, he himself does not propose any revision. Moreover, he judges that theologians cannot change the creed's basic "grammar."[26] Similarly, since Kasper is intent on anchoring the doctrine of the Trinity on a sounder soteriology, he is more engaged in giving a theological interpretation of the creed than in trying to revise the creed itself.

In conclusion, I offer three caveats. First, I have provided only a selection of the ways in which Kasper follows Rahner within the new paradigm of Trinitarian theology. Second, I have distinguished only in an *ad hoc* way those elements of Kasper's Trinitarian thought that repeat Rahner more or less exactly from those that complement him. Complementarity is just as frequent as continuity in the strict sense. Third, I have only hinted at the way in which Kasper's following of Rahner differs from other Trinitarian proposals that were influenced by Rahner.

2. Developments and Corrections

At this point, it is appropriate to consider the developments and corrections of Rahner's *The Trinity* that mark Kasper's *The God of Jesus Christ*. Let's take note of two ways in which Kasper has developed or filled out Rahner's Trinitarian theology, after which we shall consider three ways in which Kasper has corrected or overcome the deficiencies in Rahner's work, though without breaking with Rahner's new paradigm for Trinitarian theology.

(1) *Scripture's Witness to Salvation History*

Kasper's crucial development of Rahner lies in making explicit what is implicit in *The Trinity*, that is, that the commitment to salvation history goes hand in hand with a reading of the biblical text as the witness to such as history. While there is not a single biblical citation in *The Trinity*, Rahner does supply the biblical evidence for the sending of the Son and the Spirit in his article "*Theos* in the New Testament."[27]

In *The God of Jesus Christ* Kasper articulates the priority of the economic Trinity. In this endeavor, he follows the mandate of Vatican II's Dogmatic Constitution on Divine Revelation, *Dei verbum*, not only to attend to the biblical matrix of faith as a response to God's saving action in and of history but also to employ the historical-critical method, with respect to which Catholic theology had a troubled relation throughout much of the twentieth century. As Kasper exercises this option, he takes on the burden of the ambiguity and uncertainty of the historical evidence that is avoided both when there is an effective end-run around the biblical text and also when there is the deployment of a different hermeneutic regime, for example, that of Hans Urs von Balthasar's canonic and ecclesial reading in his great triptych of the Bible as scripture.[28]

Still, although the contrast here between Kasper's and Balthasar's biblical hermeneutic is illustrative, it should be noted that Kasper uses the historical-critical method itself in ways so that he avoids a positivistic reduction to historical facts that function to explain biblical attestation. As Kasper points out throughout *The God of Jesus Christ*, an irreducible circularity exists between the facts of history and the confession of faith.

One interesting consequence of Kasper's giving the biblical context of Rahner's economic and soteriological turn is the way in which Kasper transplants Rahner's transcendental reflections on mystery into divine revelation and its history. Early in part 2 of *The God of Jesus Christ*, as Kasper recalls Rahner's famous essays on mystery and the hiddenness of God, he insists that scripture renders a God who reveals his mystery with his saving will.[29] In sum, Kasper puts an exclamation point to what Rahner conveys in *The Trinity* and actually states in his essay on God in the New Testament.

(2) *Trinitarian Theology and Doxology*

A second development of Rahner's *The Trinity* in Kasper's *The God of Jesus Christ* concerns the interconnection of the Trinitarian theology and doxology, that is, the reciprocal movement between engaging in critical, systematic reflection and giving thanks and praise in worship and prayer to God. Rahner draws attention to doxology and prayer in the context of his discerning the widespread irrelevance of the doctrine of the Trinity in the contemporary period. In his view, Christian doxology and prayer have not been heard in the contemporary world but have in fact been enlisted in what amounts to a procedural monotheism.[30] While being largely pessimistic about their force, Rahner intimates that doxology and prayer might be a means of cure since they rely on first-level discourse, which is direct and primary, rather than on the doctrine of the Trinity, which belongs to second-level discourse, to conceptual explication.[31]

Kasper does not demur. Indeed, he implicitly recognizes the connection between Trinitarian theology and doxology when he stresses both Jesus' prayer to God as Father as generative with respect to the divine sonship of Jesus Christ and also the original baptismal context of the Trinitarian formula.[32] Further, Kasper insists on the link between Trinitarian theology's biblical-soteriological discourse and doxology.[33] He does not, however, make the kind of developed case for the connection prosecuted by other theologians such as LaCugna in *God for Us*.[34]

(3) *The Notion of Person in Trinitarian Theology*

One of the ways in which Kasper corrects Rahner's Trinitarian theology concerns the notion of person. Kasper gives a cool response to Rahner's recommendation in *The Trinity* to replace the use of the word "person" in Trinitarian theology with the phrase "manner of self-subsistence."[35] To be sure, Kasper is not unsympathetic to Rahner's view that, given the default understanding of person in the modern thought as a center of individual consciousness and self-consciousness, the danger is that the doctrine of the Trinity may be read tritheistically. Nonetheless, Kasper sees the hazards in Rahner's proposal, including that it has little or no pastoral value, a deficit that is far from trivial given the pastoral intent of both Rahner and Kasper.

With Kasper, it is appropriate to challenge Rahner's recommendation by posing two questions. First, just how eminent is the danger of tritheism in an era when Christians—as Rahner states—already overemphasize God's unity? Second, could not talk of the three "manners of self-subsistent existence," instead of three "persons," also be construed as a form of modalism?[36] If this misunderstanding were to occur, wouldn't it feed the overemphasis on God's unity?

(4) *History*

A crucial correction by Kasper of *The Trinity* is the evident departure in *The God of Jesus Christ* from Rahner's long-standing systematic correlation of "the transcendental" and "the categorical," which regulates Rahner's constructive discussion of the Trinity in the third and final part of his programmatic text.[37] Although Kasper does not explicitly reject the transcendental subject, he focuses his attention on history, which is regulated by the activities of the Son and Holy Spirit.[38] Insofar as Kasper employs the notion of the transcendental subject, he does so with his emphasis on history. Yet, logically and biblically this raises the question, who is the subject or human recipient of the saving activity of the Son and the Spirit?

With the caveat that Kasper does not renege on the value of the person,[39] Kasper's commitments would seem to imply that the subject of history in the final analysis is the "people of God," as expressed in Vatican II's Dogmatic Constitution on the Church, *Lumen gentium*. As is well-known, correctors of Rahner's theology such as Johann Baptist Metz have gone much further than this, at once arguing against the transcendental subject as a modern bourgeois subject and, in contrast, determining that the subject of history is the suffering communities whose voices have been silenced and whose faces have been erased.[40] Although Kasper's correction of Rahner's thought here is real, it does not reach the level of Metz's radical critique.

(5) *Explanatory Intent*

A third correction of *The Trinity* is more implied than truly explicit in *The God of Jesus Christ*. It has to do with what I call "explanatory intent" when it comes to articulating the Trinitarian economy. While throughout *The Trinity* Rahner criticizes the classical Western tradition of invidious abstraction, he himself presents in dense fashion four correlating pairs of ideas in *The Trinity*, chapter 3: origin and future, history and transcendence, invitation and acceptance, and knowledge and love. With this discussion, Rahner seems guilty in a different but related way of over-interpretation. It is not as if these correlations do not make sense, nor that they fail to rhyme with his earlier attempts at correlation such as occurs in Rahner's *Hearers of the Word* (1941). Still, Rahner is at least at odds with his own jeremiads against abstraction. Moreover, as he attempts a rough correlation between the transcendental subject (i.e., human persons) and God's self-communication in history, Rahner comes to associate the Son and Spirit univocally with truth and love, respectively. In this association, he reinscribes the positions—which he had previously dismissed as compromising the givens of revelation—articulated by Augustine and Thomas Aquinas.[41]

More than Rahner, Kasper keeps at bay the explanatory intent of classical Trinitarian theology, as happens in chapter 1 of Bonaventure's *Breviloquium* with its talk of one essence, two processions, three persons, four relations, and five marks of identification,[42] or in Hans Urs von Balthasar's discussions of intra-divine receptivity, *kenosis*, and mutuality. In his work, Kasper warns against speculative extrapolations from the economic Trinity to the immanent Trinity.[43] Given these warnings, he is likely sympathetic to Rahner's objection that Balthasar's Trinitarian theology evinces an epistemic hubris or, more particularly, a flight from what is given in history and experience.[44]

For Kasper, experience and history essentially name the same thing since all experience is historical. At the same time Kasper, who is the consummately irenic and ecclesial theologian, by no means intends to force a choice between Rahner and Balthasar on the doctrine of God.[45] Kasper expresses his admiration for Balthasar's theology, especially its spiritual depth and its strong biblical orientation.[46] Although Kasper judges that Balthasar's theology can tend in part to be overly speculative, he never accuses Balthasar's theology of being Hegelian. Indeed, he agrees with Balthasar that the statement "God is love" (1 John 4:6) is the summary of faith since it expresses who God is.[47]

Conclusion

There are two related dangers to constructing Kasper's Trinitarian theology as being in continuity with Rahner's basic orientation. The first is that it risks being a platitude. The second is that it risks underestimating Kasper's unique contribution to Trinitarian thought. As the two risks are connected, so are the answers.

To argue that Kasper works within Rahner's new paradigm is nontrivial in two different ways. First, given the biblical matrix of Kasper's Trinitarian thought, he operates to some degree in the same Trinitarian horizon as Hans Urs von Balthasar, even if there are significant differences regarding biblical hermeneutics and extrapolations to the immanent Trinity. Kasper shows considerable hospitality to Balthasar's kind of theology and thus constitutes himself as a mediating theologian of the first rank.

Second, just as important is the manner of Kasper's appropriation of Rahner, which disambiguates the relation between the economic Trinity and immanent Trinity and corrects him on a number of crucial points where Rahner might appear to be involved in either overcorrection of the theological tradition or speculative abstraction. Kasper's point of view is consistently pastoral as it is insistently ecclesial. Moreover, while fulfilling Rahner's biblical intention regarding systematic theology in general and Trinitarian theology in particular, Kasper has generated a fundamentally different kind of theology in which scripture and history mutually interpret each other.

Working in the trajectory of the Catholic Tübingen School, Kasper has moved beyond Rahner's transcendental method and method of correlation. Thus we arrive at the beginning of Kasper's work on the philosophical and religious thought of the "later" Schelling and its appropriation by the Catholic Tübingen School.[48] At the same time, we come upon the beginning of modern theology, that is, the nineteenth century's critical reflections on history and truth as well as on the activities of Christ and Spirit in the church and the world, neither of which can contain them.

According to Schelling, God is the absolute future not only in the sense that not all has yet been disclosed and not only in the sense that the church and the world live in tension toward an open future. God is the absolute future also in the sense that we live in celebration of the loving freedom of God who is the object of our faith, hope, and love. Schelling's thought is considerably easier to baptize than Hegel's, although it too falls short of Christian belief, as Kasper shows with scrupulous precision in his Habilitation, *Das Absolute in der Geschichte*. Schelling's critique of materialism and rationalistic forms of Christianity remains valid as does his emphasis on the essential character of divine freedom.

Thanks to the Catholic Tübingen School, the church's theologians have learned important lessons from Schelling, and they can continue to learn from him as long as they maintain their critical distance and anchor theological inquiry in a biblically informed faith. Among these theologians, Cardinal Walter Kasper stands tall, for he has learned much from the theologians of the Catholic Tübingen School, and he continues to teach us how to learn wisely and deeply in the service of God and the Christian faith.

Endnotes

1. Karl Rahner, *The Trinity*, trans. Joseph Donceel (New York: Crossroad, 1997); Walter Kasper, *The God of Jesus Christ*, trans. Matthew J. O'Connell (New York: Crossroad, 1982).

2. Although Rahner does not enter this caveat in *The Trinity*, he does in a number of other essays.

3. Rahner is consistent with his metaphysics of finitude as he reframes Kant's transcendentalism in his *Spirit in the World*, trans. William Dych (New York: Continuum, 1969).

4. This is a point made in Francis Schüssler Fiorenza's introduction to Rahner, *Spirit in the World*, xix–xlv.

5. Rahner, *Trinity*, 22.

6. See Bonaventure, *On the Reduction of the Arts to Theology*, trans. Zachary Hayes (St. Bonaventure, NY: Franciscan Institute Publications, 1996).

7. See Karl Rahner, "The Concept of Mystery in Catholic Theology," in *Theological Investigations*, vol. 4: *More Recent Writings*, trans. Kevin Smyth (Baltimore, MD: Helicon Press, 1966), 36–73; idem, "The Hiddenness of God" and "The

Mystery of the Trinity," in *Theological Investigations*, vol. 16: *Experiences of the Spirit: Sources of Theology*, trans. David Morland, OSB (New York: Crossroad, 1983), 227–43; 255–59. To these systematic pieces one should add Rahner's appreciative pieces on the respective apophasis of Thomas Aquinas and Ignatius Loyola. For the former, see Karl Rahner, "The Incomprehensibility of God in St. Thomas Aquinas," in *Theological Investigations*, vol. 16, 244–54; idem, "Being Open to God as Ever Greater: On the Significance of the Aphorism '*Ad Majorem Dei Gloriam*,'" in *Theological Investigations*, vol. 7: *Further Theology of the Spiritual Life*, trans. David Bourke (New York: Seabury Press, 1971), 25–46. See also Karl Rahner, *Foundations of Christian Faith: An Introduction to the Idea of Christianity*, trans. William Dych (New York: Crossroad, 1984), 44–89; idem, *The Trinity*, 46–48.

8. While there is no reason to suppose that Rahner chooses between either Aquinas and Bonaventure when it comes to the Trinity, it is interesting that the language deployed is more nearly that of Bonaventure who—without prejudice to Aquinas's indebtedness to neoPlatonism—is the more obviously neoplatonic of the two.

9. Kasper, *The God of Jesus Christ*, 273–76.

10. Ibid., 276.

11. Ibid.

12. Agreeing with Martin Heidegger, Rahner regards historicity as a fundamental element of his philosophical anthropology; it is historicity that makes human being apt for revelation, which can only be historical. See Karl Rahner, *Hearers of the Word: Laying the Foundations of a Philosophy of Religion*, trans. Joseph Donceel (New York: Continuum, 1994). The original text in German appeared in 1941.

13. Ibid., 106. It would be going too far to suggest that Kasper's work on Schelling plays a constitutive role in his insistence on the freedom of God and the gratuity of the created and redeemed order, but definitely Kasper finds in Schelling's later work an important answer, on the one hand, to naturalism, which eclipses all transcendence, and, on the other, to idealism, which proposes a form of transcendence without transcendence and also without mystery and gratuity. See Walter Kasper, *Das Absolute in der Geschichte: Philosophie und Theologie der Geschichte in der Spätphilosophie Schellings* (Freiburg: Herder, 2010).

14. Ibid., 170–71, 276–77.

15. Concerning this methodological shift, see Kasper, *The God of Jesus Christ*, 277.

16. Rahner, *The Trinity*, 10–15.

17. For Kasper's following of Rahner here, see Kasper, *The God of Jesus Christ*, 147–48.

18. On *Gaudium et spes* as articulating the challenge of atheism to Christianity, see Karl Rahner, "What Does Vatican II Teach about Atheism," trans. Theodore Westow, in *The Pastoral Approach to Atheism*, ed. K. Rahner (New York: Paulist Press, 1967), 7–24; idem, "Theological Considerations on Secularization and Atheism," in *Theological Investigations*, vol. 11: *Confrontations*, trans. David Bourke (New York: Crossroad, 1982), 166–84.

19. Rahner, *The Trinity*, 37.

20. For Augustine, see Rahner, *The Trinity*, 18–19 n. 18; 46; 115–16; 178 n. 42. For Aquinas, see especially ibid., 16–17, n. 12; 47–48. In connection with Aquinas, one should also track Rahner's references to Bernard Lonergan's *De Deo Trino*; see Rahner, *The Trinity*, 73 n. 27; 75 n. 29; 76 n. 30; 78 n. 34; 80 n. 1. Locating herself in the tradition of Rahner, Catherine Mowry LaCugna does this exegetical work in the case of Augustine's *De Trinitate* and Aquinas's treatment of *de Deo Trino* in *Summa Theologiae* (I, q. 27–43) in its relation to *de Deo Uno* (1, q. 1–26); see Catherine Mowry LaCugna, *God for Us: The Trinity and Christian Life* (San Francisco: Harper & Row, 1991), 81–109, 141–80.

21. On Manualist theology, see Kasper, *The God of Jesus Christ*, 277.

22. See Elizabeth T. Groppe, "Catherine Mowry LaCugna's Contribution to Trinitarian Theology," *Theological Studies* 63 (2002): 730–63; idem, "Creation *Ex Nihilo* and *Ex Amore*: Ontological Freedom in the Theologies of John Zizioulas and Catherine Mowry LaCugna," *Modern Theology* 21 (2005): 463–96.

23. On Kasper's agreement with Rahner, see Kasper, *The God of Jesus Christ*, 277.

24. Ibid., 311.

25. Ibid., 283–84.

26. On the ontic and grammatical or "logical" character of Trinitarian statements, see Rahner, *The Trinity*, 52–53. By "logical" Rahner means that second-order explication of what is given in the first-order expression of Christian faith.

27. Karl Rahner, *Theological Investigations*, vol. 1, trans. Cornelius Ernst, OP (Baltimore, MD: Helicon Press, 1961), 79–148. Rahner cites this article in *The Trinity*, 59 n. 7.

28. On Balthasar's use of the historical-critical method, see William T. Dickens, *Hans Urs von Balthasar's Theological Aesthetics: A Model for Post-Critical Biblical Interpretation* (Notre Dame, IN: University of Notre Dame Press, 2003).

29. Kasper, *The God of Jesus Christ*, 127–28, 119, 123–24.

30. Rahner, *The Trinity*, 10–12.

31. By "primary" here I do not mean a form that can be replaced, but rather a form rich enough in meaning to call for explication. For Rahner, "primary" in the proper and positive sense means much the same as what Heidegger would call "primordial."

32. Kasper, *The God of Jesus Christ*, 170–71, 245–46. Here, Kasper has placed less weight on Jesus' Abba experience than he does in *Jesus the Christ*, trans. V. Green (New York: Paulist Press, 1974), 72–88.

33. Kasper, *The God of Jesus Christ*, 303–4. Kasper critiques Rahner's own construction of the Trinity as insufficiently doxological; see *The God of Jesus Christ*, 302.

34. Kasper does not make the kind of developed case as occurs in LaCugna, *God for Us*, 111–42, 319–75.

35. Kasper, *The God of Jesus Christ*, 287–88, 300–302. For Rahner on the notion of the human person, see *The Trinity*, 103–14, 42–45, 56–57.

36. Kasper, *The God of Jesus Christ*, 302.

37. Ibid., 117–19.

38. Ibid., 52–53, 85.

39. Ibid., *The God of Jesus Christ*, 311–14; cf. 155–56.

40. See Johannes Baptist Metz, *Faith in History and Society: Toward a Political Fundamental Theology*, trans. David Smith (Boston: Seabury, 1980); idem, *A Passion for God: The Mystical-Political Dimension of Christianity*, trans. J. Matthew Ashley (New York: Paulist Press, 1998).

41. On Kasper's discussion of Rahner's transcendental deduction of the Trinity as the subject of grace, see *The God of Jesus Christ*, 301.

42. Bonaventure sets out in *Breviloquium* to provide a kind of shorthand for a doctrine, which he conceptually develops and spiritually explores in *Itinerarium*.

43. Kasper, *The God of Jesus Christ*, 276–77.

44. Concerning Balthasar's Trinitarian thought, Rahner writes: "I would say that there is a modern tendency . . . to develop a theory of the death of God that, in the last analysis, seems to me to be gnostic. One can find this in Hans Urs von Balthasar and in Adrienne von Speyr, although naturally more marked in her than him"; see idem, *Karl Rahner in Dialogue: Conversations and Interviews 1965–1982*, ed. Paul Imhof and Hubert Biallowons (New York: Crossroad, 1986), 126. For Balthasar's response, see *Theo-Drama: Theological Dramatic Theory*, vol. 5: *The Last Act*, trans. Graham Harrison (San Francisco: Ignatius Press, 1998), 13–14.

45. In *The God of Jesus Christ*, Kasper refers most often to Rahner among the modern Catholic theologians and secondly to Balthasar.

46. For a positive estimate of Balthasar's work, see Walter Kasper, *The Catholic Church: Nature, Reality and Mission*, trans. Thomas Hoebel (London: Blooomsbury T&T Clark, 2014), 19–20.

47. Kasper, *The God of Jesus Christ*, 308–11; cf. 299.

48. Kasper has drawn on all of Schelling's writings, but his Catholic predecessors in Tübingen did not. They did not have access to Schelling's *The Ages of the World* (1815). Johann Adam Möhler and Johann Sebastian Drey did not take account of Schelling's *Philosophie der Offenbarung* (1841), but Franz Anton Staudenmaier did.

SECTION TWO

The Church, Ecumenism, and Christian-Jewish Relations

CHAPTER 8

A Theology of Church and Ministry

Thomas F. O'Meara, OP

This sketch of Walter Kasper's writings and ideas about the church and ministry looks at a limited area of his theology and yet aspires to give access to some of its deeper intellectual and religious dynamics. Philosophical theory and ecclesiastical forms as well as Christology and pneumatology fashion and emerge from his studies over several decades of concrete structures or modes of expression in the international and the local church.

1. An Appropriation of Schelling's Late Philosophy

For his Habilitation the future professor and bishop chose the philosopher of romantic idealism Friedrich Wilhelm Joseph Schelling. He unfolded that philosopher's central theme of "the Absolute in history." The analysis of the movement of the Absolute from a primal triune self-development through its varied presence in history also included a survey of interpretations of Schelling's thought composed during the 125 years since his death and showed its numerous influences on Protestant and Catholic theologians.[1] "In this thinking about the Absolute, the infinite and the finite, the ideal and the real are identical and are present only in an absolute mutual temporality. The external world is the self-manifestation and self-presentation of Spirit setting itself in forms. . . . It is the history of self-consciousness."[2]

According to Kasper, Schelling and other modern philosophers can offer horizons and insights for interpreting the event of Jesus Christ. Without knowledge of modern thinkers "theology will run out of breath."[3] Kasper states: "I could never, as many theologians still do today, consider the modern time only as a history of downfall into a bottomless subjectivism. The modern age is far more diverse than such stereotypical characterizations can express."[4] Surprisingly, the study of "the Absolute in history" forecasts something of Kasper's subsequent interpretation of the church; transcendental and historical panentheism sends its impetuses into a theology of historical forms empowering community and service.

2. A Theology of the Church in Modern History

Kasper's 1969 book, which was translated into English as *The Crisis of Change*, offers an ecclesial reflection related to the modern cultural theory explored in Schelling's thinking. Kasper notes an observation by Ernest Troeltsch: the encounter between theology and history would in the future raise problems greater than even those raised by the encounter of theology and science.[5] The central conflict of historical and social developments in the church is the background of Kasper's ecclesiology, and it is also a fundamental dynamic in the life of American Catholicism.

Kasper, of course, observed that the Second Vatican Council brought out the interpenetration of church and history: "The problems which history poses today cannot be avoided by retreating to an imaginary 'center' of faith and rejecting historical questions as peripheral to faith."[6] Salvation history and thus ecclesial history in its depth are aspects of God's history. The theologian adds a startling idea: if human faith includes God's Word entering history, so too the church must through faith, and not in spite of it, enter history. The pulsating interplay of sacred and secular histories contributes to the unfolding of the church. The church does not automatically possess the truth but must be taught the truth in its depth and expanse by the Holy Spirit. This process happens in people and societies living out of temporality, past and present and future. The Tübingen theologian concluded in 1969: "The church is not yet the kingdom of God. Still, the forces of a new era are already at work in it."[7]

3. Seeds of Reflections on the Church

Drawing insights from Schelling's thinking on the Absolute assuming various forms in history, Kasper holds that the church continues its life in a causal interplay of seminal realities with subsequent forms and structures drawn out from times and cultures. Kasper begins with and prefers basic realities, seminal realities. His ecclesiology explores underlying realities accepted by faith and then discerned in their formative powers influential within the living church. In 1971, in the aftermath of Vatican II, Kasper, on behalf of the German bishops, treated the topic of "The Salvific Mission of the Church Today."[8] The church's mission will seek new directions and forms because there is a new understanding of grace and of the church's mission of salvation. What is the church? How does it realize itself? Who belongs to the church? That position paper, forty years ago, concluded that all Christians are bearers of the church's mission, bearers of the mission of church ministries.

Two volumes of essays from 1987 and 1999, *Theologie und Kirche*, draw together fundamental essays in ecclesiology in an approach that looks at the church developing. How should it exist today? Volume 1 treats ecclesiological aspects of faith, tradition, dogma, and grace before it turns to the church as universal sacrament and communion, two ecclesiologies drawn from dominant ideas of Vatican II. Volume 2 offers essays on the offices of bishop and deacon and on Jesus as head of the church and apostolic succession. Then theology reflects more on the life of an active church in today's societies with studies on grace and secular culture, the church and modern processes of freedom and human rights, and, finally, the church challenged by postmodernity.[9] These latter essays treat new concrete topics, although most of the chapters reflect anew on traditional areas of dogmatic theology with some contemporary attention to the individual in the church.

4. Directions for Today

The Tübingen theologian destined his ecclesiological research and reflection for the church of the present time. His writings, even those that are personal and spiritual, discuss the contemporary situation of ecclesial structures. "In the Western world, the priestly ministry and the concrete shape of the church in central and western Europe are in a dramatic period of upheaval."[10] The Catholic Church is witnessing the end of an old order, and even more it is witnessing new beginnings, sometimes hidden ones. "Not everyone has yet grasped the full extent of the upheaval, the challenge, and the new missionary orientation of pastoral work."[11] Forces outside the church pursuing human development as well as a wider study of the Gospel within the church lead to change. "Twenty years after the council, all these questions [about pluralism in the church] are still controversial in many respects."[12]

"Today" means after the Second Vatican Council. Nonetheless, the inception of this newness arrived prior to the council. "The outstanding event in the Catholic theology for our century is doubtless the overcoming of Neo-Scholasticism."[13] Inner-theological and extra-theological reasons for this shift are multiple rediscoveries: scripture as the animating principle of theology, the riches of early theologians, the true value of the thought of Thomas Aquinas and the liturgy. Also influential in this new ecclesial era are ecumenism and the presence of non-European cultures as well as a will to set aside facile estrangements between the church and modern culture. "Theology is always part of the culture of its time and of the region to which it belongs."[14]

In the opening of his *Theologie und Kirche*, volume 1, from 1987, Kasper observes that beginning with Schelling's later philosophy a fundamental characteristic of our post-idealist situation has been the growing awareness of the facticity and contingency of reality.[15] This means that the forms of the church are not capable of being deduced, not even easily or fully seen. Tradition itself has returned from being contained in books to being a varied organic life of the community. Meanwhile, ecclesiology inevitably moves into the concrete and the practical; it takes into account people's social experience of problems involved. New forms of ecclesial life will have to be accepted on their own terms. They are not subdivisions of administration or law and not illustrations of some spirituality.

5. Toward a New Theology of the Papacy

In Walter Kasper's writings, the priest, bishop, and pope are recurring themes. Let us look briefly at his theology of the papacy and then at his theology of the entire church as active.

There is no lack of studies by Kasper on the papacy. *Wozu noch einen Papst?* (*Why Still a Pope?*) from 1993 notes the emotional discussions circling around the figure and the ministry of the pope. The papacy's future involves three realities: service as the indispensable format; freedom as an unavoidable aspect of the future; the future of the papacy as the future of new forms. Is linking freedom to the future of the papacy surprising? Freedom is the milieu of modernity. People living from the nineteenth to the twentieth centuries have set aside the old structures of dominance. God's gift of human freedom is a presupposition for freedom under the New Law. "The Kingdom of God is simultaneously the kingdom of the freedom of the children of God; all external forms of mediation are subject to it."[16] Social freedom points to a freedom in Christ as well as to a liberation of human beings, and so freedom for the church and for ecclesial structures are related to the personal and social worlds of people living today. Freedom is open to grace, and grace empowers a multiple vitalization of the human person.

In terms of the papacy, Kasper ponders spirit, *Geist*, in its several meanings: "Church and Petrine office are to be first understood pneumatologically: as realities that historically have been formed out of human spirit and can be understood only in the Spirit of God. In the Spirit of God again and again the new in its charismatic way must be realized. The Spirit is given to the church in general."[17] Several of his writings take up the theme of the papacy-in-crisis. If there is a *krisis*, it can become a *kairos*, a special moment of renewal. To accomplish this, the church should locate the Petrine ministry within what is essentially Christian, as a discipleship to Christ.[18] In the papacy, as in every church office, the authority of Jesus should take on a "kenotic form." This ministry too is service. In new external forms the modality of service eschewing power encounters global societies and networks of media. One should find in church office the liberating power of the example and teaching of Jesus.

6. Ministries in the Church

Human history, communal realities animated by the Holy Spirit, old and new forms and ministries—this is the current ecclesial milieu of the Roman Catholic Church.

The Catholic Church in North America after Vatican II gave up a solitary focus on a separate sacerdotal hierarchy for a focus on community-in-service. There has been a broad rediscovery and expansion of what has come to be known in English-speaking churches by the biblical word "ministry."

Kasper's book from 2001 *Leadership in the Church: How Traditional Roles Can Serve the Christian Community Today*[19] remains with the topics of the traditional offices and roles of deacon, priest, and bishop[20] and with apostolic succession. Kasper's collection of essays, *Die Kirche und ihre Ämter. Schriften zu Ekklesiologie* ("The Church and Its Offices: Writings in Ecclesiology"), however, goes further in its discussion of office and ministry.[21] Prior to essays on priest and bishop are studies on the ecclesial community: "Collegial Structures in the Church: The Theological Place of the Councils on the Common Apostolate"; "Office and Community"; and "Pastoral Ministries in the Community." Every theology of office "must begin with the fundamental equality of all the baptized and confirmed. A specific office has its own limits. The distinction between clerics and laity should never be the point of departure for determining the essence of the church but can only have a secondary significance."[22] The community with equality for all its members precedes later official distinctions. From this reality comes the mission of the church as shared by all who are baptized. "The challenge of preaching, liturgy, and responsibility for church unity comes to all Christians together and is a function of the church as a totality. The church as a totality is the proper bearer of the ecclesial mission of salvation and every individual, including pope, priest, bishop, or lay person can be effective only in community with the totality and as its instrument."[23] The church exists through multiplicity and history. "The church and its ordering cannot be treated as a closed system. It is an open system, while in a closed system the totality can be manipulated since each aspect is derived from a generality and controlled by it."[24] There is not just one office in the church; ordained and baptismal ministries are not extensions of papal power. The charismatic dimension coming from the Spirit counters this reductionist authoritarianism.[25]

Varied activities come from graced charisms. "Through the re-emphasis of the charismatic structure of the church, the relationship of office and community receive a quite new form."[26] This wider action does not flow from the old ecclesiologies of a common priesthood or an isolated charism; nor do new ministries come from an office, an *Amt* (German). The structure of the church is not dualistic but pluriform through a "fullness of charisms." Kasper says the relationships of office and charism—even delineating what is distinctive about the priesthood—is not easy to determine. Today there is "a breaking out, a diversification" of functions in the church. "The communality of responsibility by all and the specific responsibility of the individual requires a new church structure in which the unity and diversity of all charisms come to expression."[27]

Kasper's ecclesiology works to go beyond the model of charisms and the three offices inherited from medieval and baroque ecclesiologies and canon law. Does it go far enough? Does it reach the model of organic life with many ministries? That model from Pauline theology was reemployed by the Tübingen theologian Johann Adam Möhler, who saw it rooted in Schelling's philosophy. A century later it was rehabilitated by Yves Congar and Vatican II.[28] Kasper often uses "responsibility" as a vital aspect of all of the baptized. Does this word do justice to the many public kerygmatic and sacramental activities of men and women in the church? And is his presentation of "charism" as complementing office adequate for representing ordinary expanding ministries assumed by so many men and women?

7. The Church's Ministries and the American Church

The Catholic Church in the United States is inevitably drawn to the concrete, to the practical. After 1965, ministry in parishes and dioceses found realizations leading to a new model of sharing in the organic ministerial life of the church. There are today seventy-seven million Catholics in the United States, that is, Catholics registered in parishes.[29] While the number of diocesan priests has sunk drastically, there are engaged in 17,748 parishes thirty-eight thousand educated and paid ministers, "lay ecclesial ministers," who work twenty to fifty hours per week. These lay ecclesial ministers bring to the parish ministries for religious education, for youth and young adults, and for the sick; they develop areas of peace and justice and direct initiation into the church. Added to these lay leaders are thousands of volunteers for the liturgies and service organizations. This large expansion of ministers over forty years has produced an accompanying extension of theological education, a widespread offering of university courses, special programs, and workshops joined to a proliferation of journals, books, and newsletters.

Most ecclesiologists in North America regard the ministerial model of the strict line between clergy and laity or the duality of the three ordained offices, existing over against rare charisms, to be a framework that no longer corresponds to the church's life today. There is a new model of concentric circles. That format realistically depicts various ministries in community that is the body of Christ. Those ministries are kinds of service animated by the one Spirit; they hold differences but not ecclesial and pneumatic essential distinctions.[30] Kasper's *The Catholic Church: Nature, Reality and Mission* (2011) goes further in its long fifth chapter to express the concrete form of the church as communion.[31]

This theology of the church has remained through recent decades seminal and historical, encouraging and open. It certainly stands in opposition to ideologies fearing the pneumatic life of the baptized. "The church has itself a dialogistic constitution."[32] Concrete forms of ministry other than the three ordained ones are still emerging. In the future, decade after decade, Catholic Christians will be seeking forms, new and old. To further this movement, Walter Kasper will continue to bring into the future a theology of church-in-ministry as a facet of the life of the Holy Spirit in the church, as a realization of the Absolute in history.

Endnotes

1. Walter Kasper, *Das Absolute in der Geschichte. Philosophie und Theologie der Geschichte in der Spätphilosophie Schellings* (Mainz: Matthias-Grünewald, 1965); idem, *Gesammelte Werke*, Bd. 2, new ed. (Freiburg: Herder, 2010).

2. Kasper, *Das Absolute in der Geschichte*, 54. Kasper speaks of beneficial contacts with Schelling scholars like Xavier Tilliette and Walter Schulz. Kasper's work of Schelling ensured that he saw modernity as multifaceted and as potentially aiding theological reflection; see Walter Kasper, *The Catholic Church: Nature, Reality and Mission*, trans. Thomas Hoebel (New York: Bloomsbury T&T Clark, 2014), 7–8; idem, "Ermutigung zum Denken. Von der Unerlässlichkeit der Metaphysik für die Sache der Theologie," *Theologische Quartalschrift* 168 (1989): 257–71.

3. Kasper, *The Catholic Church*, 7.

4. Ibid.

5. Walter Kasper, *The Crisis of Change: Are Church and Theology Subject to Historical Laws?* (Chicago: Argus Communications, 1969), 7. See Walter Kasper and Gerhard Sauter, *Kirche. Ort des Geistes* (Freiburg: Herder, 1976); this book is an ecumenical dialogue in which Kasper and the Protestant Tübingen theologian Gerhard Sauter develop an ecumenical and biblical theology of the Holy Spirit as the source of new directions in a renewed ecclesiology.

6. Kasper, *The Crisis of Change*, 11.

7. Ibid., 14.

8. Walter Kasper, *Die Heilssendung der Kirche in der Gegenwart* (Mainz: Matthias-Grünewald, 1971).

9. Walter Kasper, *Theologie und Kirche*, Bd 2 (Mainz: Matthias-Grünewald, 1999).

10. Walter Kasper, "Priestly Life: *Krisis* and *Kairos*," in *A Celebration of Priestly Ministry: Challenge, Renewal, and Joy in the Catholic Priesthood* (New York: Crossroad, 2007), 16.

11. Ibid., 19.

12. Walter Kasper, *Theology and Church*, trans. Margaret Kohl (New York: Crossroad, 1989), 159.

13. Ibid., 1.

14. Ibid., 12. See Walter Kasper, "Die Kirche angesichts der Herausforderungen der Postmoderne," in *Theologie und Kirche*, 2:249–66.

15. Kasper, *Theology and Church*, 10.

16. Walter Kasper, "Dienst an der Einheit und Freiheit der Kirche. Zur gegenwärtigen Diskussion um das Petrusamt in der Kirche," in *Wozu noch einen Papst? Vier Plädoyers für das Petrusamt*, ed. Walter Kasper et al. (Cologne: Communio, 1993), 54.

17. Ibid., 53.

18. Ibid. In *The Catholic Church* (p. 327) Kasper anticipates "a complex and multi-layered crisis" in the church's future.

19. Walter Kasper, *Leadership in the Church: How Traditional Roles Can Serve the Christian Community* (New York: Crossroad, 2001).

20. See Kilian McDonnell, "Walter Kasper on the Theology and the Praxis of the Bishop's Office," *Theological Studies* 63 (2002): 711–29.

21. Walter Kasper, *Die Kirche und ihre Ämter, Schriften zur Ekklesiologie* 2 (Freiburg: Herder, 2007). For similar essays, see Kasper, *Leadership in the Church*.

22. Walter Kasper, "Amt und Gemeinde," in *Die Kirche und ihre Ämter*, 51. Much earlier, Walter Kasper and Hans Küng edited a volume of *Concilium* (vol. 74) titled *The Plurality of Ministries* (Freiburg and New York: Herder and Herder, 1972). Among its essays were John L. McKenzie, "Ministerial Structures in the New Testament," treating the variety of forms of ecclesial leadership and the roles of women in the church, and also Hervé LeGrand, "The Indelible Character and the Theology of Ministry," observing that over the centuries ordination and

priestly character became superior to the influence of the community and the charisms of the Holy Spirit.

23. Kasper, "Amt und Gemeinde."

24. Ibid., 53.

25. Kasper writes that there exists "an overemphasis of the authoritative and institutional aspects of the church, or as Yves Congar says, 'an overemphasis of structure over against the life of the church' "; see Walter Kasper, "Einführung. Aspekte gegenwärtiger Pneumatologie," in *Gegenwart des Geistes. Aspekte der Pneumatologie*, ed. Walter Kasper et al. (Herder: Freiburg, 1979), 19.

26. Kasper, "Amt und Gemeinde," 54.

27. Ibid., 55. Here, Kasper adds: "Many kinds of democratic forms can be present."

28. See Thomas F. O'Meara, "Beyond 'Hierarchology': Johann Adam Möhler and Yves Congar," in *The Legacy of the Tübingen School: The Relevance of Nineteenth-Century Theology for the Twenty-First Century*, ed. Donald J. Dietrich and Michael J. Himes (New York: Crossroad, 1997), 173–91.

29. See the recent survey from the Center for Applied Research in the Apostolate (CARA) at Georgetown University in Washington, DC. For a summary of this survey, see CARA, "The Changing Face of U.S. Catholic Parishes," *Origins* (August 18, 2011): 194–208.

30. See Edward P. Hahnenberg, *Ministries: A Relational Approach* (New York: Crossroad, 2003); Thomas F. O'Meara, *Theology of Ministry* (Mahwah, NJ: Paulist Press, 1999); William Cahoy, ed., *In the Name of the Church: Vocation and Authorization of Lay Ecclesial Ministry* (Collegeville, MN: Liturgical Press, 2013); Zeni Fox, ed., *Lay Ecclesial Ministry: Pathways toward the Future* (New York: Rowman & Littlefield, 2010); Donna Eschenauer and Harold D. Horrell, eds., *Reflections on Renewal* (Collegeville, MN: Liturgical Press, 2011); Richard R. Gaillardetz, *Ecclesiology for a Global Church: A People Called and Sent* (Maryknoll, NY: Orbis Books, 2008).

31. Kasper, *The Catholic Church*, 195–287.

32. Ibid., 143. One could study the emphases in Kasper's theology in terms of Christology and pneumatology to see how the humanity of Jesus, the Christ, and the prominence of the Holy Spirit accompany and draw out the ministerial life of men and women baptized into the body of Christ and acting within an ongoing incarnation.

CHAPTER 9

Dialogue, Communion, and Unity

Brian E. Daley, SJ

"Ecumenism" (Greek, "the whole inhabited world") is a word that has slipped into favor and out again over the years in surprising ways. Ecumenism, the process toward the attainment of unity among all Christian churches, increasingly gained momentum during the first seven decades of the twentieth century. But, for the last forty years, it has advanced in small though significant steps. Some of these steps occurred in part because of the leadership of Cardinal Walter Kasper. This chapter first gives a brief history of the ecumenical movement, after which it highlights some of Walter Kasper's contributions to ecumenism.

1. An Overview of the Ecumenical Movement

At the end of the nineteenth century, young Evangelical Christians enthusiastically promoted ecumenism as a goal for the churches. During the early 1900s, more and more Protestant Christians envisioned cooperation and united missionary work among the churches, based on their common discipleship to Jesus as the key to the successful evangelization of the world. Organizations such as the World Student Christian Federation and the YMCA/YWCA grew out of this desire of young, committed Christians to get the word of Christ out to the world "in this generation." Their zeal led to the formation of the (Protestant) International Missionary Council in 1910. This impulse toward united Christian action and also a foundation for this action in united Christian prayer and worship grew still more intense after the First World War. As a result, there occurred the ecumenical or "worldwide" Christian conferences "Life and Work" in Stockholm in 1925 and "Faith and Order" in Lausanne in 1927, a theologically and liturgically focused gathering, encouraged by Canterbury's Archbishop William Temple.

Ecumenism slowly took root outside the Protestant churches. At the start, some Orthodox leaders, most notably the Patriarch of Constantinople, were cautiously positive toward it. Most Catholic officials, however, voiced little or no support for it. In fact, Pope Pius XI warned against ecumenism. In his encyclical *Mortalium animos* (January 6, 1928), Pius XI brands the new efforts at inter-Christian dialogue and cooperation as the "dangerous fallacies" of a trendy "pan-Christianity" that would result in "indifferentism"[1] and a general watering down of doctrinal commitment. He observes that a single, unified church has long existed under the pastoral guidance of the Bishop of Rome, and he declares that the only solution to Christian disunity and competition is "the return of the dissidents to the one true Church of Christ which, in the past, they so unfortunately abandoned."[2] In particular, the pope explicitly forbids Catholics from participating in ecumenical conversations with Orthodox or Protestants. "It is clear," he declares, "that the Apostolic See cannot on any terms take part in their assemblies, nor is it anyway lawful for Catholics either to support or to work for such enterprises; for if they do so, they will be giving countenance to a false Christianity, quite alien to the one Church of Christ."[3] In short, given Pius XI's ecclesiology, Christian unity is to be found only in the deliberate return of non-Catholic Christians to Roman obedience.

Despite Pope Pius XI's prohibition, much in the Catholic Church's thought and language concerning ecumenism radically changed by the mid-1960s and during the era inaugurated by the Second Vatican Council. Beginning in the 1920s, Catholic monks and scholars discreetly established informal, unofficial contacts with their Orthodox and Protestant counterparts. These Catholic pioneers included the Benedictine scholar Dom Lambert Beaudoin in Belgium and the French group *Les Dombes*, beginning in 1937. In that same year, the French Dominican theologian Yves Congar published his classic study *Chrétiens désunis: principes d'un "oecuménisme" catholique* ("Divided

Christendom: Principles of a Catholic 'Ecumenism'"). By the last years of Pius XI's pontificate, there had begun a more open Catholic theological reflection on the intrinsic need for a visible unity among all Christians, based on scripture and the church's nature as a eucharistic communion. After the Second World War, Pope Pius XII and Vatican officials cautiously encouraged "spiritual ecumenism," a phrase that Cardinal Kasper often employs (see below). That is, the pope and other church leaders urged Catholics both to take part in common prayer for unity among Christians and also, in Pius XII's words, "to extend a helping hand to all those sincerely seeking after the truth" as a manifestation of the Holy Spirit's transforming work within us.[4]

When Pope John XXIII officially announced on Christmas day 1961 a new ecumenical or worldwide council of the Catholic Church, he singled out ecumenism as he named the three principal goals for the council's deliberations: the better internal ordering of the church itself, *the promotion of visible unity among all Christians*, and the active engagement of the Catholic Church in working for world peace. Beginning in October 1962, the Second Vatican Council engaged in a reformulation of the church's self-understanding and its expression of that self-understanding in its worship and structure of life and governance. The council pursued this reformulation in the light of the church's long tradition, its interpretation of "the signs of the times," and its involvement with the political, social, and religious world of its day, including secular society and other Christian bodies. During its deliberations, Vatican II came to hold that ecumenism is not a temptation to ecclesial infidelity but rather one of the Catholic Church's first priorities. In order to promote the unity of all Christians, the council set forth ecumenism's theological foundations and guiding pastoral principles in its Decree on Ecumenism, *Unitatis redintegratio*.

During the fifteen years following the council, ecumenism was clearly in fashion among Christians, including Catholics. Formal bilateral and multilateral conversations or "dialogues" sprang up on the local, national, and international levels among believers of every description. In North America, ordinary Catholics were not always able to define or even to pronounce the word "ecumenism," but they knew that ecumenism is one of the things that a modern Catholic should care about. The euphoria of the early postconciliar years manifested itself in the dramatic gestures of mutual openness and in the charismatic words of commitment to visible reunion on the part of church leaders like Patriarch Athenagoras and Pope Paul VI as well as Willem Visser 't Hooft and Archbishop Michael Ramsey.

In the 1980s, however, a certain weariness or disillusionment seemed to settle in. Ecumenical meetings gradually tapered off into a polite but inert theological truce, marked by the repetitious drone of meetings with the mouthing of familiar phrases and the writing of minutes. Although the ideal of the reunion of Christians remained exciting, the drudgery of working toward it, step by step, seemed to take longer and to be less productive than everyone had at first hoped. Since the mid-1980s, a widespread resignation to the status quo in almost every church has increasingly replaced the initial energy and commitment to speak of and work toward Christian unity as an ideal. The World Council of Churches has more or less openly acknowledged that Christians could better use their energies to work together toward common, attainable political and social objectives, apart from strictly ecclesial or theological concerns.

Commenting on this current state of affairs, Cardinal Kasper has observed that ecumenism has moved from the energy of a sometimes wild "springtime" to "a phase of hibernation." The churches have radically scaled back the goals that Christians in dialogue initially envisioned and pursued.[5] In the mid-1960s, ecumenists dreamed of reaching the goal of Christians' "reconciled diversity" in faith and practice, a unity-in-difference analogous to the sameness and difference of "persons" in the Trinity.[6] But things have changed. Kasper writes:

> There is today a widespread interpretation that this [unity-in-difference] means that unity only requires an agreement on the fundamental understanding of the Gospel, and that church communion does not rule out differences in understanding of ministries, in institutional forms and in confessions of faith, which are sometimes even contradictory. . . . Thus, one should more properly speak of an *unreconciled* diversity and a *union* of Churches without real *unity* rather than of a reconciled diversity. Visible unity has been replaced by peaceful co-existence and friendly co-operation, full communion by intercommunion.[7]

We stand today far from the theological, pastoral, and sacramental convergence that ecumenical leaders envisioned in their activities and documents fifty years ago. In Kasper's judgment, the ecumenical movement is now in "an intermediary stage."[8] What the future holds remains unknown.

2. The Ecumenical Achievements of Cardinal Kasper

After a distinguished career, first as professor of theology and then as bishop of Rottenburg-Stuttgart, Walter Kasper was made secretary of the Pontifical Council for Promoting Christian Unity in 1999. Two years later, he was named a cardinal and promoted to be the council's president. To consider, in this brief space, his achievements in promoting the unity of Christians in the name of the Catholic Church, we can offer only a few highlights as a summary.

(1) *Ecumenism in Action*

On the practical side, we must point to Walter Kasper's long involvement in the international dialogue between Lutheran and Catholic theologians that culminated in the unprecedented "Joint Declaration on the Doctrine of Justification," received and signed by official representatives of the two Christian communities on October 31, 1999. This significant event occurred just as the then-Bishop Kasper was moving to Rome to work full time in the Pontifical Council for Christian Unity.

Further, as a member of the North American Orthodox-Catholic Consultation, I must also point to his quiet but urgent work with Metropolitan John Zizioulas of the Patriarchate of Constantinople to restart, in the fall of 2006, the stalled International Orthodox-Catholic Joint Consultation, which had once seemed so promising but whose efforts had tragically broken down in 2000. In these and so many other theological dialogues, as well as in countless visits, receptions, messages, and steady advice, Cardinal Kasper's warm, learned, judicious presence at the Pontifical Council for Christian Unity has not only kept Christian dialogue alive during this time of "hibernation" but also roused it to new energy.

(2) *Ecumenism in Theology*

On a more theological level, Kasper has provided us with a wealth of articles and addresses, as well as a pastoral guide to ecumenical engagement by Christians in his *Handbook of Spiritual Ecumenism*

(2006). This set of texts lays out a clear, doctrinally well-grounded vision for the growth of the churches toward a real unity that has yet to be achieved. Let me sketch out briefly three of the main themes articulated within this vision.

a. Ecclesiology toward Ecumenism. Cardinal Kasper emphasizes in a number of his essays that the most widespread obstacle to Christian unity is the lack of an ecumenically accepted *ecclesiology*, that is, the absence of a common, mainstream Christian understanding of what the church really *is*.

For many Christians of a more evangelical orientation, "the church" is simply a collective designation for all who confess Jesus as Lord, much as "secular society" might simply point to all humans in their nonreligious identity. Other Christians conceive of the church in a more concrete, structured way, understanding by it a particular gathering of believers in the world, with particular forms of authority and worship, particular doctrinal foundations, and particular understandings of the role and interpretation of scripture in Christian life. As Pope Pius XI and his theological advisors in 1928 stated in *Mortalium animos*, "the church" simply designates what modern Catholics had come to accept in the West:

> Christ our Lord instituted His Church as a perfect society, external of its nature and perceptible to the senses, which should carry on in the future the work of the salvation of the human race, under the leadership of one head (see Matt 16:18 and par.), with an authority teaching by word of mouth (see Mark 16:15) and [leading] by the ministry of the sacraments, [which are] the founts of heavenly grace (see John 3:5; 6:48-59; 20:22-23; Matt 18:18; etc.). . . . It follows then that the Church of Christ not only exists to-day and always, but is also exactly the same as it was in the time of the Apostles.[9]

Since the 1930s, theologians and church officials in the Catholic, Orthodox, and (to varying degrees) Protestant churches have moved steadily toward a less formal, more interpersonal, and more historically contextualized way of conceiving the totality of the Christian faithful.[10] Based on the biblical image of the body of Christ (1 Cor 12:12-30), this ecclesiology conceives of the church as a *communio*, a communion, in which there exists a sharing of life and interests that is rooted in a shared faith in the Gospel of Christ, a shared living tradition, and a shared liturgical celebration of the sacraments of baptism and the Eucharist. All of these forms of sharing make it possible for members of the church to participate in the very life of God, through the gift of the Holy Spirit. It is this understanding of the church that comes to the fore in the ecclesiological documents of the Second Vatican Council.[11]

In this ecclesiology, each community of baptized faithful who gather to hear the Word of God proclaimed by an ordained minister and to share in the eucharistic gift of Christ *is the church* in its catholic fullness, provided this community remains consciously in continuity with the apostolic faith and is in direct contact through prayer, obedience, and mutual concern with the rest of the body of Christ.[12] In the distinctively Catholic understanding of *communio*, elaborated at and since the council, the church's universal dimension is expressed and made possible by the communion of each local church (e.g., a parish) with its bishop and by the universal communion of Catholic bishops with each other and the Bishop of Rome.[13] The chief role of the Bishop of Rome, the pope, in the universal church is to promote its unity in faith and sacrament as well as to be the "watchman" and the servant of worldwide communion.[14]

In 1992, the Vatican's Congregation for the Doctrine of the Faith, led at that time by Cardinal Joseph Ratzinger, issued a document with the somewhat tentative title *Communionis notio*, that is, "On Some Aspects of the Church Understood as Communion." This text represents in rich detail the modern Catholic approach to an ecclesiology of communion. In a passage that seems to present this notion in a way particularly characteristic of Joseph Ratzinger's theology, the document states:

> In order to grasp the true meaning of the analogical application of the term *communion* to the particular Churches taken as a whole, one must bear in mind above all that the particular Churches, insofar as they are "part of the one Church of Christ" (Vatican II, *Christus Dominus* 6), have a special relationship of "mutual interiority" with the whole, that is, with the universal Church, because "in every particular Church the one, holy, catholic and apostolic Church of Christ is truly present and active" (CD 11). For this reason, "the universal Church cannot be conceived as the sum of the particular Churches, or as a federation of particular Churches" (Pope John Paul II, address to US bishops, 1987). It is not the result of the communion of the

> Churches, but, in its essential mystery, it is a reality *ontologically and temporally* prior to every *individual* particular Church.[15]

As these sentences express, *Communionis notio* explicitly holds that the universal church is "ontologically and temporally prior to" each local church. According to some church officials and theologians, however, this claim stands in need of qualification, of greater nuance. As written, it seems both to relegate the local churches to a secondary or subordinate status and also to neglect the history of the local churches in relation to the universal church.

As president of the Pontifical Council for Christian Unity, Cardinal Kasper presented a more complex understanding of the relationship between the local churches and the universal church. In a long article, written a decade after *Communionis notio*, Kasper articulates a precise list of the paradoxes of an ecclesiology of communion, anchored in the documents of Vatican II. For example, referring to *Lumen gentium* (LG), he writes:

> Although every local Church is fully Church (LG 26, 28), it is not the whole Church. The one Church exists in and out of the local Churches (LG 23), but the local Churches also exist in and out of the one Church (*Communionis notio* 9); they are shaped in its image (LG 23). Thus local Churches are not subdivisions, simple departments, emanations or provinces of the one Church; but neither is the one Church the sum of local Churches, nor just the result of their association, their mutual recognition. The one Church is real in the *communio* of local Churches, it is a *communio ecclesiarum*; but unity does not grow out of communication—it is pre-given. Taking both together, this means that the one Church and the diversity of local churches are simultaneous; they are interior to each other (perichoretic).[16]

In 2005, Cardinal Kasper again wrote about the relationship between the local churches and the universal church. In this text, he sums up in a balanced, carefully nuanced way the unique reality of a local church understood primarily as *communio* and manifested in a privileged way in the eucharistic liturgy:

> Eucharistic ecclesiology is the basis not of the independence of the local churches but of their interdependence, or more precisely, of their *perichoresis*, that is, of their mutual compenetration [*sic*]. Accordingly, the recent ecclesiology of *communio* understands

> the unity of the Church as a unity of *communion*. Her unity is not the result of a logically posterior unification of local Churches; nor do the local Churches come into being by derivation from the universal Church. The unity of the Church is not to be understood on the lines of an empire or a federation: it is a reality *sui generis*. Just as the universal Church exists only in and out of local Churches, so the local Churches in turn exist only in and out of the universal Church. (See LG 23.)[17]

As Kasper conveys, the reality of the *communio* that is the church is already present among Christians in the Gospel faith that we all share and in the common reality of our baptism, which makes us all members of Christ's body.[18] Christians experience pain and puzzlement, however, at the fact that this foundation of communion is not brought to its natural fullness: we do not yet share the Eucharist sacramentally with each other on a regular basis, even though that is the full expression and continuing nourishment of our unity. Kasper explains: "One of the reasons (but by no means the only one) is that dialogue documents may show convergence about the concept of *communio*, but on closer inspection different understandings are hidden behind the term. The common concept of *communio* has different meanings and thus calls forth different expectations and projected goals."[19]

Still, there is much promise in the fact that so many Christians now are coming to consider *communio*—that is, our common sharing of the Word and of the sacramental and social reality of salvation—as the core of the church itself. This widespread conviction makes it all the more urgent that ecumenism keep striving for what the famous statement of the World Council of Churches at New Delhi in 1961 proposes as its ideal of Christian unity: that "all in each place who are baptized into Jesus Christ and confess him as Lord and Savior are brought by the Holy Spirit into one fully-committed fellowship, holding the one apostolic faith, preaching the one Gospel, breaking the one bread, joining in common prayer, and having a corporate life reaching out in witness and service to all." Anything short of this vision is not true Christian unity.

b. Personal Transformation toward Ecumenism. Another theme that recurs in Cardinal Kasper's writings on ecumenism is his insistence that unity among the churches must begin, like all institutional renewal, as a *change within ourselves*: the change of our own views and our own actions toward a deeper assimilation of the Gospel. This emphasis on the need of personal change within us, if ecumenical progress is to happen, appears clearly in Vatican II's Decree on Ecumenism: "Every renewal of the church essentially consists in an increase of fidelity to her own calling. . . . There can be no ecumenism worthy of the name without interior conversion. For it is from the newness of attitudes of mind, from self-denial and unstinted love that desires of unity take rise and develop in a mature way."[20]

Cardinal Kasper develops this theme pointedly in his essay on "The Current Situation in Ecumenical Theology":

> Ecumenism is no one-way street, but a reciprocal learning process or—as stated in the encyclical *Ut Unum Sint*—an exchange of gifts. The way to it is therefore not a simple return of the others into the fold of the Catholic Church. In the ecumenical movement the question is the conversion not only of others but of all to Jesus Christ. Conversion always begins with ourselves. We Catholics too must be ready for an examination of conscience, self-criticism and repentance. As we move nearer to Jesus Christ, in him we move nearer to one another.[21]

This simple observation, with which most people involved in ecumenical conversation would readily agree, still seems distant from the actual mind-set of many of the theologians and church officials who engage in ecumenical dialogue. In my experience, along with our desire to communicate our own traditions faithfully and to find analogies and similarities with the traditions of those who still do not share the life of the Church with us, there always lurks an unspoken agenda of defense in ecumenical encounters. There operates a fear of unintentionally making concessions that will give away something essential to church life as we experience it in our own present theory and practice. Since the future is unknown and unpredictable, we feel the need to stay safe by protecting what we consider our treasures. As a result, our desire to preserve the status quo in substance can take precedence over our desire to grow closer with others in Christ. We speak the language of longing "that all may be one," but we tend to understand that unity only in our own present terms.

Engaging in genuine ecumenical dialogue involves committing ourselves to the risk that we will all become different in the process. And, this step is a risk that is very hard for any of us to take without the emboldening gift of the Spirit. As Cardinal Kasper reminds us, "the greater ecumenical unity for which we hope will [rightly] be the 'old' Church, indeed—but the 'old' Church in a new form."[22]

c. "Spiritual Ecumenism." Cardinal Kasper's awareness of our human tendency not to risk change may be the real reason why his writings on ecumenical dialogue emphasize that any genuine movement of Christians toward real communion must begin in the work of the Holy Spirit who alone forms disciples into the body of Christ. He observes that ecumenical progress between the churches (*ad extra*) presupposes the "inner ecumenism" of learning from each other within our own particular church (*ad intra*) and letting that openness reshape us.[23] In this regard, he remarks: "Such a conversion is also a gift of grace. So in the end it is not we who 'make' and create unity. The unity of the Churches is the gift of God's Spirit which has been solemnly promised to us. Therefore theological ecumenism must be linked to *spiritual ecumenism*, which is the heart of ecumenism."[24]

According to the cardinal, "spiritual ecumenism"—which he also occasionally refers to as "the ecumenism of life"[25]—is a gift of the unifying and sanctifying Spirit. It begins not so much in formal meetings, papers, and agreed statements but in the Christian experience of friendship, "in groups of friends where people share their lives with one another." Commenting on Vatican II's Decree on Ecumenism, *Unitatis redintegratio* (UR), he writes: "The Second Vatican Council calls spiritual ecumenism the soul of the ecumenical movement (UR 8). The council lists the following elements: personal conversion; sanctification of one's life; mutual forgiveness instead of continually reproaching the other side for its past errors; purification of the memory in view of the mistakes committed by one's own side; humble service and selfless love (UR 6–9)."[26]

In his *Handbook of Spiritual Ecumenism*, Cardinal Kasper develops this exhortation into a set of guidelines for pastors and laypersons concerned to promote reconciliation among Christians. In 2006 he wrote the *Handbook* in response to a request from the bishops serving on the Pontifical Council for Promoting Christian Unity that he write a practical guide for the ecumenically minded faithful of all the churches. Thus, in *Handbook*, he offers simple theological reflections and concrete suggestions for ways in which Christians—even in our present, ecumenically "intermediate" situation—might pray together, study scripture together, and make our common elements of liturgical life and our desire for full sacramental unity understandable to each other. Moreover, he also advises how we can harness the energies of parishes, monastic and religious communities, lay movements, and young people's groups to work together now in oneness of spirit. Significantly, before making his proposals, he reminds us that spiritual ecumenism, "indeed every act of spiritual communion, is a gift of the Holy Spirit, who binds us together and enables us to give visible expression to our Lord's desire for unity."[27]

The notion of spiritual ecumenism, which Cardinal Kasper fostered during his years as president of the Council for Christian Unity, did not fall from the sky. This recognition that the reunion of the churches must be the work of God's Spirit, enlivening hearts of faith and charismatically guiding church leaders of courage and vision, clearly has its roots in a long tradition. It was originally popularized by the great ecumenical pioneer Benedictine Abbé Paul Couturier. Also, it bore charismatically inspired fruit in 1964 when, after centuries of frosty silence on both sides, Patriarch Athenagoras of Constantinople undertook the prophetic action of boldly inviting Pope Paul VI to meet him in Jerusalem in December of that year in order to begin the "dialogue of love" between the Orthodox and Catholic churches. The patriarch's initiative was immediately and warmly accepted in Rome. As a result, the two primates met and embraced in Jerusalem. Further, they solemnly cancelled the mutual excommunications that their predecessors through representatives had pronounced in 1054 against each other and their communions.

Almost three years later, Patriarch Athenagoras and Pope Paul VI continued their conversation in Rome. In doing so, they emphasized that progress toward reunion can be found only in the common study of our traditions and in the outpouring of God's gifts within us and within our churches. Their joint statement puts it clearly: "Every element which can strengthen the bonds of charity, of communion, and of common action is a cause for spiritual rejoicing and should be promoted; anything which can harm this charity, communion and common action is to be eliminated with the grace of God and the creative strength of the Holy Spirit."[28]

The fruitful dialogue between Patriarch Athenagoras and Pope Paul VI is spiritual ecumenism in a striking form. It was the bold gesture by two charismatic leaders who were emboldened by the spirit of renewal that was suddenly sweeping the world of their day.

They took the risk of talking to each other in order to attempt the even greater risk of love.

Writing about this event thirty-five years later, Cardinal Kasper observes: "Such unity is ultimately a gift of God's Spirit and a result of his guidance." Then, moving from the breakthrough of Patriarch Athenagoras and Pope Paul VI to his own work as the Vatican's chief ecumenical officer, he states:

> Therefore the *oikoumene* is not simply an academic or diplomatic matter; its soul and heart is spiritual ecumenism. It is precisely this aspect of spiritual ecumenism that our Pontifical Council for Promoting Christian Unity wants to stress in the future. For without such a soul, ecumenism becomes either soulless activism or merely an academic exercise in which the great majority of the faithful cannot take part; unable to understand what is at stake in the ecumenical dialogue, they become estranged and indifferent or even reject the whole thing, so that a real reception of the results in the body of the Church does not take place.[29]

3. Conclusion

After thirty years of being personally involved in the Orthodox-Catholic Consultation in North America and also of watching other ecumenical dialogues progress step by step, but ever more hesitantly, I am convinced that our greatest present need is for new, equally charismatic gestures of leadership toward unity from those who guide and oversee all our churches. Such bold gestures, inspired and guided by the Holy Spirit, will lead us beyond statements and formulations toward the reception of ecumenism in daily life.

Karl Rahner once observed that we are always a little afraid of the Holy Spirit.[30] Yet, we continue to invoke the Spirit, to call down the Spirit in humble *epiclesis*. We do this because we are aware that only so will our own created gifts be transformed into living signs that make real the body of Christ.

As we all wait for the coming of the Spirit, I for one am deeply grateful to Cardinal Walter Kasper for his wisdom, his patience, and his constant reminders that our own studied efforts to unify the churches have to begin with "spiritual ecumenism," with the "ecumenism of life," the ecumenism of prayer and friendship among Christians.

Endnotes

1. Pope Pius XI, *Mortalium animos* (January 6, 1928); on "indifferentism," see 4, 5, 9.

2. Ibid., 11.

3. Ibid., 8.

4. Pope Pius XII, "Instruction of the Holy Office *Ecclesia Catholica*" (1949): "The present time has witnessed in different parts of the world a growing desire amongst many persons outside the Church for the reunion of all those who believe in Christ. This may be attributed, under the inspiration of the Holy Spirit, to external factors and the changing attitude of men's minds, but above all to the united prayers of the faithful. To all children of the true Church this is a cause for holy joy in the Lord"; in *Documents on Christian Unity*, 4th series (1948–1957), ed. G. K. A. Bell (London: Oxford University Press, 1958), 22.

5. Walter Kasper, *That They May All Be One: The Call to Unity Today* (New York: Burns and Oates, 2004), 1.

6. See Walter Kasper, "The Joint Declaration on the Doctrine of Justification," in ibid., 122–35, 129.

7. Ibid., 3; emphasis added.

8. Walter Kasper, "Ecumenism of Life and Eucharistic Fellowship," in *Sacrament of Unity: The Eucharist and the Church* (New York: Crossroad, 2004), 62.

9. Pius XI, *Mortalium animos*, 6.

10. In recent decades, "eucharistic ecclesiology" has received attention in the Christian traditions: in Orthodox circles by Nicholas Afanassiev, Alexander Schmemann, John Zizioulas; in Catholic discussions by Yves Congar and Henri de Lubac and, more recently, Jean-Marie Tillard, Joseph Ratzinger, and Walter Kasper; among German Protestants by Paul Althaus and Dietrich Bonhoeffer. See the excellent survey by Walter Kasper, "*Communio*: The Guiding Concept of Catholic Ecumenical Theology," in *That They May All Be One*, 50–74, esp. 57–60.

11. See Vatican II, *Lumen gentium* (November 21, 1964), 13, 23; *Unitatis redintegratio* (November 21, 1964), 2.

12. See Cardinal Joseph Ratzinger and the Congregation for the Doctrine of the Faith, "On Some Aspects of the Church Understood as Communion," *Communionis Notio* (1992), 9.

13. Ibid., 11–13.

14. See Pope John Paul II, *Ut unum sint* (*On Commitment to Ecumenism*) (May 25, 1995), 88–96.

15. Ratzinger, "On Some Aspects of the Church Understood as Communion," 9.

16. Kasper, "*Communio*: The Guiding Concept," 68. Cf. Ratzinger, "On Some Aspects of the Church Understood as Communion."

17. Walter Kasper, "Eucharist—Sacrament of Unity: The Essential Connection between Eucharist and Church," in *Sacrament of Unity*, 140.

18. Kasper, *Sacrament of Unity*, 51. See idem, *A Handbook of Spiritual Ecumenism* (Hyde Park, NY: New City Press, 2007), 9–15.

19. Kasper, *Sacrament of Unity*, 52.

20. Vatican II, *Unitatis redintegratio*, 6–7. Pope John Paul II develops this theme in *Ut unum sint*, 15–16.

21. Kasper, *That They May All Be One*, 17. See idem, "The Nature and Purpose of Ecumenical Dialogue," in *That They May All Be One*, 33–49. On page 44, Kasper writes: "Ecumenism *ad extra*, the dialogue with other Churches and ecclesial communities, presupposes therefore ecumenism *ad intra*, learning from each other and self-reform. Full convergence cannot be achieved by convergence alone, but also, and perhaps even more, by conversion which implies repentance, forgiveness and renewal of heart."

22. Kasper, "Eucharist—Sacrament of Unity," 146.

23. Kasper, *Sacrament of Unity*, 52.

24. Kasper, "The Nature and Purpose of Ecumenical Dialogue," 44; emphasis mine.

25. Since at least 2006, this phrase has been used by ecumenists of different churches in their speeches and writings; see Ivana Noble's report in *Signalia*, the newsletter of the Societas Ecumenica (July 2007).

26. Kasper, "Ecumenism of Life and Eucharistic Fellowship," 76.

27. Kasper, *A Handbook of Spiritual Ecumenism*.

28. Pope Paul VI and Patriarch Athenagoras, "A Common Declaration of his Holiness Pope Paul VI and the Ecumenical Patriarch Athenagoras I" (October 28, 1967).

29. Kasper, *That They May All Be One*, 17.

30. Karl Rahner, "Angst vor dem Geist. Gedanken zum Pfingsten," in *Chancen des Glaubens* (Freiburg: Herder, 1971), 52–57.

CHAPTER 10

The Catholic Tübingen School and Ecumenism

Catherine E. Clifford

No study of the Catholic Tübingen School and its influence on contemporary ecumenism would be complete without acknowledging the profound influence of Johann Adam Möhler, in particular, his two pioneering works *Die Einheit in der Kirche* (1825), titled in English *Unity in the Church, or the Principle of Catholicism Presented in the Spirit of the Church Fathers of the First Three Centuries*,[1] and *Symbolik* (1832), titled in English *Symbolism: Exposition of the Doctrinal Differences between Catholics and Protestants as Evidenced in their Symbolical Writings*.[2] Cardinal Walter Kasper acknowledges the decisive influence of Möhler's thought in a brief intellectual autobiography found at the outset of his most recent work, *The Catholic Church: Nature, Reality and Mission*.[3]

This chapter highlights the ecclesiology of Johann Adam Möhler and its significance for Walter Kasper's ecclesiology and ecumenical thought.

1. The Emergence of Contemporary Catholic Ecclesiology

The principles of the Catholic Tübingen School—that is, of a theology that is at once ecclesially conscious, scientifically rigorous, and historically minded—were instilled in Walter Kasper by his teacher Josef Rupert Geiselmann, the editor of the critical edition of *Symbolik*[4] and the foremost scholar on Möhler's work.[5] Kasper notes further that his teachers Heinrich Fries and Gottlieb Söhngen introduced him to the thought of Cardinal John Henry Newman, himself influenced by the methods of the Catholic Tübingen School, deepening his understanding of the historicity and development of dogma.

According to Kasper, Möhler and Newman are rightly considered the pioneers of twentieth-century Catholic ecclesiology, whose thought was received by the whole church in the Second Vatican Council.[6] In his 1962 doctoral thesis, *Die Lehre von der Tradition in der Römischen Schule* ("The Doctrine of Tradition in the Roman School"),[7] Kasper explores the complex reception of the thought of the Catholic Tübingen School, whose insights were carried forward by the likes of the Roman School's Giovanni Peronne, Carlo Passaglia, Clemens Schrader, and Johann Baptist Franzelin. In mid-century, Passaglia produced a two-volume work, *De Ecclesia Christi*, which develops Möhler's Christological focus and centers on the church as the body of Christ. Möhler's insights bore fruit especially in the work of Matthias Josef Scheeben, *Mysterien des Christentums* (1865), titled in English *The Mysteries of Christianity*.[8] Scheeben had studied under Perrone and Passaglia at Rome's Gregorian University and later taught dogmatics in Cologne.

(1) *The Reception of Möhler's Ecclesiology*

Despite the wide-ranging influence of Möhler and Newman, the reception of their work was hindered in part by the turn of Catholic theology to neoscholasticism during the papacy of Leo XIII in the late nineteenth century and to a baroque controversialist theology in the anti-Modernist campaign launched by Pope Pius X at the beginning of the twentieth century. This was especially the case in the Roman School. Michael J. Himes writes: "The Tübingen theologians stood apart from much of the rest of Catholic theology in the nineteenth century by their criticism of the regnant Neo-Scholasticism, openness to modern philosophical thought, and emphasis on the importance of historical critical research. In a church whose theology tended to be ultramontanist, ahistorical, and intensely hostile to modern philosophy, the Tübingen School was suspect."[9]

Nonetheless, Möhler's thought in particular was to have a significant influence in many churches, and it can be said to have laid a foundation for the outworking of the theological principles that would ground Catholic ecumenical commitment in the Second Vatican Council. It might also be seen as providing, in broad strokes, a direction for the doctrinal dialogue that would ensue between the churches in the wake of Vatican II.

Among the Russian Orthodox, both Alexei Khomiakov[10] and Vladimir Soloviev[11] were influenced by Möhler's irenic approach. Peter C. Erb notes the influence of *Unity* on English-speaking Protestantism, in particular on the development of the American High Church movement within the Reformed Church known as "Mercersburg Theology." In England, adherents of the Tractarian Movement at Oxford, including Newman, drew inspiration from Möhler's *Unity*, although it was only translated into English for the first time in 1996.[12]

Many English speakers would have read the French translation of *Unity* first published in 1835.[13] Approximately one hundred years later in 1938, a new French edition of *Unity* was among the first volumes to be published in the Unam Sanctam collection, under the direction of Yves Congar. It was chosen for the Unam Sanctam collection so that it might contribute to "the restoration of a broad, rich, living notion of the church, filled with the vitality of the biblical and traditional sources, and to a re-education of the clergy and the faithful in accord with this notion."[14] Through the work of figures such as Yves Congar[15] as well as Karl Adam,[16] who taught in the Catholic Tübingen School prior to Geiselmann, Möhler's insights were carried forward into twentieth-century ecclesiology.

A first English translation of *Symbolism* was published in 1843.[17] Subsequently, in 1997, a new edition of this same translation was issued to coincide with the English translation of *Unity*.

(2) *Möhler's Theological Groundwork for Contemporary Ecumenism*

Given that most accounts date the beginnings of the modern ecumenical movement with the International Missionary Conference held at Edinburgh in 1910 and note that official Catholic ecumenical engagement dates only from the Second Vatican Council, it is striking to consider the ecumenical intent of Möhler's project in the context of the early nineteenth century. Confessional positions in the German lands had not yet been hardened by the Kulturkampf (1871–1880) of Otto von Bismarck. The young Möhler, prior to taking up his teaching position at Tübingen in 1823, spent several months travelling to other faculties—both Catholic and Protestant—to learn from their best practices and to "gain a knowledge of other confessions."[18] As Michael Himes observes, the Protestant theological schools "seem to have created a greater and more lasting impression on Möhler than did the Catholic."[19] He was so impressed by what he saw and heard that he became convinced of the need to develop a more sympathetic understanding of other Christian communions and their doctrines. In Möhler's words: "But with those from whom we differ on the plane of doctrine and before whom we defend that doctrine, since our differences must be based on conviction, we should come together on the plane of life. This seems to me conduct worthy of a Christian." He yearned for a day when genuine dialogue would be possible: "If only the two protagonists would speak to one another again."[20]

Encounters with the historians Gottlieb Jacob Planck and Johann August Neander, of the Protestant faculties at Göttingen and Berlin, respectively, would impress upon Möhler the importance of understanding doctrines, also known as "symbols," in their historical development and directed his attention to the study of the church fathers. Further, they led him to develop a series of lectures some years later on "comparative symbolics,"[21] which formed the basis for his extensive study of the confessional statements of the various Christian churches found in *Symbolism*.[22] This work, while it remains for the most part an *apologia* for Catholic doctrine, in attempting to present doctrinal differences in as impartial and irenic a manner as possible, also notes areas of fundamental doctrinal convergence, especially in the Christological and Trinitarian confession of faith found in the classical creeds, which Möhler did not hesitate to call "the common property of the separate churches."[23] He introduces his project by explaining: "It is of course to be understood, that instruction on these points of controversy must be imparted with utmost charity, conciliation, and mildness, with a sincere love of truth, and without any exaggeration, and with constantly impressing on the minds of men, however we be bound to reject errors (for the pure doctrine of Jesus Christ and the Gospel truth is the most sacred property of man), yet we are required by our Church to embrace all [people] with love for Christ's sake, and to evince in their regard all abundance of Christian virtues."[24]

Möhler put into practice the first and most basic principle of ecumenical conversation in presupposing the good faith that led his

Protestant dialogue partners to develop their respective positions. He writes: "I flattered myself that I might do something towards bringing about religious peace, by revealing a true knowledge of the great dispute; in so far as by this knowledge [people] must come to perceive that that contest sprang out of the most earnest endeavours of both parties to uphold the truth—the pure and genuine Christianity in all its integrity."[25]

Remarkably, when confronted by the critical reactions of Protestant readers, especially the critique of Ferdinand Christian Baur of the Protestant faculty of Tübingen,[26] Möhler undertook four separate revisions in order more accurately to represent Protestant positions and to formulate a Catholic response.[27] Despite its apologetic character, *Symbolism* stands as an important antecedent to twentieth-century forms of ecumenical dialogue and as a work well ahead of its time. It is no accident that many twentieth-century ecumenists appeal to Möhler, for he laid out much of the theological groundwork that would provide the theological bases for Catholic ecumenical engagement. This becomes evident when we consider Kasper's appropriation of Möhler's insights, particularly in Kasper's recent work on the church.

2. Möhler's Influence on Kasper's Ecclesiology and Ecumenical Thought

Johann Adam Möhler is among the most frequently cited authors in Cardinal Kasper's *magnum opus* on the church: *The Catholic Church: Nature, Reality and Mission.*[28] In the space remaining, I propose to draw attention to a number of the key areas where Möhler's influence is apparent in Kasper's reflection and to consider their significance for contemporary Catholic ecumenical engagement. A brief survey of Kasper's ecumenical thought reveals him to be an unmistakable heir to this leading representative of the early Catholic Tübingen School.

(1) *A Dynamic Understanding of Tradition*

Kasper's teacher Josef Geiselmann, appropriating Möhler's dynamic understanding of tradition, revolutionized Catholic thinking on the relationship between scripture and tradition. In particular, Geiselmann's critical study of the doctrine of Trent revealed that the widely accepted "two-source" or quantitative understanding of divine revelation, conceptualized as being contained "partly" in sacred scripture and "partly" in sacred tradition, was an inaccurate representation of conciliar teaching. In fact, the council fathers at Trent rejected a draft version of the conciliar decree that proposed such a two-source theory (*partim/partim*). Kasper notes the influence of Möhler and Johann Sebastian Drey, the founder of the Catholic Tübingen School, on Geiselmann's effort to recover a dynamic notion of revelation and tradition, one that took account of the sustaining presence and action of the Holy Spirit in guiding the living community of faith.[29]

The contribution of Geiselmann constitutes an important breakthrough for contemporary ecumenical understanding. In the discussion of the Faith and Order Commission in Montreal (1963) and in the Second Vatican Council's Dogmatic Constitution on Divine Revelation, *Dei verbum*, a more dynamic notion of revelation is adopted; one that considers revelation in more personalist terms and reflects a dynamic interdependence between scripture and tradition. Cognizant of the ecumenical implications of their teaching, and integrating the insights of contemporary scholarship, the council fathers at Vatican II rejected a draft schema on revelation that attempted to solemnize a "two-source" theory of revelation. In the context of Protestant reflection, the council's more dynamic understanding of the relationship of scripture and tradition also challenges sterile notions of the sufficiency of scripture.[30]

Briefly, Catholic and Protestant scholars came to agree that before being recorded in their written form, the content of scripture belonged to a living, oral tradition. Conversely, scripture continues to exist and is interpreted in the context of a living community of faith. A common reception of this dynamic understanding of scripture and tradition marked a significant advance in Catholic-Protestant understanding and opened the door for Catholics and Protestants to read the Bible together in a joint search for a common understanding of the Bible's meaning. In the field of ecclesiology, it prepared the way for a deeper appreciation of the continuing presence of the risen Christ through the action of the Holy Spirit in enlightening the life and understanding of the community nourished by his Word.

(2) *An Ecclesiology of Communion*

Perhaps the most significant contribution to the theological foundations of contemporary ecumenism is Möhler's focus on the "Mystery of Unity" in part 1 of *Unity*. His organic image of the church, whose life force is the Holy Spirit, and his conception of the Spirit's relationship to the life of each believer draws our attention to the mystery of the church as communion, whose spiritual reality—though never dissociated from its concrete realization in history—is primary. Diversity in the outer form or expression of the church—be it in theological expression, liturgical tradition, spirituality, or canonical structure and practice—need not be antithetical to genuine unity among the particular churches. The Second Vatican Council's embrace of an ecclesiology of communion, especially in its Dogmatic Constitution on the Church, *Lumen gentium* (LG), from its opening chapter on the "Mystery of the Church," penetrates beyond the visibly and structurally separated Christian churches to recognize the spiritual bonds that unite Catholics, in varying degrees, with other Christians within the messianic people of God, through the sacrament of baptism (LG 15; cf. *Unitatis redintegratio* [UR] 3, 4, 22, 23). Moreover, one can hear an echo of Möhler's thought in Kasper's insistence that the catholicity of the church, which entails a synergetic unity in diversity, is grounded in the communion of the tripersonal God. The mystery of the church is brought about through our participation in the life of God and the indwelling of God's Spirit within us.[31]

At the First Vatican Council (1869–1870) Franzelin and Schrader were the principal drafters of the initial schema on the church, a document whose central focus was the notion of "The Church as the Mystical Body of Christ." While this idea was not ripe for reception at Vatican I, it continued to make inroads through the works of Émile Mersch, Erich Przywara, Karl Adam, and others. The notion of the church as communion was recognized as a defining theme of the Second Vatican Council's ecclesiology by the 1985 extraordinary Synod of Bishops (at which Walter Kasper served as the theological secretary, appointed by Pope John Paul II). Reflecting on the reception of the council in this period, Kasper argues: "For the Church, there is only one way into the future: the way pointed by the Council, the full implementation of the Council and its communion ecclesiology."[32]

The theme of communion has since become a central focus of ecumenical dialogue. Following the publication in 1982 of the Faith and Order Commission's historic consensus statement *Baptism, Eucharist and Ministry*,[33] it became apparent that perhaps the most intractable areas of theological divergence among the churches revolve around differing conceptions of the church and its constitutive structure. Communion ecclesiology has provided a basis on which to work toward a common understanding of the church and the unity to which the churches are called. The emergence of communion ecclesiology is evidenced in the 1982 agreed statement of the Joint Theological Commission between the Roman Catholic and Orthodox Churches, "The Mystery of the Church and of the Eucharist and of the Eucharist in Light of the Mystery of the Holy Trinity."[34]

In 1984, the Lutheran-Catholic International Commission, a dialogue that Kasper would later co-chair, looked to the theme of fellowship or communion as an important way forward, citing the words of Cardinal Johannes Willebrands: "The deepening . . . of an ecclesiology of communion is . . . perhaps the greatest possibility for tomorrow's ecumenism. . . . So far as the reintegration of the Churches into unity is concerned, we have to follow the line of this ecclesiology, which . . . is both very ancient and yet very modern."[35]

The 1992 agreed statement of the Anglican–Roman Catholic Commission "The Church as Communion"[36] established a framework for subsequent dialogue on questions relating to moral life and the exercise of authority in the church. Many other dialogues have adopted a framework of communion ecclesiology.

From 1993 onward, the World Council of Church's Faith and Order Commission has given pride of place to an ecclesiology of communion in its attempt to develop a consensus statement on the Nature and Mission of the Church. This emphasis is evident in the recently released statement *The Church: Towards a Common Vision*, which from the opening lines presents the church as the sign and fulfilment of God's design for all creation:

> The dynamic history of God's restoration of *koinonia* [communion] found its irreversible achievement in the incarnation and paschal mystery of Jesus Christ. The Church, as the body of Christ, acts by the power of the Holy Spirit to continue his life-giving mission in prophetic and compassionate ministry and so participates in God's work of healing a broken world. Communion, whose source is the very life of the Holy Trinity, is both the gift by which the Church lives and, at the same time, the gift that God calls the Church to offer to a wounded and divided humanity in hope of reconciliation and healing.[37]

Regarding the notion of the church as communion, Kasper notes Möhler's influence on the recovery of the connection between the notion of the church as a mystery or sacrament of communion and notion of the church as a eucharistic community where the whole community is the active subject of the liturgical action.[38] As Kasper observes, this understanding is reflected in the Second Vatican Council's teaching that in the liturgy "complete and definitive public worship is performed by the mystical body of Christ, that is, by the Head and his members" (*Sacrosanctum concilium* 7). Elsewhere, the Constitution on the Sacred Liturgy, *Sacrosanctum concilium* (SC), presents the eucharistic assembly as the highest manifestation of the church (SC 41). This eucharistic ecclesiology also opens the way to understanding the universal church as communion of diverse local churches,[39] or of ecclesial unity as a unity in diversity.

In spite of these developments, Cardinal Kasper has noted a certain ambiguity with regard to treatment of communion in the context of contemporary ecumenical dialogue, especially in efforts to define the conditions for full visible unity. During his tenure as president for the Pontifical Council for Promoting Christian Unity, he noted: "The common concept of *communio* has different meanings and thus calls forth different expectations and projected goals. This necessarily leads to misunderstandings on one's own part and that of the partners. Convergence about one and the same concept, however, is also—apart from other factors—the cause for confusion. The differences in understanding reflect different ecclesiologies of the various churches and ecclesial communities."[40] From a Catholic perspective, the inner reality of communion is met with a corresponding outer expression of communion in the confession of one apostolic faith, in a sharing in the sacramental life, and in the bonds of authority or hierarchical communion. The goal of Catholic ecumenism is to move from the "real, but imperfect" communion we now confess with other churches and ecclesial communities (UR 3) to full communion.

(3) *Toward an Ecumenical Catholicity*

Möhler's explorations of ecclesial unity and doctrinal difference were an attempt to uncover the roots of antithetical doctrinal positions that had become fixed and contradictory. Möhler acknowledges that in their genesis the doctrines of the Reformers were not intended to be divisive but had been advanced in the hope of preserving the integrity of the Gospel. Nevertheless, he argues, the Reformers and their communities had been overtaken by "egoism" and taken themselves as the norm of catholicity and the measure of doctrinal orthodoxy.[41] Yet far from conceiving the restoration of unity in terms of uniformity, Möhler seems to envision the possibility of a reintegration of differing yet complimentary expressions of faith within the catholicity of the whole church.

In continuity with Möhler's view, Kasper has contributed to a significant advance in ecumenical recognition as a member of the dialogue between the Catholic Church and the Lutheran World Federation, which pioneered the methodology of "differentiated consensus," to uncover, behind differing emphases and expression, a common understanding of the basic truths pertaining to the doctrine of justification by faith. In his 1987 work *Theology and Church*, he sketches out in broad strokes the principles for recognizing the existence of a differentiated consensus, without, however, using the term, by appealing to Möhler's positive appreciation of "a pluriformity of complimentary positions." Kasper writes, "There can be no such unity in truth so long as one church condemns as contrary to the faith of the gospel the faith which another church confesses—as long, that is, as the anathema formulas stand between the churches, as in fact they still do today. But this does not mean that there could not be a plurality of theologies, spiritualities, church orders, and even creedal formulas, on the foundation of the one Holy Scripture and the one creed of the ancient church which all share and are binding on us all. The concept of unity in truth does not mean that the other churches have to adopt all the creedal formulas of the Catholic Church."[42]

It was, of course, a historic breakthrough when, through the application of these very principles, the Lutheran-Catholic "Joint Declaration on Justification by Faith" could declare that, in light of a consensus on the basic truths concerning justification, "the corresponding doctrinal condemnations of the sixteenth century do not apply to today's partner."[43] We have yet to measure the full weight of this agreement on the central church-dividing issue of the Protestant Reformation. One hundred and seventy years earlier, one of the central premises of Möhler's *Symbolism* had been that the crux of disagreement between Catholic and Protestant theological systems was to be found in the understanding of the original justice and holiness of Adam, the basis of the divine-human covenant realized in the incarnation. Where Möhler sought to expose two opposing ways of comprehending theological anthropology—that is, the fundamental relationship between God and humankind—the Lutheran-Catholic dialogue discovered complementary positions.

More recently, Cardinal Kasper has described the ecumenical task as a matter of overcoming the "confessionalism"[44] of the churches and of growth toward a more wholistic understanding of Catholicity, or an "ecumenical catholicity."[45] Already, he notes, a return to the common sources of the tradition have enabled the churches to overcome the hard lines of demarcation that once characterized a rigid and exclusive notion of catholicity. Genuine catholicity is a dynamic reality with a concrete historical form that opens out onto an eschatological horizon.[46] In recognizing the effective presence of many elements of sanctification and truth in other churches and ecclesial communities (LG 8; UR 3), and in acknowledging that in some cases these are better developed in other churches than in the Catholic community (UR 17), Vatican II embraced this broader and more ancient vision of catholicity.

Kasper observes that the responsibility of Catholic engagement in ecumenical dialogue is essential to the full realization of its own catholicity. The recognition that the one church of Christ is present and operative in other Christian churches and communities obliges the Catholic Church to recognize differing degrees or densities of participation in the *Una Catholica* beyond its institutional boundaries. The path toward ecclesial unity is therefore one of repentance, renewal, and reform on which all the churches must travel toward a fuller realization of their ecclesial nature.

3. The Need for a Symbolic/Doctrinal Theology Today

Another interesting point of intersection between Möhler's thought and Kasper's reflections on ecumenism can be found in the cardinal's comprehensive overview, titled *Harvesting the Fruits* (2009), of the consensus on a host of doctrinal questions that has emerged over the last half century of sustained ecumenical dialogue.[47] Looking to the future, Kasper points to the need for "a new Symbolic Theology," noting that there exist within the churches "a wide spectrum of interpretations" of the various confessional statements and their relationship to scripture and the early creeds. "Positions akin to the *History of Religions* school of thought have emerged, together with newer liberal, social, analytical, or post-modern positions. As a result," he observes, "our dialogue partners sometimes find it difficult to formulate their own position, and what constitutes their binding and obligatory doctrine."[48]

This topic raises the complex question of doctrinal authority, which must be faced by all the churches if we are to work toward consensus with confidence in the foundations of our separate and shared positions. Even with its elaborate magisterial tradition, Catholic theology is far from being in possession of an unambiguously clear understanding of the binding character of various forms of doctrinal expression—from the councils of the early church, to the medieval councils or those of more recent memory, to liturgies and catechisms, and on to the various forms of papal teaching and documents of the dicasteries (offices) of the Roman Curia.

There is an urgent need to clarify the weight and binding character of the various expressions of Christian doctrine in their relationship to the Word of God and the broader tradition.[49] This is a question that the churches would do well to explore together, in order that they might develop a greater consensus concerning the historicity of church teaching and other forms of church life, and to elaborate a common set of criteria for discerning their normativity. In their day, both Johann Adam Möhler and John Henry Newman questioned whether any age of history or historical form of the church could stand as a "norm" against which to measure subsequent expressions of teaching and ecclesial life.[50] The church, continually engendered by God's Spirit according to what Möhler called the "law of evolution," progresses in creative tension with the circumstances and demands of each new age.

Perhaps an important key to determining the normativity of creedal and confessional statements is to be found in their interdependence with the ecclesial consciousness or the *sensus fidelium* of the global Christian community, expressed in the dynamics of reception. These realities are far more complex and challenging to ascertain than ever in our age, given the cultural diversity of each worldwide confessional family. The reconciliation of the churches in a new age of global Christianity, however, must be grounded in the assurance of a diachronic and synchronic communion in faith.

Conclusion

In this brief overview, I have sketched in broad strokes the profound influence of the Catholic Tübingen School and, in particular, the work of Johann Adam Möhler in laying out a number of foundational theological principles that ground contemporary ecumenical engagement. A glimpse at the work of Cardinal Kasper in the areas of ecclesiology and ecumenism reveals the unmistakable imprint of Möhler's thought. Kasper himself has pointed to the significance of Möhler in the appropriation of a more dynamic understanding of tradition—including the interdependence of scripture and tradition—and for the recovery of the ancient ideal of the church as a communion. Together, the notions of the living tradition of faith and of the church as a local, eucharistic community have led to a rediscovery of the true sense of catholicity as a rich diversity in unity.

Finally, Kasper suggests that in Möhler's irenic study of the creeds and confessional statements of the churches we might find a model for a new form of symbolic theology today, one that might help to clarify the weight accorded by the churches to their respective affirmations of faith, including the great creeds that were once considered the binding and normative expression of common faith. The work of Möhler and of the Catholic Tübingen School can continue to inspire our efforts of ecumenical study today, as it has so clearly marked the work of Cardinal Walter Kasper.

Endnotes

1. Johann Adam Möhler, *Unity in the Church, or The Principle of Catholicism: Presented in the Spirit of the Church Fathers of the First Three Centuries*, trans. Peter C. Erb (Washington, DC: The Catholic University Press of America, 1996). Original: *Einheit in der Kirche oder das Prinzip des Katholizismus dargestellt im Geist der Kirchenväter der ersten drei Jahrhunderte* (Tübingen: Heinrich Laupp, 1825).

2. Johann Adam Möhler, *Symbolism: Exposition of the Doctrinal Differences between Catholics and Protestants as Evidenced in Their Symbolical Writings*, trans. James Burton Robertson (New York: Crossroad, 1997); this new edition includes an introduction by Michael J. Himes. Möhler's *Symbolik* was published in 1832,

then revised and expanded in 1833, 1834, 1835, and 1838. See the critical edition prepared by Josef Rupert Geiselmann, *Symbolik, oder Darstellung der dogmatischen Gegansätze Katholiken und Protestanten nach irhen öffentlichen Bekenntnisschriften*, 2 vols. (Cologne: Jakob Hegner, 1960–61).

3. Walter Kasper, *Katholische Kirche: Wesen—Wirklichkeit—Sendung* (Freiburg: Herder, 2011), 24–27. See idem, *The Catholic Church: Nature, Reality and Mission*, trans. Thomas Hoebel (London: Bloomsbury, 2014). All references are to the original German edition; my free translation.

4. See note 2 above.

5. See, for example: Josef Rupert Geiselmann, *Die Einheit der Kirche und die Wiedervereinigung der Konfessionen* (Vienna: Beck, 1940); idem, *Lebendiger Glaube aus geheiligter Überlieferung: Der Grundgedanke der Theologie Johann Adam Möhlers und der Katholischen Tübinger Schule*, 2 vols. (Freiburg: Herder, 1966); idem, *Die theologische Anthropologie Johann Adam Möhlers: Ihr geschichtliche Wandel* (Freiburg: Herder, 1955); idem, "Der Wandel des Kirchenbewusstseins und der Kirchlicheit in der Theologie Johann Adam Möhlers," in *Sentire Ecclesiam: Das Bewusstsein von der Kirche als gestaltende Kraft der Frömmigkeit*, ed. Jean Daniélou and Herbert Vorgrimler (Freiburg: Herder, 1961), 531–675.

6. Kasper, *Katholische Kirche*, 25; idem, *The Catholic Church*, 6.

7. Walter Kasper, *Die Lehre von der Tradition in der Römischen Schule: Giovanni Perrone, Carlo Passaglia, Clemens Schrader* (Freiburg: Herder, 1962).

8. Matthias Scheeben, *The Mysteries of Christianity*, trans. Cyril Vollert (New York: Crossroad, 2008; original: Freiburg: Herder, 1865–97). See Kasper, *Katholische Kirche*, 26, 107; idem, *The Catholic Church*, 7, 63. Kasper notes the influence of the Tübingen School, especially its best-known representative, Möhler, on the Russian Orthodox thinkers Alexei Khomiakov and Vladimir Soloviev and on John Henry Newman, a protagonist of the Anglo-Catholic movement within the Church of England who was received into the Catholic Church in 1845.

9. Himes, "Introduction," in Möhler, *Symbolism*, xiii.

10. Khomiakov published little during his lifetime, due to the climate under Tzar Nikolas. He introduced the notion of *sobornost* or "synodality" as a fundamental dimension of the church. See, especially, Alexei Khomiakov, *The Church Is One*, trans. Nicolas Zernov (London: Fellowship of St. Sergius and St. Alban, 1968). In 1958, this work appeared in French in the Unam Sanctam collection, with a presentation by Yves Congar.

11. Sometimes referred to as the "Russian Newman." See Thomas J. Gerrard, "Vladimir Soloviev—The Russian Newman," *Catholic World* 105, no. 627 (June 1917): 321–36; Michel d'Herbigny, *Vladimir Soloviev: A Russian Newman, 1853–1900*, trans. A. M. Buchanan (London: R & T Washbourne, 1918).

12. See the discussion and extensive documentation in Erb's introduction to Möhler, *Unity in the Church*, 1–71, at 61–66.

13. Johann Adam Möhler, *De l'Unité de l'Église; ou, du principe du catholicisme d'après l'esprit des pères des trois premiers siècles*, trans. Philippe Bernard (Tournai: Castermann, 1835).

14. Pierre Chaillet, "Introduction," in Johann Adam Möhler, *L'Unité dans l'Église; ou, Le principe du Catholicisme d'après l'esprit des Pères des trois premiers siècles*, Unam Sanctam 2, trans. André de Lilienfeld (Paris: Cerf, 1938). My free translation.

15. Yves M.-J. Congar, "Johann Adam Möhler 1796–1838," *Theologische Quartalschrift* 150 (1970): 47–51; idem, "Sur l'évolution de la pensée de Möhler," *Revue de sciences philosophiques et théologiques* 27 (1938): 204–12.

16. Karl Adam, *The Spirit of Catholicism*, trans. J. McCann (New York: MacMillan, 1929).

17. See above, note 2, concerning Möhler, *Symbolism*.

18. Michael J. Himes, *Ongoing Incarnation: Johann Adam Möhler and the Beginnings of Modern Ecclesiology* (New York: Crossroad, 1997), 46.

19. Ibid., 45.

20. Stefan Lösch, ed. *Johann Adam Möhler*, vol. 1: *Gesammelte Acktenstücke une Briefe* (Munich: Josef Kösel & Friedrich Pustet, 1928), 74; cited in Himes, *Ongoing Incarnation*, 46.

21. Himes, *Ongoing Incarnation*, 46.

22. Note on difficulties of translating this term; see Himes, "Introduction."

23. Möhler, *Symbolism*, 1–2.

24. Ibid., xxv.

25. Ibid., xxviii.

26. Ferdinand Christian Baur, *Der Gegensatz des Katholizismus und Protestantismus nach den Principien und Hauptdogmen der beiden Lehrbegriffe mit besonderer Rücksicht auf Herrn Dr. Möhler's Symbolik* (Tübingen: Ludwig Friedrich Fues, 1934). For Möhler's reply, see Johann Adam Möhler, *Neue Untersuchungen der Lehrgegensätze zwischen den Katholiken und Protestanten. Eine Vertheidigung meiner Symbolik gegen die Kritik des Hernn Professors Dr. Baur in Tübingen* (Mainz: F. Kupferberg, 1834; rev. and exp. ed., 1835). Baur's response to the first edition is "Erwiederung auf Hernn Dr. Möhler's neuest Polemik gegen die protestantische Lehre und Kirche in der Schrift: *Neue Untersuchungen . . .*" *Tübinger Zeitschrift für Theologie* 8 (1843): 127–248. For more documentation, see Himes, "Introduction," xi–xxi.

27. See note 2 above. Also of interest are the explanations provided in the prefaces to the subsequent editions; see Möhler, *Symbolism*, xxxi–xxxiv.

28. The "Index of Names" lists thirty such references, including several extended discussions of Möhler's thought; see Kasper, *The Catholic Church*, 447ff.

29. Kasper, *Katholische Kirche*, 85–86; idem, *The Catholic Church*, 48–49. Cf. Josef Rupert Geiselmann, *The Meaning of Tradition*, trans. W. J. O'Hara (New York: Herder, 1966).

30. Kasper, *Katholische Kirche*, 86; idem, *The Catholic Church*, 48–49.

31. Kasper, *Katholische Kirche*, 242; idem, *The Catholic Church*, 163.

32. Walter Kasper, *Theology and Church*, trans. Margaret Kohl (New York: Crossroad, 1989), 150.

33. Faith and Order Commission, *Baptism, Eucharist and Ministry* (Geneva: WCC Publications, 1982).

34. Joint Orthodox–Roman Catholic Theological Commission, "The Mystery of the Church and of the Eucharist in the Light of the Mystery of the Holy Trinity," at http://www.vatican.va/roman_curia/pontifical_councils/chrstuni/ch_orthodox_docs/rc_pc_chrstuni_doc_19820706_munich_en.html.

35. Lutheran-Catholic International Commission, "Facing Unity," 6, at http://www.prounione.urbe.it/dia-int/l-rc/doc/e_l-rc_facing.html#txt6; cf. Johannes Willebrands, "The Future of Ecumenism," *One in Christ* (1975): 323.

36. Anglican–Roman Catholic International Commission, "The Church as Communion," at http://www.vatican.va/roman_curia/pontifical_councils/chrstuni/angl-comm-docs/rc_pc_chrstuni_doc_19900906_church-communion_en.html.

37. Faith and Order Commission, *The Church: Towards a Common Vision; Faith and Order Paper No. 214* (Geneva: WCC Publications, 2013), 1, 5. Kasper was appointed as a member of the Faith and Order Commission in 1979.

38. Kasper, *Theology and Church*, 190.

39. Cardinal Kasper vigorously defended the importance of the local churches and their simultaneity with the universal church in a friendly rejoinder to Cardinal Joseph Ratzinger in "Zur Theologie und Praxis des bischöflichen Amtes," *Auf neue Art Kirche Sein: Wirklichkeiten—Herausfoderungen—Wandlungen* (Munich: Bernward bei Don Bosco, 1999), 32–48. For a more extensive discussion, see Killian McDonnell, "The Ratzinger/Kasper Debate: The Universal and Local Churches," *Theological Studies* 63 (2002): 227–50.

40. Walter Kasper, "Present Situation and Future of the Ecumenical Movement," *Information Service* 109 (2002): 11–20, 15.

41. See Möhler, *Unity in the Church*, 122–65. On p. 161, Möhler explains the impetus for "heresy": "It wishes to build a common life on the foundation of egoism; but this cannot be done."

42. Kasper, *Theology and Church*, 144–45.

43. Lutheran World Federation and the Catholic Church, "Joint Declaration on the Doctrine of Justification," 13, http://www.vatican.va/roman_curia/pontifical_councils/chrstuni/documents/rc_pc_chrstuni_doc_31101999_cath-luth-joint-declaration_en.html. Kasper served as co-chair for the Lutheran-Catholic Commission on Unity from 1967 to 1972 and again from 1995 to 2001.

44. Kasper, *Katholische Kirche*, 258–59; idem, *The Catholic Church*, 175.

45. Kasper, *Katholische Kirche*, 262–65; idem, *The Catholic Church*, 178–80.

46. Kasper, *Katholische Kirche*, 265; idem, *The Catholic Church*, 180.

47. Walter Kasper, *Harvesting the Fruits: Aspects of Christian Faith in Ecumenical Dialogue* (New York: Continuum, 2009).

48. Kasper, *Harvesting the Fruits*, no. 107, pp. 201–2.

49. An important study of the complex question of doctrinal authority that sketches out the many dimensions of this issue that must be faced by the churches is Groupe des Dombes, *One Teacher: Doctrinal Authority in the Church*, trans. Catherine E. Clifford (Grand Rapids: Eerdmans, 2010). Original version: Groupe de Dombes, *Un seul maître: l'autorité doctrinale dans l'Eglise* (Paris: Bayard, 2005).

50. See Himes, *Ongoing Incarnation*, 147–51; Kasper, *Katholische Kirche*, 263; idem, *The Catholic Church*, 179.

CHAPTER 11

Catholicism in a New Key

John R. Sachs, SJ

During the last fifty years, the University of Tübingen has enjoyed international renown because of its creative Catholic and Protestant theological faculties. In particular, Walter Kasper's *Jesus the Christ* (1974 in German, 1976 in English) certainly played a big role in drawing the attention of English-speaking theologians to both Kasper himself and the Catholic Tübingen School.[1] In order to understand Kasper's theology in general and his theological approach to ecumenism in particular, it is necessary to locate his thought in relation to the work of the Catholic Tübingen School's two early great theologians, Johann Sebastian Drey and Johann Adam Möhler.[2]

This chapter sheds light on the understanding of the church and tradition that Drey and Möhler introduced and on which Kasper has drawn in his theology of the church and in his leadership in ecumenism.

1. Johann Sebastian Drey's Theology of the Church

After the Reformation, the idea of a Protestant faculty of theology and a Catholic faculty of theology at the same university in a German-speaking land was unimaginable. Yet, this breakthrough happened for the first time in 1817 when the state of Württemberg's government moved the fledgling Catholic theological faculty at Ellwangen to the already existing university in Tübingen with its Protestant theological faculty.[3] Of course, then "Catholic" denoted a particular denomination and, unlike the climate today, the relationship between the faculties was not all that friendly. For a variety of cultural, historical, political, and theological reasons, apologetic and polemical spirits were high. In response to the Reformation and the Enlightenment, the first generation of Catholic theologians at Tübingen saw it as their responsibility to give a credible defense of the Catholic Church as it had developed since its apostolic foundation. Thus, they set out to identify and espouse the essence or nature of Catholicism that lies at the heart of its unfolding over the centuries.[4]

(1) *The Church's "Essence"*

Johann Sebastian Drey, the first Catholic professor of dogmatic theology in Tübingen, took up this challenge in 1819 in his programmatic essay, "On the Spirit and Essence of Catholicism," which appeared in the first issue of the Catholic journal *Theologische Quartalschrift*.[5] He argues that Catholicism is the "truthful, objective, uninterrupted, pure and enduring continuation of primitive Christianity."[6] As Walter Kasper has noted, according to Drey the church's essence is found neither merely in a concept nor in a privileged historical period but in a living, organic reality. The church is a living act of tradition, rooted in the Christ event, that is, in divine revelation as received by the apostolic community, and in this event's ongoing mediation into the future.[7]

Drey was not the kind of "ecumenical" theologian who was irenic and played down the real points of difference. Rather, he sought intellectual clarity precisely where there were important theological differences. Yet, he was at the same time respectful of Protestantism in his arguments and criticisms.[8] There were two reasons for this, both of which are important for today's ecumenism and also for understanding Cardinal Kasper, whose episcopal motto is "Truth in Love," *Veritatem in caritate* (Eph 4:15). First, for Drey, theologians must never forget that humility is "the deepest thing in religion, deeper than faith and love, for only through it is it possible for a person resolutely to dedicate one's understanding to service of the faith and one's will to service of love."[9] Second, Drey had the sure vision and hope that, as a living, historical reality, the church is ever living into the fullness of its true unity and catholicity and that the conflicts and contradictions which all life entails are ultimately embraced by God's providence.

In Drey's *Brief Introduction to the Study of Theology* (1819) we find a remarkable insight characteristic of Drey's sensibility for the historical development of the truth into which the Spirit leads the church.[10] Drey writes:

> One can distance oneself from the truth either by falling away from it or by failing to keep up with it. The first is error plain and simple; the second leads to error. Error is a moving outside the boundary of the truth. It sets its own boundary and so diverges from the truth. Falling behind the truth is sluggishness, which happens when the vitality of the religious principle in its forward-moving development begins to die. Thus, it becomes truncated and one way or the other it comes to the point where the imperfect, the part, is mistaken for the perfect, the whole.[11]

According to Drey, truth is on the move. For this reason, the church as a living, historical reality is being pulled forward into the truth by the Holy Spirit. Abiding in "the fullness of truth," as Jesus puts it in John 16:13, is not a matter of sitting still, of staying put. Drey's way of understanding the *dynamis* of the Spirit, who leads the church into the fullness of its truth in history, is quite different from the view, which we might prefer, that the Spirit enlightens us to appreciate with deeper insight and unction what we already know and are convinced about. For Drey, the Spirit presses the church not only to go *deeper* into what it already knows but also to go *forward* into what it does not yet know. Thus, historical development is not a mere chronological unfolding of a reality already completely present and familiar. Instead, it is an organic, even dramatic process in which something new appears, often evoking consternation and disagreement.

(2) *The Church's Living Tradition*

Whenever there is change, there is disagreement and conflict. Accepting this process, Drey took a hopeful view of polarization, even though it had led in the church's history to heresy and schism and to the anomaly of Christianity's differing confessions or denominations. In Drey's early diaries, reflecting the influence of F. W. J. Schelling's philosophy of history, there are the beginnings of Drey's theory concerning life's dialectical process. This notion of the movement from conflict to resolution, the *Gegensatzlehre* in German, comes to fuller expression in Drey's *Brief Introduction to the Study of Theology* when he states that the historical necessity and aptness of conflict and division are ultimately fruitful aspects of life in general. He writes: "Every temporal form calls forth its antithesis and only through it receives its own determinate character."[12]

While Drey rejects the use of this theory to excuse ecclesial indifferentism in the face of a divided church, he employs it to see a positive significance in the divisions among Christians. In his view, it is only in the working out of such oppositions that the church comes to a clearer consciousness of itself and its tradition. Theologically, he believes that the differences or conflicts among Christians are accepted and eventually made fruitful by divine providence for the church's self-realization and knowledge of the truth.[13] Drey voices this idea, as Kasper has noted, in his essay of 1822 titled "On the Church That Alone Leads to Salvation." He urges all Christians to "reverence in faith and humility the Spirit of providence, who has gathered up the division of the church into sects into his plan, even as the division of all the nations."[14] As Christians cooperate with the Spirit, they eventually move beyond their specific differences to a new, fuller realization of the church. According to Drey, one example of Christians' failure to keep up with the Spirit is the Great Schism of 1054 between the Eastern Church and the Western Church.

In Drey's perspective, Christians err not only when they fail to cooperate with the Spirit in overcoming their differences but also when they depart from the truth, when they make an error in thought or judgment. Such occurred to some degree, Drey holds, in the Protestant Reformation. In part, the Reformers went astray because of their doctrinal willfulness and obduracy. But Drey adds nuance to this view, as Kasper points out, when he observes that error can occur when there is a "premature rushing ahead" of the truth. In this light, the Reformers were correct in many of their concerns, but they were wrong in moving too quickly to address these concerns. According to Drey, the Reformers rightly glimpsed aspects of the church's possible future authentic development. But they rashly anticipated this development so that the newness for which they called came into conflict with the existing state of the church. While Christians fail at times to keep up with the Spirit, they also make the mistake at other times of racing ahead of the Spirit.[15]

According to Drey, the church's tradition is a living, organic process, not the dead product of a past age. It is not the dead faith of the living but the living faith of the dead. For this reason, authentic development in the church requires the ability to discern the church's essence or identity amid change and the differences among Christians. This discernment is facilitated in part by the church's teachings, its doctrines. But these doctrines when taken as a historical, systematic whole exhibit two elements, that which is "fixed" and that which is "flexible." Some doctrines have reached a point of finality in their development. These teachings, at least in their content, though perhaps not in their form, are fixed or permanent. Other doctrines are still in the process of development; they have the status of theological opinions or judgments. These teachings, in their content and their form, are flexible, open to improvement. The former, which are also called dogmas, serve as principles of the identity of the church's faith.[16]

According to Drey, theologians contribute to the church's life when they assist in differentiating between what is fixed and what is flexible among and within the church's doctrines. While a doctrine's content may be permanent, its mode of formulation may need revision. There exists flexibility or mutability in the variety of concepts and philosophical systems at work in the historical expressions of dogmas. Further, when a teaching stands in the realm of opinion or judgment, then it can change in ways that contribute to the vitality of the church and the unfolding of its tradition. In this case, theologians must serve "as teachers in their church since such opinions are not merely accidental but necessary subjects of investigation and presentation for dogmatic and moral theology."[17] Theologians must be proactive because the "impulse for further development and greater conceptual clarity can only come from individuals." When they make this kind of contribution to the church, they rightly prepare the way for a developing doctrine to reach its final and fixed form.[18]

Finally, Drey holds that Christians in general and theologians in particular must recognize both the fixity and the flexibility of the church's doctrines. On the one hand, when some people insist on changing what is fixed or permanent, they fuel heterodoxy. On the other hand, when other people deny the flexible aspects of doctrines or elevate mere opinion to the status of dogma, they generate hyperorthodoxy.[19] This dynamic is at work today in the ongoing debate concerning the church's reception of the Second Vatican Council.

(3) *Johann Adam Möhler's Clarification*

While Drey's ideas were rich and original, they were also in some cases in need of refinement. For this reason, Drey's colleague Johann Adam Möhler took up Drey's seminal insight about historical, organic development in the church and its tradition. Affirming it, he simultaneously advanced it by clarifying the two dimensions of this development or movement: the church is both anchored in the past, in particular, in the event of Jesus Christ, and also coming to full realization in the future through the Holy Spirit's guidance and inspiration. Highlighting and agreeing with Möhler's clarification, Walter Kasper writes:

> Tradition is not merely the organic unfolding of the beginning. The Church is much more of a dialectical double-movement in relationship with its "origin in fullness." *Retrospectively* it must always take as its norm the truth revealed once and for all: it needs constant renewal from its origin, especially constant renewal from the witness of scripture. At the same time, the Church must *prospectively* enter into each new situation and pay attention to the "signs of the time." In this double-movement, the Spirit leads in ever-new ways into the fullness of truth.[20]

In other words, the church in every age must live in relation both to Jesus Christ as known in scripture and tradition and also to the Holy Spirit as encountered in its contemporary life and encounters with the world. On the one hand, the church must continue to learn from the Gospel. Yet, on the other hand, it has something new to receive as it enters each new situation, something that in some way it stands in need of. This receptivity to the present and the future is crucial today with respect to ecumenism. In its own ecclesial poverty of spirit, the kind that Jesus praised (Matt 5:3), the church must still receive the fullness of its unity and catholicity from and with others so as to actualize it concretely. As Kasper has noted, this movement forward entails a real sharing of gifts among all Christians.

According to Möhler, the church's twofold movement toward Christ in scripture and the Spirit in contemporary life functions as the heart and norm of authentic new development. Unlike Drey, Möhler views heresies or schisms not as necessary phases in the church's self-realization in history but as legitimate oppositions to the status quo that went astray, as evils that should not have occurred.

In this perspective, things went wrong because there was a refusal to heed the Spirit who not only leads the church forward in its development but also holds the church together. In Kasper's words, the Holy Spirit "fills and enlivens all believers, binding them all into one life shared, to one spirit-filled communion," in which there is room for real difference and opposition.[21] Yet, in the judgment of Möhler and also Kasper, the Christians who have departed from the church's all-embracing unity still carry within their communities something of this unity and also the longing for a new all-embracing unity. Only by returning to the whole, in which all Christians are reconciled in unity, can these estranged communities be transformed into fruitful polarities in the church's rich diversity.[22]

This idea that the church's true unity includes diversity, which Möhler introduced and which Kasper has pursued, anticipates the concept of *unity as reconciled diversity* that has become important in ecumenism. Indeed, it is central in Kasper's own understanding of the goal of ecumenism and in his vision of the church. Of course, Christian reconciliation of this kind is, in the end, not simply an achievement of human effort but also the work of the Holy Spirit.[23]

2. A Vision of Church Unity

What will Christian unity look like concretely? And what will it require of us? Let us consider Walter Kasper's answers to these questions.

(1) *Not Restoration*

Kasper rejects the kind of "return" and "restoration" ecumenism that sees union as reabsorption by the Catholic Church, itself remaining more or less unchanged. The unity to which Christians are moving in the Spirit is not a return to the past. Rather, it will be a new form of unity in which there exists genuine differences.

Kasper highlights a warning against the notion of Christian unity as a restoration in Möhler's classic work, *Unity in the Church, or the Principle of Catholicism as Presented in the Spirit of the Church Fathers of the First Three Centuries* (1825). According to Möhler, reconciliation will include diversity that does not jeopardize the unity. This reality will exist as the work of the Spirit. Möhler specifically employs this idea of unity-in-difference to shed light on the relationships among the bishops and the pope, that is, among the local churches and the universal church. While agreeing with this use of the concept, Kasper also applies it frequently to the new situation of ecumenism. He writes:

> Two extremes in church life are possible, and both are named egoism. One is when each one wants to be all; the other is when only one wants to be all. In the latter situation, the bond of unity becomes so tight and the love so warm, that one cannot help but to suffocate. In the former situation, everything falls apart and it becomes so cold that one freezes. The one kind of egoism gives rise to the other; but it does not have to be that only one or each one wants to be all. All can only be all together and the unity of all can only be a whole. That is the idea of the Catholic Church.[24]

In speaking here of two tendencies in ecumenism, Kasper is implicitly associating the view that "only one wants to be all" with the idea that unity requires a return of all Christians to the Catholic Church. A unity of this sort would be a restoration, characterized by uniformity. At the same time, Kasper is linking the view that "each one wants to be all" with the idea that unity would be an external fusion of what is now divided. There would result an ecclesial polity similar to a confederacy. In Kasper's judgment, both forms of unity are extremes and unacceptable.

Appealing to the theologies of Drey and Möhler, Kasper holds that the way "back" to a lost unity is not the restoration of a past time. Rather, the Spirit calls Christians forward into the future, into a new unity that will result from real change and conversion in all churches. This reconciliation may assume a form that neither Drey nor Möhler could have imagined. Although it will entail the transformation of all parties, it will not bring about the destruction of the various ecclesial identities. Kasper writes: "Ecumenism is not a losing deal, not a process of becoming poorer, in which one gives up one's own identity and carelessly throws overboard what earlier generations held to be holy. Ecumenism is a living process of growth."[25]

(2) *A Future Reality*

The unity to which the Spirit is calling all Christians requires a much deeper and experiential knowledge of how the Holy Spirit, which is fruitful not only in the Catholic Church but in other churches as well, has given to each and to all holy gifts to share and to receive from one another.[26] In this regard, the church is a pilgrim, ever on the road of conversion and renewal. In Kasper's view, if the Catholic Church is to realize its catholicity, its genuine universality, it must undergo a change of heart and mind and become reconciled with other Christian communities. Kasper writes: "Wounded by the divisions of Christians, the Catholic Church, too, is unable in a condition of division to concretely actualize its own catholicity. Many aspects of being-church are better actualized in other churches. For this reason, ecumenism is not a one-way street, but a mutual learning process or, as the encyclical *Ut unum sint* puts it, an 'exchange of gifts.' The way there is not a simple return of the others to the fold of the Catholic Church."[27]

In Kasper's vision, the ecumenical movement toward true Christian unity will enable each of the churches and Christian communities to discover elements of the Christian life that had been dormant or inadequate and then to incorporate these elements in new forms into its Christian life. Referring to the Catholic Church, he states that it can expect to find that "aspects of being church, which in the Catholic Church are fundamentally present but little developed or atrophied, will be further developed through ecumenical dialogue with other churches in which such aspects are more richly and fully displayed."[28] In other words, it is not only the non-Catholic Christians who have not kept up with the Spirit. The Catholic Church too has, to put it in Drey's words, in some ways "fallen behind the truth." Also, it is not only the Catholic Church that has valuable gifts of the Spirit to share with other Christians. Non-Catholic Christians are also recipients of the Spirit's gifts, which they would gladly pass on to Catholics.

Further, as Kasper holds, the church's unity and catholicity are not static and merely juridical realities. Rather, they are eschatological realities. Christian reconciliation and universality already partially exist, but they are not yet fully attained in the church. Thus, Kasper observes that the "unity and catholicity of the church are always and in every period still coming to be and remain forever a task."[29] In its concrete history, the church's catholicity always "falls short of its own final perfection."[30] Correlatively, "the unity of the church in the Catholic Church presently exists only in a historical deficient way because in its present form it does not afford room for the necessary diversity that should be."[31] Nevertheless, there are occasions or situations in which the church manifests and thus anticipates the full catholicity and unity to which God calls it. Kasper holds:

> The Catholic Church is there, where it is not a pick-and-choose gospel or a partisan ideology that is held onto, but rather the whole faith of all times and places in its fullness, without curtailment. It is there, where one witnesses to the faith world-wide among all peoples and in all cultures for everyone, regardless of their station in life, their race, their ethnicity and their culture. It is there, where the faith is holistically related to and lived out in all dimensions of human life. It is there, where unity affords the greatest possible room and where, in the Holy Spirit, one is ready to listen for and learn about the fullness of Jesus Christ that is ever-greater and ever-new.[32]

Referring to Vatican II's Decree on Ecumenism, *Unitatis redintegratio* (UR), Kasper insists that the church's striving for full visible unity is "a duty that arises from the innermost meaning of the church's catholicity." Insofar as it lacks this unity, "the Catholic Church is hindered from actualizing its catholicity fully. This means that the Catholic Church can actualize its catholicity fully only ecumenically."[33] In this perspective, the great contribution to ecumenism made by the council's decree was not its recognition of elements of truth and holiness outside the Catholic Church but the "distinction between full and imperfect communion" (UR 3).[34] To be specific, the Catholic Church has attained only "imperfect communion," not the "full communion" of the church of Christ. This recognition by Vatican II occurs when in its Dogmatic Constitution on the Church, *Lumen gentium*, the council states that the church of Christ "subsists in" the Catholic Church.[35] The import of this famous expression is the council's recognition that while the church of Christ is fully actualized in the Catholic Church, it does not exist completely in the Catholic Church, which lacks the full communion spoken of in the Decree on Ecumenism. Reflecting on this acknowledgment, one wonders whether the significance of the council's teaching on this point has, even yet, made a broad impact among Catholics, though it surely influences the theologians involved in ecumenical dialogues.[36]

Cardinal Kasper's emphasis on models of ecumenism in which Christian unity is an eschatological reality undergirds his stress on the conversion that is required of all Christians if this reconciliation is to come about.[37] This call to transformation brings to mind Paul's admission, "I have been crucified with Christ; and it is no longer I who live, but it is Christ who lives in me" (Gal 2:19-20). Paul discovered his true personal unity and identity in Jesus Christ, which he received after he underwent a death of self. This personal change did not involve a loss of his true self; quite the contrary. Something like this must happen to us as individual believers and to our respective churches if we are to allow ourselves to be drawn in the Spirit's tether toward fuller unity and catholicity. This transformation is required of *all* of the churches and Christian communities if we will ever be able to discern the Spirit's lead and follow it into the future that the Spirit so earnestly desires.

(3) *Discovering Christian Unity*

According to Hebrews 11:1, it is not easy to hope for what we cannot see. Although these words apply to the coming of Christ, they also describe our search for Christian unity. We do not find it is easy to speak of and labor for the full unity and catholicity of the church when we cannot yet conceive or imagine it concretely. Yet, this endeavor is precisely what the Spirit of Christ calls us to do. Speaking to this challenge, Walter Kasper has observed that today's lack of agreement on the goal of ecumenism may in fact manifest profoundly different understandings of the church's essence or nature.

In his younger days, several years after his move from Münster to Tübingen, Walter Kasper wrote a book with Gerhard Sauter, a distinguished Protestant theologian, titled *Kirche—Ort des Geistes* ("Church—Place of the Spirit") in which he defines the church as the sacrament of the Spirit.[38] The church, he writes, is an "improvisation of the Spirit," and it therefore "must have the courage to be open to the unforeseeable and the new, what we can neither plan nor bring about ourselves."[39] Indeed, the church is an "open system that cannot be captured and conceptualized from a single point."[40] No doubt, some readers consider this a startling admission from a German theologian.

Today, an older and even wiser Kasper still lives and gives voice to this same conviction and hope. In the last chapter of *The Catholic Church: Nature, Reality and Mission* (2011), he reiterates that the Spirit remains at the center of his theology, including his ecclesiology.[41] As he states, the church is more than an institution; it is always a "new event in the Holy Spirit."[42] This is true not only in the sense that the Holy Spirit is the divine gift of God's self-communication in the lives of the faithful. It is also true in the sense that the church as a whole, in all its dimensions, is a new event, in which the Spirit is constantly seeking to renew and re-form it. Again and again, Kasper warns that such a renewal and the conversion it requires is a movement into the future. As such, it is never merely the continuation of what was and is; it is a future that cannot simply be extrapolated in advance but that must ultimately be received as the Spirit's gift.[43]

The ongoing, forming work of the Spirit Creator is not imposed on us. Rather, we must discern and receive it. This acceptance requires courage because the Spirit, who is the ever-greater, ever-newer God, leads us into the truth of being church, a living truth that is on the move. According to Drey, it is a truth that we may find hard to keep up with. It is a truth that we might give up on or even refuse to imagine as possible. Think of the disciples on the road to Emmaus (Luke 24:13-25). Think of Peter and Paul, the mission to the Gentiles, and the issue of circumcision (Acts 15:1-35). As Lisa Sowle Cahill has recently written in another context, "Perhaps the most important task of theology is to sustain hope that change is really possible."[44]

As Kasper notes, our acceptance of the Spirit's call to Christian unity requires courage. It requires us to let go of much that is familiar to us and treasured by us. Yet we must find this courage if we are to be true to the new breaking forth of Vatican II and if we are to follow the Spirit who leads the church into a future we cannot yet see.[45] The council has "pointed us in the direction of a new way of being church. It has given us a light for the journey, not a floodlight that illumines the whole road into the future, but a lantern we can carry, which like every lantern can only illumine to the extent that we ourselves move forward. It gives light for each next step, which can and must then be followed by other steps."[46]

According to Cardinal Kasper, this movement in the Spirit can happen only if the renewed *communio* ecclesiology of Vatican II leads to the renewal and reform of the church as an institution.[47] If we do not quench the Spirit, such letting go leads to a new beginning, a gift of the Spirit, who already "has freed the church many times in its history from what had become narrow and hardened and led it back to the catholic breadth of its origin."[48] This theology of Cardinal

Kasper presents the Catholicism of Drey and Möhler in a new key. It is rooted in scripture and tradition, and yet it is also open to a new future that we cannot yet imagine. Kasper grounds his vision and hope for ecumenism in the paradoxical movement of the Spirit, who leads the church back to its origin and simultaneously forward into a future way of being church that cannot be fully known in advance, a way of being church that will require conversion and reform of *all* of the churches and make possible the mutual recognition and reception of the different gifts that all the churches have received from the Spirit for the building up of the one church of Christ.

3. Toward an Ecumenical Spirituality

No doubt the fifty years since the "big bang" of the Second Vatican Council have been a time of reception, hope, and discernment about new possibilities and challenges. There are impressive and heartening signs of the fruitfulness of ecumenical hope and hard work, which Kasper has documented in *Harvesting the Fruits: Aspects of Christian Faith in Ecumenical Dialogue* (2009).[49] But after an initial period of rapid expansion of ecumenical and interreligious hopes, labors, and successes, there has been a slowing down, even a cooling of ecumenism not only in the Catholic Church but also in other churches and ecclesial communities. It is disturbing that the compass and direction of the council of which Kasper speaks has become such a *quaestio disputata*. It is disheartening to see efforts to deepen catholic identity that seem oppositional and, paradoxically, sectarian. As Kasper himself observes, fifty years into its reception of the council the council's enthusiasm for ecumenism seems paralyzed and almost gone. Once again, we need the kind of new Pentecost that Pope John XXIII spoke of when he convoked the council.[50]

It is now clear that the hard work of ecumenical dialogue, including dispute, can have real success only when it is done *in* the Spirit. For this reason, Kasper's insistence on the need for an ecumenical spirituality is so important.[51] It is a call for Christians to find new ways of living, praying, studying, and serving the world together that embrace not only individuals but also intentional communities, churches, and ecclesial communities as a whole. Perhaps through this common process we can learn "to think and feel with the church" (*sentire cum ecclesia*)—ecumenically. Kasper reminds us that the great divisions of the church did not come about simply because people argued about doctrine and *talked* past each other. Perhaps even more significant were and are the ways that people end up *living* past one another religiously, culturally, and socially.[52] This is where we can and must do something at all levels.

But this is difficult, because it means that ministry to the unity and catholicity of the church is not something that we can delegate to a small group of professional ecumenists. It means that individuals, parishes, local churches, and the churches themselves must honestly face questions such as: Do I really desire Christian unity? What am I willing to do for it? Why do so many generous Christians not consider ecumenism to be a top priority?

If we do truly desire it, if we truly desire to become ecumenically Catholic in a new way, then, as Ignatius of Loyola says in the *Spiritual Exercises*, we must beg for the grace that we desire. If we do not honestly find this desire within ourselves, perhaps we can hear the needling voice of Ignatius asking us if we at least have the desire for the desire! Moreover, if we desire a new Pentecost for the church, Cardinal Kasper reminds us that

> the Spirit can come as on the first Pentecost (Acts 2:2f.), in storm and fire; in the storm that sweeps away and the fire that burns up much of what today still seems important. But the Spirit can also come, as it did to the Prophet Elijah, in a soft breeze (1 Kg 19:12f.) and purify us and the world from within with its glowing embers. He can make us realize once again that we need not worry; on the contrary, our strength is our joy in God.[53]

Today, the pursuit of Christian unity requires the humility and the courage both to have faith in the Spirit who is leading the church forward and also to envision the hoped-for reality, even if the concrete vision remains hidden. When Christians have this faith and this vision, they give prophetic witness to the possibility of deeper "unity in reconciled diversity" and to the importance of actively waiting and working for it, even when we seem to lack the freedom and desire to do so. When Christians hope that their theological labors might evoke in others the joy in God and in the church that they so clearly live, they are a real blessing. In Cardinal Walter Kasper, we are grateful to recognize such a Christian.

Endnotes

1. Wayne L. Fehr, *The Birth of the Catholic Tübingen School: The Dogmatics of Johann Sebastian Drey* (Chico, CA: Scholars Press, 1981), 1.

2. In September 1978, I arrived in Tübingen to undertake doctoral studies with Professor Walter Kasper, who months earlier had responded positively via mail to my request to work with him in Christology and Spirituality. After unpacking my bags, it took me a week to get up the nerve to telephone Professor Kasper. He immediately responded with the warmth and enthusiasm of a *Mensch*, a genuine person. He invited me to his home, the home in which Kasper's Doktorvater Josef Rupert Geiselmann had lived on a street high above the Neckar River.

When I came to Kasper's home, he welcomed me into his library and engaged me for about twenty minutes in informal conversation about the beautiful Swabian countryside. Then he said, "Well, let's talk about your dissertation topic. Given your interests, I think it should be pneumatology. There is a lot of interesting work being done by Orthodox theologians. But the difficulty is, there's no one here who is really an expert on that." I can't remember how I responded but it couldn't have been enthusiastically, because without skipping a beat, he continued, "Perhaps something more classical; for example, the pneumatology of Bonaventure." After another long pause on my part, he came up with another suggestion.

Finally, Professor Kasper said, "I was talking to Yves Congar recently, and he told me that if one wanted to do pneumatology today, one should really do Balthasar." (Now the only thing by Balthasar I had read was his book on prayer, eight years previously, while a Jesuit novice). Kasper continued, "The great advantage would be that the scope is limited (*begrenzt*)." Now you have to imagine how I saw him sitting there, with a wall full of books behind him. As he gestured with his hands at least two feet apart to indicate what *begrenzt* might mean, my eyes were drawn through his outstretched hands to a span of about four yards of books, all by Balthasar, on the shelf behind him. I realized with a sinking feeling that this was the *good* news of a "good news/bad news" joke. The (really) bad news was yet to come. "The difficulty with such a topic," he continued, "is that Balthasar was never really an academic theologian. One reads him and is taken up into it; it is fascinating and compelling. Yet, when one tries to put his thought into traditional categories, it seems to go . . . poof," now rubbing his fingertips together and lifting his hands in the air. I thought all was lost. "But Father Sachs, you don't have to decide this now," he continued. Just as the sweetest relief began to settle in my soul, he concluded, "Give me a call next week to tell me what you decide!"

Five days later I had decided on Balthasar. So began six wonderful years in Tübingen and a lasting friendship with my Doktorvater Walter Kasper.

3. See Rudolf Reinhardt, "Die Katholisch-theologische Fakultät Tübingen im ersten Jahrhundert ihres Bestehens. Faktoren und Phasen der Entwicklung," in *Tübinger Theologen und ihre Theologie: Quellen und Forschungen zur Geschichte der Katholisch-Theologischen Fakultät Tübingen*, ed. Rudolf Reinhardt (Tübingen: Mohr, 1977), 1–42; Max Seckler, "Weltoffene Katholizität: Ein Modell," in *Die schiefen Wände des Lehrhauses: Katholizität als Herausforderung* (Freiburg: Herder, 1988), 156–77; Bradford Hinze, "Roman Catholic Theology: Tübingen," in *The Blackwell Companion to Nineteenth-Century Theology*, ed. David Fergusson (Oxford: Blackwell, 2010), 187–213. On Tübingen's Protestant theological faculty, see Horton Harris, *The Tübingen School* (Oxford: Clarendon Press, 1975).

4. Walter Kasper, "Vom Geist und Wesen des Katholizismus. Bedeutung, Wirkungsgeschichte und Aktualität Johann Sebastian Dreys und Johann Adam Möhlers Wesensbestimmung des Katholizismus," *Theologische Quartalschrift* 183, no. 3 (2003): 196–212; idem, "Verständnis der Theologie damals und heute," in *Theologie im Wandel*, ed. Katholisch-theologische Fakultät an der Universität Tübingen (Munich: Erich Wewel Verlag, 1967), 90–115. All translations are mine.

5. Johann Sebastian Drey, "Vom Geist und Wesen des Katholizismus," *Theologische Quartalschrift* 1, nos. 1, 2, 3, and 4 (1819): 3–24, 193–210, 369–92, 559–75; reprinted in *Geist des Christentums und des Katholizismus. Ausgewählte Schriften Katholischer Theologie im Zeitalter des deutschen Idealismus und der Romantik*, ed. Josef Rupert Geiselmann (Mainz: Mattias-Grünewald-Verlag, 1940), 193–234. Further references to Drey's "Vom Geist und Wesen des Katholizismus" are to this text in Geiselmann, ed., *Geist des Christentums und des Katholizismus*.

6. Ibid., 196.

7. Kasper, "Vom Geist und Wesen des Katholizismus," 198.

8. Kasper, "Die Einheit der Kirche im Licht der Tübinger Schule," in *Theologie als Instanz der Moderne. Beiträge und Studien zu Johann Sebastian Drey und zur Katholischen Tübinger Schule*, ed. Michael Kessler (Tübingen: Francke Verlag, 2005), 189–206, 191–92.

9. Drey, "Vom Geist und Wesen des Katholizismus," 204–5.

10. Johann Sebastian Drey, *Kurze Einleitung in das Studium der Theologie mit Rücksicht auf den wissenschaftlichen Standpunkt und das katholische System* (Tübingen: Heinrich Laupp, 1819), photographically reproduced in *Theologie, Kirche, Katholizismus. Beiträge zur Programmatik der Katholischen Tübinger Schule*, ed. Michael Kessler and Max Seckler (Tübingen: Francke Verlag, 2003), which includes essays by Joseph Ratzinger, Walter Kasper, and Max Seckler. References are to paragraphs. For a fine English translation and introduction, see *Brief Introduction to the Study of Theology with Reference to the Scientific Standpoint and the Catholic System*, trans. Michael J. Himes (Notre Dame, IN: University of Notre Dame Press, 1994).

11. Drey, *Kurze Einleitung*, 240.

12. Ibid., 247.

13. Ibid., 244.

14. Kasper, "Die Einheit der Kirche," 199–200, citing Johann Sebastian Drey, "Über den Satz von der alleinseligmachenden Kirche," in Geiselmann, ed., *Geist des Christentums und des Katholizismus*, 335–57, at 355.

15. Kasper, "Die Einheit der Kirche," 199, citing Drey, *Kurze Einleitung*, 245. See also Drey, "Vom Geist und Wesen des Katholizismus," 232.

16. Drey, *Kurze Einleitung*, 256–58.

17. Ibid., 258.

18. Ibid., 259. On the significance of Drey's theory of doctrinal development as a theological task, see John E. Thiel, "J. S. Drey on Doctrinal Development: The Context of Theological Encyclopedia," *Heythrop Journal* 27, no. 3 (1986): 290–305. See also John E. Thiel, *Senses of Tradition: Continuity and Development in Catholic Faith* (New York: Oxford University Press, 2000); idem, *Imagination and Authority: Theological Authorship in the Modern Tradition* (Minneapolis: Fortress Press, 1991).

19. Drey, *Kurze Einleitung*, 260.

20. Kasper, "Vom Geist und Wesen des Katholizismus," 209–10; emphasis added.

21. Ibid., 200.

22. Kasper, "Die Einheit der Kirche," 200–201.

23. Ibid., 204–5, 211. See also Walter Kasper, "Einheit in Versöhnter Verschiedenheit" and "Ökumene und Spiritualität," in *Wege zur Einheit der Christen* (Freiburg: Herder, 2012), 222–33 and 592–612. For the development of this model of unity in Catholic theology, Kasper acknowledges Heinrich Fries and Karl Rahner, *Einigung der Kirchen—reale Möglichkeit*, Questiones Disputatae 184 (Freiburg: Herder, 1983).

24. Kasper, "Vom Geist und Wesen des Katholizismus," 208, citing Johann Adam Möhler, *Die Einheit in der Kirche oder das Prinzip des Katholizismus dargestellt im Geist der Kirchenväter der drei ersten Jahrhunderte*, ed. Johann Rupert Geiselmann (Darmstadt: Wissenschaftliche Buchgesellschaft, 1957), 237.

25. Walter Kasper, "Ökumene des Lebens," in *Wege zur Einheit der Christen*, 575–91, at 581. See also Walter Kasper, "Konfessionelle Identität—Reichtum und Herausforderung," in *Wege zur Einheit der Christen*, 433–52.

26. Walter Kasper, "Situation und Zukunft der Ökumene" in *Wege zur Einheit der Christen*, 343–64, at 363.

27. Walter Kasper, "Die gegenwärtige Situation der ökumenischen Theologie" in *Wege zur Einheit der Christen*, 398–418, at 401. See Walter Kasper, *Katholische Kirche: Wesen—Wirklichkeit—Sendung* (Freiburg: Herder: 2011), 436; idem, *The Catholic Church: Nature, Reality and Mission*, trans. Thomas Hoebel (London: Bloomsbury T&T Clark, 2014), 306.

28. Kasper, *Katholische Kirche*, 435–36; idem, *The Catholic Church*, 305–6.

29. Walter Kasper, "Der ekklesiologische Charakter der nichtkatholischen Kirchen," in *Wege zur Einheit der Christen*, 64–84, at 83.

30. Kasper, *Katholische Kirche*, 260; idem, *The Cathoilc Church*, 176.

31. Walter Kasper, "Der ekklesiologische Charakter der nichtkatholischen Kirchen," 82.

32. Kasper, *Katholische Kirche*, 260; idem, *The Catholic Church*, 176.

33. Walter Kasper, "Kircheneinheit und Kirchengemeinschaft in katholischer Perspektive," in *Wege zur Einheit der Christen*, 85–104, at 89–90. See also idem, "Communio: Die Leitidee der katholischen ökumenischen Theologie," in *Wege zur Einheit der Christen*, 137–67, at 157–58.

34. Walter Kasper, "Das Ökumenismusdekret—nach 40. Jahren neu gelesen," in *Wege zur Einheit der Christen*, 125–36, at 135.

35. For this reason, Kasper often emphasizes the point that when the council refers to "ecclesial communities" in distinction to churches, this does not mean that they are *not* churches in any sense but that they *are* churches in a way analogous to the Catholic Church. This is an important and contentious issue in ecumenical dialogues. Kasper notes, on the one hand, that other Christian denominations clearly understand and speak of themselves as churches differently from how the Catholic Church understands itself as "church." On the other hand, he points out that Vatican II recognizes essential *ecclesial* elements of the Church of Christ in other churches. Referring to John Paul II's *Ut unum sint* 13, Kasper observes that "outside the boundaries of the Catholic Community there is not an *ecclesial* vacuum"; see idem, *Wege zur Einheit der Christen*, 401; my emphasis. In other words, the contrast is between the full actualization of the Church of Christ in the Catholic Church and the real, if imperfect, actualization of the Church of Christ in the other churches. Just how difficult it can be to express the desired nuance is shown in Kasper's statement that outside the Catholic Church, "there is not 'the' church, but there is ecclesial reality. Consequently, *Dominus Iesus* does not mean to say that the ecclesial communities that arose from the Reformation are not churches, but only that they are not churches in the proper sense [*im eigentlichen Sinn*]. Positively, this means: in an improper sense [*in einem uneigentlichen Sinn*] analogous to the Catholic Church, they are churches. As a matter of fact, they have a different understanding of church and do not even want to be church in the Catholic sense"; see Kasper, *Wege zur Einheit der Christen*, 156. Again and again, Kasper emphasizes that the full unity and catholicity of the Church of Christ will entail a profound conversion for all churches concerning what it really means to be Christ's Church.

36. See the analysis of *Unitatis redintegratio* in a *Festschrift* for Kasper's seventieth birthday: Bernd Jochen Hilberath, "'Förderung der Einheit'—oder favorisiert das Ökumenismusdekret eine Rückkehr-Ökumene?," in *Kirche in ökumenischer Perspektive*, ed. Peter Walter, Klaus Krämer, and George Augustin (Freiburg: Herder, 2003), 178–95. Bernd Jochen Hilberath, Kasper's successor in Tübingen, defends the point repeatedly made by Kasper that the "restoration," *redintegratio*, of ecclesial unity of which the decree speaks is a true reintegration into a new and fuller unity; it is not a "restoration," *restauratio*, in the sense of a return of non-Catholic churches and ecclesial communities to the (Roman) Catholic Church, especially in its present form. In order to move to the form of church that will more fully actualize the fullness of unity inspired by the Holy Spirit will require conversion and change of *all*.

37. Walter Kasper, *That They May All Be One: The Call to Unity Today* (London: Burns and Oates, 2004), 90–91.

38. Walter Kasper and Gerhard Sauter, *Kirche—Ort des Geistes* (Freiburg: Herder, 1976).

39. Ibid., 50.

40. Ibid., 53.

41. Kasper, *Katholische Kirche*, 487–88, 102–31, 201–15; idem, *The Catholic Church*, 344–45, 59–80, 133–42.

42. Kasper, *Katholische Kirche*, 475; idem, *The Catholic Church*, 335.

43. Kasper, *Katholische Kirche*, 464–65; idem, *The Catholic Church*, 328–29.

44. Lisa Sowle Cahill, "*Caritas in Veritate*: Benedict's Global Reorientation," *Theological Studies* 71, no. 2 (2010): 291–319, at 316.

45. Kasper, *Katholische Kirche*, 466; idem, *The Catholic Church*, 329.

46. Kasper, *Katholische Kirche*, 487; idem, *The Catholic Church*, 344.

47. Kasper, *Katholische Kirche*, 484; idem, *The Catholic Church*, 342. See idem, "Communio: Die Leitidee der katholischen ökumenischen Theologie," 137–67. In Kasper's view, the next phase of ecumenical dialogue must include discussion of *communio*-ecclesiology as well as what the different churches and ecclesial communities mean when speaking of the church's unity as a *communio*-unity; see Kasper, *Katholische Kirche*, 436; idem, *The Catholic Church*, 306.

48. Kasper, *Katholische Kirche*, 467; idem, *The Catholic Church*, 330.

49. Cardinal Walter Kasper, *Harvesting the Fruits: Aspects of Christian Faith in Ecumenical Dialogue* (London: Continuum, 2009).

50. Kasper, *Katholische Kirche*, 467, 487; idem, *The Catholic Church*, 330, 344.

51. In 1965, hence immediately after the council, Walter Kasper highlighted the importance of an ecumenical spirituality; see idem, "Das Gespräch mit der protestantischen Theologie," in *Wege zur Einheit der Christen*, 237–61. Moreover, ecumenical spirituality became a central theme after Kasper's appointment to the Pontifical Council for Promoting Christian Unity. See idem, *Wege zur Einheit der Christen*, 575–663.

52. Kasper, "Ökumene und Spiritualität," 592–612, at 596.

53. Kasper, *Katholische Kirche*, 488; idem, *The Catholic Church*, 345.

CHAPTER 12

Unity at the Table

Susan K. Wood, SCL

The Eucharist is a recurring theme in the theological writings of Cardinal Walter Kasper. Kasper began to write about the Eucharist long before his appointment in 1999 to the Pontifical Council for Promoting Christian Unity. In 1985, he published his essay "Aspects of the Eucharist in Their Unity and Variety: On the Recent Discussion about the Fundamental Form and Meaning of the Eucharist."[1] As the bishop of the Diocese of Rottenburg-Stuttgart (1989–99), he reflected on the Eucharist in his 1995 Lenten letter to the parishes and again in his pastoral letter of May 21, 1998, titled "Die Feier der Eucharistie" ("The Celebration of the Eucharist"). In 2004, Kasper gathered much of his occasional writings on the Eucharist into his *Sacrament of Unity: The Eucharist and the Church*, which he dedicated to the Diocese of Rottenburg-Stuttgart.[2]

The Eucharist became a guiding theme in Kasper's theology of ecumenism.[3] In numerous writings, he directly comments on both the ecumenical problems of mutual recognition of the Eucharist and also the goal of ecumenical unity at the eucharistic table.[4] In the Pontifical Council for Promoting Christian Unity (1999–2010), he pursued aspects of this theme and culminated his years of work on the council with the publication of his book *Harvesting the Fruits: Basic Aspects of Christian Faith in Ecumenical Dialogue* (2009), which summarizes the results of the Catholic Church's official dialogues with the Lutheran, Reformed, Anglican, and Methodist churches over forty years.[5] A major topic of these dialogues has been the Eucharist, especially the themes that enable the dialogue partners to reach substantial, even if not yet full, agreement on the Eucharist. Two such themes concern the recovery of the biblical category of anamnesis or memory/remembrance and the renewed understanding of the Eucharist's epiclesis, that is, its prayer asking the Spirit to descend upon the gifts to change them into the body and blood of Christ for the well-being of those who receive them. This prayer conveys that the Holy Spirit is the main agent of the liturgy. Significantly, these themes also appear in Kasper's earlier pastoral writings.

In considering the ecumenical problem of our Christian divisions at the eucharistic table, it is tempting to rush in and focus on our disagreements about eucharistic doctrine, for example, concerning the nature of eucharistic sacrifice or the real presence of Christ in the Eucharist. This approach would, however, short-circuit the theological context in which Kasper considers the Eucharist as the sacrament of unity. To appreciate why disunity at the eucharistic table is not only a scandal but also a tragedy and simultaneously to realize the full imperative to work for the unity of all Christians, one must grasp Kasper's vision of the Eucharist as the center and synthesis of all Christian unities. Thus, drawing on Kasper's writings, this essay considers the Eucharist in relation to four unities: the unity of doctrines, particularly the doctrines of creation, redemption, and eschatology; the unity of eucharistic theology; the unity of the church as communion or *communio*; and, finally, the ecumenical unity of all Christians united at one table. It will become clear that according to Walter Kasper ecumenical unity is but one facet of the church's eucharistic unity.

1. The Eucharist within the Unity of Doctrines

The Eucharist is, Kasper holds, the sacrament that makes present and synthesizes the entire Christian mystery of salvation. It is at once personal, social, universal, and cosmic. Kasper writes that the Eucharist "embraces the creation and the eschatological new creation; it expresses both God's movement toward us human beings and the movement with which we respond to him, as individuals and as humankind. It is the comprehensive testament of the life, dying, and resurrection of Jesus Christ. It is the glorification of God and the salvation of the human person. It is personal and ecclesial, a gift that is given and a task that is assigned."[6]

Guided by this inclusive view, Kasper observes that the Eucharist is connected to the doctrine of creation, for it takes basic elements of creation, namely, wheat and grapes, the "fruit of the earth," made bread and wine "through the work of human hands," and transforms them into the body and blood of Christ. In the Eucharist, "the entire creation is drawn by means of the sacramental symbolism into the proleptic celebration and anticipation of the heavenly nuptial feast."[7] Moreover, the consecration of the bread and wine manifests the mystery of the Word become flesh (John 1:14). For this reason, Kasper observes: "In the Eucharist the incarnation continues in a new, that is, sacramental manner."[8] This change of the elements of creation is accomplished through the epiclesis, which Kasper calls "the innermost soul of the Eucharist," for in the Eucharist the assembly prays for "the sending of the Spirit" so that he may bring about the deeds of salvation that become a present reality in the anamnesis, the remembrance.[9] In remembering, we simultaneously reach toward the future, because this same Spirit "is the eschatological gift."[10]

The Eucharist is the eschatological sign of the nuptial banquet and anticipates "the eschatological glorification of God by all his creation."[11] The transformation of the world at the end of time "is anticipated when these gifts are transformed into the body and blood of Christ."[12] In this regard, Kasper points to how the good gifts of creation are explicitly drawn into the great closing doxologies of the first, third, and fourth canons of the Mass. Within this great cosmic and eschatological vision, the Eucharist is "the liturgy of the world" in the words of Karl Rahner and the "Mass of the World" according to the thought of Pierre Teilhard de Chardin.[13] The Eucharist is the "anticipation of eschatological praise which will be offered by the whole of creation, . . . a proleptic realization of the heavenly glorification of God and of the eschatological perfecting of the world."[14] In the Eucharist, "the world has become one in the praise of the Creator," which is to say that it has become "whole."[15]

Thus, the Eucharist unites the doctrines of creation, redemption, and eschatology in the church's worship. It directs us to recall our origin and our destiny. Creation is the "going out" or *exitus* from God, and redemption is the "returning" or *reditus* to God, the returning to the Father as members of the body of Christ in the power of the Spirit through the salvation wrought by the blood of the lamb. Jesus Christ is the beginning and the end of creation. Final fulfillment or *eschaton* is not individual but social, the reconciliation of all in Christ. The tradition has used the image of the body of Christ united with its head, Christ, to reflect this social unity. The Eucharist sacramentally signifies and realizes this cosmic reality.

2. Unity within Eucharistic Theology

According to Kasper, three aspects of the Eucharist—the eucharistic real presence of Jesus Christ, the Eucharist as sacrifice, and the Eucharist as sacrament—form "one single, indissoluble, inherent unity." In explaining this unity, he stands apart from scholastic theology, which juxtaposed these three aspects of the Eucharist without shedding light on how they are mutually related. As Kasper points out, when the liturgical renewal of the twentieth century revived the categories of anamnesis or remembrance and of epiclesis, it facilitated the recovery of the unity of these three aspects of Eucharist as well as the new ecumenical agreement on these themes.

Kasper links the institution of the Eucharist by Jesus with the anamnesis of his salvific work in the context of thanksgiving, since thanksgiving is the basic attitude of persons "who receive the deeds and the gifts of salvation."[16] Thus, the basic form of the Mass is a "celebration of remembrance which gives praise to God."[17] The anamnesis is the sacrifice and death of Jesus made present under the form of sacramental symbol. For Kasper the sacrificial nature of the Eucharist gives the Eucharist its true depth, preserving it from banal trivialization. A world deformed by sin can achieve unity and peace in no other way. Further, rather than pitting the Eucharist as meal and the Eucharist as sacrifice against each other (as often occurs), Kasper sees that these two views are complementary. Indeed, the latter, the Eucharist as sacrifice, is a necessary condition of the former, the Eucharist as meal. In this regard, Kasper recalls the New Testament's sacrificial language concerning the Last Supper: for example, "my blood poured out for the many" and the "blood of the covenant" (Mark 14:24; Matt 26:28). The result of sacrifice is reconciliation and the restoration of the unity that was lost. Here, Kasper cites two significant biblical verses: "For he is our peace; in his flesh he has made both groups into one and has broken down the dividing wall, that is, the hostility between us" (Eph 2:14) and "In Christ God was reconciling the world to himself, not counting their trespasses against them" (2 Cor 5:19).

The category of anamnesis has also enabled ecumenical breakthroughs regarding the sacrificial character of the Eucharist, for it emphasizes the once-for-all character of Christ's sacrifice on the cross, which in sacramental remembrance through the category of "real symbol" is present under sacramental modality in another time and place. More difficult ecumenically is the Catholic Church's conviction that the Eucharist not only makes present the sacrifice of Jesus Christ but is also a sacrifice offered by the church. Christian communities issuing from the Reformation readily assert that in the Eucharist the church offers a sacrifice of praise and thanksgiving. But they find it foreign to say that in the Eucharist the church gives thanks and offers sacrifice as the "sacrament of the presence of Christ's sacrifice." Kasper expresses the two dimensions of the Eucharist as a katabatic or "descending" movement of blessing and also as an anabatic or "ascending" movement "whereby the church, as the body of Christ, is drawn into his one sacrifice and as the bride of Christ shares in obedient submission in offering his sacrifice."[18] The Eucharist unites the reciprocal action of giving and receiving. It is both gift and prayer.[19] That is, the Eucharist affords us the opportunity in the Spirit both to receive Christ and also to offer ourselves in, with, and through Christ to the Father.

As already noted, according to Kasper, Christians should not set the Eucharist as sacrifice and the Eucharist as meal against each other. Yet, such can implicitly happen in eucharistic devotions. In an oblique reference to eucharistic adoration, Kasper discusses the primary purpose of the Eucharist when he says: "Bread is not meant to be looked at, but to be eaten. The Eucharist too is given to us so that we may eat it."[20] Surpassing mere fellowship, when we share in the Eucharist, we enter into the most intimate personal fellowship possible with Jesus Christ. Christ becomes our nourishment, and the Eucharist becomes a foretaste of the heavenly wedding banquet.

At the same time, referring to the Reformers' talk of the Eucharist as the "Lord's Supper," Kasper says that "instead of speaking of the Eucharist in terms of a meal," we ought rather to speak of its "fellowship character" and its "ecclesial dimension."[21] In light of the early church's detachment of the Eucharist from a normal meal (1 Cor 11:17-34) and also of the reasoning that led to the celebration of the Eucharist in the early morning, Kasper judges that the use of the phrase "Lord's Supper" is an innovation.[22] Such talk, he holds, sets up a contrast between the Eucharist as a meal or "supper" and the Eucharist as a celebration of community, an ecclesial event. This juxtaposition stands separate from the contrast between the Eucharist as meal and the Eucharist as sacrifice.

As Kasper explains, the epiclesis at the Eucharist transforms the bread and wine into the body and blood of Christ and simultaneously transforms the assembly into the ecclesial body of Christ. In this twofold change, the invoking of the Holy Spirit makes possible the sacramental presence of Christ. The body of Christ present sacramentally is none other than the one who was sacrificed and is now risen. In sum, the epiclesis is the lynchpin of the unity of the eucharistic real presence, the Eucharist as sacrifice, and the Eucharist as sacrament.

In summary, the use of the categories of anamnesis and epiclesis sheds light on the unity of eucharistic theology. It holds together the Eucharist as sacrifice and the Eucharist as meal as well as integrates the Eucharist as meal and the Eucharist as an ecclesial celebration of community. This appreciation of the unifying character of the Eucharist fills out the discussion in part 1 above of the Eucharist as the unifying point of the doctrines of creation, redemption, and eschatology. Through Kasper's reflections, the synthetic and integrative power of the Eucharist comes to light. Further, as we shall now see, the Eucharist manifests the church's nature and unity.

3. The Eucharist and the Church's Unity

The Eucharist, along with baptism, is the sacramental foundation and summit of both personal and ecclesial unity.[23] It effects both individual participation in Christ and also communal solidarity in Christ. In this regard, Kasper often stresses the importance of 1 Corinthians 10:16-17: "The cup of blessing that we bless, is it not a sharing in the blood of Christ? The bread that we break, is it not a sharing in the body of Christ? Because there is one bread, we who are many are one body, for we all partake of the one bread." Community or *koinonia* (Greek) in the Eucharist is the source and sign of *koinonia* in the one body of Christ. As Augustine attested, the Eucharist is a sign of unity and a bond of love.[24]

The reality of the Christian community in the Eucharist is the foundation of what has been termed a "eucharistic ecclesiology" and, more recently, "communion ecclesiology." The 1985 Synod of Bishops, at which Walter Kasper was the theological secretary, identified "communion" or *communio* as "the central and basic idea" of the documents of the Second Vatican Council.[25] "Communion ecclesiology" encompasses a "vertical" communion with God as the basis and support for the "horizontal" communion among Christians. The communion of Christians does not precede their incorporation into the church but is the result of their incorporation into a sacramentally constituted communion.[26]

This link between the sacramental body of Christ and the ecclesial body of Christ was lost sight of between the first and second millennia, especially in the eucharistic controversy with Beranger of Tours. Illuminating this oversight, Henri de Lubac has traced the shift from calling the Eucharist the *corpus mysticum*, the "mystical body," because it was received spiritually, to speaking of the Eucharist as the *corpus verum*, the "true body," which emphasizes Christ's real presence, the presence that was uncontested before the controversy. This emphasis brought to the fore the unity of the historical body of Jesus Christ with Christ's sacramental body in the Eucharist, but it simultaneously disassociated the Eucharist from the ecclesial body of Christ, the church. Correspondingly, the church shifted its self-designation from *corpus verum* to *corpus mysticum*, thereby highlighting its spiritual nature but overlooking the link between the church and the Eucharist.[27]

In Kasper's judgment, the shift away from the unity of the Eucharist and the church resulted in "a fatal individualization and privatization of the understanding and the praxis of the Eucharist" through much of the church's second millennium. The recovery of this unity has happened, Kasper observes, because of a few factors: the ecclesiology of Johann Adam Möhler, the liturgical movement of the late nineteenth and twentieth centuries, the recent retrieval of an understanding of the liturgical assembly as the subject of the eucharistic liturgy, and the recovery of the liturgical principle concerning the "active participation" of all persons present at the Eucharist.[28] Unfortunately, another result of the shift away from the unity of the Eucharist was that the church came to be considered more in sociological and juridical categories than in terms of the sacraments.[29]

As often occurs in reform movements, the pendulum sometimes swings too far to the other extreme. In this case, according to Kasper, the liturgical renewal's emphasis on the "community Mass" may have sometimes led to the neglect at the Eucharist of personal prayer, conversion, personal thanksgiving, and adoration. Kasper concludes: "we have not yet succeeded in finding the correct equilibrium between personal and ecclesial *communio*."[30]

4. The Eucharist in Ecumenical Relations

In light of the eucharistic theology outlined above, we can see more clearly the requirements, accomplishments, and uncompleted tasks necessary for eucharistic communion among separated Christians. Today, the chief points at issue in ecumenical dialogues concern Christ's real presence in the Eucharist, the Eucharist as memorial and sacrifice, the role of the Holy Spirit in the sacrament, and the relationship between the Eucharist and the church. As already noted, Walter Kasper "harvested" the results of the international dialogues with Anglicans, Lutherans, Reformed, and Methodists in *Harvesting the Fruits: Basic Aspects of Christian Faith in Ecumenical Dialogue*.[31] Here, we shall examine the two topics that have received the most sustained attention: Christ's presence in the Eucharist and the Eucharist as sacrifice.

(1) *Presence of Christ in the Eucharist*

Ecumenical points of agreement or convergence concerning Christ's real presence in the Eucharist have emerged for at least two reasons. First, there now exists an enriched understanding of the category of sacrament as a mode of personal presence. This notion leads to an understanding of the Eucharist that is distinctly different from the view of Eucharist as involving Christ's physical-historical presence, on the one hand, and also from the view of sacrament as involving Christ's spiritual non-substantial presence, on the other hand. The former does not sufficiently take into account the fact that the *risen* Christ is present in the Eucharist. The latter does not sufficiently clarify a real presence of Christ in the Eucharist.

Second, a renewed appreciation of epiclesis emphasizes the action of the Holy Spirit through whose power the body and blood of Christ are made present in the eucharistic elements. The work of the Holy Spirit removes any automatic or mechanical notion of sacramental efficacy by transforming the bread and wine into the body and blood of Christ and also by effecting our union with Christ.[32]

An area not explored by the dialogues, but which could be fruitful in the future, would be the development of a theology of the presence of Christ as the firstfruit of the new creation. This theology would synthesize the work of the Holy Spirit with a Christology of Christ's resurrection and not only emphasize the incarnational aspects of the real presence as a substantial "enfleshment," as it were, of the eucharistic elements but also stress the fact that it is the *risen* Christ who is present in the Eucharist. In this perspective, the Eucharist not only looks to the past in anamnesis but also to the future in anticipation; it is the pledge of eschatological fulfillment in Christ. This point is developed in Kasper's discussion of the cosmic dimension of the Eucharist.

One other area of unfinished ecumenical business concerns the issue of the effect of Christ's presence on the substances of bread and wine in the Eucharist. Does it somehow eliminate or annihilate the bread as bread and the wine as wine?

(2) *The Eucharist as Sacrifice*

Each of the ecumenical dialogues has generated its own statements concerning the sacrificial character of the Eucharist. It is appropriate, therefore, that we review these statements, which came about, in part, through the efforts of Cardinal Kasper.

The most significant breakthrough on the issue of sacrifice occurred in the Catholic-Anglican dialogue. The agreement on eucharistic sacrifice was achieved through the retrieval of the notion of memorial or anamnesis. In 1971 the Anglican–Roman Catholic International Commission (ARCIC) agreed that "the notion of *memorial* as understood in the Passover celebration at the time of Christ—i.e., the making effective in the present of an event in the past—has opened the way to a clearer understanding of the relationship between Christ's sacrifice and the Eucharist. The Eucharistic memorial is no mere calling to mind of a past event or of its significance, but the Church's effectual proclamation of God's mighty acts."[33]

In 1979, ARCIC reiterated that the notion of anamnesis "enables us to affirm a strong conviction of sacramental realism and to reject mere symbolism." Working with this notion, it shed light on the relationship between sacrifice and memorial by saying:

> It is possible to say at the same time that there is only one unrepeatable sacrifice in the historical sense, but that the Eucharist is a sacrifice in the sacramental sense, provided that it is clear that this is not a repetition of the historical sacrifice. There is therefore one historical, unrepeatable sacrifice, offered once for all by Christ and accepted once for all by the Father. In the celebration of the memorial, Christ in the Holy Spirit unites his people with himself in a sacramental way so that the Church enters into the movement of his self-offering.[34]

ARCIC also clarified that the category of anamnesis enables a distinction between a historical event and its sacramental representation. In effect, the once-for-all historical event of the sacrifice on the cross exists under a different modality, that of sacrament, which makes present that one unrepeatable historical event. The Eucharist is a sacrifice in a sacramental way.

In 1994, ARCIC advanced the Catholic-Anglican agreement in its *Clarifications of Certain Aspects of the Agreed Statements on Eucharist and Ministry*. In particular, it affirmed that the Eucharist as a propitiatory sacrifice applies to the faithful departed.

The Reformed-Catholic dialogue has also worked with the notions of anamnesis and sacrament. In 1977, it employed these notions to associate Christ's real presence in the Eucharist and Christ's sacrifice. It states:

> In its joyful prayer of thanksgiving, "in the Eucharist," when the Church of Christ remembers [Christ's] reconciling death for our sins and for the sins of the whole world, Christ himself is present who "gave himself up on our behalf as an offering and sacrifice whose fragrance is pleasing to God" (Eph 5:2). Sanctified by his Spirit, the Church through, with and in God's son, Jesus Christ, offers itself to the Father. It thereby becomes a living sacrifice of thanksgiving, through which God is publicly praised (cf. Rom 12:1; 1 Pet 3:5). The validity, strength and effect of the Supper are rooted in the cross of the Lord and in his living presence in the Holy Spirit.[35]

The Reformed-Catholic dialogue has also agreed that in the Eucharist we participate in Christ's self-offering to the Father:

> He [Christ] is both Apostle from God and our High Priest (cf. Heb 3.1) who has consecrated us together with him into one, so

> that in his self-offering to the Father through the eternal Spirit (cf. Heb 9.14), he offers us also in himself and so through our union with him we share in that self-offering made on our behalf. It is the same Spirit who cries "Abba, Father" (cf. Mk 14.36) in him who cries "Abba, Father" in us, as we in the Eucharist take the Lord's Prayer into our own mouth (Rom 8.15f., 26f.).

The Lutheran-Catholic dialogue has also reaffirmed the use of the category of memorial as understood in the ancient Passover celebration as the way to understand the difference between Christ's sacrifice on Golgotha and the Eucharist as sacrifice.[36] In 1978, it linked its understanding of the sacrificial character of the Eucharist and the notion of the real presence for Christ, who "is present as the Crucified One who died for our sins and rose again for our justification, as Jesus Christ's once-for-all sacrifice for the sins of the world. This sacrifice can be neither continued, nor repeated, nor replaced, nor complemented; but rather it can and should become effective ever anew in the midst of the congregation."[37] Because Christ who is present is the Sacrificed One, the sacrifice of the Eucharist is inseparable from his presence. Once again, the category of sacrament provides the modality of this sacrifice, so that Christ's once-for-all sacrifice is present with the mode of sacrament. The Eucharist as sacrifice is not a repetition or continuation of Christ's sacrifice.

The Methodist-Catholic dialogue affirmed in 1996 that the eucharistic sacrifice is truly Christ's sacrifice; it is not a mere calling to mind of the past event of his sacrifice or its significance. It stated: "Jesus Christ instituted the Eucharist as a holy meal, the memorial of his sacrifice. As the baptized partake of it they share the sacrament of his body given for them and his blood shed for them; they present and plead his sacrifice before God the Father; and they receive the fruits of it in faith."[38] With these words, the dialogue reaffirmed its statement of 1971: "In this celebration we share in Christ's offering Himself in obedience to the Father's will."[39]

In conclusion, notable agreements among these four dialogue partners concerning the sacrificial character of the Eucharist include these four affirmations. First, Christ is present in the Eucharist as the Crucified One who died for our sins as the once-for-all sacrifice for the sins of the world. This Crucified One gives himself to us in the Eucharist. Second, the church's celebration of the Eucharist is a sacrifice of praise and thanksgiving. Third, in the Eucharist Christ's offering of himself to the Father in the power of the Holy Spirit is sacramentally present. This sacramental presence of Christ's sacrifice is neither an extension nor a repetition of his once-for-all sacrifice on the cross. Fourth, the category "anamnesis" or "memorial" describes a celebration that is not a mere recalling of a past event but a making present of that unique past event.

At this point in the ecumenical dialogues, a major obstacle to a shared Eucharist is undoubtedly not eucharistic doctrine *per se*, on which—as we have seen—much progress toward agreement has taken place. Rather, the movement toward a shared Eucharist is currently blocked by the question of who may be the minister or presider of the Eucharist. This question itself is related to the question of apostolic succession.[40] Further, even though the ecumenical dialogues have advanced toward convergence on understanding the church as communion, they still face major differences concerning the nature of the church. These topics, however, lie beyond the scope of this essay.

Conclusion

Since Catholics and other Christians are now experiencing a real but imperfect communion, all of us are moving through what Walter Kasper calls an "intermediary situation."[41] The operative principle is that "one receives the Eucharist in that church fellowship to which one belongs."[42] Nevertheless, since the highest "law" concerns the salvation of God's people, the Catholic Church's Ecumenical Directory of 1993 gives four limited conditions for separated Christians to receive the Eucharist from a Catholic minister or priest. The relationship is asymmetrical, however, for the Ecumenical Directory includes no provision for Catholics to receive the Eucharist from a Protestant minister. It withholds this permission because of differences concerning teachings on the Eucharist and also on account of the lack of the Catholic Church's recognition of the ministry of these other churches and Christian communities. Finally, while the Ecumenical Directory does permit Catholics, under limited conditions, to receive the Eucharist from an Orthodox minister or priest, the ecclesial polity of the Orthodox does not permit this intercommunion.

The pain of disunity at the eucharistic table impels us to work for the unity of Christians. Among the most diligent workers for this unity stands Cardinal Walter Kasper. As this essay has shown, he has advanced the movement toward Christian unity in general and toward unity at the eucharistic table in particular through his theological writings and his pastoral leadership. To be sure, he intensified his efforts for Christian unity when he served as secretary for the Pontifical Council for Promoting Church Unity, beginning in 1999, and as president of the Pontifical Council from 2001 until his retirement in 2010. As Kasper himself has often observed, ecclesial unity among Christians is not so much a task to be achieved by us. Rather, it is a gift that God will bestow on Christians. In this perspective, we can clearly see that Cardinal Walter Kasper, with his passion and skills for ecumenical unity, is a God-given gift for Christian unity.

Endnotes

1. Walter Kasper, "Aspects of the Eucharist in their Unity and Variety," in *Theology and Church*, trans. Margaret Kohl (New York: Crossroad, 1989), 177–94. This essay originally appeared in *Communio* 12 (1985): 115–38. It also appears in idem, *Sacrament of Unity: The Eucharist and the Church* (New York: Crossroad, 2004), 84–116.

2. Kasper's emphasis on the Eucharist in *Sacrament of Unity* occurs again in Walter Kasper, *The Catholic Church: Nature, Reality and Mission*, trans. Thomas Hoebel (London: Bloomsbury T&T Clark, 2014), 20–22.

3. Walter Kasper, "*Communio*: The Guiding Concept in Catholic Ecumenical Theology," in *That All May Be One: the Call to Unity Today* (London: Continuum, 2004), 50–74.

4. See Walter Kasper, "Ein Herr, ein Glaube, eine Taufe: Ökumeische Perspektiven der Zukunft," in *Von der "Gemeinsamen Erklärung" zum "Gemeinsamen Herrenmahl"?*, ed. Ernst Pulsfort and Rolf Hausch (Regensburg: Pustet, 202), 217–38; idem, "Taufe, Eucharistie und Amt in der gegenwärtigen ökumenischen Diskussion: Bemerkungen zum Lima-Papier," in *Praesentia Christi*, ed. Johannes Betz and Lothar Lies (Düsseldorf: Patmos Verlag, 1984).

5. Cardinal Walter Kasper, *Harvesting the Fruits: Basic Aspects of Christian Faith in Ecumenical Dialogue* (New York: Continuum, 2009).

6. Kasper, *Sacrament of Unity*, 113.

7. Ibid., 112.

8. Ibid., 53.

9. Ibid., 101.

10. Ibid., 103.

11. Ibid., 112.

12. Ibid.

13. See Pierre Teilhard de Chardin, "The Mass on the World," in *The Heart of Matter*, trans. René Hague (New York: Harcourt Brace Jovanovich, 1978), 119ff.

14. Kasper, *Sacrament of Unity*, 126.

15. Ibid., 127.

16. Ibid., 96.

17. Ibid., 9

18. Ibid., 99.

19. Ibid., 102.

20. Ibid., 54.

21. Ibid., 106.

22. Ibid.

23. Kasper, "*Communio*: The Guiding Concept," 55; see Kasper, *Sacrament of Unity*, 105–11.

24. Kasper, "*Communio*: The Guiding Concept," 55, citing Augustine of Hippo, *Commentary on John*, 26.6 and 13. See Vatican II, *Unitatis redintegratio* (November 21, 1964), 2.

25. Extraordinary Synod of Bishops, *The Final Report* (1985), II. C. 1. See Vatican II, *Lumen gentium* (November 21, 1964), 3, 11.

26. Kasper, *That They May All Be One*, 59.

27. Henri de Lubac, *Corpus Mysticum: L'Eucharistie et l'Église au Moyen Age* (Paris: 1944). See Kasper, *Sacrament of Unity*, 107–8.

28. Kasper, *Sacrament of Unity*, 108.

29. Kasper, *That They May All Be One*, 57.

30. Kasper, *Sacrament of Unity*, 109.

31. In *Harvesting the Fruits*, Kasper summarizes and quotes from the ecumenical texts to which the notes below refer.

32. See ARCIC, *Eucharistic Doctrine* (1971), 9, 11; idem, *Clarifications of Certain Aspects of the Agreed Statements on Eucharist and Ministry* (1998); Lutheran-Catholic Dialogue, *The Ministry in the Church* (1981), 1, 22, 23; Reformed-Catholic Dialogue (Phase 1), *The Person of Christ in Church and World* (1977), 81, 82, 85; Methodist-Catholic Dialogue (Nairobi), *Towards a Statement on the Church* (1986) 15, 16; idem (Rio de Janeiro), *The Word of Life* (1996), 15.

33. See ARCIC, *Eucharistic Doctrine*, 5; cf. 3.

34. See ARCIC, *Eucharistic Doctrine: Elucidation* (1979), 5.

35. See Reformed-Catholic Dialogue, *The Presence of Christ in the World*, 81; cf. 87, 69, 75.

36. See Lutheran-Catholic Dialogue, *The Eucharist* (1978), 36.

37. See ibid., 56.

38. See Methodist-Catholic Dialogue, *The Word of Life*, 102.

39. Methodist-Catholic Dialogue, *The Denver Report* (1971), 83.

40. See Lutheran-Catholic Dialogue, *The Apostolicity of the Church: Study Document of the Lutheran-Catholic Commission on Unity* (Minneapolis: Lutheran University Press, 2006).

41. Kasper, *Sacrament of Unity*, 143.

42. Ibid., 144.

CHAPTER 13

New Paths of Shalom in Christian-Jewish Relations

Elizabeth T. Groppe

"Traveler, there is no road; the road is made by walking."[1] These words of the poet Antonio Machado describe the work of Christian-Jewish dialogue in our time. The Second Vatican Council's affirmation that "the Jews remain very dear to God" (*Nostra aetate* 4) initiated a new era in relations between Christians and Jews, an era for which Catholics were not theologically well prepared.

The relationship of the Catholic Church to the Jewish people was not on the mind of Pope John XXIII when he convened the Second Vatican Council on January 25, 1959, nor was this relationship an area of scholarly inquiry among the theologians who served as advisers (*periti* in Latin) to the bishops who gathered in Rome. The council would not have even engaged the topic were it not for Jules Isaac, the French Jewish scholar who lost his wife and daughter to the Nazi genocide. In June 1960, at the age of eighty-one, Isaac traveled to Rome for an audience with Pope John to present historical documentation of the theology of "contempt" (French, *mépris*) for Jews that runs through the Christian tradition and to appeal for its reform. Isaac testified that this theology, rooted in the assumption that God has revoked the covenant with the Jewish people, is inconsistent with the Gospel of love, and his appeal ultimately gave rise through a complex process to Vatican II's Declaration on the Relation of the Church to Non-Christian Religions, *Nostra aetate*. The declaration condemns anti-Semitism in all forms and affirms that the Jews remain beloved by God.

Nostra aetate inspired a new Catholic outreach to the Jewish community. In 1967, the Holy See instituted the Office for Catholic-Jewish Relations, and in 1974, it replaced this office with the Commission for Religious Relations with the Jews, established within the Pontifical Council for Promoting Christian Unity. At the request of Pope John Paul II, Kasper became the secretary for this Pontifical Council on March 3, 1999. And on February 21, 2001, Pope John Paul II appointed Cardinal Walter Kasper to succeed Cardinal Edward Cassidy as the president of this pontifical council, a position from which Kasper retired on July 1, 2010. In order to appreciate Cardinal Kasper's extraordinary work over almost ten years, this chapter highlights five contributions to Christian-Jewish relations that are the legacy of his years of service as president of the commission, and it concludes with the reflections of several Jewish scholars and leaders in Christian-Jewish dialogue.

1. Five Contributions to Catholic-Jewish Relations

Cardinal Kasper's many contributions to Catholic-Jewish relations include his call to repentance, his cultivation of relationships and friendships with Jewish colleagues, his clarity about what it means to engage in religious dialogue, his humility, and his reflections on the theological significance of the developing new relationship between Christians and Jews.

(1) *Repentance*/Teshuvà

"*Teshuvà*," Kasper stated in his first address to the Catholic-Jewish Liaison Committee in his capacity as president of the Commission for Religious Relations with the Jews, "is an indispensable step on our path." *Teshuvà* is the term used in Jewish liturgy to speak of repentance and return to God. "For us, Catholics," Kasper continues, "Pope John Paul II has set the example."[2] The example to which the cardinal refers is likely the pope's visit to Jerusalem in March 2000. Mindful of the history of the theology of contempt that Jules Isaac had chronicled and its real consequences for the Jewish people, the pope placed in a crevice of Jerusalem's Western Wall this prayer that had been offered at St. Peter's Basilica on the first Ash Wednesday of the new millennium:

> God of our fathers,
> You chose Abraham and his descendants
> to bring your Name to the Nations:
> we are deeply saddened
> by the behavior of those
> who in the course of history
> have caused these children of yours to suffer,
> and asking your forgiveness
> we wish to commit ourselves
> to genuine brotherhood
> with the people of the Covenant.

Acting in the spirit of this penitential prayer, Kasper calls for a culture of memory within the church. He emphasizes that there are wounds from the past that must still be healed[3] and that remembrance is not a matter of recording information but is rather a branding of the soul.[4] We are linked, he explains, to the sins as well as the merits of all the members of the church, present and past, and "we are all, therefore, called to share in our inner attitudes, prayers and actions in this same journey of conversion and reconciliation [exemplified by Pope John Paul II], because it is a question of the need to live *in capite et in membris* (in the head and in the members)."[5] *Teshuvà* cannot be limited merely to a few authoritative, meaningful gestures or even high-level documents but must be an act of the whole church. Kasper's own *teshuvà* is evident in his commitment to work for a reconciliation of the Christian and Jewish faith communities that is grounded in "a total mutual respect for our respective traditions and convictions."[6]

(2) *Nurturing New Relationships and Friendships*

The Christian-Jewish schism is a saga of broken relationships. A full chronicle of the history that Jules Isaac documented in his presentation to Pope John XXIII would fill volumes.[7] Among the events in this chronicle are the Council of Elvira (ca. 304 CE), which issued a canon that required any member of the faithful who eats with Jews to abstain from eucharistic communion. The history includes the actions of Christian rulers who expelled the Jewish population from

England in 1290, from France in 1306, from Spain in 1492, and from Portugal in 1496. It includes as well the decision of Pope Paul V to segregate the Jews in Rome within a ghetto in 1555, a practice that continued for more than three centuries. These and other forms of social segregation made it difficult for Christians to form real relationships with Jews, leaving a void in the Catholic imagination that was filled with New Testament accounts of those Jews who handed Jesus over to the Romans for crucifixion and theological constructs of the blind and wandering Jew. The new relationships formed between Catholics and Jews after *Nostra aetate* (1965) challenged these derogatory images. "The paradigm change after the Council," writes David Neuhaus, "insisted that the imaginary, textual, and often mythic Jew of Catholic traditional teaching had to make way for the real Jew."[8]

Kasper reached out to "real Jews," establishing friendships with members of the Jewish community. Many of these friendships came through his work with the International Catholic-Jewish Liaison Committee established in 1970 as a bridge between the Vatican's Commission for Religious Relations and the International Jewish Committee for Interreligious Relations. The friendships that have originated through this liaison, the cardinal reminisces, "belong to the most wonderful experiences of the past years."[9] The ecclesial documents that guide interreligious relations are important "but they are not all. Documents can become dead letters; in contrast, dialogue thrives on personal face to face encounter."[10]

Nurturing real relationships is more challenging than issuing statements, and Kasper describes his work as president of the Commission for Religious Relations with the Jews as "anything other than boring and anything other than easy."[11] He was committed, nonetheless, to these relationships. "I have tried to do my best," he stated upon receiving the American Jewish Committee's Isaiah award, "to ensure that *Nostra aetate* did not remain a dead letter, but that it became flesh, blood and bones not only in many interfaith conferences, dialogues, symposiums and workshops, but—more importantly—in personal relations and networks of friendships . . . and concrete forms of cooperation aimed at promoting common values of justice, freedom and charity, peace and health care, education, and the preparation of new youth leadership."[12]

One example of these relationships is Kasper's friendship with Rabbi David Rosen, international director of interreligious affairs for the American Jewish Community. Rosen invited Kasper to share

Shabbat dinners at his home in Israel and in a hotel room in Rome. "It is not possible to really understand contemporary Jewish reality," Kasper observes, in light of these meals, "without experiencing a traditional Shabbat celebration."[13]

In 2005, Rosen was invested with papal knighthood in the Order of Saint Gregory the Great, and Kasper was given the responsibility of decorating him on behalf of Pope Benedict XVI at a ceremony in Jerusalem. The character of their friendship is evident in the exchange that took place on this occasion:

> "Now that you are a Papal Knight," Kasper said warmly to Rosen, "you have the right to ride a horse inside the Vatican!"
>
> "Your Eminence," Rosen replied graciously, "perhaps you might like to update this right—and provide me instead with a nice red Ferrari."
>
> "No!" Kasper responded firmly, with a smile. "With the traffic in Rome, you are much better off on a horse!"[14]

The late John S. Dunne described interreligious encounter as a process of "passing over" into the reality of another and then "coming back" into one's own.[15] That Kasper is truly able to pass empathetically into the reality of Jewish colleagues is evident in his response to the reception of *Dominus Iesus*. This declaration from the Congregation of the Doctrine of the Faith on the "Unicity and Salvific Universality of Jesus Christ and the Church" (August 6, 2000) sparked international controversy. Much of the negative reaction to *Dominus Iesus* was, according to Kasper, the result of misunderstandings that occurred because of the declaration's highly technical language that was compounded by misleading media coverage. For Jews, moreover, the statement evoked painful memories of past eras. "It was not its intention to hurt or offend," the cardinal stated. "But it did, and for this I can only express my profound regret. My friends' pains are also my pains."[16]

The empathy and friendship that Kasper extended to Jewish colleagues on this and other occasions was reciprocated. "It was not an easy decision for me as a German," he reflected in 2010, "to accept this duty [of presidency of the Pontifical Commission for Religious Relations]."[17] "But very soon I was surprised, for instead of finding suspicious partners I discovered friends, and this friendship not only helped me to do what I had to do but made what I had to do not merely a duty, but rather a personally engaging and fulfilling task."[18] There was "never even the least indication of reservation from their side about my [German] provenance, which was for me a positive sign and an encouragement that even after a sad history a new beginning can be possible."[19]

(3) *The Meaning of "Religious Dialogue"*

As Christians, we have a long history of conducting disputations with Jews—and much less experience engaging with them in true dialogue. One of Kasper's contributions is his clarification as to what precisely dialogue is and what it is not. Leading us on a *via negativa*, he explains that religious dialogue is not small talk, nor exchange of information, nor even academic discussion, although progress does require academic exchange.[20] Religious dialogue is not indifferentism, and its end is neither relativism nor syncretism.[21]

What, then, is religious dialogue? True dialogue, the cardinal explains, is an encounter between persons who meet as equal partners, an encounter in which one freely witnesses to one's own faith and conviction and receives in turn the witness of the other, bearing and respecting the "otherness" of the other,[22] a theme that Philip Cunningham probes in his contribution to this volume (see chap. 14). Invoking the personalist philosophy of Pope John Paul II, Kasper notes that it is through this receptive openness to others and generous self-giving that human persons come to maturity. He cites the work of Martin Buber, Emmanuel Levinas, and others who help us see "that it is in the countenance of the other, in confronting the otherness of that other, that we discover ourselves."[23]

In dialogue, Kasper continues, "I want to communicate something that is important for me and for my life . . . what gives meaning to my life, what supports me, what inspires, encourages and also consoles me. Because it is important to me and makes me happy, I want to share it with others so that they too may be blessed. Dialogue, in this deeper sense, implies witness of my deepest faith, a witness which proposes but by no means imposes one's own faith; on the contrary, it implies respect for every other conviction and every other faith. So in dialogue Jews give witness of their faith, witness of what supported them in the dark periods of their history and their life, and Christians give account of the hope they have in Jesus Christ. In doing so, both are far away from any kind of proselytism, but both can learn from each other and enrich each other."[24]

When Jews and Christians meet in dialogue, they realize not only their differences but also their common faith in the one God and common commitment to walk on God's paths. "We should have no fear to respectfully go near the faith experience of one another," Kasper explains, "to respectfully see one another's face 'as one sees the face of God' (cf. Gen. 33:10), feeling blessed by it. We are partners, we are 'others', but we are also 'brothers.' "[25] Christians have forgotten that we are grafted into the good olive tree of Israel (Rom 11), and Kasper believes "that the discovery, or the rediscovery, of this essential link between both our religious traditions, is basically the agenda for our dialogue."[26]

One of Kasper's own experiences of this rediscovery occurred in 2001 on a flight to Rome from Montevideo, Uruguay. Upon departure, a rabbi handed the cardinal a Jewish prayer book. Reading the book during the long trip home, Kasper found himself in prayer. "It is true," he realized in this experience, "what a group of Jewish theologians formulated in the statement '*Dabru emet*' (September 15, 2000) . . . 'Jews and Christians worship the same God.' This is the God of Abraham, Isaac, and Jacob, who for us Christians is also the God of Jesus Christ."[27]

Dialogue and the nurturance of interfaith relations, Kasper emphasizes, is not only or even primarily for the sake of our own spiritual discoveries. Rather, religious dialogue offers hope to a world suffering from cultural and moral deprivation. Christians and Jews "both want to share our deepest concerns to an often disoriented world that needs such witness and searches for it."[28] We "cannot waste time," the cardinal states, "with useless, superficial, transparently self-promoting public quarrels." This is a "high and holy task."[29]

One example of this holy witness is an action initiated by delegates to a meeting of the Jewish World Congress that took place in Buenos Aires during Argentina's financial crisis. The Jewish delegates saw children standing hungry in the streets; their parents did not have the money for bus fare that was necessary to send the children to schools where regular meals were being served. The Jewish World Congress raised ten million dollars and asked Kasper how to best use the funds in service of the children in this predominantly Catholic country, and the cardinal facilitated collaboration with the Catholic organization Caritas International, which has offices in every city in Argentina.[30]

Another story of holy witness comes from Cape Town, South Africa, where the International Catholic-Jewish Liaison Committee met in November 2006. Members of the committee visited schools, Jewish and Catholic health service organizations caring for people with HIV/AIDS, and other facilities. Judith Hertz, co-chair of the Commission on Interreligious Affairs of Reform Judaism, tells this story about a visit to a children's hospital: "The children were accustomed to visitors and greeted us with big smiles. Cardinal Kasper was in my group. A small boy, about four years old, had an especially winsome smile. Cardinal Kasper returned his smile, reached out his arms to the child and picked him up. The child cuddled in his arms and proceeded in this way with us through the 'tour.' Each of the visitors followed the cardinal's example and picked up a child. It was not pathos that moved us but joy—joy that came with the recognition that it is possible to add pleasure to children's lives even in painful and sad circumstances."[31]

(4) *Humility*

Humility, explains Bernard of Clairvaux, is the ground on which we as mortal creatures can seek truth, and Cardinal Kasper exemplified this humility as he grappled with the theological complexities of the Christian-Jewish relationship. The theory of the substitution of the old covenant by the new, he explains, "is gone since the Second Vatican Council,"[32] replaced by a theology of what Pope John Paul II termed God's "unabrogated covenant" with the Jewish people.[33] This affirmation is the foundation for the new relationship between the church and the Jewish people that is emerging in the postconciliar era, but it has also raised many difficult questions about the relationship between God's covenant with the Jewish people and the covenant in Christ. Kasper approached these questions with genuine humility and an openness of mind and spirit. "We are only *at the start of a new start* of a 'Christian theology of Judaism,'" he affirms. "Many decisive questions still remain open."[34] Centuries "of anti-Judaic theology cannot be overcome in only forty years. *Nostra aetate* was only the beginning of a new beginning."[35]

Kasper encouraged open theological exploration of the implications of this new beginning. After Jewish scholars published "*Dabru Emet*:

To Speak the Truth" (2000), Kasper supported the work of an international group of Christian theologians who undertook a five-year study of the relationship of the universal saving significance of Jesus Christ to Israel's ongoing covenantal life. In a foreword to the book *Christ Jesus and the Jewish People Today* (2011) that was the fruit of this study, Kasper notes that there will be different positions on the open questions before us and invites readers to join in the conversation in order to advance the discussion.[36] He also acknowledges that the questions that we face are eschatological and, for this reason, even the theological labor of multiple generations will be limited in its expression. The full realization of the covenant will come only at the end of time and "therefore, our theological knowledge in such issues will always be fragmentary and partial."[37]

(5) *Toward a Theology of the Jewish-Christian Relation*

With eschatological humility, Cardinal Kasper grappled with the theological challenges of the Christian-Jewish relationship, and his own contributions to the ongoing discussion include ten constructive points.

(1) The covenant has its concrete historical reference point in the people of Israel. In the course of their history, the covenant is reinterpreted and sealed anew in new contexts: the postdiluvian covenant with Noah, the covenant with Abraham and Sarah, the covenant mediated through Moses on Sinai, the entrance into the Promised Land, the anointing of King David, the return from Babylonian exile, and the prophetic promise of an everlasting covenant.[38] The new covenant in Christ is continuous with this history as the "final and definitive reinterpretation of the covenant which God has sealed with his people once and for all."[39]

(2) The new covenant accomplishes the universality of redemption that was implicit in the old covenant since its inception. "Christ has rescinded the exclusion of the Gentiles and given them access to the covenant; he has created peace and united and reconciled Jews and Gentiles in his person (cf. Eph 2:11-22)."[40] The universality of Christ's redemption for Jews and for Gentiles, Kasper emphasizes, is fundamental throughout the entire New Testament (Eph 2:14-18; Col 1:15-18; 1 Tim 2:5; Rom 3:24; 8:32; and others).

(3) At the same time, the seals of the original covenant remain. "From the Christian perspective the covenant with the Jewish people is unbroken (Rom. 11:29) for we as Christians believe that these promises find in Jesus their definitive and irrevocable Amen (2 Cor. 1:20) and at the same time that in him, who is the end of the law (Rom. 10:4), the law is not nullified but upheld (Rom. 3:31)."[41]

(4) The new covenant is "new" not in the sense of historical innovation, nor in the sense of the replacement of something old, nor even a reform or renewal of the old, but in an eschatological sense. The new covenant is "the eschatological fulfillment and therefore definitive reinterpretation of the Old Testament covenant promise."[42]

(5) This eschatological fulfillment of the covenant in Christ is universal and therefore includes the Jewish people in its embrace. "From a Christian perspective," Kasper writes, "the death and resurrection of Christ also means salvation for the Jews."[43] With empathy, he appreciates "that it must be painful for Jews to listen to such words," and this causes him no small distress.[44] He immediately adds that the Christian conviction of the universality and "unicity" or absolute singularity of the redemption wrought in Christ does *not* imply a replacement of the old covenant by the new unless the Christological affirmation becomes an ecclesiological claim and the difference between what is already accomplished in Christ and the still anticipated eschatological consummation is abrogated.[45]

(6) Carefully maintaining these differences, Kasper affirms that Jews and Christians are together one covenant people who exist each in their own distinctiveness without confusion but also without separation.[46] Kasper's acknowledgment of this difference within the unity of the people of God is a significant theological contribution that goes beyond Vatican II. *Lumen gentium*, the Dogmatic Constitution on the Church, states that the church is the new people of God to which non-Christians (including the Jews) are called and ordained (LG 13; cf. 16), and *Nostra aetate* describes the church as "the new people of God" (4).[47] Cardinal Kasper affirms, in contrast, that Jews and Christians are together "the one people of God."[48]

(7) Members of the new covenant exercise evangelization in relationship with Jews in the proper technical sense of this term: i.e., bearing witness to the Gospel through prayer, liturgy, and life. Mis-

sion, in contrast, refers to an invitation to conversion from false gods or idols to the one true God—the God whom the Jews worship. The church therefore has no mission to the Jewish people, and Jews need not become Christian to participate in salvation. "If they follow their own conscience," Kasper writes, "and believe in God's promises as they understand them in their religious tradition they are in line with God's plan, which for us comes to its historical completion in Jesus Christ."[49]

(8) The relationship between Judaism and Christianity is so complex and dialectic that it cannot be reduced to a concise formula.[50] "Rabbi Professor Michael Signer is certainly right," the cardinal notes, "when he states that this highly tense relation can only be expressed through images and symbols."[51] Kasper himself often employs Paul's image of the Jewish people as the stock of the good olive tree onto which the Gentiles have been grafted: "In the Epistle to the Romans, Paul uses the image of the root of the olive tree for Israel, into which the church of the Gentiles is grafted like a branch. The root bears the branches and gives them sustenance (cf. Rom. 11:16-24). With this image Paul resists any Christian triumphalism: 'It is not you that support the root, but the root that supports you' (11:18)."

The church, the cardinal explains, is dependent on Israel, for "salvation is from the Jews" (John 4:22). The presence of the Old Testament in the canon of sacred scripture preserved Christianity from sliding into Gnosticism and sharpens its awareness of the historicity and physicality of the salvation story. "Traditional theological anti-Judaism has cut the church off from its bearing and sustaining root, and has led to its impoverishment and weakening."[52] The Jewish people, in turn, need the church to extend the worship of God to the Gentiles. Franz Rosenzweig, Kasper notes, knows the "danger posed by Judaism cutting itself off in its self-sufficiency and closing the door to dialogue. For Judaism cannot simply be indifferent to the branch of Christianity which was grafted into the Jewish rootstock and has in the meantime grown into a great tree, without denying a part of itself. For the promise given to Abraham that all the nations are blessed in him (cf. Gen. 12:3 etc.) has made its way toward fulfillment by way of Christianity."[53]

(9) Christians and Jews stand together as a covenant people who bear witness to the absolute singularity or "unicity" of the one and

only God (Deut 6:4; Mark 12:29).[54] This affirmation of God's radical uniqueness is not simply a metaphysical statement but a "qualitative, *existential* statement"; it is "a demand for a radical and integrated decision to belong to God with all one's heart, soul and understanding (Mark 12:30 and parallels)."[55] In a postmodern world that so often seems to have lost values and convictions, a world where many doubt the reality of universal truth and norms of justice, a common witness by Christians and Jews to the one God whom we worship offers hope for the future. The unicity of God that we affirm does not produce totalitarianism or imperialism as some fear, for the one God is a God of self-giving Trinitarian and kenotic love, a love that *is* "precisely in this self-giving."[56] Moreover, God's absolute uniqueness implies that we are all irrevocably sisters and brothers of one family. Kasper urges Christians and Jews to testify together within our secular and sometimes even cynical world to the sanctity of God's name, the sanctity of human life, the grace of forgiveness and reconciliation, and the need for the preservation of God's creation. "In today's world," the cardinal affirms, "we, Jews and Christians, have a common mission: together we should give an orientation. Together we must be ambassadors of peace and bring about *Shalom*."[57]

(10) Finally, it should be noted that although Kasper served as president of the Pontifical Commission for Religious Relations with the Jews, he was keenly aware of the importance of building relationships with Muslims "who share our sonship with Abraham and our monotheistic faith." He calls for the establishment of interreligious trialogues or three-way conversations and hopes for that day when Jerusalem will be "a place of peace for Jews, Muslims and Christians and a sign of hope for peace for all humankind."[58]

Given that Cardinal Kasper has made at least ten distinct contributions to a theology of the relationship between the Catholic Church and the Jewish people, one can scarcely ask for more. Yet, as John T. Pawlikowski has noted, Kasper wrote his major works in systematic theology prior to his service as president of the pontifical commission. Should the cardinal be inspired to continue his work in systematic theology in his retirement, it would enrich the church were he to revisit books such as *The God of Jesus Christ* (1982) and *Jesus the Christ* (1974) in light of his deepened engagement with Judaism. This would add yet another dimension to his constructive Christian theology.

2. Jewish Perspectives on Kasper's Contributions to Christian-Jewish Dialogue

In celebration of Cardinal Kasper's eightieth birthday, Jewish scholars wrote reflections on Cardinal Kasper's contributions to the dialogue between Christians and Jews. Abbreviated versions of their statements appear below.

(1) *Susannah Heschel, Eli Black Professor of Jewish Studies at Dartmouth College*

"Cardinal Kasper is a pastoral figure and a figure of great warmth. From the Jewish perspective, the warmth that he exudes as a person is very important. It matters not only what one says but how one says it. The warmth that Kasper expresses has made a big impression on Jews. He interprets *Nostra aetate* in a wonderful positive direction, but he did so not only as a Catholic theologian but also as a defender of Jews and of Jewish concerns, someone who could articulate a Jewish perspective even as a Catholic. I am reminded of Isaiah: 'Here I am, send me' (Isa 6:8). God trusted Isaiah to speak in God's name, and Isaiah had the ability to speak on behalf of another. That is important and very precious."

(2) *Adam Gregerman, Jewish Scholar at the Institute of Christian and Jewish Studies*

"Cardinal Walter Kasper has done remarkable work to improve Jewish-Catholic relations. He has skillfully led the Roman Catholic Church's efforts at reconciliation by offering a theologically sophisticated and also compassionate view of Jews and Judaism. Above all, he has steadfastly aimed to solidify and to build on the path-breaking work of the Second Vatican Council. The Jewish community has come to value greatly the process begun with *Nostra aetate*. Cardinal Kasper's efforts to translate the declaration into life and into reality are therefore deeply appreciated. Against those who would weaken these changes, he has insisted that there is no turning back.

"We should not forget how much has been accomplished in a short period of time. As Cardinal Kasper has observed, 'No one could have foreseen forty-five years ago where we are today in the relationship between Jews and Christians.'[59] Not only does Cardinal Kasper remind us of these changes but he himself has done much to make them possible. He has steadfastly endeavored to make his own hope, and that of the Catholic Church, a reality, to move to a new stage in an often bitter and painful millennia-long relationship.

"Cardinal Kasper has directly addressed some of the most difficult and complex issues in our relationship with insight and subtlety. Above all, he has grappled fruitfully with the tension between universal salvation in Christ and the ongoing Jewish covenant. While recognizing that complete agreement is neither possible nor desirable, this type of serious engagement holds the most promise for greater understanding. As perhaps the best tribute to him, Jews and Catholics together can show our appreciation by continuing this vital work."

(3) *Shira Lander, Anna Smith Fine Senior Lecturer of Jewish Studies at Rice University*

"Throughout his career, Cardinal Kasper argued for the uniqueness of the Christian-Jewish relationship. Commenting on the significant yet controversial *Dominus Iesus*, he said: 'We, both Jews and Christians, are on the same side, on the same boat, if I am allowed to say so; we have to fight, to argue and to bear witness together. Our common self-understanding is at stake.'[60] Cardinal Kasper also affirmed the eternality of the Jewish covenant with God as their valid path to salvation: '[T]he Church believes that Judaism, that is, the faithful response of the Jewish people to God's irrevocable covenant, is salvific for them, because God is faithful to his promises.'[61] One Jewish objection to *Dominus Iesus* involved a misunderstanding of the term 'evangelization,' which Cardinal Kasper reassured his Jewish friends 'if understood in its proper and theological meaning, does not imply any attempt at proselytism whatsoever.'[62]

"Cardinal Kasper continued to uphold his deep respect for Judaism while also promoting sincere and authentic dialogue between Roman Catholics and Jews throughout the papacy of Benedict XVI. Upon receiving the esteemed Isaiah Interreligious Award from the American Jewish Committee, Cardinal Kasper reaffirmed that 'Judaism and Christianity stand in a relationship which is unique in all the history of religions. Jews and Christians are together the new people of God.'[63] He restated his conviction that Judaism was a valid expression of faith in the one God for Jews while at the same time avowing his church's eschatological hope in the fullness of God's grace to extend to all humankind, including Jews. This position is evident in his explanation of the changes made in 2007 to the 1962 Tridentine Rite for Good Friday's petition for the Jews.[64] While many in the Jewish community remain dissatisfied by his response to this difficult chapter in Catholic-Jewish relations, others understood that the cardinal was breaking new ground and clearing the way for a more honest conversation. This new stage of Jewish-Christian dialogue is epitomized in the culminating work of an international group of Christian theologians who undertook a five-year study of how to relate 'the universal saving significance of Jesus Christ to Israel's ongoing covenantal life with God.'[65] This volume *Christ Jesus and the Jewish People Today: New Explorations of Theological Interrelationships* (2011) marks the capstone to Cardinal Kasper's legacy. In the book's foreword, he writes that 'dialogue must . . . be the realization that Jews and Christians differ on these issues and must respect and appreciate each other in their otherness. But precisely for the sake of mutual respect and appreciation, in the newly generated climate of trust it must be a primary goal to actively reduce old misunderstandings and develop possible approaches to understanding each other's positions.'[66]

"With these words, Cardinal Kasper has bequeathed the dialogue to a new generation of theologians and scholars. This new generation, standing on the shoulders of the giants who before them established a bond of trust and commitment between Catholics and Jews, will follow the cardinal's lead in breaking new ground. As he averred on many occasions, 'We stand only at the beginning of a new beginning.' "[67]

(4) *Ruth Langer, Professor of Jewish Studies and Associate Director of the Center for Jewish-Christian Learning, Boston College*

"My first—and I think only—meeting with Cardinal Kasper in a small-group setting was when he participated in the meeting of the Christian Scholars Group in Jewish-Christian Relations at a retreat house before coming back with us to Boston College where he delivered the public lecture 'The Commission for Religious Relations with the Jews: A Crucial Endeavour of the Catholic Church' (November 6, 2002).[68] In this lecture, he expresses several of the important themes that echoed through his leadership of the Pontifical Council for Religious Relations with the Jews, most memorably for me his metaphor that *Nostra aetate* took the form it did, as a document about the world's major religions and not just Judaism, 'to save the furniture from the burning house.' In other words, there remained and remains more to do.

"Another theme that echoes in his writings is his emphasis that *Nostra aetate* was only the 'beginning of the beginning,' and we are in many ways still at the 'beginning.' This gives us a mandate for undertaking the challenging tasks that are necessary in order for dialogue at all levels between Jews and Catholics to move forward grounded on a firmer foundation.

"At the meeting of the Christian Scholars Group in 2002, I experienced a personal side of Cardinal Kasper. . . . He clearly rejoiced in the opportunity to sit back and think together with a group of theologians. The perpetual smile on his face was clearly genuine and reflected deeply his emotions as he joined in the group's work."

(5) *Rabbi David Rosen, International Director of Interreligious Affairs for the American Jewish Community*

"The Mishnah identifies the age of eighty with *gvurah* which is usually translated as 'great strength' but may also be translated as 'heroism.' Indeed, Cardinal Kasper is one of the heroes of the blessed transformation in Catholic-Jewish relations in our time and together with my congratulations I pay tribute to him for all he has done and all he is."

Conclusion

In his reflections on the Christian-Jewish relationship, Cardinal Kasper emphasizes not only the Pauline image of the olive tree with its spreading roots and branches (Rom 11) but also an image of Jews and Gentiles standing shoulder to shoulder. This vision, he explains, originated in Jewish exegesis of Zechariah's prophecy of that day when "the Lord will be one and his name one" (Zech 14:9). The prophet looks into the messianic future where the peoples are taken into covenant with Israel. "According to rabbinical interpretation all of us, Jews and all people, will stand shoulder to shoulder. . . . Jews and Christians together maintain this hope. For they can testify from the bitter and painful lessons of history that—despite otherness and foreignness and despite historical guilt—conversion, reconciliation, peace and friendship are possible. May the new century become a century of brotherhood—shoulder to shoulder. Shalom!"[69]

Endnotes

1. Cited in Mary C. Boys, "The Road Is Made by Walking," in *Faith Transformed: Christian Encounters with Jews and Judaism*, ed. John C. Merkle (Collegeville, MN: Liturgical Press, 2003), 162. Boys renders Machado's *caminante* as "walker," whereas I translate this as "traveler."

2. Walter Kasper, "Welcoming Address to the 2001 ILC Meeting" (New York: May 1, 2001); see http://www.ccjr.us/dialogika-resources/documents-and-statements/roman-catholic/kasper/644-wk01may1; accessed April 20, 2013.

3. Walter Kasper, "Welcome to the Vatican's Commemoration of the 40th Anniversary of *Nostra Aetate*" (Rome: October 27, 2005); see http://www.ccjr.us/dialogika-resources/documents-and-statements/roman-catholic/kasper/654-wk05oct27; accessed April 20, 2013.

4. Walter Kasper, "The Theology of the Covenant as Central Issue in the Jewish-Christian Dialogue" (Sacred Heart University, Fairfield, CT: December 4, 2001); see http://www.ccjr.us/dialogika-resources/documents-and-statements/roman-catholic/kasper/648-wk01dec4; accessed April 20, 2013. See idem, "The Commission for Religious Relations with the Jews: A Crucial Endeavor of the Catholic Church" (Address at Boston College: November 6, 2002); see http://www.ccjr.us/dialogika-resources/documents-and-statements/roman-catholic/kasper/642-kasper02nov6; accessed April 20, 2013.

5. Kasper, "Antisemitism: A Wound to Be Healed" (Reflections for the Fourth European Day of Jewish Culture: September 5, 2013); see http://www.ccjr.us/dialogika-resources/documents-and-statements/roman-catholic/kasper/656-wk03sept5; accessed April 20, 2013.

6. Kasper, "Welcoming Address to the 2001 ILC Meeting."

7. For surveys of this history, see Anna Foa, "The Difficult Apprenticeship of Diversity," in *The Catholic Church and the Jewish People: Recent Reflections from Rome*, ed. Philip A. Cunningham, Norbert J. Hofmann, and Joseph Sievers (New York: Fordham University Press, 2007), 41–53; Edward H. Flannery, *The Anguish of the Jews: Twenty-Three Centuries of Antisemitism*, rev. ed. (New York: Paulist Press, 1985); Robert Michael, *A History of Catholic Antisemitism: The Dark Side of the Church* (New York: Palgrave Macmillan, 2008).

8. David M. Neuhaus, "Engaging the Jewish People: Forty Years since *Nostra Aetate*," in *Catholic Engagement with World Religions: A Comprehensive Study*, ed. Karl Josh Becker and Ilaria Morali (Maryknoll, NY: Orbis, 2010), 398–99.

9. Walter Kasper, *Wo das Herz des Glaubens Schlägt* (Freiburg: Herder, 2008), 282. Here and below, translations by Robert A. Krieg.

10. Kasper, "The Commission for Religious Relations with the Jews: A Crucial Endeavor of the Catholic Church" (Boston College, Boston, MA: November 6, 2002); see http://www.ccjr.us/dialogika-resources/educational-and-liturgical-materials/classic-articles/496-kasper02nov6; accessed April 20, 2013.

11. Ibid.

12. Walter Kasper, Address upon receiving the American Jewish Committee's Isaiah Interreligious Award (Washington, DC: April 30, 2010); see http://www.ccjr.us/dialogika-resources/documents-and-statements/roman-catholic/kasper/945-kasper2010apr30; accessed April 20, 2013.

13. E-mail communication with Rabbi David Rosen (April 24, 2013).

14. E-mail communication with Rabbi David Rosen (April 26, 2013).

15. John S. Dunne, *The Way of All the Earth: Experiments in Truth and Religion* (New York: MacMillan, 1972), ix.

16. Walter Kasper, "*Dominus Iesus*" (Address at the seventeenth meeting of the International Catholic-Jewish Liaison Committee, New York: May 1, 2001); see http://www.ccjr.us/dialogika-resources/documents-and-statements/analysis/497-kasper01may1; accessed April 20, 2013.

17. Walter Kasper, "Recent Developments in Jewish-Christian Relations" (Address at Liverpool Hope University: May 24, 2010) ; see http://www.ccjr.us/dialogika-resources/documents-and-statements/roman-catholic/kasper/814-kasper2010may24; accessed April 20, 2013.

18. Kasper, Address upon receiving the American Jewish Committee's Isaiah Interreligious Award.

19. Kasper, "Recent Developments in Jewish-Christian Relations."

20. Kasper, "The Theology of the Covenant."

21. Kasper, "The Commission for Religious Relations with the Jews: A Crucial Endeavor."

22. Ibid.

23. Ibid.

24. Walter Kasper, "The Jewish-Christian Dialogue: Foundations, Progress, Difficulties, and Perspectives" (Lecture at the Israel Museum in Jerusalem, under the sponsorship of the Interreligious Coordinating Council in Israel: November 21, 2001); see http://www.ccjr.us/dialogika-resources/documents-and-statements/roman-catholic/kasper/647-wk01nov21; accessed April 20, 2013.

25. Kasper, "Welcoming Address to the 2001 ILC Meeting."

26. Ibid.

27. Kasper, *Wo das Herz des Glaubens Schlägt*, 286. The text of *Dabru Emet*, which was originally published in *The New York Times*, is reprinted in *Christianity in Jewish Terms*, ed. Tikva Frymer-Kensky, David Novak, Peter Ochs, David Fox Sandmel, and Michael A. Signer (Boulder, CO: Westview, 2000), xvii–xx.

28. Kasper, "The Jewish-Christian Dialogue."

29. Ibid.

30. Kasper, *Wo das Herz des Glaubens Schlägt*, 285.

31. For an account of this meeting, see http://interreligious.rj.org/ILC19thMeeting.htm; accessed April 20, 2013.

32. Kasper, "*Dominus Iesus*." See also "The Theology of the Covenant."

33. Walter Kasper, "The Relationship of the Old and New Covenant as One of the Central Issues in Jewish-Christian Dialogue" (Address at the Centre for the Study of Jewish-Christian Relations, Cambridge, United Kingdom: December 6, 2004); see http://www.ccjr.us/dialogika-resources/documents-and-statements/roman-catholic/kasper/652-kasper04dec6; accessed April 20, 2013.

34. Ibid. My emphasis.

35. Kasper, "The Commission for Religious Relations with the Jews: A Crucial Endeavor."

36. Walter Kasper, "Foreword," in *Christ Jesus and the Jewish People Today: New Explorations of Theological Interrelationships*, ed. Philip A. Cunningham et al. (Grand Rapids, MI: William B. Eerdmans, 2011), xiii–xiv.

37. Kasper, "The Theology of the Covenant."

38. Kasper, "The Relationship of the Old and New Covenant."

39. Ibid.

40. Ibid.

41. Kasper, "The Commission for Religious Relations with the Jews: A Crucial Endeavor."

42. Kasper, "The Relationship of the Old and New Covenant."

43. Kasper, "Foreword," in *Christ Jesus and the Jewish People Today*, xv.

44. Kasper, "The Commission for Religious Relations with the Jews: A Crucial Endeavor."

45. Kasper, "The Relationship of the Old and New Covenant."

46. Kasper, "Foreword," in *Christ Jesus and the Jewish People Today*, xv.

47. On this point, see Elizabeth T. Groppe, "Revisiting Vatican II's Theology of the People of God after Forty-Five Years of Catholic-Jewish Dialogue," *Theological Studies* 72 (2011): 586–619.

48. Kasper, Address upon receiving the American Jewish Committee's Isaiah Interreligious Award.

49. Kasper, "Commission for Religious Relations with the Jews: A Crucial Endeavor."

50. Kasper, "The Relationship of the Old and New Covenant."

51. Kasper, "The Commission for Religious Relations with the Jews: A Crucial Endeavor."

52. Kasper, "The Relationship of the Old and New Covenant."

53. Ibid.

54. Walter Kasper, "The Unicity and Universality of Jesus Christ" (October 17, 2000); see http://www.ccjr.us/dialogika-resources/documents-and-statements/roman-catholic/kasper/657-wc00oct17; accessed April 20, 2013.

55. Ibid.

56. Ibid.

57. Kasper, "*Dominus Iesus*."

58. Kasper, "The Jewish-Christian Dialogue: Foundations, Progress, Difficulties and Perspectives."

59. Kasper, "Foreword," in *Christ Jesus and the Jewish People Today*, xviii.

60. Kasper, "The Jewish-Christian Dialogue: Foundations, Progress, Difficulties and Perspectives."

61. Ibid.

62. Ibid.

63. Kasper, Address upon receiving the American Jewish Committee's Isaiah Interreligious Award.

64. Walter Kasper, "Striving for Mutual Respect in Modes of Prayer," *L'Osservatore Romano* (April 16, 2008): 8–9.

65. Kasper, "Foreword," in *Christ Jesus and the Jewish People Today*, xiii.

66. Ibid.

67. Ibid, xiv.

68. Kasper, "The Commission for Religious Relations with the Jews: A Crucial Endeavor."

69. Ibid.

CHAPTER 14

Celebrating Judaism as a "Sacrament of Every Otherness"

Philip A. Cunningham

On March 3, 2001, Walter Kasper—whom Pope John Paul II had elevated the previous month to the College of Cardinals—became the president of the Pontifical Council for Promoting Christian Unity. In accepting this office, he also assumed leadership of the Commission for Religious Relations with the Jews (CRRJ). Coincidentally, around this time Catholic-Jewish research and interreligious dialogue were beginning to plumb new theological depths. In May 2001 in New York City at the seventeenth meeting of the International Catholic-Jewish Liaison Committee (ILC), Kasper acknowledged that the time was ripe "for a dialogue which goes beyond the discussion of problems and enters into the very heart of what constitutes our identities as faith communities."[1]

It would, however, be a series of interconnected "problems" during Kasper's nearly ten years as the CRRJ president that would stimulate deeper Catholic theological self-reflection on the relations between the two faith communities. This essay focuses on Cardinal Kasper's own theological contributions in grappling with the emerging questions.

1. Judaism as "Unique among the World's Religions"

One "problem," in particular, formed the backdrop to the meeting of the ILC in 2001. On August 6, 2000, the Congregation for the

Doctrine of the Faith (CDF) issued *Dominus Iesus* ("A Declaration on the Unicity and Salvific Universality of Jesus Christ and the Church") with the aim of combating an extreme relativism that sees all religions as essentially the same. Unfortunately, the CDF had not considered what its text implied about Judaism. For example, the text asserted that Christian "*faith*" is "the acceptance in grace of revealed truth" from God, whereas "the other religions," the results of human yearnings, are based on mere "*belief*," understood as "that sum of experience and thought that constitutes the human treasury of wisdom and religious aspiration" but which is still searching for God.[2] As a result, the adherents of non-Christian religions were "in a gravely deficient situation in comparison with those who, in the Church, have the fullness of the means of salvation."[3]

To Jews, who naturally understand themselves as an "other religion" in relation to Christianity, *Dominus Iesus* seemingly communicated that the Jewish people do not have "faith" and are unacquainted with divine revelation. By failing to note God's election of Israel or God's establishment of the Mosaic covenant at Sinai, the CDF's declaration apparently discounted the entire Jewish tradition as a legitimate faith. Given the history of Christian hostility to Judaism, an understandable fear of Catholic reversion to long-lived habits inclined some readers to interpret *Dominus Iesus* in the worst possible light.

Since it was not evident, especially to Jewish readers, that the authors of *Dominus Iesus* had taken for granted that Judaism is a true "faith," Vatican officials acted quickly to correct this oversight. In the following months, Cardinal Joseph Ratzinger, then the head of the CDF,[4] and Cardinal Edward Idris Cassidy, the retiring CRRJ president,[5] and Cardinal Kasper explained that "Judaism, in the mind of the Church, is unique among the world's religions."[6]

2. Jewish Covenantal Life as "Salvific for Them"

In his formal remarks at the May 2001 ILC meeting, Kasper also noted that Judaism's unique character relates to the Christian understanding of salvation:

> Jews and Christians, by their respective specific identities, are intimately related to each other. It is impossible now to enter the complex problem of how this intimate relatedness should or

> could be defined. Such a question touches the mystery of Jewish and Christian existence as well, and should be discussed in our further dialogue.
>
> The only thing I wish to say is that the Document *Dominus Iesus* does not state that everybody needs to become a Catholic in order to be saved by God. On the contrary, it declares that God's grace, which is the grace of Jesus Christ according to our faith, is available to all. Therefore, the Church believes that Judaism, i.e. the faithful response of the Jewish people to God's irrevocable covenant, is salvific for them, because God is faithful to his promises.[7]

To my knowledge, this statement was the first time a Vatican spokesperson had explicitly linked Judaism's covenantal life to salvation. Yet, this association between God's covenant and salvation is unavoidable. How could people in a biblically attested, loving relationship with a saving God—a relationship that is so intimate as to be called "covenantal"—not be "saved" by virtue of that relationship? Unsettled by Kasper's statement, some Catholics would later claim that Christ's universal significance was being compromised by such formulations. But, in Cardinal Kasper's careful construction, it is the "grace of Jesus Christ" itself that is somehow involved in the mystery of Israel's covenantal life with God.

In fact, *Dominus Iesus* itself made a similar but more general point by quoting from John Paul II's encyclical *Redemptoris Missio*: "salvation in Christ is accessible by virtue of a grace which, while having a mysterious relationship to the Church, does not make [non-Christians] formally part of the Church, but enlightens them in a way which is accommodated to their spiritual and material situation. This *grace comes from Christ*; it is the result of his sacrifice and is communicated by the Holy Spirit."[8] Similarly, the Second Vatican Council upheld the universality of God's salvation through Jesus Christ. In *Nostra aetate*, the council asserted that the various "beliefs" of humanity "often reflect a ray of that truth which enlightens all men and women."[9] Commenting on this teaching during the council, Archbishop John Carmel Heenan observed that if the rays of truth, God's Word, illumine all people, then "how much more luminous is the Jewish religion which is, at the same time, the root of our faith!"[10]

Thus, Cardinal Kasper reiterated and clarified the church's recognition of the theological significance of God's covenant with the Jewish people. He appealed not only to church teachings but also to history in light of the Bible. Time and again, Kasper has insisted that God has never revoked the divine covenantal bond with Jews.[11]

Further, according to Kasper, since God's covenant with Jews is eternal, Christians must affirm Judaism's self-understanding of its own covenantal experiences in history.[12] In his public lecture at Sacred Heart University (Fairfield, Connecticut) in December 2001, the cardinal declared:

> God's Covenant with Israel has not simply been replaced by the new Covenant. God has not rescinded his contract with Israel; He has not repudiated and forsaken his people. Israel is still God's partner. God is still devoted to his people with love and loyalty, mercy, justice and pardon; God is always with his people especially in the most difficult moments of history. Every Jew, as one of His people, lives in promise.[13]

3. Judaism as a "Sacrament of Every Otherness"

Cardinal Kasper has often expressed his reverence for Judaism's covenantal vitality and his consequent respect for Jewish self-understanding as God's people. In his remarks on the thirty-seventh anniversary of *Nostra aetate* on October 28, 2002, he stated:

> Since 1965 many things have occurred. In our memory we want to especially retain the meeting in Assisi fifteen years ago, the pilgrimage of the Pope to Jerusalem, the many encounters that at every level have made possible a respectful and blessed exchange: through these, rediscovering fraternity, we Catholics became aware with greater clarity that the faith of Israel is that of our elder brothers, and, most importantly, that *Judaism is as a sacrament of every otherness that as such the Church must learn to discern, recognize and celebrate*.[14]

Kasper's use of the language of sacrament in relation to Judaism is surely deliberate. The Catholic principle of sacramentality understands that the presence of God can be mediated in all manner of experiences, for example, through our attentiveness to Creation and also in our outreach to people in need. This sacramental view of God's relationship with God's people culminates in the view that Christians come into God's presence most potently in the seven formal sacramental rites of Catholicism.

In light of this sacramental theology, Kasper's assertion that Judaism is like a "sacrament of every otherness" resonates deeply with Catholic spirituality and theology. As the cardinal holds, it means that Judaism can mediate to Christians the divine presence that is at work beyond the borders of the church. In other words, Christians may encounter the living God as they communicate with and learn from Jews and the Jewish tradition. By extension, they may also benefit from their respectful relationships with people of other beliefs as well.[15] Far from being contemptuous of Jewish "otherness," Kasper respects it. Indeed, he acknowledges that Judaism's difference from Christianity can itself mediate the divine and so deserves to be celebrated. This insight informs all of the cardinal's theological work regarding Judaism.

4. "No Organized Catholic Missionary Activity towards Jews"

A few months before Cardinal Kasper spoke at Sacred Heart University in December 2001, several evangelical Christian organizations in the United States launched new campaigns to convert Jews to Christianity. News of these efforts prompted some of us who responded to the cardinal at Sacred Heart to ask if the CRRJ could issue an official statement on why the Catholic Church does not engage in missionary action toward Jews.[16] In reply, Kasper suggested that religious leaders in the United States could more immediately respond to the American situation.

Acting on Kasper's suggestion, Rabbi Gilbert Rosenthal and Cardinal William Keeler—then the co-chairs of the dialogue between the National Council of Synagogues and the US Bishops' Committee for Ecumenical and Interreligious Affairs—decided to explore the topic of "Covenant and Mission" at the meeting of the Jewish and Catholic delegates in March 2002. Toward this endeavor, they asked Jewish and Catholic participants to present scholarly papers at this meeting.

At the request of Cardinal Keeler, several people prepared the Catholic position paper concerning Christian missionary efforts toward Jews. Along with the cardinal himself, there were Catholic university theologians. Also, there were staff members from the United States Conference of Catholic Bishops (USCCB)—specifically, from the USCCB's Office for Ecumenical and Interreligious Affairs and from its Office on Doctrine.[17] Working together, they generated a text that reviewed the developments in Catholic teachings on Judaism since *Nostra aetate*. They concluded: "A deepening Catholic appreciation of the eternal covenant between God and the Jewish people, together with a recognition of a divinely-given mission to Jews to witness to God's faithful love, lead to the conclusion that campaigns that target Jews for conversion to Christianity are no longer theologically acceptable in the Catholic Church."[18]

This Catholic reflection was well received by the Jewish and Catholic delegates, including bishops, rabbis, and academicians, at their meeting in March 2002. All present agreed that both the Jewish and Catholic papers should be made public. Together with an introduction, the combined papers appeared on August 12, 2002, titled "Reflections on Covenant and Mission."

The publication was intended to promote further discussion on the issue of Christian missionary efforts toward Jews, and it surely did this. Space does not allow for a detailed analysis of the public responses to "Reflections on Covenant and Mission."[19] It suffices to note that some readers had the mistaken impression that this set of papers was a formal statement by the USCCB. Other readers incorrectly read it as positing the existence of two parallel covenants, one between God and Christians and the other between God and Jews, but it actually did not discuss this subject.[20]

On November 6, 2002, Cardinal Kasper addressed the issue of a Christian mission toward Jews. In a public lecture at Boston College, he stressed that the new relationship since Vatican II between Catholics and Jews is only at "the beginning of a new beginning."[21] Then he spoke of "Reflections on Covenant and Mission" as "an invitation and a challenge for further discussion" and went on to convey four important points.

First, Kasper reiterated the church's recognition of the irrevocable character of the Mosaic covenant:

> [A]s Christians we know that God's covenant with Israel by God's faithfulness is not broken (Rom 11:29; cf. 3:4), mission understood as call to conversion from idolatry to the living and true God (1 Thess 1:9) does not apply and cannot be applied to

> Jews. They confess the living true God, who gave and gives them support, hope, confidence and strength in many difficult situations of their history. There cannot be the same kind of behavior towards Jews as there exists towards Gentiles. This is not a merely abstract theological affirmation, but an affirmation that has concrete and tangible consequences such as the fact that there is no organized Catholic missionary activity towards Jews as there is for all other non-Christian religions.

Second, Kasper acknowledged the church's respect for the Jewish interpretation of the Hebrew Bible. He insisted that the common, though differently interpreted, scriptural heritage of Jews and Christians "is an open text pointing to a future which will be determined by God alone at the end of time. Both our faiths are open towards this future."

Third, the cardinal viewed the relationship between Christians and Jews in an eschatological perspective. That is, he spoke of it in relation to the coming of God's "new age":

> But whilst Jews expect the coming of the Messiah, who is still unknown, Christians believe that he has already shown his face in Jesus of Nazareth, whom we as Christians therefore confess as the Christ, he who at the end of time will be revealed as the Messiah for Jews and for all nations. The universality of Christ's redemption for Jews and for Gentiles is . . . fundamental throughout the entire New Testament. . . . So from the Christian perspective the covenant with the Jewish people is unbroken (Rom 11:29), for we as Christians believe that these promises find in Jesus their definitive and irrevocable Amen (2 Cor 1:20) and at the same time that in him, who is the end of the law (Rom 10:4), the law is not nullified but upheld (Rom 3:31).

Fourth, Cardinal Kasper affirmed God's saving relationship with the Jewish people. He declared: "This does not mean that Jews in order to be saved have to become Christians; if they follow their own conscience and believe in God's promises as they understand them in their religious tradition they are in line with God's plan, which for us [Christians] comes to its historical completion in Jesus Christ."

In this highly nuanced presentation, Cardinal Kasper manifested once again his profound respect for God's saving outreach in Judaism and stressed that both Jews and Christians are hoping for the ultimate fulfillment of all God's promises at the "end of days." In this regard, quoting the Pontifical Biblical Commission's eschatological statements in a 2001 study that had been "signed [and thus endorsed] by Cardinal Ratzinger," Kasper observed:

> What has already been accomplished in Christ must yet be accomplished in us and in the world. The definitive fulfillment will be at the end with the resurrection of the dead, a new heaven and a new earth. Jewish messianic expectation is not in vain. It can become for us Christians a powerful stimulus to keep alive the eschatological dimension of our faith. Like them, we too live in expectation. The difference is that for us the One who is to come will have the traits of the Jesus who has already come and is already present and active among us.[22]

Kasper here made the point that since God is ever-faithful, God will unquestionably realize the hopes of Jews at the eschaton. Jews as Jews will enter into God's new age. They need not become Christians in historic time in order "to be saved."

5. "Two Concurrent Parts of God's One People" in the "Eschatological Interim"

Cardinal Kasper subsequently further developed these eschatological ideas in relation to the Jewish people. In December 2004, he set Christ's universal significance in an end-times context, thereby avoiding a supersessionist disregard for Judaism:[23]

> At the heart of the Christian faith is the affirmation of Jesus as the Christ in whom all the promises of the old covenant have become Yes and Amen (cf. 2 Cor 1:20). Therefore it is *the* fundamental hermeneutical presupposition of Christian theology to read the promises of the old covenant in the light of their Christological fulfillment. . . . That does not lead back to the substitution theory . . . if the balance of promise from the Old Testament is taken seriously and the eschatological difference between the fulfillment which has *already* been accomplished in Christ Jesus and the *still* anticipated consummation is held open. This difference leaves room for the "still" of the continuing validity of the covenant with Israel. . . . Regardless of [their] Christological

> difference [Jews and Christians] are, in the current eschatological interim, two concurrent parts of God's one people.[24]

In other words, although the end times have commenced with the resurrection of Jesus, by which he was "introduced to the 'world to come,'"[25] the ultimate culmination of all things is yet to occur in the future when the expectations of God's People—both Jews and Christians—will be fully realized.

6. "God Decides When and How"

In February 2008, Pope Benedict XVI revised the Tridentine Rite's Good Friday intercession for Jews, written in Latin. He took this initiative in order to remove this sixteenth-century prayer's offensive references to Jews as veiled in blindness. Nevertheless, the prayer ignited a controversy both within the church and among Jews. Cardinal Kasper as the CRRJ president immediately took steps to resolve this "problem."

In 1984, Pope John Paul II had granted so-called traditionalist Catholics permission to celebrate the Tridentine Rite—the liturgical prayers in Latin that the church had adopted in 1570 and used until the liturgical reforms of Pope John XXIII, the Second Vatican Council, and Pope Paul VI. John Paul II had not, however, implemented a new version of the Tridentine Rite's Good Friday prayer for "the conversion of Jews" to belief in Jesus Christ. This prayer stood in sharp contrast to the 1970 Roman Missal's Good Friday intercession, which said nothing about the conversion of Jews to Jesus Christ. Rather, it expressed the Christian desire that Jews "may continue to grow in the love of [God's] name and in faithfulness to his covenant [and that they] may arrive at the fullness of redemption."[26]

Concerned about traditionalist Catholics' anti-Jewish sentiments, Benedict revised the rite's intercession to read: "Let us also pray for the Jews. May the Lord our God illuminate their hearts so that they may *recognize Jesus Christ as savior* [italics added] of all men. . . . Almighty and everlasting God, you who want all men to be saved and to gain knowledge of the Truth, kindly allow that, as the fullness of peoples enter into your Church, all of Israel may be saved."[27]

Not surprisingly, when this revised prayer was made public in February 2008, it sparked a storm of protest from Catholics as well as from Jews. This criticism grew even greater when the reformulated intercession appeared in the Tridentine Rite's new missals under the title "for the conversion of the Jews" (*pro conversione Iudaeorum*) instead of under the title "for the Jews" (*pro Iudaeis*). Vatican officials immediately announced that "for the conversion of the Jews" was printed in error, but this did little to dispel the confusion and distress among Christians and Jews. Fueling the controversy was the fact that various cardinals issued conflicting statements about the new prayer's meaning.[28]

A month or so after the publication of Pope Benedict's revision, Cardinal Kasper published what has become the Vatican's definitive commentary on this text. His essay, under the title "God Decides When and How: The Good Friday Prayer," initially appeared on March 21, 2008, in the German newspaper *Frankfurter Allgemeine Zeitung*.[29] A few weeks later, at the request of the pope, Kasper's analysis was reprinted in the Vatican newspaper *L'Osservatore Romano*, titled "Striving for Mutual Respect in Modes of Prayer."[30]

In his commentary, Cardinal Kasper gave a balanced response to the "problem." On the one hand, he cautioned that Jews should not in principle object to the church's Christological prayers. On the other hand, he observed: "In the past the belief in Christ which distinguishes Christians from Jews has frequently been made a 'language of contempt' (Jules Isaac), with all the evil consequences that have arisen from that." Therefore, both Jews and Christians have still "much to learn" in terms of respecting one another's modes of prayer.[31]

The cardinal pointed out further that the new prayer should not be read "through the lens" of the mistaken and subsequently retracted heading "For the conversion of the Jews." In this vein, he gave assurance that "in contrast to some evangelical circles, the Catholic Church has no organized or institutionalized mission to the Jews."[32]

Appealing to Romans 11:25ff., Kasper explained why: "God will bring about the salvation of Israel in the end, not on the basis of a mission to the Jews but on the basis of the mission to the Gentiles, when the fullness of the Gentiles has entered." In other words, the church sees its relation to the Jewish people within the horizon of God's end time.[33] In this perspective, the Tridentine Rite's revised Good Friday prayer is an expression of eschatological hope, akin to "Thy Kingdom come" in the Lord's Prayer (Matt 6:10). Kasper observed: "Such petitions for the coming of the Kingdom of God and for the realization of the mystery of salvation are not by nature a call to the Church to undertake missionary action to the Jews. . . . So in this prayer the Church does not take it upon herself to orchestrate the realization of the unfathomable mystery. She cannot do so. Instead, she lays the *when* and the *how* entirely in God's hands. God alone can bring about the Kingdom of God in which the whole of Israel is saved and eschatological peace is bestowed on the world."[34]

In what perhaps proved to be a significant reference for Pope Benedict XVI, Cardinal Kasper then noted: "In order to support this interpretation one can refer to a text of St. Bernard of Clairvaux which says that we do not have to concern ourselves with the Jews, for God himself will take care of them."[35] The cardinal added: "The exclusion of an intentional and institutional mission to the Jews does not mean that Christians should sit about with their hands in their laps." Rather, they should give witness to their faith in Christ, "tactfully and respectfully," just as Jews should share their faith openly with Christians. In conclusion, Kasper conveyed his hope that the controversy over the Good Friday intercession would lead to a "deepening of the dialogue" between Catholics and Jews.[36]

In mid-May 2008, about a month after Kasper's article appeared in *L'Osservatore Romano*, the Vatican's secretary of state, Cardinal Tarcisio Bertone, sent a letter to the Chief Rabbinate of Israel, stating that Cardinal Kasper's commentary on the new Good Friday prayer for the Jews also spoke for Pope Benedict. Adding a further clarification, Bertone wrote: "As Cardinal Kasper clearly explains, the new *Oremus et pro Iudaeis* ['And let us pray for the Jews'] is not intended to promote proselytism to Jews, and it opens up an eschatological perspective."[37]

Three years later, Pope Benedict XVI himself expressed Cardinal Kasper's eschatological view of the church's relationship to the Jewish people. In *Jesus of Nazareth*, volume 2 (2011), the pope wrote:

> We realize today with horror how many misunderstandings with grave consequences have weighed down our history. Yet a new reflection can acknowledge that the beginnings of a correct understanding have always been there, waiting to be rediscovered, however deep the shadows.
>
> Here I should like to recall the advice given by Bernard of Clairvaux to his pupil Pope Eugene III on this matter. He reminds the Pope that his duty of care extends not only to Christians, but:

> "You also have obligations toward unbelievers, whether Jew, Greek, or Gentile" (*De Consideratione* III/i, 2). Then he immediately corrects himself and observes more accurately: "Granted, with regard to the Jews, time excuses you; for them a determined point in time has been fixed, which cannot be anticipated. The full number of the Gentiles must come in first . . ." (*De Consideratione* III/i, 3).
>
> Hildegard Brem comments on this passage as follows: "In the light of Romans 11:25, the Church must not concern herself with the conversion of the Jews, since she must wait for the time fixed for this by God, 'until the full number of the Gentiles come in' (Rom 11:25). . . ."
>
> . . . In the meantime, Israel retains its own mission. Israel is in the hands of God, who will save it "as a whole" at the proper time, when the number of the Gentiles is complete.[38]

In this text, Benedict XVI clearly drew on Cardinal Kasper's citation of Bernard of Clairvaux. Bernard's insight, to which Kasper had called the pope's attention, confirmed for the pope that the "beginnings of a correct understanding" about the church's relationship with the Jews, which had remained hidden in the past, are now coming to light.[39]

7. Let Us "Tackle the Many Questions That Are Still Waiting"

In October 2006, two dozen scholars from around the world gathered in Ariccia, Italy, at one of the sites used by the drafters of *Nostra aetate* over forty years earlier. At this meeting, they embarked on a five-year study in response to the question: How might we Christians in our time reaffirm our faith claim that Jesus Christ is the savior of all humanity, even as we affirm the Jewish people's covenantal life with God? As the group convened, Cardinal Kasper came to encourage the project and to offer some procedural suggestions. Over the next few years, as he received the reports he had requested of the group's progress, he repeatedly stressed the importance of this study. In 2011, the scholars assembled their respective papers and published an anthology titled *Christ Jesus and the Jewish People Today: New Explorations of Theological Interrelationships*.[40] The book's foreword, written by Kasper, is perhaps the cardinal's final substantive writing on Catholic-Jewish relations during his tenure as president of the CRRJ.

In the foreword, the cardinal observes, as he had often said before, that *Nostra aetate* poses many new questions that the Catholic Church is only now beginning to address in a serious way. According to Kasper, as the church follows through on *Nostra aetate*, it should consider six trajectories or points of reference that set the parameters for its inquiry and reflection. What follows is a succinct summary of Kasper's six points of reference.

(1) Israel is the divinely chosen and beloved people of the covenant, which was never revoked or terminated. The New Covenant is the definitive Yes and Amen to all of God's promises but not their suspension or abolition.

(2) Christian-Jewish relations involve not only the relationship of the Old and New Covenants but also the church's relationship with postbiblical rabbinic and Talmudic Judaism. Rabbinic and Christian readings of the Tanakh/Old Testament developed in parallel and are both possible.

(3) Postbiblical Judaism and the church do not represent two parallel ways of salvation; they are the one-covenant people. The two are dialectically related to each other in their difference, which can hardly be reduced to a formula or catchy phrase.

(4) The church remains faithful to its identity and mission only insofar as it remains connected with its Jewish roots (see Rom 11:16-24). The church simultaneously gives the rootstock new vitality and fertility as it spreads Israel's monotheism and the Ten Commandments universally among the nations.

(5) Christians should undertake no mission toward the Jewish people, and yet they must bear witness among all people, including Jews, to their faith in Jesus Christ.

(6) As Jews and Christians look to the future, they should give witness together to the hope for the perfect justice and the universal *shalom* that God alone will usher in at the end of time.[41]

Cardinal Kasper has here presented six guideposts for the future. At the same time, they represent much of what Cardinal Kasper accomplished as president of the CRRJ. From 2001 to 2010, the cardinal affirmed and developed each of these six points by means of his words, actions, and personal relationships.

Unfortunately, this abbreviated review of Kasper's six points does not do justice to the personal warmth and the intellectual curiosity of the person who proposed them in his foreword to *Christ Jesus and the Jewish People*. Cardinal Kasper succeeded in improving the ties between Christians and Jews in part because of his open-mindedness. In 2002 when he was asked about the criticisms being leveled at the time against the idea that the church ought not to sponsor missionary campaigns to Jews, he observed that "the problem is that for [the critics] there are no questions." Walter Kasper himself accepts questions as they arise and pursues them in his theological reflections. As the CRRJ's president, he did not shrink from the tough issues that surfaced amid the Catholic Church's *rapprochement* with Judaism. Rather, he highlighted these issues. Moreover, he supported and collaborated with everyone seeking to celebrate Judaism "as a sacrament of every otherness." As such, he is a model bishop-theologian and an exemplary Christian. May Cardinal Walter Kasper inspire us, as he has put it, "to continue on the path and to tackle the many questions that are still waiting."[42]

Endnotes

1. Walter Kasper, "Welcoming Address to the 2001 ILC Meeting" (New York: May 1, 2001); see http://www.ccjr.us/dialogika-resources/documents-and-statements/roman-catholic/kasper/644-wk01may1. On July 12, 2001, at a meeting of the International Council of Christians and Jews in Montevideo, Uruguay, Kasper stated: "Our dialogue needs intensification; it needs to discover its very existential and religious depth." See http://www.ccjr.us/dialogika-resources/documents-and-statements/roman-catholic/kasper/646-wk01july12.

2. Cardinal Joseph Ratzinger and the Congregation for the Doctrine of the Faith, *Dominus Iesus* (August 6, 2000), 7.

3. Ibid., 22.

4. Cardinal Joseph Ratzinger, "The Heritage of Abraham: The Gift of Christmas," trans. Murray Watson, *L'Osservatore Romano* (December 29, 2000); see http://www.ccjr.us/dialogika-resources/documents-and-statements/roman-catholic/pope-benedict-xvi/348-b16-00dec29.

5. Cardinal Cassidy, "The Future of Jewish-Christian Relations in the Light of the Visit of Pope John Paul II to the Holy Land" (Address delivered at the Annual General Meeting of the Interreligious Coordinating Council in Israel: March 13, 2001), 4; see http://www.ccjr.us/dialogika-resources/educational-and-liturgical-materials/classic-articles/1238-cassidy2001mar13.

6. Walter Kasper, "On *Dominus Iesus*" (Address to the seventeenth meeting of the International Catholic-Jewish Liaison Committee, New York: May 1, 2001). See http://www.ccjr.us/dialogika-resources/documents-and-statements/roman-catholic/kasper/641-kasper01may1.

7. Ibid. In his address in Montevideo on July 12, 2001, Kasper said: "Now we are aware of God's unrevoked covenant with his people and of the *permanent and actual salvific* significance of Jewish religion for its believers" (my emphasis). See http://www.ccjr.us/dialogika-resources/documents-and-statements/roman-catholic/kasper/646-wk01july12. On November 21, 2001, Kasper repeated this sentence at Jerusalem's Israel Museum. See http://www.ccjr.us/dialogika-resources/documents-and-statements/roman-catholic/kasper/647-wk01nov21.

8. *Dominus Iesus*, 20; emphasis added.

9. Vatican II, *Nostra aetate* (October 28, 1965), 2.

10. For Archbishop Heenan's intervention of September 29, 1964, on Schema XIII (which became *Nostra aetate*), see http://www.ccjr.us/dialogika-resources/documents-and-statements/roman-catholic/second-vatican-council/na-debate/1020-v21964sept29b#Heenan.

11. By this time, Pope John Paul II had spoken of God's irrevocable covenant with the Jews on many occasions, specifically in Mainz on November 17, 1980; in Sydney on November 26, 1986; in Miami on September 11, 1987; in Vienna on June 24, 1988; in the Vatican on September 26, 1990, on November 8, 1990, on April 28, 1999, and on June 29, 1999; and at Mount Sinai on February 26, 2000. See http://www.ccjr.us/dialogika-resources/documents-and-statements/roman-catholic/pope-john-paul-ii.

12. As earlier stated, the Council for Religious Relations with the Jews includes this statement in the preamble of its "Guidelines and Suggestions for Implementing the Conciliar Declaration *Nostra Aetate*, No. 4" (1974): "Christians . . . must strive to learn by what essential traits Jews define themselves in the light of their own religious experience."

13. Walter Kasper, "The Theology of the Covenant as Central Issue in the Jewish-Christian Dialogue" (December 4, 2001), 2; see http://www.ccjr.us/dialogika-resources/documents-and-statements/roman-catholic/kasper/648-wk01dec4.

14. Walter Kasper, "Address on the 37th Anniversary of *Nostra Aetate*" (October 28, 2002); emphasis added; see http://www.ccjr.us/dialogika-resources/documents-and-statements/roman-catholic/kasper/650-wk02oct28. See Alberto Melloni, "*Nostra Aetate* and the Discovery of the Sacrament of Otherness," in *The Catholic Church and the Jewish People: Recent Reflections from Rome*, ed. Philip A. Cunningham, Norbert J. Hofmann, and Joseph Sievers (New York: Fordham University Press, 2007), 129–51, esp. 150–51.

15. In a similar vein, see Anna Foa, "The Difficult Apprenticeship of Diversity," in Cunningham et al., *The Catholic Church and the Jewish People*, 41–53. She observes that the toleration of a Jewish presence in Christendom "laid the foundations for an apprenticeship of diversity, or in other words, found itself forced to

face an instance of diversity, a diversity that was blindfolded, distraught, subordinate, and in perpetual servitude [as in religious depictions of Ecclesia and Synagoga], but a diversity that even the most monolithic Christian societies had to face wherever there were Jews" (p. 43).

16. On this discussion at Sacred Heart University in December 2001, see: http://www.bc.edu/dam/files/research_sites/cjl/texts/center/conferences/12301.htm.

17. There is a significant omission in the USCCB's statement of 2009: "A Note on Ambiguities Contained in 'Reflections on Covenant and Mission' "; it omits that the USCCB's Office of Doctrine as well as its Office for Ecumenical and Interreligious Affairs contributed to the writing of "Reflections on Covenant and Mission." The omission is in this sentence: "The Catholic part of the document was written by scholars who made up an advisory group to the Committee on Ecumenical and Interreligious Affairs."

18. For the statement by Cardinal Keeler and the other participants on the Catholic Church's opposition to Christian missionary efforts toward Jews, see http://www.ccjr.us/dialogika-resources/themes-in-todays-dialogue/conversion/1093-ncs-bceia02aug12.

19. For relevant primary texts, see http://www.ccjr.us/dialogika-resources/themes-in-todays-dialogue/conversion. For a detailed analysis of the "neo-supersessionist" arguments raised over the next few years, see Philip A. Cunningham, "Official Ecclesial Documents to Implement Vatican II on Relations with Jews: Study Them, Become Immersed in Them, and Put Them into Practice," *Studies in Christian-Jewish Relations* 4, no. 1 (2009): 1–36, which is available at http://ejournals.bc.edu/ojs/index.php/scjr/article/view/1521/1374.

20. If a discussion of the issue of one covenant or two covenants had occurred, it would have acknowledged the statement in the CRRJ's "Notes on the Correct Way to Present Jews and Judaism in Preaching and Catechesis in the Roman Catholic Church" (1985): "The Church and Judaism cannot, then, be seen as two parallel ways of salvation and the Church must witness to Christ as the Redeemer for all" (1.7).

21. Walter Kasper, "The Commission for Religious Relations with the Jews: A Crucial Endeavour of the Catholic Church" (November 6, 2002); see http://www.ccjr.us/dialogika-resources/documents-and-statements/roman-catholic/kasper/642-kasper02nov6.

22. Pontifical Biblical Commission, *The Jewish People and Their Sacred Scriptures in the Christian Bible*, trans. Maurice Hogan (Vatican City: Libreria Editrice Vaticana, 2002), 21. A striking resonance occurs between this document's phrase that the "One who is to come will have the traits of the Jesus who has already come and is already present and active among us," and Kasper's wording that the Messiah has already "shown his face in Jesus of Nazareth." Although this document is referring to the traits of the eschatological messiah being recognizable by Christians because of traits belonging to Jesus, Kasper was speaking of Jesus as having proleptically manifested and as continuing to manifest the eschatological messiah to the church.

23. A precedent for this move occurs in the CRRJ's "Notes on the Correct Way to Present Jews and Judaism in Preaching and Catechesis in the Roman Catholic Church" (1985), 2.8-11.

24. Walter Kasper, "The Relationship of the Old and the New Covenant as One of the Central Issues in Jewish-Christian Dialogue" (Lecture at the Centre for the Study of Jewish-Christian Relations, now in the Woolf Institute, Cambridge, United Kingdom: December 6, 2004), 5–6; see http://www.ccjr.us/dialogika-resources/documents-and-statements/roman-catholic/kasper/652-kasper04dec6; emphases in the original.

25. Pontifical Biblical Commission, "Instruction on the Bible and Christology" (1984), 1.2.6. For this instruction, see Joseph A. Fitzmyer, *Scripture and Christology: A Statement of the Biblical Commission with a Commentary* (New York: Paulist Press, 1986).

26. For the texts of the three Good Friday intercessions, see http://www.ccjr.us/dialogika-resources/documents-and-statements/roman-catholic/pope-benedict-xvi/425-b1608feb5.

27. See http://www.ccjr.us/dialogika-resources/themes-in-todays-dialogue/pasttopics/good-friday-prayer/440-b1608feb5.

28. For the Vatican's statement on this error, see http://www.ccjr.us/dialogika-resources/themes-in-todays-dialogue/good-friday-prayer.

29. Walter Kasper, "Für Bitte—Das Wann und Wie Entscheidet Gott," *Frankfurter Allgemeine Zeitung* 68 (March 21, 2008): 39. See http://www.faz.net/aktuell/feuilleton/debatten/karfreitagsfuerbitte-das-wann-und-wie-entscheidet-gott-1512132.html.

30. Walter Kasper, "Striving for Mutual Respect in Modes of Prayer"; see http://www.ccjr.us/dialogika-resources/documents-and-statements/roman-catholic/kasper/651-kasper08apr16; originally published in *L'Osservatore Romano* (April 16, 2008): 8–9

31. Ibid., II.

32. Ibid., III.

33. Kasper's eschatological reasoning echoes the deliberations of the Second Vatican Council in September 1964. At that time, a public controversy arose over a leaked draft of Schema XIII (later titled *Nostra aetate*) that seemed to promote missionary efforts toward Jews. In response, the council fathers called for the careful expression in Schema XIII of "the church's eschatological hope, since it concerns the mystery [of Israel], [and so that] any appearance of proselytism must be avoided." See *Acta Synodalia*, 3.8, 648.

34. Kasper, "Striving for Mutual Respect in Modes of Prayer," IV.

35. Ibid.; citing Bernard of Clairvaux, *De consideratione*, III, 1, 3.

36. Ibid., V.

37. For Cardinal Bertone's letter, see http://www.ccjr.us/dialogika-resources/themes-in-todays-dialogue/good-friday-prayer/445-bertone08may14.

38. Benedict XVI, *Jesus of Nazareth*, vol. 2: *Holy Week: From the Entrance into Jerusalem to the Resurrection*, trans. Vatican Secretariat of State (San Francisco: Ignatius Press, 2011), 44–45, 47.

39. For other Christian thinkers in history who might offer additional "flashes of light" on this question, see Joseph Sievers, "A History of the Interpretation of Romans 11:29," *Annali di storia dell'esegesi* 14 (1997): 381–442.

40. Philip A. Cunningham, Joseph Sievers, Mary C. Boys, Hans Hermann Henrix, and Jesper Svartvik, eds., *Christ Jesus and the Jewish People Today: New Explorations of Theological Interrelationships* (Grand Rapids, MI: Wm. Eerdmans, 2011).

41. Ibid., xiv–xviii.

42. Ibid., xviii.

CHAPTER 15

Faith Seeking Understanding

John C. Cavadini

This chapter is my expression of gratitude to indicate what dimension of my vocation as a theologian I have seen more clearly as a result of Cardinal Walter Kasper's writings.

In a famous but perhaps permanently elusive passage of the *De doctrina christiana*, Augustine of Hippo comments on the pleasure of finding hidden meaning in a text of scripture. He asks why it gives more pleasure to the hearer if, instead of a discursive lecture on ecclesial life as beginning with baptism and bearing fruit in the love of God and neighbor, the teaching is presented as the sense of a passage in the Song of Songs.[1] Augustine repeatedly emphasizes the pleasure gained at finding the teaching about the church hidden as an allegorical meaning of the Song of Songs. This conviction cannot be explained simply as feeling the reward of hard work in searching out the hidden meaning of the Song, for the pleasure comes, Augustine says, not simply in finding the meaning but in contemplating the various moments of ecclesial life using the imagery from the Song of Songs.

One must remember that for Augustine the meaning hidden in scripture is not hidden because God is playing games with us and is intentionally obscurantist. Rather, the meaning is hidden because the scriptural text is a unique locus of God's self-emptying love. That divine love lies hidden *as* the text. The joy of discovering the hidden meaning is not primarily the joy of accomplishment but the pleasure of discovering the depth of God's self-emptying love. It is not the joy of mastering a puzzle but of realizing that we are loved by God.

"Understanding" a scriptural text involves the pleasure of discovering oneself as loved by God in a way that makes one want to share that love with others. But that very desire makes us want to articulate it clearly. Hence, we find that there are the two "phases" of theology, as Augustine explains it, the phase of discovery (*modus inveniendi*) and the phase of communication (*modus proferendi*).[2] These two moments are linked. But they are linked not because the first phase of research or "understanding" is the job of the theologian, and the second phase, the job of the preacher. They are connected because *both* of these steps are the job of the theologian who is both scholar and preacher. Has one really "understood" a biblical text if one cannot articulate it in a way that will engender understanding in others?

1. The Theologian's Job

It is the gift of Walter Kasper's theology to challenge us theologians to see ourselves always at the interface of the *modus inveniendi* and the *modus proferendi*. The cardinal challenges us not to think that the task of theology is complete until both of these jobs are accomplished. He has just exhorted us as *theologians*—not as preachers—to realize that in the secular culture surrounding us people are asking some basic questions, including questions about God, and that they need intelligible answers. Speaking vaguely about a divine being will not be enough.

I recall a passage in *The God of Jesus Christ* where Kasper says: "In the final analysis the divine Trinity is the interpretation of the statement that God is love."[3] He also reminds us that "the proclamation of the triune God is of the greatest *pastoral* importance in the present-day situation."[4]

In other words, Kasper—to use the Augustinian idiom I invoked above—has drawn attention to the intimate connection between the *modus inveniendi* and the *modus proferendi*. In doing so, he has revealed that the space "in between" the *modus inveniendi* and the *modus proferendi* is not real but only a virtual space. Have I really completed the work of discovery, for example, if, having recognized a difference between modern uses of the word "person" and the ancient meaning of "person," I conclude that in stating the doctrine of the Trinity, the word "person" ought, as Karl Barth held, to be replaced with "mode of being" or, as Karl Rahner judged, to be replaced with "distinct manner of subsisting"?[5] As Kasper points out, these expressions would paralyze preaching on the Trinity (assuming it isn't paralyzed already). It would also, I might add, paralyze teaching too.

In the Augustinian idiom, what Kasper is showing us is that the two phases of theology are only notionally distant, and he has placed us precisely in this notional distance. Have we really "discovered" the understanding we need if we have not yet articulated it in a way that can be used to engender an understanding of the Christian proclamation in those who need it most? At least we can take comfort in the intrinsic difficulty of the task, for theologians of the stature of Barth and Rahner can be invoked as examples of possible failure!

Kasper is also reminding us, as Augustine did, that the *modus inveniendi* and the *modus proferendi* are not two separate job descriptions, for example, one the job of the theologian and the other the job of the preacher. Placed in the notional space between them, we theologians are invited to remember that they are one job, in fact, *our* job, precisely as theologians.

This view does not mean that theology is not complete unless it is articulated in every instance to make it accessible for the average person without a theological education. But it means that theology is not complete unless it really does help a teacher or a preacher explain or proclaim the teaching to others in a way that engenders genuine understanding. Theology should be oriented toward preaching and teaching, such that it fully realizes its inner intention only when God's Word is preached or explained.

How can we work in this notional space between discovery and communication? In the Augustinian idiom, I believe, it is by contemplating the teachings of the church, the "rule of faith," *as* interpretations of the biblical text. The pleasure of discovery of which Augustine speaks is a pleasure in the discovery that the biblical text really *is* revelation. For this reason, the most precise articulations of Christian teaching are the ones that show the biblical text as revelation. That is, they enable us to understand both *that* and also *how* God's Word is actually active in this scriptural text in some way. Also, they teach us that in this biblical text we encounter first and foremost God's compassionate love, God's mercy.

This claim is not to construe theology as a biblical positivism. Kasper himself makes this point in *The God of Jesus Christ*. Speaking of the word "person" in the doctrine of the Trinity, Kasper states: "The decisive question is not whether a concept [of person] as such occurs in scripture, but whether [this concept] represents an objectively valid interpretation of the biblical testimony. The tradition undoubtedly regarded the concept of person as that kind of valid interpretation."[6]

Further, this claim about discovery and communication does not imply a positivist view of tradition. What it expresses is that theology renounces itself as theology if it is content to develop systems of self-enclosed jargon, if it works in "exclusively metalinguistic concept[s] antecedently unsuited for use in preaching" as a kind of replacement for, rather than an interpretation of, the biblical idiom of image, story, and law.[7] In sum, for Kasper as for Augustine, it is our job as theologians to work toward, not against or with indifference to, the church's proclamation of the living Word.

2. Teaching the Doctrine of the Trinity

Here's a case in point. During this semester, I am teaching a course titled "The Catholic Faith." When it came time to study the doctrine of the Trinity, I told the students something in accordance with Kasper's view of the theologian's job. I said that "to say that 'God is Trinity, that is, three persons, one God' is the exact same thing as saying that 'God is love.'"

I made this statement in part for a pastoral reason. The pastoral importance of communicating that the Trinity is the God of love comes from the urgency of clarifying that this teaching *is* the only doctrine of God that adequately represents and articulates the freedom of God to love us. It affirms, therefore, the centrality of love itself in our world. This affirmation is crucial today because so often authentic love is treated with contempt and disdain by the kingdoms of this world and their accompanying ideologies of materialism and un-freedom.

All that said, I did not adequately communicate in my lecture the point concerning the identity between "There are three persons in the one God" and "God is love." I say this because one student immediately commented, "But it loses something in translation!" He meant, of course, that some of the meaning is lost when we move from "There are three persons in one God" to "God is love."

The student's comment was a little deflating. With it, the student was implicitly calling the bluff of my exaggerated way of making my point. Further, he was communicating that my abrupt, simplified claim lacked pastoral sensitivity.

The student did not need to be told that the doctrine of the Trinity, as classically expressed, is so outdated as to be almost irretrievable. Rather, he needed the "translation" of the doctrine into contemporary terms, and he was implicitly chiding me for not providing it. He wanted to be shown how the traditional formulation "There are three persons in one God" *is* a way of saying "God is love." He sought the instruction that the latter statement is an appropriate translation of the former because it provides insight into the biblical testimony and demonstrates this testimony's distinctiveness and depth.

To return to Augustine's way of putting it, the student was craving the "pleasure" of finding the hidden meaning in the biblical text. He was yearning for the delight of the Word, the "understanding" that makes the doctrine of the Trinity come alive because this doctrine truly *is* an interpretation of the biblical witness. At the same time, this understanding of the doctrine brings the awareness that the biblical witness lives with all of its warmth in the church's traditional teaching, formulated precisely as an interpretation of the biblical testimony.

If the student were to attain this understanding of the Word, then he would have an encounter simultaneously with the church and the biblical text. This experience is the "pleasure" that the student was craving, namely, an awareness of God's revelation, of the Word in scripture and tradition. In this, the student would realize that the doctrinal formulation concerning the Trinity is not a heteronymous imposition on the biblical testimony. Rather, this formulation arose because it captures and clarifies the biblical witness that we are loved by God—indeed, that God *is* love. In particular, this formulation attests that God is truly self-emptied in Christ into scripture, tradition, and community.

Moreover, the encounter between the student and the living Word in the biblical text would not be left in the past. It would not be a happening that afterward had little or no significance for the present. If this were the case, it would be self-defeating! No, the "pleasure" of discovering a biblical text's hidden meaning moves us to express our discovery in language intelligible for us today.

So, for example, we learn that the word "person" involves a dialogical relation between the biblical testimony and contemporary language. Yet, the past witness cannot be replaced with a language so impenetrable that it seems to declare that the past testimony was a mistake. A translation of this sort would wrongly convey that the Bible can be explained only by replacing its language. Rather, what is required is that we never tire of interpreting God's Word in scripture into discourse that is intelligible and pastorally appropriate to today's Christians.

3. Cardinal Kasper's Gift to Us

As we celebrate Cardinal Kasper's eightieth birthday, we acknowledge that the cardinal has in fact given *us* a gift. In his writings, he has presented us with a lovely vision of our vocation as theologians. Thus, he has reminded us that the most beautiful gifts are sometimes the most terrible, the most awesome, and the most difficult. In his introduction to the new edition of *The God of Jesus Christ*, he says: "The question of how we can speak today about the God of Jesus Christ in an understandable way is not only an urgent pastoral question, but also a deeply theological fundamental problem, which requires hard thinking."[8]

The *modus inveniendi* is hard because the *modus proferendi* demands that it be so. As Kasper writes, theology is "least of all . . . an easy chat about God." Rather, it is the "rational service of God (*logike latreia; rationale obsequium*) (Rom. 12.1), which commits us to giving an account (*apologia*) of the hope that is in us (1 Pet. 3.15)."[9] With these words, Kasper challenges us to a new apologetics which we might style as the apologetics of love. It would show to a world desperately in need of this message of love that the basic Christian mystery is the most profound mystery of God as love. This is the divine reality that—if we theologians have done our job—when encountered, is its own apologia, the drop of sweetness so craved by a world all too familiar with a surfeit of bitterness, of emptiness, and of strife.

Cardinal Kasper, thank you for this gift. With great gratitude, we accept it!

Endnotes

1. Augustine, *De doctrina christiana*, 2.6.7-8. See Augustine, *On Christian Doctrine*, trans. with intro. D. W. Robertson Jr. (Upper Saddle River, NJ: Prentice Hall, 1997, 1958).

2. Ibid., 1.1.1.

3. Walter Kasper, *The God of Jesus Christ*, trans. Matthew J. O'Connell (New York: Crossroad, 1984), 265.

4. Ibid., 315; emphasis added.

5. Ibid., 287.

6. Ibid., 286.

7. Ibid. See Vatican II, *Dei verbum* (November 18, 1965), 24: "The sacred scriptures contain the word of God, and, because they are inspired, they truly are the word of God; therefore, the study of the sacred page should be the very soul of sacred theology."

8. Walter Kasper, "Introduction to the New Edition," trans. Dinah Livingstone, in *The God of Jesus Christ*, trans. Matthew J. O'Connell, new ed. (London: Continuum, 2012), ix–xxvi, xiii–xiv.

9. Ibid., xiv.

CHAPTER 16

How to Do Theology Today

Cardinal Walter Kasper

As all speakers before me have done, I too want to express my deep gratitude for this wonderful symposium. I have to thank all who prepared and organized it and all who gave the excellent papers I've heard. Often I was reminded of the books and articles I wrote in my "preexistence" half a century ago. So I can only agree that, since then, many problems within theology have changed. Therefore, in what follows I do not want to teach younger theologians how to do theology today. I can only explain how I understood and now understand my theological craftsmanship and then leave it to a younger generation whether and to what degree they can profit from it.[1]

Let me start with a quotation of Karl Rahner. Even though I don't consider myself to be a Rahnerian, all theologians of my generation are deeply indebted to Rahner. None of us could do theology today without his enormous achievements of opening up doors and windows. Once, when I had to present a *Laudatio* (tribute) on the occasion of his seventy-fifth birthday, Karl Rahner answered with his dry charm: "Who I am sadly greets who I ought to be." This phrase came to my mind as I listened during this symposium to what was said about me. (I do not say this in order to imitate a priest who on his eightieth birthday said: "My main virtue is my humility, and in this no one can match me.") I remember Rahner's comment only because in the same context he said: "I hope that, what is called *my* theology is only to its smallest degree *my* theology."

1. Theology in the Christian Tradition

This comment brings me to my first thesis: Theology, rightly understood, is never only my theology, nor is it only a theology of today. We theologians stand in the long line of tradition and are like dwarfs on the shoulders of giants. With this view of tradition, I have already indicated where I come from, i.e., from the Catholic School of Tübingen: Johann Sebastian Drey, Johann Adam Möhler, Johann Evangelist Kuhn, and others.[2] John R. Sachs and Robert A. Krieg presented this context in an illuminating way. There is only one aspect that I would like to add. Often Tübingen theology is put in contradiction with Roman theology. Surely there are differences. But already in my doctoral dissertation on the understanding of tradition in the Roman School, I gave evidence that there are also strong relations between Tübingen theology and Roman theology.[3]

The Tübingen theology of the nineteenth century is all but liberal theology, an epithet that some have tried to hang on me. I like to pass not as a liberal but as a radical and even more as an open-minded theologian. For "radical" does not mean "fanatical." The word radical means to go back to the *radices*, "to the roots." Only a tree with deep roots can withstand the storms. Only by going back to the origins can we go ahead. For going back to the roots and the sources means leaving the stagnant waters and drawing fresh water from the spring. All reforms within church history started from such a turning back to the apostolic origins. In this sense, conservative and progressive theologies are not contradictory but complementary.

Rooted in apostolic faith transmitted through the ages, theology can never be only my theology, just as faith is never only my faith. In my faith I am indebted to many persons: my parents, my family, my teachers, my pastors, many uncomplicated faithful people, and my friends. Finally, we are indebted to the apostolic faith that is transmitted to us through history by the church, our mother in the faith. The ancient creeds did not initially begin "I believe" but "we believe." So theology can only "re-flect" what it has received; it lives and proceeds in manifold contexts of tradition, reception, and communication within the community of the faithful, which is one of the oldest definitions of the church.

This conception of theology stands in analogy with one fundamental insight of the different post-idealistic philosophers such as Martin

Heidegger, Hans-Georg Gadamer, Paul Ricoeur, Ludwig Wittgenstein, and Jürgen Habermas. As they agreed, all of our reflections are based on language. Nobody invents his or her language. We are indebted for our language to our respective language communities, and we are heirs of our respective cultural traditions. For the language that we use is not only an instrument of communication; language is also a symbolic system through which we take over a certain interpretation of reality.

So the correctly understood ecclesial character of theology has nothing to do with following a party line. Ecclesial faith is not a line; it is an ocean. According to Melchior Cano, there are many *loci theologici*, i.e., places and instances where faith can be found: sacred scripture whose study and interpretation comprise the soul of all theology (*Dei verbum* 24), the ancient creeds shared by all mainline churches of the East and the West, the liturgy, the church fathers, the great theologians of the past, the witness of the saints, and the witness and praxis of the whole people of God as well as religious literature and poetry, and religious art and music. As one of my colleagues in Tübingen, Max Seckler, has made clear, it is only in this large context that the church's magisterium has its specific role and authority as *locus theologicus*.[4] As a consequence of this broad setting, the ecclesial character of theology cannot be reduced to a simple repetition and explication of magisterial documents, as important as they are. Christian truth is symphonic, as Hans Urs von Balthasar has shown.

As language is a living realty, also tradition is a living tradition. We have the tradition we received only in the act of transmission, i.e., in tradition in its active sense. Tradition is not a package and a burden that we have to drag along; it is much more a fresh spring which never is exhausted. In the last analysis, tradition is the self-tradition of the exalted Lord through the Holy Spirit who guides us into all truth (John 16:13). So tradition is always young and keeps young. The church and, in a special way, theology are instrumental to translate the original sense of the Gospel into the present day. This endeavor is the very meaning of *aggiornamento*, i.e., to bring the original message, transmitted by tradition, up to date. Kristin M. Colberg has explained this point very well.

The theologian's task of "mediation," *Vermittlung*, will often lead to conflict with current opinions. Christian faith is never obvious. We cannot avoid the scandal of the cross (1 Cor 1:23) and become everybody's darling. There can exist tensions within the church about different interpretations of the one and same Gospel. All life is constituted by tensions; where tensions end, life comes to an end. We don't want a boring, dead church but a living church. Tensions when they don't become deadly contradictions can be enriching complementary aspects. It is in this context that I see my debate with the then-Cardinal Joseph Ratzinger.[5] We are Catholics and remain friends. Theologians should not become stumbling blocks of division but agents of diversity within unity in a synchronic and in a diachronic way. As theologians, we should build up communion and speak the truth in love (cf. Eph 4:15).

2. Theology in Relation to Philosophy

To understand tradition as living tradition tells us that theology has to think. Theology is indebted to the axiom "*Fides quaerens intellectum*," that is, "faith seeking for understanding" (Anselm of Canterbury). Theology has to be *apologia* of "the hope" that is within us, and as theologians we have to give "an accounting" of our faith (1 Pet 3:15). Theology is *logike latreia*, a rational liturgy (Rom 12:1). Thus, theology has two eyes: a historical one, relying on tradition, and a speculative one, relying on philosophy.

Speculation does not mean a departure from the realm of faith to a region of free speculations. Speculation is derived from *speculum*, mirror; "specu-lation" brings different truths in a mirror into relation, i.e., it brings them into correspondence with one another. The First Vatican Council mentioned three possibilities: (1) the *analogia* between faith and human knowledge; (2) the *nexus mysteriorum*, that is, the inner relation of the various aspects of faith; and, (3) finally, the relation of these aspects to the ultimate eschatological goal of human existence.[6] The individual Christian truths are not isolated statements; they do not constitute a sum or a codex of statements. Rather, they are a whole and interpret one another. In this sense, the Second Vatican Council speaks of "the hierarchy of truths" (*Unitatis redintegratio* 11), which demands that we interpret each theological statement in relation to its Christological foundation and center. So, in the last analysis, theology becomes an introduction to friendship with Jesus Christ and an explanation of the one mystery of Jesus Christ.

Speculation of this kind needs contact with philosophy. The first paper I did as a young student was on Plato's doctrine of the ideas in his dialogue with *Phaidon*, and the second paper was on Thomas Aquinas's theology, specifically, on The concept of truth in the *Quaestiones disputatae de veritate*. In my later theological work, Thomas Aquinas was always present; he has remained for me one of the great masters of theology. But Thomas was not a Thomist; he was an open thinker with a large horizon. This view gave me the freedom to dedicate my Habilitation to a modern philosopher who was fundamental for the Catholic Tübingen School in the nineteenth century. Under the title "The Absolute in History," I wrote on the philosophy and theology of history in the thinking of the late Schelling.[7]

In his paper Thomas F. O'Meara has pointed out how much Schelling's later thought was influential also for my ecclesiological thinking. Yet, as Francis Schüssler Fiorenza has observed, I was never a mere disciple of Schelling. Already in my Habilitation I criticized Schelling, who wanted to overcome idealism but did not fully achieve it. For me it was fundamental to show that God is freedom in love. So it is impossible to interpret, as Schelling did in his "positive philosophy," divine revelation within the categories previously developed in his negative philosophy, which ascends from below and ends up with a kind of negative theology. Only God as absolute freedom can fulfill our human freedom. So I agree with Anthony J. Godzieba's interpretation: Grace is God's free self-communication, which fulfills and transcends all our natural desires.

Some scholars may be of the opinion that idealistic philosophy is no longer up to date. For, since the nineteenth century, we have moved from the modern era to the postmodern era with its tendency to call into question many of the ideals of the Enlightenment and of idealistic philosophy. But already Schelling in his late philosophy was at the same time the highpoint of idealism and a turning point to the post-idealistic thinking of Kierkegaard, Marx, and Nietzsche. Heidegger as well as Habermas did studies on Schelling's late philosophy. Schelling had also great significance for prerevolutionary Russian thinking, especially for Vladimir Soloviev, who already at that time intended to bridge the gap between Eastern Orthodox theology and Western Latin theology.

So Schelling as a thinker of transition remains interesting for us in our postmodern situation. He brings us into contact with the modern philosophy of freedom and subjectivity (which is quite different from subjectivism), and he also points to this philosophy's limits. As we have to take seriously a postmodern critique of a one-sided conceptual and notional idealistic understanding, theology in a critical sense has also to take seriously the legitimate concerns of the modern age. Just as theology defends the faith against postmodern pluralism and relativism, it must also defend it against antirationalist, fundamentalist tendencies. In this critical and at the same time constructive sense, theology becomes (in a quite unexpected way) an ally of a properly understood Enlightenment. This commitment was important to Pope John Paul II, as expressed in his encyclical *Fides et ratio* (1998), an encyclical that became central for Pope Benedict XVI. We dare not fall under the spell of a fundamentalist or emotional and sentimental understanding of the faith and withdraw into a falsely understood pious corner; we must give everyone "an accounting," an *apologia*, of "the hope" that is in us (1 Pet 3:15) and in dialogue argue as advocates for the faith. Therefore, the church even today needs good theologians with deep insight into the greatness and in the limits of the modern age.

3. Speaking of God Who Is Mercy

After this fundamental reflection on theology's two eyes, let us ask now: what is the main challenge to theology today? Already Thomas Aquinas taught at the beginning of his *Summa theologica* that the subject (in modern terms, the object) of theology is God and everything else insofar as it relates to God. Theology is *logos* on *theos*; it is God-talk. Theologians who do not speak about God do *allotria*, "something strange"; they miss their theme or object and go astray.[8]

This position brings me to the challenge facing today's theology: how are we to talk about God? In *Gaudium et spes*, Vatican II counted atheism in its various forms as one of the serious phenomena of this age; it also had the humility to confess the share of blame Christians bear for this situation (GS 19). Since the council, the situation in our secularized Western world has worsened dramatically. The problem is not so much the theoretical atheism of the nineteenth century nor the so-called new atheism, which proceeds from an ideology based in evolutionary theory. The problem is practical atheism, that is, today's indifference regarding the question of God. Many people now consider the secular option to be normal.

So we can no longer worry only about the social, cultural, and political effects of faith and take belief in God for granted. And, above all, we cannot engage today's new pagans with questions of internal church reform. The questions of church reform are interesting for insiders. But the people outside the church have other questions. They ask: where do I come from, and where am I going? Why and for what purpose do I exist? How do I find happiness? Why is there evil and suffering in the world? Why must I suffer? Why do so many innocent people have to suffer, not only from unjust situations, but also from natural upheavals, e.g., tsunamis, earthquakes, drought, etc.? How can a God who is almighty and all merciful permit all of this misery? Is not belief in God, especially in the monotheistic God, the very cause of many evils such as intolerance, violence, xenophobia, and oppression?

To answer these questions we as Christian theologians cannot speak vaguely about a divine being or a divine dimension, as all forms of religion do more or less. Rather, we must speak of the God who in history didn't reveal something to us, but revealed and communicated himself, speaking to us "as his friends" (*Dei verbum* 2). We must talk about the God who in Jesus Christ committed himself to become "flesh" (John 1:14), a human being who has shared our life, our joys and hopes, our anxieties and sorrows; we must discuss the God whom Jesus revealed to be God as our Father, the God for us and with us. This is the God whom the First Letter of John defined as "love" (1 John 4:8-16), a statement that the Christian tradition has interpreted to mean the self-communication of the triune God.

Unfortunately, the systematic theology of the nineteenth and early twentieth centuries' theological manuals represents a one-sided metaphysical vision of God, and it mostly overlooks and forgets the central and fundamental message of God's mercy, i.e., God's unshakable faithfulness to his love.[9] Schelling discovered a fundamental point in the biblical understanding of God when he interpreted the biblical name Yahweh to mean that God in divine love and mercy is the power of an ever new future. To speak of "the mercy of God" is to say that in every situation, even the worst situation, God concedes us a new chance, gives us a new beginning. Thus, in every situation, we can call out, "Abba, Father" (Gal 4:6), and, even if nobody else hears us or wants to hear us, God will listen to us. God's mercy, God's *misericordia*, (i.e., God's heart, *cor* in Latin, for the suffering and the poor, *miseri* in Latin) is—as Pope Francis has said—the name of our God and our fundamental message for today.

Mercy is God's preferential option for the poor. To be sure, mercy has personal and private consequences; we must be merciful with our neighbors. Yet, mercy has—as Johann Baptist Metz and the liberation theologians point out—also a political and public dimension. As Christians, we can change the world by bringing a beam of mercy into our world and making the world warmer and brighter for all people.

4. Speaking of God Who Is Love and Truth

To talk about God means to talk about the ultimate all-encompassing reality as love. So we cannot talk about God as a reality only outside the world. To talk about God includes talking about the world as God's creation, as Elizabeth A. Johnson has reminded us. We have to protect and cultivate creation as the fruit of God's love. Further, since talking about God includes commitment to all other people—people created in the "image" and "likeness" of God and belonging to the one human family (Gen 1:16-27)—so our talk about God must also have social and pastoral dimensions. Further, in a particular way, we cannot talk about God without talking about ourselves. Theology presupposes conversion and the opening up of our hearts to God. We cannot talk about God without talking to God in prayer. This insight brings me to the subjective dimension of theology.

Perhaps at this point I may insert a short biographical note. Already as a little boy I wanted to become a parish priest. I never achieved it. Already after one year as an associate pastor in Stuttgart, I was asked by the bishop to return to the university, where I stayed more than half of my life. But theology has always been a dimension of my priestly pastoral vocation. During my whole academic life, I was pastorally committed, for example, in the medical clinics in Tübingen and in parishes in Münster, Tübingen, and elsewhere. Often, during the week I would wrestle with a theological problem and try to express it in simple words in my Sunday sermon, but I would fail to do so; then, I would become aware that I myself did not understand the problem well enough. My theological master, Josef Geiselmann, during my last encounter with him in a memorable walk on Tübingen's Österberg, told me: "When you have understood something, you can express it in simple words." Thus, doing pastoral work and listening to people and their problems has helped me to do my theological work.

In this regard, I found an interesting section in the writings of Thomas Aquinas. Thomas makes the distinction between three kinds of crowns or halos as symbols of holiness. The first kind of crown goes to the virgins, for they had to withstand lifelong the challenge and temptation of the flesh and the evil that comes out of our bad desires. The second type of crown belongs to the martyrs, for they gave witness to Christ even to the point of giving up their lives for Christ. The third kind goes—and this is for me very consoling—to the theologians because they have to struggle with the devil, the father of lies, and to give witness to the truth.

The truth that we as theologians have to confess and teach does not consist only in correct dogmatic formulas. Rather, it concerns a living reality; Jesus Christ is the truth in person (John 14:6). He is the light of the world (John 8:12), the light of life (John 1:4; 8:12). Christ is the truth that all people need in order to find the right way to live in this world's darkness, night, twilight, and fog. As theologians, we can help people so that a little more light may shine in their lives, and we can help the church to give witness so that Christ becomes the *Lumen gentium*, the light of the peoples.

This light of truth isn't like a floodlight on the runway. Rather, it is like a lantern, which gives light only to the degree that we go forward. Yet, this truth gives enough light to walk the next step. In this sense, after the anthropocentric turning point that has occurred in theology, we now need to undergo a theocentric turning point in theology. We have to give witness that the joy of the Lord is our strength (Neh 8:10). Therefore, let's be joyful theologians.

Endnotes

1. See Walter Kasper, *The Methods in Dogmatic Theology*, trans. J. Drury (Dublin: Ecclesia, 1969); idem, "Was heißt Theologie zu treiben? Dankrede nach der Verleihung des Theologischen Preises der Salzburger Hochschulwochen," in *Gott im Kommen*, ed. Gregor Maria Hoff (Innsbruck: Tyrolia Verlag, 2006), 250–58; idem, *The Catholic Church: Nature, Reality and Mission*, trans. Thomas Hoebel (London: Bloomsbury T&T Clark, 2014), 41–59.

2. Kasper, *The Catholic Church*, 5–7, 347–48 notes 6–10.

3. Walter Kasper, *Die Lehre von der Tradition in der Römischen Schule* (1962), ed. George Augustin and Klaus Krämer, *Gesammelte Schriften*, vol. 1 (Freiburg: Herder, 2011).

4. Max Seckler, "Die ekklesiologische Bedeutung des Systems der 'loci theologici'. Erkenntnistheologische Katholizität und strukturale Weisheit," in *Die schiefen Wände des Lehrhauses. Katholizität als Herausforderung* (Freiburg: Herder, 1988), 79–104.

5. Kasper, *The Catholic Church*, 271–75.

6. Vatican Council I, *Dei Filius*, 4.4: "Now reason does indeed when it seeks persistently, piously and soberly, achieve by God's gift some understanding, and that most profitable, of the mysteries, whether by analogy from what it knows naturally, or from the connexion of these mysteries with one another and with the final end of humanity." Available at: http://www.papalencyclicals.net/Councils/ecum20.htm.

7. Walter Kasper, *Das Absolute in der Geschichte. Philosophie und Theologie der Geschichte in der Spätphilosophie Schellings* (1965), ed. George Augustin and Klaus Krämer, *Gesammelte Schriften*, vol. 2 (Freiburg: Herder, 2010).

8. Walter Kasper, "Introduction to the New Edition," trans. Dinah Livingstone, in *The God of Jesus Christ*, trans. Matthew J. O'Connell (London: Bloomsbury Continuum, 2012), ix–xxvi.

9. Walter Kasper, *Mercy: The Essence of the Gospel and Key to Christian Life*, trans. William Madges (New York: Paulist Press, 2014).

SECTION THREE

Reflections on Forgiveness, Vatican II, and Hope

CHAPTER 17

Forgiveness and the Purification of Memory

Cardinal Walter Kasper
Tantur Ecumenical Institute, Jerusalem
May 25, 2004

1. Pope John Paul II's Request for Forgiveness

When Pope John Pope II asked for forgiveness for the sins committed throughout history by the church's sons and daughters—on the First Sunday of Lent of the Jubilee Year 2000 during an uplifting Mass in St. Peter's in Rome—the echo that resonated from his message was not unanimous.[1]

Many expressed approval and satisfaction: "Finally! The time has come!" With statements like these, they perceived this recognition of fault as a sign of truth and sincerity that would endow the church with a new credibility. This act of repentance and prayer for forgiveness would free the church from the burden of the past and enable the church to start afresh its journey into the new millennium. I was deeply moved when, at the end of the ceremony, the pope approached a large cross at the foot of which he symbolically laid down this sin where it not only belongs but in the only place where, according to Christian faith, it can be washed away. I felt that I had experienced a significant event of history.

Nevertheless, there were also different opinions, embodying doubt and critical reservations. They came partially from within the church. These voices expressed concern about whether the church had started to doubt its divine mission and infallibility, whether it was surrendering to anti-church propaganda that reiterates the same allegations over and over again: the crusades, the Inquisition, witch hunts, phobia toward science and progress as well as women, ignorance, and intolerance. With its self-accusation, does not the church admit that its detractors are right, and, in doing so, does it not create confusion and perplexity among faithful Christians? Is not such an act a unilateral act? Have not others also made mistakes?

Yet again other people judged that the pope's prayer for forgiveness was simply a clever propaganda trick to appease the adversary and defuse further criticism against the church. Moreover, the pope was accused of referring to the sin of the church's sons and daughters but not to the sin of the church as an institution. This is a critique to which we will come back later on.

To start with, we should bear in mind that popes and bishops are also the church's sons who, as human beings, just as all other sons and daughters of the church, share not only the apostolic heritage but also the history and mentality of their common family, i.e., the church. But can we who are living today ask for forgiveness for the sins committed by those who lived before us? Is not sin something personal? Do we have the right to judge acts undertaken in totally different spiritual and political circumstances by individuals who lived even centuries ago?

Historians warn us against the danger of oversimplifying the way we judge an earlier era's events, which cannot be simply measured according to our contemporary outlook. What today seems more or less obvious, or at least conforming to our idea of political correctness, was considered differently in the past and judged according to arguments that were, in good faith, convincing at the time. Historians refer to the problems of historical hermeneutics and question whether the church's teaching can effectively assume the responsibility for or have the competence to evaluate historical events. By asking for forgiveness, should a specific and particular understanding of history be given a definitive and official status in the church?

Other urgent and relevant questions also arise. For example, can the church, in this way, confront the moral, theological, and spiritual problems arising from such an appalling crime as the state-planned and state-implemented annihilation of European Jews, namely, the Shoah? Is it possible at all to find answers to these questions?

2. A Unique Request

Pope John Paul II's prayer for forgiveness and also for the purification of memory has raised fundamental questions. This is especially so since this act is unique and unprecedented in its form.

Certainly, all Jubilee Years, since the first one proclaimed in the year 1300 by Pope Boniface VIII, have been inspired by the idea of forgiveness and mercy, which characterized the Jubilee referred to in the Old Testament (Lev 25:8-13); they have always been connected to acts of repentance. In fact, when we speak of indulgences in this context, we should not think immediately of the ecclesial abuses that fuelled the Reformation. The underlying idea in an indulgence is that the whole church prays for the individuals involved and spiritually supports them in their overcoming the punishment for sins, i.e., the healing of the wounds caused by sin which God has forgiven but which continues to have an effect. The Jubilee Years, therefore, have always been linked to personal sin and personal repentance, but they had never been an opportunity for the church to examine its conscience and to discern its past faults and even to ask for forgiveness.

Not even Pope Hadrian IV's famous admission—in 1522 in front of the Reichstag in Nuremberg—of the misuses and misdeeds committed by the church's leader and members can be considered as a precedent. At that time, in fact, Hadrian blamed his predecessor and the Roman Curia for their sins but did not add to this accusation a prayer for forgiveness.

The first traces of John Paul II's new approach can be found in the Second Vatican Council when at the beginning of its second session (September 29, 1963) Pope Paul VI asked God and the divided Christians of the East for forgiveness for the wrongs committed by the Catholic Church, and he declared himself in turn willing to forgive. The pope's subsequent gesture—in 1965 during the visit to Rome of Metropolitan Meliton as the delegate of the Ecumenical Patriarchate—of kneeling in the Sistine Chapel and asking for forgiveness was most eloquent. After centuries of defensive attitudes, Paul VI inaugurated a new, reconciling tone that found a clear echo in several documents of the Second Vatican Council.

Vatican II's Decree on Ecumenism, *Unitatis redintegratio* (UR), expresses regret for sins against unity and asks for forgiveness (UR 7). The Pastoral Constitution on the Church in the Modern World, *Gaudium et spes* (GS), speaks of the co-responsibility of Christians for the emergence of modern atheism (GS 19) and regrets the attitude that has not recognized the legitimate autonomy of science and culture (GS 36). In the Declaration on the Relation of the Church to Non-Christian Religions, *Nostra aetate* (NA), the council also condemned all forms of anti-Semitism (NA 4), however, it did not combine this recognition of sins and repentance with any prayer for forgiveness.

Even before the First Sunday of Lent in 2000, Pope John Paul II made gestures that went further than those of the Second Vatican Council and of his predecessors. I will mention only a few examples. In 1984, during his visit to the World Council of Churches in Geneva, he spoke of the shortcomings committed on the Catholic side. In 1985 in Yaoundé (Cameroon) the pope asked the African people for forgiveness for the slavery of black people. He repeated the same prayer for forgiveness in his message addressed in 1992 to Native Americans as well as to the black people deported to America. In 1995, in his encyclical letter on ecumenism, *Ut unum sint* (88), the pope followed the example of Paul VI and asked for forgiveness for the aspects of papal history that have left painful memories for other Christians. Also, in 1995, on the occasion of the canonization of Jan Sarkander, he asked for forgiveness for the injustice perpetrated on non-Catholics in Moravia.

Besides these appeals, two other more recent acts come to mind. The first is well-known. In 2000, during his visit to Jerusalem, Pope John Paul II left a paper with a prayer for forgiveness at the Western ("Wailing") Wall. The second occurred in 2001; while in Athens, the pope asked forgiveness for the offenses committed during the conquest and destruction of Constantinople in 1254. (Such prayers for forgiveness belonged also to the style of Pope Benedict XVI.)

3. A Call for Reform and Holiness

These prayers for forgiveness are more than a matter of "style." They show Pope John Paul II's constant effort to interpret the deep theological meaning of the biblical and ecclesial tradition in line with the teaching of the Second Vatican Council. The council confessed "one holy catholic and apostolic church" (*una sancta catholica et apostolica ecclesia*), as these words were formulated in the confessions of faith of the Councils of Nicaea in 325 and Constantinople in 381. Thus, according to the common creed of Eastern and Western Christianity, holiness is one of the fundamental characteristics of the church's identity.

This confession has nothing to do with triumphalism, for the above-mentioned phrase is contained in the creed's third part, which speaks of the Holy Spirit. The church's holiness is something objective; that is, it is founded on the gift of the Holy Spirit who dwells in and leads the church. Also, at least since Augustine of Hippo's dispute with the Donatists, the church has understood that among its members are people whose personal sanctity cannot be taken for granted; to the people needing repentance, the church offers the sacrament of reconciliation. At the same time, the church has known that reform is necessary for its institutions as well as for individual Christians. Calls for reform were frequent in the late Middle Ages. The Council of Trent (1545–63) reacted to the turmoil of the Reformation not only dogmatically but also through its extensive reform of the institutional church.

The Second Vatican Council referred to this need for reform and extensively studied the question. On the one hand, in its Dogmatic Constitution on the Church, *Lumen gentium* (LG), it reaffirms the profession of the church's holiness (LG 39, 48). On the other, it states that the church is one complex reality, comprising a divine and a human dimension: "the church . . . clasping sinners to its bosom, at once holy and always in need of purification, follows constantly the path of penance and renewal" (LG 8). The call to renewal is a constant *leitmotiv* of the Second Vatican Council; it can be found in the Dogmatic Constitution on the Church (LG 4, 7, 9) and also in other conciliar documents (UR 4, 6; GS 21, 43; *Ad gentes divinitus* 37, etc.).

It is upon these foundations that Pope John Paul II was able to undertake theological reflection. His thoughts are expressed especially in his *Tertio millennio adveniente* (1994), written in preparation for the Jubilee Year 2000, in which he develops a rigorously coherent program. In this apostolic letter (33–35), he speaks in detail of the need for an examination of conscience and mentions in concrete terms sins against unity, acquiescence to intolerance, and even the use of violence.

In his Bull of Indiction of the Jubilee Year, *Incarnationis mysterium* (1998), John Paul II explicitly talks about the purification of memory (11), which he sees as an act of humility, recognizing one's faults and as an act of conversion, emanating from one's examination of conscience. Church history recounts, next to its pages engraved with the marks of holiness, many events that constitute a "counter-testimony to Christianity." John Paul II goes on to say: "Because of the bond which unites us to one another in the Mystical Body, all of us, though not personally responsible and without encroaching on the judgement of God who alone knows every heart, bear the burden of the errors and faults of those who have gone before us." The pope adds that these sins "have hindered the Bride of Christ from shining forth in all her beauty. Our sin has impeded the Spirit's working in the hearts of many people." Elsewhere, the pope also mentions "sinful structures" as the consequences of personal sins (*Reconciliatio et Paenitentia* 16; *Ut unum sint* 34).

Therefore, Pope John Paul II distinguishes between the personal sins of an individual Christian, for which only the individual is responsible, and the consequences of those sins, i.e., the darkening of the church's radiance and message. The sins of an individual become a burden for the whole community because of the deep inner links that bind together the parts of the mystical body of Christ. Such a burden cannot be relieved simply by human effort. We cannot ignore it, nor can we build a new church from scratch. It is only God who can free us from the burden of the past through divine forgiveness.

4. The Bible on Purification from Sin and the Purification of Memory

What has been said so far is deeply rooted in sacred scripture as well as in church tradition. In the light of scripture, we can understand forgiveness and the purification of memory in a deeper and more comprehensive way. We will proceed in three steps. First, we shall consider the social dimension of sin. Second, we will speak of purification from sin. And, third, we will discuss the purification of memory. In the last two sections, after some brief references to church tradition, we shall focus on whether and how the biblical concepts can be understood today.

(1) *Sin's Social Dimension*

The ancient world conceived sin not merely as a subjective act committed by an individual but also as an act belonging to a much wider sacred and social context.[2] Sin was understood as a wound to an all-comprehensive sacred order, causing a disruption to this order and becoming a burden for the whole community. It is intertwined in a community's connective tissue, constituting a kind of collective responsibility and permeating the whole community like a curse. In his regard, biblical exegetes speak of act-consequence, i.e., of a sin-curse bond.

In order to break the evil chain of sin and stop its evil consequences, atonement was needed, i.e., the disruption to sacred order had to be counterbalanced. For serious transgressions, this was possible only by banning the guilty person from the community, which in practice was like a death sentence. One could atone for one's sins also by proxy, by laying the guilt upon an animal; this scapegoat was then sent away into the wilderness to die (Lev 16:20-22). It was also possible to sacrifice an animal (Lev 4–5), so that it would endure death in the place of the sinner. In this way, the sin-curse bond was broken. The great day of atonement, Yom Kippur, which was an atonement also for sins that had been committed unconsciously, allowed the reconciliation of the whole people with God every year (Lev 16:29-34; 23:26-32).

These concepts are also present in the New Testament. In particular, they can be found in two key places. First, they are fundamental for the four accounts of Jesus' last supper.[3] The idea of proxy is expressed when the accounts speak of the body of Christ that is given for us (1 Cor 11:24; Luke 22:19) and of his blood that is poured out for us (Matt 26:27f.; Mark 14:24; Luke 22:20). The version of Matthew and Mark also refers to Exodus 24:8, mentioning the blood of the covenant (Matt 26:28; Mark 14:24). The second key place is the Letter to the Romans when Paul says that God appointed the cross of Christ as a new sacrifice to show his righteousness (Rom 3:25; cf. Heb 9:11ff.).

This view corresponds to the idea that Jesus himself had of his death, which he understood as a ransom for many, i.e., for all (Mark 10:45). He did not unburden himself of sin but took it on himself and died for sinners. For our sake, Jesus made himself to be sin and curse (2 Cor 5:21; Gal 3:13). In doing so, he broke the chain of the curse and the power of sin. He set a new beginning and gave way to life and love.

This freedom from the cycle of sin does not concern only the individual isolated from the rest of the community. This freedom through baptism (1 Cor 12:13) is inscribed in the new solidarity of salvation, in the body of Christ: "If one member suffers, all suffer together with it; if one member is honored, all rejoice together with it" (1 Cor 12:26; cf. Rom 12:15). The sentence "Bear one another's burden" (Gal 6:2) can thus be understood in a positive way. This is the foundation of the "communion of saints," *communio sanctorum*, of the Apostles' Creed.

(2) *Purification from Sin*

In the Old Testament, besides atonement rites we find also purification rites. They are based on the idea that sin brings a person in contact with what is impure and causes a stain that disrupts his or her capacity to worship and live within the community. This stain can be removed through ablutions or baths. Such aspersion with purifying water takes place, for example, during Yom Kippur.[4] The forgiveness of sins can therefore be described as a washing away or a purification. "Wash me thoroughly from my iniquity, and cleanse me from my sin" (Ps 51:2); "wash me, and I shall be whiter than snow" (Ps 51:7; cf. Isa 1:16; Jer 2:22; 4:14). The prophets reiterate this concept and await the definitive purification of the people by the Spirit of God (Isa 6:5ff.; 13:1f.).

The New Testament also speaks of such purification (2 Tim 2:21; Heb 1:3; 9:22f.; 10:2; 2 Pet 1:9; 1 John 1:7, 9). Baptism, in particular, is described as purification (Eph 5:26; 2 Pet 1:9). We also find the purification of one's heart (Acts 15:9; Jas 4:8) and also of one's conscience (Heb 9:9, 13f.). "If the blood of goats and bulls, with the sprinkling of the ashes of a heifer, sanctifies those who have been defiled so that their flesh is purified, how much more will the blood of Christ, who through the eternal Spirit offered himself without blemish to God, purify our conscience from dead works to worship the living God!" (Heb 9:13-14).

This sentence is the main biblical foundation of the *purificatio memoriae*. The purification of conscience from "dead works" should not be understood in a moral way as the appeasement of a guilty conscience and the gift of a clear one. The purification is rather a cathartic freedom from works belonging to death. It brings about a new eschatological existence and a renewal of individuals in their entirety.[5] The purification of sins means the death of the old self and the gift of a new life (Rom 6:1-11); through it, we are a new creation (2 Cor 5:17; Gal 6:15).

(3) *The Purification of Memory*

The breaking of the sin-curse bond can be also expressed with the category of memory. *Zakar*, *zikkaron*, *anamnesis*, and *memoria* are fundamental, key biblical categories.[6] God is the God who remembers human persons (Ps 8:4-6; Heb 2:5-8). The Bible continuously refers to the fact that God remembers the covenant made with the ancestors (Gen 9:15f.; Exod 2:24; 6:5; etc.). Especially in the book of Deuteronomy, we find a whole theology of memory (Deut 5:15; 7:18; etc.).

Such memory creates a connection that binds different generations. Whoever is forgotten is like one who is dead (Ps 31:12). God's remembering is a powerful event, capable of creating a new situation. Likewise, the people should remember the events of the history of salvation in order to make them always present. It is especially in the feast of Passover (Exod 12:14; Deut 16:3) that God lays the foundation of the memory of his salvific events (Ps 111:4). The New Testament uses the expression: "Do this in remembrance of me" (1 Cor 11:25; Luke 22:19) in the eucharistic context. It is, above all, the role of the Spirit to remind us of the words and works of Jesus, to make them present, and to lead us to their deeper understanding (John 14:26).

Evil acts are also remembered by God, but God's mercy is expressed precisely by his lack of rancor. According to Exodus 34:6-9, God forgives sins in order to give future generations the possibility to convert; he immediately punishes sinners in order to leave the following generation the chance to convert (Deut 7:10). Thus, God limits the sin-curse cycle or even breaks it by not taking into account sins committed in the past (Isa 43:25; 64:8; Jer 31:34). In doing so, he cancels the power of the past and gives the future a new chance. Thanks to the divine gift of forgiveness, the past is prevented from poisoning the present and burdening the future. Forgiveness is freedom from the power of past sins and the gift of a new future. It is no longer the past but the future that has an impact on the present.

God's gift also gives the human person the opportunity to remember "before God" his or her guilty past, to recognize and account for it. This remembering happens in the form of the confession of sin (Ps 38:18; Dan 9:4, 20). Since we know that God is merciful, we can judge the past in a different way. Confessing our sins does not mean, therefore, to erase them or forget them. Sin will be explicitly remembered as such "before God," but it will receive a new qualification from God: it is now a forgiven sin.

Today it has become difficult for us to understand the underlying idea of purification of memory, especially in the rites. We tend to perceive them as magical practices. We are inclined to see the atonement and purification rites as human attempts to influence God and merit divine favor. The Old and New Testaments present a different conception. They teach that it is God who, in his mercy, has established the order of rites and has appointed Christ as the sacrifice of reconciliation (Rom 3:25). Thus, the holiness of God and his desire for reconciliation express themselves in ritual. God does not act like human beings; God does not seek revenge. God acts as God, the One who forgives (Hos 11:9). Instead of the deserved death, God gives life (Ezek 18:21-23; 31:10f.). Forgiveness therefore is the creation of a new heart (Ps 51:10-12; Ezek 11:19; 36:26f.), the gift of a new life (Rom 6:4) and a new creation (2 Cor 5:17; Gal 6:15).

The biblical concepts of forgiveness and purification are therefore an expression of God's transcendence. God is not the guarantor of any established order: he is above the order of the world and can create a new order. God breaks the sin-curse cycle and initiates a new beginning. He can free humankind from the past and bestow a new future. Forgiveness thus means both that God is God and not a human being and also that God is the God of humans. God is merciful and compassionate, slow to anger, rich in kindness and faithfulness (Exod 34:6).

5. Theological Teachings on Sin, Repentance, and Memory

It would be highly interesting and illuminating as well to explain how traditional theological doctrine developed and interpreted these biblical insights. This study would imply among other aspects the explanation of the whole doctrine of penance and the sacrament of reconciliation, but in this context I can only offer some indications.

We could refer to the meaning of repentance, which implies conversion and real turning away from the bad deeds of the past, resolving for the good in the future, and making good for wrongs wherever possible. We could remember the deep meaning of confession, which does not mean only confession of sins but first of all confession as praise of God's greatness in abundant mercy and love. We also could call to mind the doctrine of original sin—not an easy concept—which implies solidarity in sin and in the consequences of sin, and the doctrine of the communion of saints, which implies solidarity in grace.

We could further delve into the traditional distinction between the "guilt of sin" (*culpa peccati*) and the eternal and temporal consequences or "punishments deriving from sin" (*reatus peccati*). Whereas eternal punishments of guilt are forgiven by the forgiveness of sins, temporal consequences can endure and offer the opportunity for atonement. According to Catholic doctrine, confession and forgiveness of sins is often connected with the gift of inner joy, spiritual peace, and consolation. In this context it would be highly interesting to have an understanding of the meaning of purification in the ascetic and spiritual experience of the saints and of corresponding spiritual theology. Finally, we could develop the fundamental meaning and importance of memory (*memoria*), which in the context of liturgy means not only the subjective memory of the past but an objective making present and making effective of God's salvific deeds in the past through proclamation and sacramental symbols.

All these doctrines show that what today is called the purification of memory has deep roots in theological tradition and is at the same time a creative development and an actualization of that tradition. But to explain all these aspects not superficially but in an adequate way would take us much more time than we have in this context. Therefore, I prefer to commit a methodological and hermeneutical "sin" by jumping immediately from the biblical witness, over two thousand years of tradition and interpretation, to our present-day problematic.

6. Sin's Social and Institutional Consequences

The question arises whether those biblical notions can still be understood today. Should we not demythologize these sacral and mythical ideas and interpret them in an existential way, as Rudolf Bultmann suggested? In reality, such a proposal is influenced by the polemics of the Reformation concerning the sacrifice of the Mass as well as by the contemporary shift to subjectivity and the tendency to see sin as something merely subjective and intimate. From a philosophical perspective, Paul Ricoeur studied this process of the "subjectivation" of sin and guilt but simultaneously reaffirmed, like others, the still relevant and powerful meaning of myth.[7]

Therefore, the question is not whether we can reverse these modern developments, which is clearly not possible, but whether we will remain stuck in the modern "subjectivation" of sin. Do the experiences of humankind in the twentieth century allow us to hold on to the modern idea of the merely subjective and intimate nature of sin and guilt? Is it enough to become aware of our guilt and sin in our private conscience with a feeling of shame and regret and then to ask God for forgiveness? Our experience from recent history clearly shows that this is not possible. Two examples can be mentioned.

Let me start with the following. All that white colonial powers inflicted for centuries upon African and other peoples (often without being really aware of it and thus without the personal guilt of individuals) still has negative consequences today from a cultural, social, and political point of view. An evil cycle emerged. These wronged peoples, whenever and wherever possible, have sought revenge. This process is particularly clear in some parts of the Arab world, where there is a widespread hatred against Western civilisation. The problem with revenge lies in the fact that old guilt is erased with new guilt, thus perpetuating the sin-curse cycle. The answer put forward by the Christian message is a different one. Christ has assumed the sins of the whole of humankind, has made atonement once and for all, and thus has given a new future to justice and love. Nevertheless, we—Europeans and Westerners—still have to learn how to activate the strength of justice and love. This is why the evil cycle persists. Can we therefore expect something positive from the future?

The second example refers to the Shoah, the Nazis' state-planned and state-implemented annihilation of European Jews. The consequences of this abominable crime affect not only the victims and the culprits; they affect not only Germans. The consequences have an impact on the current world situation, the state of Israel, and the conflict in the Middle East, which, in turn, fuels the conflict between the Arab and the Western worlds. After 1945 in Germany, reparation was extensively spoken of, and much was undertaken in its cause. But nobody can seriously think that it is possible to compensate for the deaths of millions of people.

Emmanuel Levinas was of the opinion that, according to Jewish thought, crimes against people can be forgiven only by the victims.[8] How, though, can the dead forgive, and how can one be forgiven for the death of people? The Christian answer is that, if the guilt is immeasurable, it is only before God, the Lord of life and death, that we can place it. There would not be any hope without the hope of judgement and resurrection from the dead. Without judgement, the murderer would triumph over his innocent victim. It is only through resurrection that justice can be done for the victim.[9] Such hope should not be understood as an escape from our responsibility and from what we can actually do in this life. Rather, the hope based on God's promise should encourage us to start afresh and help others also to draw hope.

These are only two examples among many. They clearly show that the biblical understanding of guilt, in which sin causes a vicious cycle in the community and in history, which cannot be broken simply by human effort, is far from being obsolete; this understanding is as valid today as it was in the past. Political theology and liberation theology, in particular, drawing on the neo-Marxist ideas of the Frankfurt School, have overcome the limits of a narrowly understood anthropological and existential concept of guilt, which is exclusively focused on the individual, and they have brought back into the foreground the social and interrelated dimension of sin. Political theology has spoken of structures of sin and of sinful structures.[10] Catholic theology has dealt with these ideas not only in a critical but also in a constructive way, as demonstrated by the church's official documents.[11]

The starting point for Catholic reflection is that sin, in its deep and true sense, is always an act of the person, not the act of a community. It is not possible to lay the blame on structures or systems without undermining the dignity and freedom of the person. We need to make a distinction, however, between personal responsibility for sins and the social consequences of sins. Our human interrelatedness means that the act of a single person has an impact also on others. There is not only a community of saints but also a community of sinners. Through the accumulation of many personal sins, there emerge situations of sin, not sinful situations. Collective behaviors and mentalities can develop in more or less large ethnic or social groups, and even in nations and blocks of states, constituting a phenomenon that can take on enormous proportions and have a fatal impact on society.

These situations of sin can be described as sinful only by analogy. They should not be understood as equal to personal sins. The individual is still personally responsible when he or she accepts, silently approves, or does not oppose (whenever possible) such situations. This is why in the long run a change in these situations of sin cannot be brought about only through institutional and structural changes or revolutions; it can occur only with the conversion of the people who are responsible for those situations. Just as the vicious circle of sin is based on a series of personal decisions, so it is through personal decisions—and especially through the prophetic gestures and words of individuals—that such cycles can be broken.

7. Purifying Memory for the Future

The continuing influence of past actions has been discussed in the history of philosophy since Plato with the help of the concept of memory.[12] In the thinking of St. Augustine, memory is the center of the human person. In fact, the specificity of the human person is that he or she is not simply bound to the present instant but can transcend it; the person can make the past present through memory and anticipate the future. With the capacity to experience together the three dimensions of time, a human person is a temporal image of eternity, an atom of eternity (Søren Kierkegaard).

We should not, however, consider memory simply in an anthropological perspective as the capacity of a single person. Memory has also a historical and philosophical meaning. It forms not only the identity of a person but also the historical identity of a group, of a people, and of a culture. It is especially in the philosophy of G. W. F. Hegel that memory becomes constitutive of reason; reason becomes itself only by remembering and working its way through history. In post-idealistic philosophy—from Wilhelm Dilthey through Martin Heidegger to Hans-Georg Gadamer—memory becomes a hermeneutic category: understanding occurs when, through memory, we make the past present. The mediation of reason and history occurs through memory.

Walter Benjamin and the Frankfurt School added a new aspect.[13] They recognized the "Dialectic of the Enlightenment" (Theodore W. Adorno) and rejected a one-sided and one-dimensional philosophy of progress. They revealed the other side of the history of progress and presented a vision of history from the perspective of the victims, of the marginalized, and of forgotten people, of the losers. Memory is the memory of suffering; it discovers the unrealized opportunities of the past and creates solidarity with the dead and the victims of history. In this way, it brings about dangerous insights that break down the current oversimplifications, trivializations, and camouflages of reality. Memory as memory of suffering (*memoria passionis*) becomes dangerous memory. It is a category of interruption and resistance. It frees one from the imprisonment of the present and opens up the future. Memory is a future-oriented memory; it impels us forward by going back to the roots.

Memory is a *conditio sine qua non* for reason, namely, for critical reason; it is resistant to a one-sided scientific and technical thinking that is mindless of history as well as to the loss of historical awareness. It makes clear that forgetting the past leads to the decline of reason, to arbitrary relativism, and to addiction to the present. To forget history is to renounce not only a fundamental biblical and theological category but also a fundamental category of human, social, and cultural identity. The neglect of history leads to the isolation of the individual, to the atomization and the disintegration of society. It promotes a one-sided philosophy of progress, deprived of orientation and criteria.

The church, which has the task of preserving the *memoria passionis Christi*, is opposed to this decline of the person and society. This ecclesial commitment appears in the title of the document on the Shoah by the Pontifical Commission for Religious Relations with the Jews: "We Remember."[14] Indeed, to forget the injustice of the past would mean to do new injustice to those who were its victims. At the same time, the *memoria passionis Christi* offers the church the possibility and the task of reassessing historical memory in the light of the memory of the death and resurrection of Christ. The message of forgiveness and new life purifies memory. It purifies bad memories, which entail feelings of revenge, hatred, bitterness, pain, disappointment, discouragement, resignation, and frustration. It allows us to see a painful history with reconciled eyes and with a reconciled heart, not to forget, but to forgive the suffered injustices and to start a common journey into the future together with the enemy of the past.

Therefore, the *purificatio memoriae* should neither idealize the memory of past events nor make them harmless—as occurs in the memories of old age that often idealize the recollections of childhood and youth—nor should it, in a false sense, calm and appease these memories. The purification of memory is faithful to reality, but it is also aware of the higher reality of God's forgiveness and reconciliation and also of God's promise. Thus, the purification of memory spurs and activates forgiveness and reconciliation, which are God's gifts, and helps to make hope real. In this process, *purificatio memoriae* becomes *memoria futuri* (Yehuda Bauer). It becomes what Pope John Paul II was striving for by opening up and tracing the way forward into the twenty-first century.

Endnotes

1. For Pope John Paul II's homily, Mass of Pardon (March 12, 2000), see John Paul II and the International Theological Commission, *Memory and Reconciliation: The Church and the Faults of the Past* (Boston: Pauline Books, 2000).

2. On sin's social impact, see Gerhard von Rad, *Old Testament Theology*, vol. 1, trans. D. M. G. Stalker (Louisville, KY: Westminster John Knox Press, 2001, 1962); Ulrich Wilckens, *Brief an die Römer*, vol. 1 (Zurich: Benziger, 1978), 233–43; Helmut Merklein and Josef Schuster, "Sühne," in *Lexikon für Theologie und Kirche*, vol. 9, ed. Walter Kasper et al. (Freiburg: Herder, 2000), 1097–1104.

3. On the theme of atonement in Jesus' Last Supper, see Heinz Schürmann, *Ursprung und Gestalt: Erörterung und Besinnungen zum Neuen Testament* (Düsseldorf: Patmos Verlag, 1970), 77–198; Thomas Söding, "Das Mahl des Herrn," in *Vorgeschmack: ökumenische Bemühungen um die Eucharistie*, ed. Theodore Schneider and Bernd Jochen Hilberath (Mainz: Matthias Grünewald, 1996), 134–63.

4. See Erich Grässer, *An die Hebräer*, vol. 2 (Zurich: Benziger Verlag, 1993), 156–60.

5. See ibid., 161–65.

6. See *Theological Dictionary of the New Testament*, ed. Gerhard Kittel, Gerhard Friedrich, and Geoffrey W. Bromiley (Grand Rapids, MI: W. B. Eerdmans, 1985); Wunibald Müller, Arno Schilson, Hans Bernhard Meyer, "Anamnesis," in *Lexikon für Theologie und Kirche*, vol. 1, ed. Walter Kasper et al. (Freiburg: Herder, 1997), 590–92.

7. See Paul Ricoeur, *Symbolism of Evil* (Boston: Beacon Press, 1967); Jürgen Habermas, *The Future of Human Nature* (Cambridge, UK: Polity Press, 2003).

8. For Emmanuel Levinas's statement, see Adrian Schenker et al., "Vergebung der Sünden," in *Theologische Realenzyklopädie*, vol. 34, ed. Gerhard Müller et al. (Berlin: Walter de Gruyter, 2000), 663–90, at 669.

9. See Max Horkheimer and Hellmut Gumnior, *Die Sehnsucht nach dem ganz Anderen* (Hamburg: Furche, 1970).

10. See Johannes Baptist Metz, *Faith in History and Society: Towards a Practical Fundamental Theology*, trans. David Smith (New York: Crossroad, 2007, 1980), chap. 3.

11. See Pope John Paul II, Apostolic Exhortation "Reconciliation and Penance" (December 2, 1984), 16; available at http://www.vatican.va/holy_father/john_paul_ii/apost_exhortations/documents/hf_jp-ii_exh_02121984_reconciliatio-et-paenitentia_en.html.

12. See *Historisches Wörterbuch der Philosophie*, vol. 2, ed. Joachim Ritter et al. (Darmstadt: Wissenschaftliche Buchgesellschaft, 1972), 636–43; Metz, *Faith in History and Society*, chap. 11.

13. Walter Benjamin, "On the Concept of History," in *Walter Benjamin: Selected Writings*, vol. 4, ed. Edmund Jephcott et al. (Cambridge, MA: Harvard University Press, 2003).

14. Commission for Religious Relations with the Jews, "We Remember: A Reflection on the Shoah" (March 16, 1998), available at http://www.vatican.va/roman_curia/pontifical_councils/chrstuni/documents/rc_pc_chrstuni_doc_16031998_shoah_en.html. See Johannes Baptist Metz, "Zwischen Erinnern und Vergessen: Die Schoah im Zeitalter kultureller Anamnesie," in *Zum Begriff der neuen Politischen Theologie* (Mainz: Matthias Grünewald Verlag, 1997), 149–55.

CHAPTER 18

Renewal from the Source: The Interpretation and Reception of the Second Vatican Council

Cardinal Walter Kasper
Keeley Vatican Lecture, Nanovic Institute for European Studies
University of Notre Dame
April 24, 2013

1. The Council: An Unfinished Story

The evening of January 25, 1959, has remained fixed in my memory. I was a young priest then, and I was listening to the radio news with some friends. Television did not yet exist. We could not believe our ears when we heard that Pope John XXIII had convoked a Vatican council that day. It was like lightning from a blue sky. After the Second World War, I had grown up in the Catholic youth movement of that time. In it, I heard about and absorbed the concerns of the liturgical movement, the biblical movement, and the beginnings of the ecumenical movement. During my studies in Tübingen I learned from the great nineteenth-century theologians of the Catholic Tübingen School that tradition has to be understood not as a static but as a living tradition. Pope Pius XII, who was greatly revered in Germany, opened doors with his encyclicals *Mystici corporis* (1943), *Divino afflante Spiritu* (1943), and *Mediator Dei* (1947), but toward the end of that pontificate we felt stagnation in the church. Nevertheless, we held great hopes and expectations. But none of us had ever dreamed of a council.

The sense of a new start, the discussions, and the enthusiasm that Pope John XXIII's announcement stimulated is hard for young people today to imagine. When I was studying theology at Tübingen University from 1952 to 1956, it was forbidden for us Catholics to attend lectures by the faculty of Protestant theology. Because it was forbidden, it was, of course, very enticing. But with John XXIII it was as though a dam had been opened; everything happened in a rush. We met Protestant theologians and talked the whole night long. We kept hearing news from Rome that the forces in the Roman Curia were trying to quickly blow out the little light of progress that had been lit. Then on October 11, 1962—now sitting in front of a television—we were relieved and enthusiastic once more as we heard the pope's opening address at the council in which he warned against "the prophets of doom" and spoke of the church's *aggiornamento* (Italian, "bringing up to date").

For my generation the Second Vatican Council has remained a formative influence. The experiences of that time continue to be a fixed point of reference for my theological thinking. But for most people today the council has long been past history. All who are younger than the age of sixty did not consciously experience the new departure of those days. For them, the council belongs to another age and another world. It was the age of the Cold War; the Berlin Wall was built a year before the council's start; and during the council's first session the Cuban missile crisis took the world to the brink of nuclear war. In that situation Pope John XXIII published his famous encyclical *Pacem in Terris* (1963).

Today, fifty years later, we live in a totally different and rapidly changing globalized world with many new challenges. The optimistic belief in progress of those days and the spirit of a new departure toward new boundaries that pervaded the Kennedy era disappeared long ago. For most Catholics, the developments set in train by the council, such as the liturgical renewal, have become part of the church's everyday life. But what we now experience, at least in Europe, is not a great new departure and not the springtime of the church that we expected then but instead a stagnating church with signs of crisis. Now many people hope that the new pontiff, Francis, who calls himself "Bishop of Rome," will bring back enthusiasm and a vision of the future.

Already beginning last year, in connection with the jubilee of Vatican II, there is a lot of talk about the council.[1] People are asking, where do we go from here? Back to before the council or forward beyond it? Pope John Paul II and Pope Benedict XVI both called the council a trustworthy compass for the course of the church in the twenty-first century. But the needle of the compass is still wavering restlessly. With a little exaggeration, a Roman newspaper in 2005 published an article on the fortieth anniversary of the closing of Vatican II with the headline "È guerra sul concilio" ("At War over the Council"). A German newspaper said something similar: there is a battle raging over the liberal agenda of the council. It is clear that the interpretation of the council is disputed in many respects and that the council has left us an agenda that is still a long way from being completely worked through.

Anyone who knows the history of the church's twenty councils recognized as ecumenical will hardly be surprised. Postconciliar times were almost always turbulent times. Think of the Arian controversies following the first general council of Nicaea (325), or the secession of the Oriental Orthodox churches (Coptic, Syrian, Armenian, etc.) after the fourth general council of Chalcedon (451). Most councils were able to prevail only after a difficult reception process. In the case of the Second Vatican Council, it is no different.[2]

But the Second Vatican Council is still a special case. Unlike the previous councils, it was not called to discern false doctrine or to reconcile a schism; it did not proclaim any formal dogma or pass any formal disciplinary resolutions. John XXIII had a much more comprehensive perspective. He did not want any condemnations or delimitations. Instead, he saw the coming of a new age and sought an *aggiornamento* of the church, bringing it up to date. By that he did not mean any trivial conformity to the spirit of the times. He spoke of the council's pastoral goal. He intended the council to express the church's traditional faith, the abiding validity of which he did not doubt, in a new contemporary form so that it could reach people's hearts and shed light on the problems of the day. *Lumen gentium*, the "Light of nations," are the opening words of Vatican II's Dogmatic Constitution of the Church: Christ should once more be the light of the peoples of the world. And, according to the Pastoral Constitution on the Church in the World, the church is to share the *Gaudium et spes*, the "joy and hope," and the sorrows and fears of humanity, especially of the poor and oppressed.

The overwhelming majority of the council fathers grasped John XXIII's vision. For them the pastoral intention did not mean that they wished to deny its teachings' dogmatic character. Even though the council did not proclaim any new formal dogma, the intention was to speak of the faith in an authentic, magisterially binding manner and to renew it. In view of the "signs of the times," the council's participants wanted to proceed from sacred scripture and the tradition of the first millennium and to see the church in the first instance not as an institution or organization but as a mystery, as the people of God, the body of Christ, and the house of the Spirit. They wanted the liturgy to be understood not simply as a solemn and sacral rite but as the representation of the paschal mystery of Christ, with "the active participation" of the whole people of Christ. They wanted to overcome the Constantinian era's symbiosis of the church and the state, the one-sided antireform and antimodernist mentality of the last centuries, and to take up the concerns of the biblical, liturgical, patristic, pastoral, and ecumenical renewal movements between the two world wars, to open a new chapter in the burdened history of the church with Judaism, and to enter into dialogue with the other religions and with modern culture. It was to a certain extent a modernization program that did not want modernism but a renewal from the sources. Pope John Paul II made the point precisely in his program for the new third millennium. He said it involved a *ripartire da Cristo*,[3] a new departure with Christ as the starting point.

That was a fascinating program. An influential minority, however, resolutely opposed this attempt by the majority. They remained captive to the structure of neoscholasticism and defended the post-Tridentine tradition in a one-sided manner. Pope John XXIII's successor, Pope Paul VI—unjustly a too much forgotten pope—was in principle inclined toward the concerns of the majority but also sought (in accordance with the ancient conciliar tradition) to achieve, if at all possible, a united consensus on the passing of the council documents. He succeeded: all sixteen documents were passed almost unanimously. But that came at a cost. In many places, as in previous councils, there were found compromise formulations in which the position of the majority often stands directly side by side with the position of the minority with their concern for demarcation.

So the council's texts contain enormous conflict potential; they open the door for a selective reception in one or the other direction. Vatican II was a council of transition. It wanted renewal without giving up the old. For this synthesis of old and new, however, the council could only set the framework for the postconciliar reception. So the question arises: In which direction does the compass of Vatican II point, and where is the church heading in this still young third millennium? Will it maintain the confident trust of John XXIII and the renewal from the sources or take the path back to defensive antireform and antimodernist attitudes? That is the question facing postconciliar reception.

2. Three Phases of Reception

We can distinguish three overlapping phases of reception so far. At first there was a phase of enthusiasm. In a lecture immediately after his return from the council, the Jesuit theologian Karl Rahner spoke of "the beginning of a beginning."[4] But Rahner remained cautious regarding further developments. Others went further and wanted, as they felt, to set aside the baggage of tradition as an unnecessary compromise, and—leaping over almost two thousand years of church history—to interpret the church's doctrine anew on the basis of scripture. They felt that after the first-stage rocket had been ignited by the council, it was now time for the second stage. But this second-stage rocket soon looked like a spaceship beyond the reach of ground control.

The reaction was not long in coming. It came not only from the Society of Saint Pius X, founded by Archbishop Marcel LeFebvre, but also from theologians who had been counted among the council's progressives, for example, Jacques Maritain, Louis Bouyer, and Henri de Lubac. Unlike LeFebvre, they criticized not the council itself but its reception. In 1966, Joseph Ratzinger, who as a young theologian played a significant part in the council as a *peritus*, already struck a cautionary note at the first German Catholic Assembly. Later, as a cardinal, he arrived at an on-the-whole critical evaluation of the postconciliar situation in his report "The Situation of the Faith" (1985). And with good reason! In the first two decades after the council an exodus of priests and members of orders had taken place; in many spheres there was a noticeable decline in ecclesial praxis; and protest movements had arisen among both laity and priests, above all, after Pope Paul VI's encyclical *Humanae vitae* (1968) concerning the transmission of human life. In this official teaching, the pope speaks of the smoke of Satan that had penetrated into the temple of God through some kind of cracks.

Some critics went so far as to consider the council to be an accident and the greatest catastrophe in recent church history. But it would be a knee-jerk reaction to consider that everything that happened after the council happened because of Vatican II. The critics fail to recognize the long-term trends in religious sociology that were having an effect on society and the church even before the council and that erupted in the social upheavals connected with the student and youth protests of 1968, from San Francisco to Paris, Frankfurt, and Berlin. The emancipatory tendencies of that time also had consequences in the ecclesial realm. The progressives during the council were in fact the true conservatives: they turned back to the older traditions in order to break up the later encrustations. But now progressives of a new kind began to speak out: they did not take their orientation so much from the earlier tradition but from the "signs of the times," and they wanted to interpret the Gospel with a view to humanity today and the changed social situation. This concern is in principle legitimate for the council itself. But it becomes problematic if the doctrine of the faith threatens to become a doctrine of a purely secular salvation, as occurred in some—but not all—forms of liberation theology.

The Extraordinary Synod of Bishops of 1985 had the task of drawing the balance twenty years after the end of the council. This episcopal assembly led to a third phase of reception. The synod was aware of the crisis but did not want to join in the widespread lamentation.[5] They spoke of an ambivalent situation in which, beside the unmistakable negative aspects—such as increasing secularization and a worrying superficiality as well as an ideological reinterpretation of the faith—there were also the council's many good fruits. The liturgical renewal led to a greater emphasis on the word of God and to a more active participation of the whole celebrating congregation, the ecumenical *rapprochements*, the opening up to the modern world and its culture, and much more. In principle the synod emphasized that the church was the same in all councils and that Vatican II was to be interpreted in the context of all other councils.

With this principle, the synod became a crystallization point for the third phase of reception, the magisterial reception. The first official step toward reception was the liturgical reform, above all, the introduction of the new missal, which came into force on the First Sunday of Advent 1970. This reform was accepted with gratitude by the overwhelming majority of the faithful, but it also encountered criticism, partly for theological reasons, but partly also because many missed the previous rite's sacred and aesthetic character. Therefore, in 2007, Pope Benedict XVI permitted, as an exception to the rule, the use once more of the preconciliar rite, the Tridentine Rite. That solved some problems, but it also gave rise to new problems with which Pope Francis must now deal.

One further step was that Pope John Paul II in 1983 promulgated the new Code of Canon Law initiated by John XXIII, with the intention of translating the conciliar doctrine of the church into canonical language and legal forms. Some canonists understand the new Code as the ultimate magisterial interpretation of the council,[6] a position that I do not share because canon law, as important as it is, treats only the institutional and not the inner and mystic aspect of the church, which was fundamental for the conciliar renewal. Others criticize the fact that in spite of many improvements, the new canon law lags behind the council (for example, in the question of collegiality and the participation of the laity) and has not fully received the council.[7]

Finally in 1992, on the thirtieth anniversary of the council's opening, Pope John Paul II published the *Catechism of the Catholic Church*, initiated by the synod of 1985. He understood the *Catechism* as a contribution toward the renewal of ecclesial life as the Second Vatican Council intended it.

This official phase of the reception without doubt led to a consolidation of the ecclesial situation. It has in the meantime, however, reached its limits. The council unleashed a dynamic that goes on and calls for a further step in the realization of the conciliar agenda within a world of rapid change. Let us ask: Where do we stand now after three phases of reception?

3. The Light and Shadows in Our Postconciliar Situation

In the first place, one should acknowledge, in spite of the widespread discontent, that there is no lack of positive aspects. The council documents are not dead letters. They have shaped the life of the dioceses, parishes, and local communions through the renewal of the liturgy as well as through a stronger biblically based spirituality and the active participation of the laity, and they have stimulated ecumenical and interreligious dialogue. Also, they have led to a charismatic renewal. The multiplicity of charismas and the general call to holiness were given a new radiance and many evangelical (in the original meaning of the word) elements and concerns were taken up. There are attentive observers of church development who predict a future evangelical Catholicism.[8]

Nor did the official reception of Vatican II stand still. To some extent, it went above and beyond the council. That occurred, for example, in the case of the liturgical reforms: the council had still retained the Latin language as the rule for liturgical language and had not yet discussed the orientation in the celebration with the priest facing the people. It is similar also in the case of the implementation of the religious freedom proclaimed by the council after lengthy debates and of the "policy" of human rights, with which John Paul II made an essential contribution to overcoming the Communist dictatorships in Eastern Europe. Moreover, the encyclical *Ut unum sint* (1995), the first ecumenical encyclical ever, added depth to the council's ecumenical statements and energetically took them further. The various international, interreligious prayer encounters at Assisi (1986, 1993, 2002, 2011) extended the interreligious dialogue prompted by the council. All of this has brought positive change to the face of the church both within and without.

At the same time, the shadows must also be mentioned. Many of the impulses given by the council have so far only been implemented halfheartedly, such as the significance of the local church, the collegiality of the episcopate, the shared responsibility of the laity, especially the role of women in the church. And, in contrast, the centralism of the Roman Curia has increased. A series of recent events have also shown how much the Curia is itself in urgent need of reform and modernization, a need clearly expressed by the cardinals preceding the last conclave and now taken up by Pope Francis.

Ecumenism, another important concern of Vatican II, has borne many good fruits, more than could have been expected at the time of the council. In the interim, a noticeable cooling off has occurred in the official conversations with the churches both of the East and of the West. The causes are many and are located on all sides. In the relationship with the churches of the Reformation it has become clear that the different understandings of the church result in different notions of the church's unity, so that to a large extent there remain irreconcilable views of ecumenism's goal: is it full communion in truth and love, or is it a mutual recognition amid remaining differences?

There are also pastoral problems, for example, ethical questions that directly touch the real lives of many faithful Catholics. Many of these questions have in fact led to a kind of horizontal schism between that which is taught "from above" as obligatory and that which is actually practiced "from below" and is mostly silently tolerated. One must also mention the lack of priests, which is becoming increasingly obvious in many local churches, often leading to the merger of parishes into a new kind of mega-parish. Last but not least, the abuse crisis has led to a substantial loss of the church's credibility.

Both laity and theologians have presented many concrete demands for reform. Some of these demands, like the improvement of the church's juridical culture and greater transparency, merit consideration, and yet others such as the ordination of women cannot be accepted by the church, which is bound by the existing foundations of the faith. Other churches and ecclesial communities that have conceded to a large extent to such wishes—churches that have no pope, no curia, and no celibacy, that ordain women and grant their blessing to second or third marriages or same-sex partnerships—are no better off when it comes to making the Gospel contemporary and moving people to faith. Obviously, the church's sustainability does not in the first instance depend on these issues. On the contrary, a church that leans on the social mainstream becomes ambivalent in the literal sense of the word and, in the end, superfluous. The church is interesting only when it stands up for its cause credibly and convincingly and gives voice to social criticism when it must.

Further, we cannot envision the future of the church from only a typical Western perspective and forget that many, many Christians suffer persecution and oppression in other parts of our world. The blood of these martyrs is—as it was in the first Christian centuries—the seed of new Christians and of the church's new future. These faithful Christians, living in the dark, are the very light of the church.

Concluding this part of our reflection we can state: The light and the shadows show that the impetus of the council is still far from being exhausted even fifty years after it was opened. So we have to ask, what is the responsible way ahead beyond restorative and nostalgic dreams or utopian visions? In order to answer this question we have to deal anew with the council's documents. Many people talk about the council without having ever read its texts. We must not turn the council into a myth or reduce it to a few cheap slogans.

We should read the texts and ask for the adequate hermeneutic of the council, that is, look for the right method of interpreting it. Only then can we unearth the council's undiscovered treasures.

4. In Search of the Council's Hermeneutic

Recently a vigorous debate has arisen regarding the question of the hermeneutic of the council. All serious interpreters are agreed that it is not permissible to turn the council into a quarry for finding the required answer to every question. But at the same time it is not permissible to cite some vague spirit of the council. The starting point must be the council's texts, and they must be interpreted according to the generally recognized rules and criteria for the interpretation of the council.[9]

It is crucial to extract the meaning of a conciliar statement carefully from its often complicated editorial history, and then to set that meaning within the complex and tension-filled totality of all the conciliar statements, and then to understand this totality in turn within the totality of the church's tradition and its historical development as well as in relation to its subsequent reception. Finally, each individual statement must be interpreted within the framework of "the hierarchy of truths" (*Unitatis redintegratio* 11), that is, from its Christological foundation and center.

A council is, however, not an assembly concerned with the production and editing of documents. Each council has its place in a specific historical situation; it is an extraordinary event that accrues symbolic significance. Such symbolic actions and symbolic events imprint themselves on the church's collective memory even more strongly and more deeply than the dogmatic formulae, which are mostly difficult for the average Christian to understand.[10] So the simple fact alone that the Second Vatican Council (1962–65) took place following the First Vatican Council (1869–70), with its definition of the pope's primacy of jurisdiction and infallibility, has a symbolic significance. Vatican II makes it clear that the church is not a monarchist institution but is, as *communio*, essentially concerned with communication. Therefore, in critical situations the successors of the apostles follow the example of the first century's Jerusalem Apostolic Council in assembling in order to seek, under the leadership of St. Peter and the other apostles, a consensus in the Holy Spirit. But they did so, of course, with the involvement and the approval of the whole congregation (Acts 15). This grassroots involvement and approval could be an important indicator for the further progress of the reception of Vatican II. The council's reception, under the leadership of the *magisterium*, is a matter for the whole people of God.

Pope Benedict XVI initiated the latest phase of the council's hermeneutic in his address to the members of the Roman Curia on December 22, 2005. Adhering to the synod of 1985, he made it clear that consensus must run not only synchronically (referring to the present church) but also diachronically (referring to the church of all ages). In this sense he contrasted two hermeneutics with one another: the hermeneutic of breaks and discontinuity, which he rejected, and the hermeneutic of reform and renewal. In this confrontation it is important that the pope did not, as is often claimed, set the hermeneutic of discontinuity against the hermeneutic of continuity. Benedict XVI spoke not of a hermeneutic of continuity but of a hermeneutic of reform and of a "renewal of the Church, while maintaining continuity."

This formula is important. It involves a continuity that does not simply repeat tradition. Rather, it means an innovative continuity that does not make the tradition look old but proves it to be forever young. In the sense of Johann Adam Möhler and John Henry Newman, continuity involves a living tradition that allows the never consumed, always inexhaustible newness of Jesus Christ constantly to shine anew (cf. Irenaeus of Lyon). The tradition is indeed in the end a work of the Holy Spirit who leads the church into all truth (John 16:13).

When the pope spoke of a hermeneutic of reform, he meant reform in the sense of the medieval tradition, which involves not just the constantly necessary practical adaptation of individual paragraphs. Anyone who speaks of reform assumes that there exist deficits and failings that make it necessary to fulfill the call of the prophets and Jesus to conversion, that the church is always in need of purification and must abidingly walk the path of repentance, renewal, and reform (*Lumen gentium* 8; *Unitatis redintegratio* 4). The Dominican theologian Yves Congar, one of the most influential *periti* during the council, distinguished between the one tradition (singular) and the many traditions (plural) that give expression to the one tradition in a historically determined manner and that must therefore be deepened, interpreted, and in part corrected again and again.[11]

In which direction such an interpretation can lead us Pope Francis already indicated in the first days of his pontificate. He spoke of a poor church for the poor. This vision is his hermeneutical key for Vatican II. For the council said, in an unfortunately seldom-quoted paragraph of *Lumen gentium*, that as Jesus carried out the work of redemption in poverty and oppression so the church is called to follow the same path. It must not seek earthly glory but proclaim the living Christ through its example, humility, and self-denial and through its closeness to all people who are afflicted by human misery (*Lumen gentium* 8, 3). This reference to the cry of the poor recurs in many instances and should give rise to an interpretation of the council that is focused not on the church but on those whom in the Sermon on the Mount Jesus calls "Blessed" (Matt 5:1-12).

So Pope Benedict's address and Pope Francis's interpretation could help to rekindle the council's fire and give once more new force to the council's innovative impulse. According to an often-quoted phrase of St. Thomas More, tradition is to pass on not the ashes but the fire. So let us consider what it might mean to speak of a new beginning in the council's footsteps. Where can and should this path lead us?

5. A New Beginning in the Footsteps of the Council

In what follows I can only suggest a few viewpoints that seem important to me.[12] The Second Vatican Council took up some of modernity's important concerns in a critically constructive manner. Today, half a century later, we have moved from the modern to the postmodern era, which calls into question many of the Enlightenment's ideals. The mid-twentieth century's belief in progress and trust in reason have been shaken. This shift does not mean, however, that the council is no longer relevant. On the contrary! The Christian faith by its very nature seeks understanding. It was Anselm of Canterbury who established the axiom, "Faith seeking understanding" (*Fides quaerens intellectum*). The church must therefore continue to take seriously the legitimate concerns of the modern age. Just as it defends the Christian faith against postmodern pluralism and relativism, it must also defend it against today's antirationalist and fundamentalist tendencies. Thus, the church becomes an ally in a quite unexpected way of the Enlightenment, properly understood. This viewpoint was important for John Paul II in his encyclical *Fides et ratio* (1998), and for Benedict XVI it has become absolutely central.[13] We dare not fall under the spell of a fundamentalist or emotional or sentimental understanding of the faith and withdraw into a falsely understood pious corner; we must give everyone an account (*apologia*) of the hope that is in us (1 Pet 3:15) and in dialogue argue as advocates for the faith. The church needs good theologians.

This first thought leads to a second. Since the Second Vatican Council, the church has become universal in a new way. It is the one church of Jesus Christ, and yet it must make itself at home in varied and diverse cultures. The world in which we live is economically, technologically, and in its media a globalized network. At the same time, it is a culturally and religiously diverse world in which intolerable social differences persist and political and military conflicts lie in wait. Today's world is afflicted by the plague of international terrorism and by a new wave in the persecution of Christians in many countries. Following the evangelization of Europe in the first millennium and the evangelization of Africa and the Americas in the second millennium, there is occurring in the third millennium the evangelization of Asia with its ancient, advanced cultures and its growing economic and political power. This orientation confronts the church with the issue of Christian unity and diversity in a totally new way.

Unity through the Petrine office is a great good for us and a gift from the Lord to his church. But advocating a center does not mean accepting excessive centralism. Already in 1963, as a professor, Joseph Ratzinger pointed out that unity in the Petrine office need not necessarily be understood as an administrative unity but leaves room for a range of administrative, disciplinary, and liturgical structures.[14] In the encyclical *Ut unum sint* (1995), John Paul II proposed the consideration of new forms in exercise of papal primacy. This consideration is of fundamental significance not only for ecumenical dialogue but also for the Catholic Church itself. The church's unity cannot be understood as anything but unity in diversity and diversity in unity. It is here that the core problem in the reception of Vatican II still remains unresolved.

Thus there arises a third thought. The problem of unity and diversity is epitomized today in the question of the freedom of each individual human being, including each individual Christian. Immanuel Kant defined the Enlightenment's program in this way: "Have the courage to use your own reason." Today, we often speak of the individualization of life choices and of faith. We speak of mature citizens and mature Christians. The council addressed this issue in its statements on conscience. It defined conscience as the center and sanctuary of humanity, in which a human person is alone with God and hears God's voice in his or her inmost being (*Gaudium et spes* 16). Joseph Ratzinger analyzed this statement meticulously already in 1968 and arrived at the conclusion that the council had not thought its statement through to the end.[15] He was of the opinion that one should follow the problem further in the footsteps of John Henry Newman. Newman concludes his famous letter of 1874 to the Duke of Norfolk as follows: "Certainly, if I am obliged to bring religion into after-dinner toasts, (which indeed does not seem quite the thing) I shall drink,—to the Pope, if you please,—still, to Conscience first, and to the Pope afterwards."[16]

For Newman the conscience is the real representative of Christ, the place where the authority of the church reaches its internal limits. The church cannot take the place of the personal conscience. Yet, in order to distinguish the quiet voice of God in us from the loud voices around us, we must listen to the church's voice and take note of what other Christians who preceded us or who are contemporaries have heard as God's voice. In order to arrive at a responsible decision, each of us must receive advice while at the same time engaging in the formation of conscience. Following one's "informed conscience" (as we say) is not the easy way on the broad highway of current opinion and the applause of the masses; it is often a narrow, steep, and lonely path. That is shown by the many martyrs of the past century and our century who risked and gave their lives at the call of conscience. The call of conscience is not an easy matter but a very serious and, indeed, often a deadly serious one.

The notion of conscience as the echo of God's voice brings me to the final and most important point, the question of God. This question seems to me to be today's fundamental question. The council counted atheism in its various forms as one of the serious phenomena of this age; it also had enough humility to confess the share of blame Christians bear for this situation (*Gaudium et spes* 19). Since then, the situation has intensified dramatically in our secularized Western world. The problem is not so much the theoretical atheism of the nineteenth century nor the so-called new atheism that proceeds from an ideology based on evolutionary theory or brain research.[17] Rather, today's urgent issue is a practical atheism, a pervasive indifference regarding the question of God.

Many people now consider the secular option to be normal. They are no worse morally than the average Christian; they live more or less like you and me, and they do not seem to feel that anything is lacking.[18] But, according to our understanding, something important is lacking. They are experiencing what Thomas Aquinas calls *acedia*, which means not only laziness but spiritual listlessness, a kind of sadness and desperation that do not reach the very measure of the human person.[19]

We can no longer worry about only the social, cultural, and political effects of the faith and take belief in God for granted. Above all, we cannot engage these new pagans with questions of internal church reform. The issues of church reform are interesting for insiders. But the people outside have other questions. They ask: Where do I come from, and where am I going? Why and for what purpose do I exist? How to find happiness? Why is there evil and suffering in the world? Why must I suffer? How can I come to terms with evil and suffering and live with it?

The present situation demands that Christians be theologians, theologians whose task is to speak (*logos*) of God (*theos*). This is not a new agenda. It is the agenda of one of the greatest theologians of Christianity, Thomas Aquinas, who said already in the thirteenth century at the beginning of his *Summa theologica* that the subject of theology is God and everything else insofar as it relates to God.[20] As we do this, we as Christian theologians must not speak vaguely about a divine being as all forms of religion do more or less. Rather, we must speak concretely of the God revealed in Jesus Christ as love (1 John 4:8, 16), as God with us and for us, as God infinitely merciful who respects us, who in every situation concedes us a new chance and to whom we can in all situations say, "Abba, Father." In sum, we must speak about the mercy (*misericordia*) that is—as Pope Francis has said—the name of our God.[21]

Without a personal foundation of faith and without a personal life born out of faith and committed in love and mercy for the poor, everything else leads nowhere. The old trench warfare between conservatives and progressives does not lead anywhere. Without a solid foundation of committed faith, everything else floats in the air. We must in the first instance awaken new faith, hope, and love. We need a theocentric turn in the church's pastoral life. As a result of which, those outside the church will observe that "the joy of the Lord is your strength" (Neh 8:10).

To conclude: the council dared to take a step into a new era of church history. It did not point the way to a liberal conformist church but to a church spiritually renewed from its sources, which is at the same time a church open to dialogue and engaged in the cause of humanity. Our pursuit of the council's path has not yet reached its end. We have perhaps not even completed half of the course. We have to continue along this path with patience and courage and overall with joy in order to overcome the sadness of the world (2 Cor 7:10). Joy is contagious, whereas laments are repulsive. When we renew the joy of being the church that the council intended to enflame, then we shall pass this joy on to others. As this occurs, the church can proceed with a new prophetic power in a rapidly changing and profoundly insecure world. Then, too, the church can be a compass and an encouraging sign of hope for many. This confident faith is what we should learn from Vatican II, so that we can engage in theology and form the church on the basis of a new joy in faith. For that goal I wish to all of us, especially to the growing younger generation, above all, strength, patience, courage, and joy!

Endnotes

1. Recent interpretations of Vatican II include: Giuseppe Alberigo and Joseph A. Komonchak, *History of Vatican II*, trans. Matthew J. O'Connell (Maryknoll, NY: Orbis Books, 1995–2006); Peter Hünermann, ed., *Das II. Vatikanum—christlicher Glaube im Horizont der globalen Modernisierung* (Paderborn: Schöningh, 1998); Peter Hünermann and Bernd Jochen Hilberath, eds., *Herders Theologischer Kommentar zum Zweiten Vatikanischen Konzil*, 5 vols. (Freiburg: Herder, 2004–2006); Giuseppe Alberigo and Matthew Sherry, *A Brief History of Vatican II*, trans. Matthew Sherry (Maryknoll, NY: Orbis Books, 2006); Agostino Marchetto, *The Second Vatican Ecumenical Council*, trans. Kenneth D. Whitehead (Scranton, PA: Scanton University Press, 2010); John W. O'Malley, *What Happened at Vatican II?* (Cambridge, MA: Harvard University Press, 2008); Otto Hermann Pesch, *Das Zweite Vatikanische Konzil*, new ed. (Würzburg: Echter, 2010, 1993); Walter Kasper, *The Catholic Church: Nature, Reality and Mission*, trans. Thomas Hoebel (London: Bloomsbury T & T Clark, 2014), 10–15; Roberto De Mattei, *Il Concilio Vaticano II. Una storia mai scritta* (Turin: Lindau, 2010); Walter Brandmüller et al., *Le "chiavi" di Benedetto XVI per interpretare il Vaticano II* (Siena: Cantagalli, 2012); Jan-Heiner Tück, ed., *Erinnerung an die Zukunft. Das Zweite Vatikanische Konzil* (Freiburg: Herder, 2012); Kurt Koch, *Das Zweite Vatikanische Konzil. Eine Bilanz: Die Hermeneutik der Reform* (Augsburg: Sankt Ulrich, 2012); Agostino Marchetto, *Il Concilio*

ecumenico Vaticano II. Per la sua corretta ermeneutica (Vatican City: Libreria editrice vaticana, 2012); Joseph Ratzinger / Benedict XVI, *Zur Lehre des Zweiten Vatikanischen Konzils*, 2 vols. (Freiburg: Herder, 2012). For research on Vatican II, see Hermann Josef Pottmeyer et al., eds., *Die Rezeption des Zweiten Vatikanischen Konzils* (Düsseldorf: Patmos, 1986); Franz Xavier Bischof, ed., *Das Zweite Vatikanische Konzil (1962–1965). Stand und Perspektiven der kirchen-historischen Forschung im deutsch-sprachigen Raum* (Stuttgart: Kohlhammer, 2012).

2. On the notion of reception in the church, see Yves Congar, "La 'réception' comme réalité ecclésiologique (1972)," in *Église et Papauté* (Paris: Editions du Cerf, 1994), 229–66; Alois Grillmeier, "Konzil und Rezeption," in *Mit ihm und in ihm* (Freiburg: Herder, 1975), 303–34; Gilles Routhier, *La réception d'un concile* (Paris: Editions du Cerf, 1993); Wolfgang Beinert, "Die Rezeption und ihre Bedeutung für Leben und Lehre der Kirche," in *Verbindliches Zeugnis*, vol. 2, ed. Wolfgang Pannenberg and Theodore Schneider (Freiburg: Herder, 1995), 193–218; Christoph Theobald, *La réception du concile Vatican II* (Paris: Cerf, 2009); Hermann Josef Pottmeyer, "reception of doctrine," and Ladislas M. Orsy, "reception of law," in *The HarperCollins Encyclopedia of Catholicism*, ed. Richard P. McBrien (New York: HarperCollins, 1995), 1081–82.

3. John Paul II, Apostolic Letter *Novo millennio ineunte* (January 6, 2001), 29.

4. See Karl Rahner, *Das Konzil—ein neuer Beginn*, introduction by Cardinal Karl Lehmann (Freiburg: Herder, 2012); Günther Wassilowsky, *Universales Heilssakrament Kirche. Karl Rahners Beitrag zur Ekklesiologie des II. Vatikanum* (Innsbruck: Tyrolia, 2001).

5. See Walter Kasper, *Zukunft aus der Kraft des Konzils. Die außerordentliche Bischofssynode `85. Die Dokumente mit einem Kommentar* (Freiburg: Herder, 1986).

6. See Norbert Lüdecke, "Der Codex Iuris Canonici von 1983: 'Krönung' des II. Vatikanischen Konzils?," in *Die deutschsprachigen Länder und das II. Vatikanum*, ed. Hubert Wolf and Claus Arnold (Paderborn: Schöningh, 2000), 209–37; Georg Bier, *Rechtsstellung des Diözesanbischofs nach dem Codex Iuris Canonici von 1983* (Würzburg: Echter, 2001); Bernd Jochen Hilberath, "Der CIC als authentische Rezeption des Zweiten Vatikanums," *Theologische Quartalschrift* 186 (2006): 40–49.

7. See Herve Legrand, "Vierzig Jahre danach. Wie steht es mit den kirchlichen Reformen, die das II. Vaticanum beabsichtigt hatte," in *Concilium* [German Edition] 41 (2005), 397–411; Günther Wassilowsky, ed., *Zweites Vatikanum—vergessene Anstöße, gegenwärtige Fortschreibungen* (Freiburg: Herder, 2004); Franz Xavier Bischof, "Steinbruch Konzil? Zu Kontinuität und Diskontinuität kirchlicher Lehrentscheidungen," *Münchener theologische Zeitschrift* 59 (2008): 194–210.

8. See John Allen, *The Future Church* (Garden City, NY: Doubleday, 2009); George Weigel, *Evangelical Catholicism: Deep Reform in the 21st-Century Church* (New York: Basic Books, 2013).

9. On conciliar hermeneutics, see Walter Kasper, "The Continuing Challenge of the Second Vatican Council: The Hermeneutics of Conciliar Statements," in *Theology and Church*, trans. Margaret Kohl (New York: Crossroad Publishing, 1989), 166–76; Otto Hermann Pesch, *Das Zweite Vatikanische Konzil. Vorgeschichte-*

Verlauf-Ergebnisse-Nachgeschichte, 3rd ed. (Würzburg: Echter, 1994), 148–60; Karl Lehmann, "Hermeneutik für einen künftigen Umgang mit dem Konzil," in Wassilowsky, *Zweites Vatikanum*, 71–89; Karl Lehmann, "Das II. Vatikanum—ein Wegweiser. Verständnis-Rezeption-Bedeutung," in *Das Zweite Vatikanische Konzil und die Zeichen der Zeit heute*, ed. Peter Hünermann (Freiburg: Herder, 2006), 11–26. On the differing starting points, see Jan-Heiner Tück, "Eine 'reines Pastoralkonzil'? Zur Verbindlichkeit des Vatikanum II," *Internationale katholische Zeitschrift: Communio* 41 (2012): 441–57.

10. The difficulty in understanding dogmatic formulae has been noted both by the reform-inclined Giuseppe Alberigo and the restoration-inclined Roberto de Mattei; see note 1 above for their respective books.

11. See Yves Congar, *The Tradition and the Traditions*, trans. Michael Naseby and Thomas Rainborough (New York: Macmillan, 1967). On how to understand tradition, see Walter Kasper, "Vorwort zur Neuausgabe," in *Die Lehre von der Tradition in der Römischen Schule* (Freiburg: Herder, 2011), 13–19.

12. See Kasper, *The Catholic Church*, 342–46.

13. See Pope Benedict XVI, "Faith, Reason and the University: Memories and Reflections," Lecture at the University of Regensburg (September 12, 2005); idem, Motu proprio *Porta fidei* (October 11, 2011); idem, General Audience (November 21, 2012). Available at http://www.vatican.va/holy_father/benedict_xvi/index.htm.

14. See Joseph Ratzinger, "Primat," in *Lexion für Theologie und Kirche*, vol. 8, ed. Josef Höfer and Karl Rahner (Freiburg: Herder, 1963), 761–63.

15. See Joseph Ratzinger, "Pastorale Konstitution. Erster Hauptteil: Kommentar zum I. Kapitel. Artikel 16," in *Lexikon für Theologie und Kirche. Das Zweite Vatikanische Konzil*, vol. 3, ed. Heinrich Suso Brechter et al. (Herder: Freiburg, 1968), 328–31.

16. See John Henry Newman, Letter to the Duke of Norfolk (1874), 5. Conscience, n. 261, which is available at http://www.newmanreader.org/works/anglicans/volume2/gladstone/section5.html.

17. On the earlier problematic, see Walter Kasper, *The God of Jesus Christ*, trans. Matthew J. O'Connell (New York: Crossroad Publishing, 1984), 65–115; on the recent problematic, see Magnus Striet, *Wiederkehr des Atheismus. Fluch oder Segen für die Theologie?* (Freiburg: Herder, 2008).

18. See Charles Taylor, *A Secular Age* (Cambridge, MA: Harvard University Press, 2007).

19. See Thomas Aquinas, *Summa theologica*, I/II, q. 35 a. 8; II/II, q. 20 a. 4, q. 35.

20. See Thomas Aquinas, *Summa theologica*, I, q. 1 a. 7.

21. See Walter Kasper, *Mercy: The Essence of the Gospel and the Key to Christian Life*, trans. William Madges (New York: Paulist Press, 2014).

CHAPTER 19

Be Joyful in Hope: A Homily

Cardinal Walter Kasper
Basilica of the Sacred Heart, University of Notre Dame
April 27, 2013

Readings: Acts 14:21b-27; Revelation 21:1-5a; John 13:31-33a, 34-35

Dear brothers and sisters in Christ!
Dear friends!

It gives me great joy and profound satisfaction to celebrate this Eucharist with you on this Fifth Sunday of the Easter season. The readings of this Sunday fit well with the celebration that God has given to me now at eighty years of life and, among them, my priestly ordination fifty-six years ago and my ministry as a pastor, as a bishop, and as a theologian within the church.

1. "Continue in the Faith" (Acts 14:22a)

I feel myself in a similar situation as the apostle Paul who, according to the first reading, together with Barnabas returned to Antioch where they had been first commended for the task that they had now completed. They gathered the church together and told the faithful what God had done through them.

St. Paul had to face many difficulties, trials, and obstacles during his first missionary journey through Asia Minor. What was much more important to him, however, was to give witness that God despite all these difficulties opened a door to spread the Good News, the Gospel. God was with them.

So too for me, the twentieth century, into which I was born, did not start as a happy century. No, it was a dark and bloody century. I grew up in Germany during the Nazi time and amid the horrors of the Second World War. But afterward the twentieth century evolved into a century with many ecclesial movements of renewal. Very early, I learned about the liturgical, biblical, patristic, and pastoral renewals that eventually converged in the Second Vatican Council. The council raised new enthusiasm in the church and showed us to be a young church that is on the way of renewal and of reaching out to other Christians and to the world. Vatican II became for me a fixed point of reference. Pope John XXIII understood the council as the dawn of a new epoch, as the beginning of a new spring, and as a new Pentecost.

After dark centuries there happened the ecumenical movement, and in Christians' steps toward reconciliation with the Jewish people there has occurred a new beginning. Though we are still far away from the final mark, the results we have already achieved exceed all of our original expectations. God's Spirit has opened anew a door and is preparing a new future. But difficulties and trials within the church and in our relations to our present society continue. What Paul told the people in Lystra and Iconium is true also today: "It is through many persecutions that we must enter the kingdom of God" (Acts 14:22b). In a similar way, this is true also in our days and in our lives.

Personally, I am far from the pessimism and skepticism with which elderly people often suffer. I am convinced that God is present also in our time and in our world. God's work goes on. Nobody can stop it. Thus: Never lose courage! By God's mercy, there is no situation where there is no way out. There will always be a chance. Every difficulty can turn into a new *kairós*, the gift of a new God-given chance and opportunity. So, as Paul said, we have reason "to continue in the faith" (Acts 14:22a), which is the light illuminating and encouraging us on life's way. One who believes is never alone. God is with him or her.

2. "I Am Making All Things New" (Rev 21:5)

Today's second reading, which is taken from the New Testament's last book, the book of Revelation, also urges us to stand firm in the faith. But it doesn't look back to what happened in the past; it looks forward to the future, a future that God prepares for us. It sees the

New Jerusalem, the holy city, coming down from God, out of heaven, adorned as a bride for her bridegroom. And then there come the infinitely comforting words that God "will wipe every tear from their eyes. Death will be no more; mourning and crying and pain will be no more, for the first things have passed away." Then "the one who was seated on the throne said, 'See, I am making all things new'" (Rev 21:3-5).

What strikes me in this text is the word "new," which is a key term in the Old and New Testaments. It doesn't mean innovations that fill our curiosity, nor the innovations of science and technology, in which our time takes pride. Some of these innovations may be useful and may be real progress, others can turn to become dangerous or at least ambiguous. Frequently, what is new today and what seems to be the last cry can be tomorrow out of fashion. Whoever marries in this fashion will be a widower very soon. Whereas the new that God promises is somewhat different; it is the absolute new, the newness which is God, the Almighty. For God is never the old God; God is—as St. Augustine says—the youngest of us all. Although God is always the same, for us God is nevertheless every day new and surprising in never-ending love and mercy. God does not forget the good things we do. In the end of time, when God will be all in all (1 Cor 15:28), God will purify us, perfect what is deficient, and bring us into the eternal reality. The Almighty will make all things new in a fundamental renewal that is radically more than our innovations.

For us today it is important to look forward. For often our expectations end up in delusions and frustrations that lead to greater skepticism among more and more people. Hope becomes a scarce commodity. But without hope nobody can live. Without hope suicide is, as the French philosopher Albert Camus said, the only honest answer. Today, the mission of the church and of all Christians is to be a counteracting force opening up the horizon to give hope, a hope which conquers even death, a hope which gives us back the joy to live. Christian hope tells us that in the end we have to leave everything, except the good we did. Our tears will be wiped out; only love will remain (1 Cor 13:8), and so also the works of love will remain. That which is good works as a rich harvest that opens into the eternal reality. The good that we do will not be done in vain.

When I reflected on my eightieth birthday and the good (and less good) that I've done in my life and in my theology, I came to the conclusion that to the degree that I have helped people find hope and joy in God, I achieved at least something. Joy and hope are indeed available to us because God is always new and always greater than our expectations, greater than our hearts. Given the divine promise of "a new heaven and a new earth" (Rev 21:1), God far exceeds our most keen imaginations. This hope in God accompanies me also in my old age. The Old Testament prophet tells us that "the joy of the LORD is your strength" (Neh 8:10), and the New Testament announces good and joyful news concerning "the love of God in Christ Jesus our Lord" (Rom 8:39). Thus: Be joyful in hope!

3. "Love One Another" (John 13:34)

While today's first reading looks back and the second looks forward, the third reading, the Gospel according to St. John, looks from both perspectives to the present and tells us what to do today. It speaks of the new commandment, the commandment of love: "I give you a new commandment, that you love one another. Just as I have loved you, you also should love one another" (John 13:34).

Many people believe that Christian faith is a complex and difficult thing. No, on the contrary, it is easy to speak about. One word suffices: "love." "God is love" (1 John 4:8). "God so loved the world that he gave his only Son" (John 3:16) who loved us "to the end," until death (John 13:1). So we should love one another. Only with love and mercy can we illuminate and penetrate the world and make it a little warmer. It is never in vain and never too late to do works of love and works of mercy. Love and mercy should be the very marks of the church and of every Christian.

There are many personal and ecclesial consequences of the works of mercy. The church—as Pope Francis reiterates—should not be a self-referential reality; the church has a mission and has to go forth until the end of the world and to the boundaries of our society: to the poor, the marginalized, the sick, the homeless, the hopeless, and the suffering.

Here I'll limit myself to only one consequence. The Second Vatican Council opened up dialogue with non-Catholics and non-Christians, especially with Jews, the people of the First Covenant. After dark centuries where we considered one another as enemies, we are discovering one another again as friends, as sisters and brothers. I am very grateful that Pope John Paul II and Pope Benedict XVI entrusted and charged me with this important mission.

Yet, it is an unfinished mission. We didn't totally achieve filling up the ditches, but we achieved bridges of friendship and trust above the ditches, where from both sides we can meet one another. There is a new atmosphere of friendship, of effective cooperation and common witness, based on common being in Jesus Christ through the one baptism. Also, we did not achieve full unity among Christians, but the one Christian community became a reality. The global community of Christians is the largest peace movement in the world. Christians from different cultures and from all continents, more than 2.1 billion of us,[1] share the same convictions on fundamental questions of human existence. The followers of Jesus Christ are all committed to the message of peace proclaimed on the Sermon of the Mount (Matt 5:5, 7, 10), a peace which is more than the silence of arms; it is the fruit of justice for everybody in the world.

This justice is the minimum of love, whereas love and mercy are the maximum and the optimum of justice. Without love and mercy, the highest law is in danger of becoming the greatest injustice (as Cicero observed). Justice without mercy becomes a soulless reality and a soulless society. For it is love that everybody needs the most and as human persons deserves the most.

Mercy is the Christian newness. Mercy gives a foretaste and an anticipation of what we hope for, the coming of the heavenly Jerusalem. Only through mercy does our Christian message of the merciful God become credible, plausible, and authentic. In our church we should start being merciful. In our church we should give a good example. One beam of mercy makes the world warmer and brighter for all people.

Remain firm in faith! Be joyful in hope! Be merciful with your neighbor! That's the message of this Fifth Sunday after Easter, and that's all that is necessary to be a Christian. There remains still much to pray for and more to do. Even when someone becomes eighty years old, there is still time to begin anew. Amen.

Endnote

1. See http://www.pewresearch.org/daily-number/number-of-christians-rises-but-their-share-of-world-population-stays-stable/.

Contributors

Dr. John C. Cavadini (PhD, Yale University, 1988). Professor of patristic theology and McGrath-Cavadini Director, Institute for Church Life, University of Notre Dame. Member of the International Theological Commission. Author, editor, and translator of books and articles on the theology of Augustine of Hippo, contemporary theology, and the renewal of Catholicism, including *Augustine through the Ages* (1999), *Who Do You Say That I Am?* (2004), and *Explorations in the Theology of Benedict XVI* (2013).

Dr. Catherine E. Clifford (PhD, University of St. Michael's College, 2002). Professor of systematic and historical theology and director, Research Centre for Vatican II and 21st Century Catholicism, St. Paul University (Ottawa). Author, editor, and translator of books and articles in ecclesiology, ecumenism, and sacramental theology, including *The Groupe des Dombes: A Dialogue of Conversion* (2005), *A Century of Prayer for Christian Unity* (2009), *Keys to the Council: Unlocking the Teaching of Vatican II*, with Richard Gaillardetz (2012), and *Decoding Vatican II* (2014).

Dr. Kristin M. Colberg (PhD, University of Notre Dame, 2009). Assistant professor of historical-systematic theology, College of Saint Benedict/ Saint John's University. Member of the Catholic-Reformed Dialogue. Author of articles on the Second Vatican Council, appearing in *The Heythrop Journal*, *Horizons*, and *Missiology*, and author of *Becoming a Modern Church: The Relationship between Vatican Council I and Vatican Council II* (2015).

Dr. Philip A. Cunningham (PhD, Boston College, 1992). Professor of theology and director, Institute for Jewish-Catholic Relations, Saint Joseph's University (Philadelphia). Author and editor of books and articles on Christian-Jewish relations, biblical studies, and religious education, including co-editor of *The Catholic Church and the Jewish People: Recent Reflections from Rome* (2007) and *Christ Jesus and the Jewish People Today: New Explorations of Theological Interrelationships* (2011).

Rev. Brian E. Daley, SJ (DPhil, Oxford University, 1978). Catherine Huisking Professor of Patristic Theology, University of Notre Dame. Author, editor, and translator of books and authors on patristic theology and the early church, including *The Hope of the Early Church* (1991), *Gregory of Nazianzus* (2006), *God in Early Christian Thought* (2009), and *Light on the Mountain: Greek Patristic and Byzantine Homilies on the Transfiguration of the Lord*, with John Behr (2013).

Dr. Francis Schüssler Fiorenza (ThD, Westphalia Wilhelms University, Münster, 1972). Charles Chauncey Stillman Professor of Roman Catholic Theological Studies, Harvard Divinity School. Author and editor of books and articles in systematic theology and theological hermeneutics, including *Modern Christian Thought*, 2 volumes (2006), *Systematic Theology: Roman Catholic Perspectives* (2nd rev. ed., 2011), and *Political Theology: Contemporary Challenges and Future Directions* (2013).

Dr. Anthony J. Godzieba (PhD, Catholic University of America, 1992). Professor of theology and religious studies, Villanova University, and editor of *Horizons: The Journal of the College Theology Society.* Author of books and numerous articles on fundamental theology, systematic theology, and philosophy of religion, including *Bernhard Welte's Fundamental Theological Approach to Christology* (1994) and *Christology: Memory, Inquiry, Practice*, with Anne M. Clifford (2003).

Dr. Elizabeth T. Groppe (PhD, University of Notre Dame, 1999). Associate professor of theology, Xavier University (Cincinnati). Author of books and articles on the doctrine of God, Jewish-Christian relations, and the theology of the environment, including *Yves Congar's Theology of the Holy Spirit* (2004) and *Eating and Drinking: Christian Explorations of Daily Living* (2010).

Rev. Gustavo A. Gutiérrez, OP (PhD, Catholic University of Lyon, 1985). John Cardinal O'Hara Professor of Theology, University of Notre Dame. Author of books and articles on Latin American liberation theology, including *A Theology of Liberation: History, Politics and Salvation* (1971), *On Job: God-Talk and the Suffering of the Innocent* (1986), and *We Drink from Our Own Wells* (2003).

Dr. Mary Catherine Hilkert, OP (PhD, Catholic University of America, 1984). Professor of systematic theology, University of Notre Dame. Author and editor of books and articles on theological anthropology, preaching, and feminist theology, including *Naming Grace: Preaching and the Sacramental Imagination* (1997), *The Praxis of the Reign of God: An Introduction to the Theology of Edward Schillebeeckx* (2002), and *Speaking with Authority: Catherine of Siena and the Voices of Women Today* (rev. and exp. ed., 2008).

Dr. Elizabeth A. Johnson, CSJ (PhD, Catholic University of America, 1981). Distinguished professor of theology, Fordham University. Author of books and articles on the doctrine of God, Christology, Mariology, and feminist theology, including *She Who Is: The Mystery of God in Feminist Theological Discourse* (1992), *Quest for the Living God: Mapping Frontiers in the Theology of God* (2007), and *Ask the Beasts: Darwin and the God of Love* (2014).

Cardinal Walter Kasper (ThD, Eberhard Karls University, Tübingen, 1958). Emeritus professor of theology, Eberhard Karls University. Emeritus bishop of Diocese of Rottenburg-Stuttgart. President emeritus of the Pontifical Council for Promoting Christian Unity and of the Pontifical Commission for Religious Relations with the Jews. Author of many books and articles on the doctrine of God, Christology, the church, and ecumenical and interreligious relations, including *Harvesting the Fruits: Aspects of Christian Faith Ecumenical Dialogue* (2009), *The Catholic Church: Nature, Reality and Mission* (2011), and *Mercy: The Essence of the Gospel and the Key to Christian Life* (2012).

Dr. Robert A. Krieg (PhD, University of Notre Dame, 1976). Professor of systematic theology, University of Notre Dame. Author, editor, and translator of books and articles on Christology, the Catholic Church in Germany, and German theologians, including *Romano Guardini: A Precursor of Vatican II* (1997), *Catholic Theologians in Nazi Germany* (2004), and *Treasure in the Field: Salvation in the Bible and in Our Lives* (2013).

Dr. William P. Loewe (PhD, Marquette University, 1974). Associate professor of theology, Catholic University of America. Author of articles on Christology, soteriology, and fundamental theology in *The Anglican Theological Review*, *The Catholic Biblical Quarterly*, *The Heythrop Journal*, *Horizons*, *Theological Studies*, and *The Thomist*. Author and editor of books, including *The College Student's Introduction to Christology* (1996) and *Theology and Sacred Scripture* (2002).

Rev. Thomas F. O'Meara, OP (ThD, Ludwig Maximillian University, Munich, 1967). Emeritus Warren Professor of Theology, University of Notre Dame. Author, editor, and translator of books and articles on the theology of grace, Thomas Aquinas, and the history of modern Catholic theology. Publications include *God in the World: The Theology of Karl Rahner* (2007), *Vast Universe: Extraterrestrials and Christian Revelation* (2012), and *Scanning the Signs of the Times: French Dominicans in the Twentieth Century*, with Paul Philibert, OP (2013).

Dr. Cyril J. O'Regan (PhD, Yale University, 1989). Huisking Professor of Philosophical-Systematic Theology, University of Notre Dame. Author of books and articles in philosophical theology, systematic theology, and postmodern thought, including *Gnostic Apocalypse* (2002), *Theology and the Spaces of Apocalyptic* (2009), and *Anatomy of Misremembering: Von Balthasar's Response to Philosophical Modernity*, volume 1 (2014).

Rabbi A. James Rudin (DD, Hebrew Union College–Jewish Institute of Religion, 1960). Senior religious advisor, American Jewish Committee. Emeritus director, Interreligious Affairs Department, American Jewish Committee. Distinguished professor, St. Leo University. Author of numerous books and articles, especially concerning Jewish-Christian relations, including *The Baptizing of America: The Religious Right's Plans for the Rest of Us* (2009), *Christians and Jews: Faith to Faith* (2011) and *Cushing, Spellman, and O'Connor: The Surprising Story of How Three American Cardinals Transformed Catholic-Jewish Relations* (2012).

Rev. John R. Sachs, SJ (ThD, Eberhard Karls University, Tübingen, 1984). Associate professor of theology, Boston College School of Theology and Ministry. Author of articles on creation and eschatology, theological anthropology, the doctrine of God, Ignatian spirituality, and the theology of Karl Rahner appearing in *Gregorianum*, *Theological Studies*, and *The Way Supplement*. Author of *The Christian Vision of Humanity: Basic Christian Anthropology* (1991).

Dr. Susan K. Wood, SCL (PhD, Marquette University, 1986). Professor of systematic theology, Marquette University, and editor, *Pro Ecclesia*. Editorial advisory board, *Ecclesiology*. Member of the International Lutheran-Catholic Dialogue, the US Lutheran-Catholic Dialogue, and the North American Orthodox-Catholic Dialogue. Author and editor of books and articles on the church, ecumenism, sacramental theology, and Henri de Lubac, including *One Baptism: Ecumenical Dimensions of the Doctrine of Baptism* (2009) and *Critical Issues in Ecclesiology* (2011).

Index of Persons